# A MORAL ART

# A MORAL ART

## GRAMMAR, SOCIETY, AND CULTURE IN TRECENTO FLORENCE

## PAUL F. GEHL

CORNELL UNIVERSITY PRESS

ITHACA AND LONDON

First published 1993 by Cornell University Press.


Library of Congress Cataloging-in-Publication Data

Gehl, Paul F.
    A moral art : grammar, society, and culture in Trecento Florence / Paul F. Gehl.
        p.   cm.
    Includes bibliographical references and index.
    ISBN 0-8014-2836-X (alk. paper)
        1. Latin philology—Study and teaching—Italy—Florence—History.   2. Latin language, Medieval and modern—Italy—Florence—Style.   3. Latin literature—Appreciation—Italy—Florence.   4. Language and culture—Italy—Florence—History
5. Latin language—Italy—Florence—Grammar.   6. Florence (Italy)—Intellectual life.
7. Florence (Italy)—History—To 1421.   8. Renaissance—Italy—Florence.
9. Humanists—Italy—Florence.   I. Title.
PA2065.l7G44   1993
470'.7'04551—dc20                                                          92-47067


Printed in the United States of America


♾ The paper in this book meets the minimum requirements
of the American National Standard for Information Sciences–
Permanence of Paper for Printed Library Materials, ANSI Z39.48-1984.

*For Dick Brown*

# CONTENTS

# ACKNOWLEDGMENTS

L arge projects produce large debts, and I cannot even count everyone who has helped in making this book come about. The individuals do group themselves into families, however, and these can be named. Above all, my work has been nurtured by the extended family of the Newberry Library, whose community of scholars is presided over by its paterfamilias, Richard H. Brown, to whom this volume is dedicated. I cannot list all the others at the Newberry who helped, but very special thanks are due to Peggy McCracken, Ronald Witt, Richard Mallette, John Marino, Rob Carlson, and Mary Carruthers, who patiently read the entire manuscript at several stages. Many other Newberryans have contributed directly, and still other friends at the library have been part of the effort just by being here. I thank you all from the bottom of my heart.

Thanks are also due to many other Chicagoans who belong to my Hyde Park and South Loop families. I think most of Braxton Ross, who has been a constant inspiration since my early graduate school days. From my immense Roman family, I must single out Katherine Gill, Lucilla Marino, Armando Petrucci, and Franca Nardelli Petrucci. The broader Italian landscape holds another group of my creditors, too diffuse to call a family. Particular thanks to Robert Black, Charles Davis, Paul Grendler, Jane Langton, Alfonso Mirto, Renato Pasta, and Kevin Stevens. Many others did not know they were helping, or would not now admit to it, or never told me their names. As always happens, this last group contains a disproportionate number of library workers and archivists, for whom all historians are thankful. Most of their institutions are listed in the Appendix; other libraries that extended help and hospitality are those of the Gregorian University, Northwestern University, the American Academy in Rome, and the universities of Chicago, Illinois, London, and Florence.

Research support for this project was granted by the American Council of Learned Societies, the British Academy, and the Newberry Library. I could not have done without, and I am very grateful. Parts of the book were presented in forums presided over by James Melchert of the American Academy in Rome; Julius Kirshner of the University of Chicago; Jan Ziolkowski of Harvard University; Ned Rosenheim of the Caxton Club of Chicago; Christopher Kleinhenz, John Tedeschi, and Robert Rodini of the University of Wisconsin. I thank them for the opportunity to speak to and learn from their colleagues and students.

For permission to reproduce photographs, I acknowledge the courtesy of the Newberry Library, the Biblioteca Medicea-Laurenziana, the Biblioteca Nazionale Centrale di Firenze, the Biblioteca Riccardiana, and the Biblioteca Guarnacci. Portions of the Appendix and Chapter 2 appeared in my article "Latin Readers," in *Scrittura e civiltà* 13 (1989); portions of Chapter 4 appeared in my "Augustinian Catechism," *Augustinian Studies* 19 (1988). These are reproduced with the permission of the editors.

PAUL F. GEHL

*The Newberry Library*
*Chicago*

# INTRODUCTION

Grammar is often characterized as a conservative discipline, and there is no doubt that it sometimes is. But there are times when staid Dame Grammar and her elder sister Philology are the agents of intellectual revolution. This was certainly the case during the Renaissance, which saw the recovery of classical latinity and the creation of a new, scientific philology. The study of education in the earliest stages of Italian humanism, however, has been hampered by too keen an appreciation of this spirit of change. If we look closely at the educational practices that created the public for early humanism, we see that Grammar remained a sturdy disciplinarian, stubbornly resistant to change, well into the fifteenth century.

This book concerns the education of one part of the reading public of the early Renaissance, those who studied Latin grammar at Florence. It provides a case study of educational conservatism in action. We will discover that, far from fostering the progress of stylistic and philosophical classicism, the grammar masters of Florence acted as a brake on the new humanism, in the name of the moral needs of an educated citizenry. They did so by stressing the integrity of a universalizing Latin tradition embodied in moral texts that had for centuries promoted Christian communitarian values. They responded to challenges offered by vernacular literacy and by humanism with a restriction of the Latin course. This moralizing sort of education, and not some vaguely defined theological conservatism or reactionary clerical culture, provided traditionalist opponents of early humanism with the conviction of their opinions and with many of their arguments.

The humanists defended themselves by agreeing, sincerely enough, that

I

Latin and the literary studies that followed it were moral arts and that the purpose of the *studia humanitatis* was the moral reform of the individual and even of society. The trecento humanists consistently put their reforms in a Christian context, not just for political expediency or to advance their careers, but also because they had a deep commitment to the spiritual life. However radical their claims for the active, political function of the new classical studies, they felt the pull of a more contemplative ideal. Historians have noted, sometimes with puzzlement, the religious conversions of the greatest early humanists. Petrarch, Boccaccio, and Salutati each renounced at some stage the most radical implications of the classicizing literary and linguistic program. These men did not relapse into medieval patterns of thought under social pressure. Rather, they were giving expression to an ancient longing implicit in the notion of the moralizing ends of language with which they had grown up. They could not achieve a radical recovery of an ancient philosophy of language because they were thoroughly imbued with Christian notions of the meaning of Latin.

In this book I explore, on the basis of the records of a single region, some of the sources of this underlying tension in early humanism, specifically those embedded in the way Latin was studied and taught on the elementary level. Considerable attention has been paid over the years to the education of the early humanists and to the pedagogical programs they devised in the first part of the fifteenth century; but our understanding of trecento programs of Latin study in Italy is still limited, especially for the elementary course. The full meaning of the humanist achievement is unclear because we have missed an important part of its background. In particular, we do not have a good record of how the Italian situation differed from that in the rest of Europe, nor have we explored what regional variations in educational programs existed in Italy. We do not really know what linguistic and philosophical assumptions underlay the education the first humanists received from their medieval grammar masters.

To study this important background for humanism, we must leave behind some of the prejudices of the humanists themselves, above all the assumption that there was a sharp and sudden contrast between the pedagogy introduced by the second generation of humanists about 1400 and the medieval program against which they polemicized. Even if the claims for novelty made by these humanists were true, their claims alone would not tell us what the polemic was really about, for these writers did not characterize the old pedagogy in any detailed way. We would still need to recover what it was the early humanists claimed to hate about their own educations. Detailed recent studies, moreover, have pointed to many continuities between medieval and humanist pedagogy; these studies seriously undermine the validity of the humanists' claims to originality.[1]

We must turn away from the humanists in another way too, for studying pedagogy means concentrating not on the intellectual leaders, the poets and philosophers, but on some very humble figures, the elementary grammar masters. Such masters lived and worked in every Italian city and town, but they rarely achieved fame or even local notoriety. These fourteenth-century grammarians have a great deal to tell us about Italian society, independent of any interest we may have in humanism. We learn from them that Latin pedagogy was a shifting, changing field long before the humanist reforms, and that the public for grammar instruction, especially the parents who payed the bills, affected deeply the nature of the medieval curriculum.

The grammar master *was* an humble figure. Often he had no university training himself, and yet one part of his job was to prepare students for the university or for other advanced study in the form of a legal apprenticeship or clerical school. He also had an even more fundamental social mission, that of passing on classical and Christian Latin traditions to the lay elites of rapidly urbanizing Italy. He did this not by imparting literacy but by teaching students how to read in a latinate way, that is, with memorial techniques and for moral ends. The grammarian was a professional linguist charged with the formal initiation of educable young men to Latin high culture.[2] As such, he educated the public for all new Latin literature; his students were the reading public for nascent humanism.

In this book, then, I address the social status and cultural role of the elementary teacher of grammar as well as the larger, symbolic value of Latin as vehicle of high culture in a bilingual society. I concentrate on Latin education, because almost every attempt to be "educated" (as opposed to merely literate) in fourteenth-century Italy involved confronting the Latin heritage. An understanding of the meaning of Latin education can best be achieved on the level of regional culture, and so I concentrate on grammar masters and grammar teaching in a single trecento city, Florence, and to a lesser extent the surrounding region of Tuscany.

Before considering the Florentine evidence, however, we must try to

1. A brief introduction to the state of the field is offered by Black, "Italian Renaissance Education," to be used with the cautions offered in the accompanying "Reply to Robert Black" by Grendler.

2. Ong, "Latin Language Study"; Klapisch-Zuber, "Le chiavi"; and Carruthers, *Book of Memory*, develop these ideas at length. I present new evidence in Chapters 3–7.

picture the overall educational situation in thirteenth- and fourteenth-century Italy. Italian teachers of Latin adapted a medieval tradition of grammatical teaching that emphasized the ethical preparation of the student to enter a textual community. In the older, monastic version of this tradition, the textual community in question was the monastery itself, and more broadly the monastic elite of the whole church. In law-oriented, high medieval Italy and its flourishing universities, the textual community was an academic and professional one. A profound distortion of the older tradition of literary studies took place between the eleventh and thirteenth centuries for the sake of creating a new forensic and diplomatic Latin.[3] Obviously, the textual communities that concerned school teachers of the trecento were broader and more diverse still, but the deeply internalized notion of a rhetorically defined community persisted, and many of the strategies for initiating the student into such a community through the study of Latin remained in place. In the course of the thirteenth and fourteenth centuries, the character of this linguistic and spiritual initiation gradually changed so that by the end of the period the Latin course at Florence had achieved a clearly political meaning and a strongly pre-professional character, while remaining the first initiation of the boy student into moral thought.[4]

Elementary moral principles were inculcated in the grammar classroom at all periods. But in the early and central Middle Ages, the controlled conditions of the monastic classroom and the needs of monks and clerics for an education to the common, conventual life had created a tradition of language study that was normative not only in the linguistic sphere but in the moral one as well. Outside the monasteries, advanced study of ethics had traditionally been the province of rhetoric and dialectic. Within the walls, where advanced philosophical study was less common and less useful, grammar was entrusted with a much broader moral mission than had been usual in classical schools.[5]

---

3. Best described in the various essays of Wieruszowski, *Politics and Culture*. See also the important observations of Bruni in "Boncompagno da Signa," 83–87, 99–108, and those of Witt, "Medieval Italian Culture," 35–47. Witt also discusses this theme in his forthcoming *Medieval Italian Culture and the Origins of Humanism*. Throughout this book I employ the notion of textual communities developed by Brian Stock in his important *Implications of Literacy*, esp. 88–92, 233–40.

4. Klapisch-Zuber, "Le chiavi," 769–75. There is a growing consensus among scholars working on medieval language arts that the peculiar usages and doctrines of medieval masters cannot be explained without reference to moral categories and goals; see, e.g., Law, "Originality," 43–47; Bruni, "Boncompagno da Signa," 106–8; Reeve, "Circulation," 115–16; and Bagni, "Artes dictandi," 204–20.

5. On normative language study, see Law, "Originality," 44–46; Carruthers, *Book of*

Grammar thus became a forum for private, contemplative literary study. Its aims were both personal, moral improvement and elementary instruction in language skills needed for further professional work. Meanwhile, the goals of rhetoric were narrowed; it became a fully professional discipline concerned with public pronouncements, especially legal ones. Ronald Witt aptly remarks the end product of this centuries-long development when he notes that the fourteenth-century humanists used a fully medieval rhetorical style in their public letters while reserving a grammatical classicism for poetry and private correspondence, "depending on the public or private character of the apparent audience."[6] Only in the fifteenth century was a classicizing sort of rhetoric recreated, as an add-on to a grammar course that slowly retreated into a skills orientation. In our period, grammar and rhetoric (in the ancient, distinct sense of these fields) had been thoroughly telescoped into the sole available arts course outside the university, the moral art of grammar.

The matter of audience is crucial here. The medieval grammar course was not designed for professional education. To be sure, it *could* be pre-professional, and students frequently gave it up with an effective minimum of accomplishment in order to move on to legal training. Grammar as a field of study, however, had long since become a literary form of education. Such an education had meaning for parents only if it could also provide a firm grounding in the moral conduct of private life. This form of grammar, intended to educate a moral literary public, is the subject of this book.

The tradition of moral-rhetorical pedagogy was weak in the Italian universities, oriented as they were to the study of law. With the breakdown of the university-level trivium under the pressures of preparing canon and civil lawyers, notaries, and civil servants for the expanding Italian city governments, grammar was left as the single "arts course" in the common curriculum. Logic became a preparatory discipline, rarely studied for its own sake. Meanwhile, rhetoric was increasingly focused on epistolary theory and notarial training; it became a professional course equivalent to law, medicine, or theology. In the early trecento, Italian universities responded to this literary impoverishment by establishing chairs of grammatical studies, whose occupants concentrated on the study of the ancient poets. Somewhat later, they also appointed professors of rhetoric in the classical mold who used Cicero, Pseudo-Cicero, and Quin-

---

*Memory,* 156–81; Copeland, *Rhetoric, Hermeneutics,* 42–52, 154–58, 221–23; Amsler, *Etymology,* 82–132, 177–95; Bagni, "L'inventio," 108–11.

6. Witt, "Medieval Italian Culture," 54.

tilian as their central texts. These rhetoricians sometimes lectured on the Roman poets as well.[7]

Before the mid-fourteenth century, however, and even later in some places, literary study was largely relegated to extra-university "preparatory schools" or, more properly, grammar schools, since most of the students in such courses did not actually go on to the university. Modern scholars, judging the disappearance of Latin classics from the university arts curriculum by the standards of the great twelfth-century renaissance, have tended to think that grammar was in eclipse and that classical studies generally decayed.[8] Although this view certainly reflects the priorities of the thirteenth- and fourteenth-century university-trained elites, it does not give us a good sense of what happened at the pre-university level or among students who were not bound for the university at all.

The relegation of Latin grammar to grammar schools probably worked to broaden the literary public, especially in such cities as Florence which did not have a strong university tradition. Without such university influence, Latin schools and teachers responded to other social and intellectual pressures. Although this book is directed toward Latin education, it is important to recognize what Werner Raith has justly called the multi-layered nature (*Mehrschichtigkeit*) of Florentine education.[9] The traditional Latin curriculum inherited from the monastic Middle Ages was only one of several kinds of formal schooling available in Florence. Grammar masters and students saw themselves as a latinate, internationally oriented elite; but they lived in a society dominated by manufacturing and commercial interests. One result was the flourishing schools of *abbaco* (business arithmetic). Outside any schools, however, by far the largest number of Florentines got nonformal educations in homes, churches, and workshops. These women and men received training that was just as clearly goal-oriented, practical, and moralistic as the Latin or *abbaco* courses.

This broad and variegated backdrop was never far from the minds of Latin educators. Grammar masters were answerable to fathers with commerical or professional ambitions for their sons and to mothers who daily went to school to mendicant preachers and confessors. Even the immense class of unschooled wage earners had an infuence on the Latin school, via the ideals of the mendicants. One goal of trecento Latin study was to

---

7. Cf. Banker, "*Ars dictaminis*," 159–65; Bagni, "Artes dictandi," 211–20.

8. See, e.g., Witt, "Medieval Ars Dictaminis," who in general follows Kristeller on this subject.

9. Raith, *Florenz*, esp. 116–21.

create a reader who could interpret the wisdom of Latin texts for broad, unlettered audiences. The paradigm for such a popularizing Latinist was the mendicant preacher. As we see in the following chapters, mendicant ideals informed many of the peculiarly Florentine modifications of the Latin course.

Grammar schools, because they retained some of the ideals of earlier monastic schools with a comparable curriculum, continued the older tradition of integrated grammatical teaching. Grammar masters were thus able to accommodate the demands of urban parents for a firm grounding in Christian catechesis. In this way, formal study of the ancient Christian moral rhetoric, loosely based on the Augustinian corpus, became widely available to the growing urban upper classes. Very few Florentines completed a grammar course and fewer still went on to university study. But many studied *grammatica* for a few years and were exposed to its principal lesson, the power of moral rhetoric. People like these made up the largest if not the most articulate part of the literary public for Dante and Petrarch.

This new public had a broad appreciation of both the formal qualities of literature and its moral impact. It was an educated audience but not a learned one. It possessed strong preferences for stern moralizing in most contexts, the capacity to understand allegory and spiritual analogy when skillfully presented, and a deep appreciation of ironic and satirical treatments of moral hypocrisy, especially as evidenced in the institutions of the church. For urban grammar masters and students, and perhaps more important still for the students' parents, the value of the Latin course resided both in imparting an ethical education and in providing entrée to the major professions. Whether or not the humanists wrote *for* this public, these people were the largest part of the literate classes, and their tastes and priorities often determined what succeeded in the literary marketplace. Their education was the instrument by which the market for books was fueled, both before and after the invention of printing. Tuscany, with its high literacy rate and flourishing vernacular tradition, was a literary marketplace unto itself. It is important to our understanding of the halting start and uneven success of early humanism to see how this market differed educationally from the rest of Italy.

My approach in this book differs considerably from the existing studies of medieval and Renaissance education. Although I have relied heavily and gratefully on the work of other scholars, I have also written with a firm conviction that the present literature is often too ambitious, too quick to generalize from limited sources, and insufficiently cognizant of the possibility of regional variation. Even the best and most sophisticated modern treatments do not address Italian schooling of the *buon secolo antico* on its own terms. Two approaches are discernible. The first typically takes polemical writings on medieval education by humanist authors stretching from Petrarch to Ramus at face value and thereby creates a strawman, "medieval pedagogy," which is pilloried for its shortcomings, most notably a total lack of feeling for classical Latin style. This is the basic approach of the classic in the field, Eugenio Garin's *L'educazione in Europa (1400–1600)*, which expressly excludes the trecento from consideration and thus fails to confront the meaning of the medieval teaching tradition for the early humanists. Such a view has the merit of giving weight to the reform of Latin stylistics, a major concern of the humanist movement. But it truncates unnaturally the continuity in moral and pedagogical thought that underlay the transition from trecento to quattrocento schools.

A similar but more inclusive view, more judiciously stated, is to be found in Paul F. Grendler's *Schooling in Renaissance Italy: Literacy and Learning, 1300–1600*, which, as its very title shows, attempts a broader study than did Garin. Grendler draws together documentation from archives and literary sources across northern and central Italy, and he provides several useful comparisons of individual cities at different periods during the Renaissance broadly defined. Grendler subscribes, nonetheless, to Garin's fundamental picture of the early fifteenth century as one of thoroughgoing reform, and in so doing he treats the trecento rather monochromatically. This is not to belittle Grendler's achievement. Indeed, he fills out and renders more convincing than ever the thesis of Garin. Garin based his argument chiefly on the humanists' own writings. Grendler is also able to estimate the penetration of humanist ideals into schools in provincial towns by marshaling evidence from such documents as teachers' letters of appointment, city council debates, official professions of faith required by local inquisitors, and surviving printed schoolbooks. He provides as well a good structural analysis of grammatical education and coherent descriptions nowhere else to be found of its content at various levels.[10]

10. Grendler's book has been widely reviewed. See especially the evaluations of Melissa Bullard in *The Historian* 53 (1991), 785; my own in *Modern Language Review* 85 (1990), 221–22; D. S. Chambers in the *Journal of Ecclesiastical History* 42 (1991), 310–12; and Robert Black's essay "Italian Renaissance Education." Grendler defends his overall approach and the use of the humanist polemics as sources in "Reply to Robert Black."

An alternative approach is that of Anthony Grafton and Lisa Jardine in their *From Humanism to the Humanities*, which also locates educational reform in the fifteenth century, though rather later than for Garin and Grendler and with a different meaning and content. In particular, Jardine and Grafton propose a gradual evolution of the grammar and rhetoric curriculum, as classicizing teachers sought an influential place for the new latinity in the service of increasingly absolutist states. For them, the product of the new humanist education possessed "the sort of personality traits that any Renaissance ruler found attractive, above all, obedience and docility."[11]

In this view the Italian humanist program for grammar was not really complete until near the end of the fifteenth century and underwent further, profound changes in northern Europe. The thesis of Grafton and Jardine has the advantage that it accords better than Garin's with the limited evidence about when humanist thought effectively took over the elementary classrooms of Renaissance Italy. Because they concentrate on a few highly successful figures, however, and do not deal with the abundant archival sources for everyday teachers in the fifteenth century, their study does not go very far in explaining how the humanist reform took hold. Their opening chapters on the fourteenth and early fifteenth centuries, moreover, are not useful for our purposes in studying the trecento. They overrate the positive, disputational qualities of medieval education so as to cut down to size the reformers of the early fifteenth century. They seem to imagine that the tedium, repetitiveness, and conformism of primary education in the Renaissance was the creation of the humanists, although it had characterized elementary Latin education throughout the Middle Ages. The ideal medieval pedagogy they describe, if it ever existed, was a northern European phenomenon and primarily concerned with advanced levels of study, not an Italian or elementary pedagogy at all.[12]

Whichever of these approaches is taken, the trecento presented is monolithically "medieval" and remains in the past tense, well in the background of a fifteenth-century, "Renaissance" experience. Both views portray the earlier Italian educational experience as essentially the same as, or merely a local variant of, the scholasticism of high medieval France. In a review article that treats Garin and several other works, Robert Black has correctly pointed out that all these scholars assume too sharp a contrast, too radical a break between medieval and humanist pedagogy.[13]

11. Grafton and Jardine, *From Humanism*, 24.
12. Ibid., esp. xi–xvi, 1–18.
13. Black, "Italian Renaissance Education," 333–34.

There exist, however, many detailed studies on the training and cultural outlook of the early literary and philosophical humanists. The authors of these studies have been my guides in the present work. Charles Davis, Vittore Branca, Giuseppe Billanovich, Paul Oskar Kristeller, Ronald Witt, Francesco Bruni, Werner Raith, and their numerous students have painted a picture of early humanist culture that has little to do with the commonplaces of the historiography of medieval education. They do not consider humanism a radical break with the culture of the late Middle Ages. Instead, they portray a humanistic worldview built on a native Italian learning that was profoundly rhetorical, deeply urban in outlook, and oriented toward the study of law.[14] Typically they have also assumed that some or all of the classicizing interests of the early humanists were imported from France in the course of the thirteenth and early fourteenth centuries. Witt, for example, has called attention to the impetus provided by both northern Latin culture and the many vernacular literatures of Italy, especially in French and Provençal, for the creation of the new classicizing Latin style.[15] Davis has also rightly stressed the importance of the mendicant orders in Tuscany in shaping the sort of education the great authors of the trecento received. Raith, by contrast, has emphasized the way Florence in the thirteenth and fourteenth centuries stood apart from international cultural norms and developed its own highly localized merchant worldview that received and modified influences from outside freely and autonomously.[16] These insights become major themes of what follows here.

Our picture of Italian grammatical culture in the trecento can be filled out and made more precise by recent, often detailed studies of pedagogical phenomena, textbooks, and single schools or local groups of schools. Christine Klapisch-Zuber, Robert Black, Christian Bec, Silvia Rizzo, Piero Lucchi, Gian Carlo Alessio, Paolo Bagni, and others have presented new sources—textbooks, archival documents about grammar masters and students, and literary treatments of educational issues—in important studies.[17] The social historians among them have helped elucidate the

14. The seminal studies are Davis, "Education in Dante's Florence," and "The Florentine *Studia*"; Billanovich, "Auctorista, humanista, orator"; Kristeller, *Renaissance Thought*; Witt, "Medieval Ars Dictaminis"; and Bruni, *L'italiano*. Witt's "Origins" and "Medieval Italian Culture" offer brief previews of a more comprehensive study in progress. The most up-to-date bibliography on education in the period is that in Grendler, *Schooling*, 431–61.

15. Witt, "Origins," 98–101, and "Medieval Italian Culture," 44–45; for this interpretation, see also Ullmann, "Some Aspects," 29–34.

16. See Raith, *Florenz*, esp. 111–35.

17. The studies by these scholars are described in part by Black, "Italian Renaissance Education." I am thinking especially of Alessio, "Le istituzioni scolastiche"; Klapisch-Zuber,

milieux and *mentalités* of the individuals who taught and studied Latin, and the philologists, paleographers, and literary historians have given us new critical approaches to the surviving texts.

Above all, these scholars have proved that we can understand the fourteenth century neither as a period of radical change nor yet as the staging area for some radical break to come. Texts and the communities that gather around them are the conditioning factor in the study of any strongly rhetorical culture like that of the trecento. In such communities, radical breaks are rare if they occur at all; in pedagogy they are especially rare.

Our understanding of elementary education in the Middle Ages has also been handicapped by an almost obsessive search by scholars for order and standardization. It is hard to understand why this is so. Surely we have long since learned that there were many Middle Ages, and that no five-hundred- or even two-hundred-year period can be very uniform in cultural terms. In education particularly, the talents and preferences of individual teachers have always resulted in wide variations of practice within even the most rigidly standardized curricula. So, although we may badly want to generalize, we need to realize the limits of any such attempt. Medieval education, and especially grammar, was an essentially conservative field, but its conservatism functioned first on a social and ethical level, secondarily on the level of technique and preference for individual texts, and only in a very weak and inconsistent way in the matter of systematic curricula.

In the matter of curricula particularly, the existing literature is seriously deficient because of a common misreading of sources. One recent scholar of medieval pedagogy, James McGregor, goes so far as to say that there are only "five major sources of information on grammar curricula" for the entire Middle Ages. He means that we have five systematic lists of authors and textbooks for lengthy courses of personal reading. He dismisses numerous other reading lists and curricula, representing what individual teachers actually "taught at various times" as being "of almost no value." Instead he tallies the frequency of occurrence of the school authors in library catalogues and *libri manuales*.[18] There is nothing wrong, certainly, with these latter sources, nor with consulting the great twelfth-century curricular theorists Conrad of Hirsau, Alexander Neckham, Aimeric, and the two anonymous writers who make up McGregor's "big five" sources.

---

"Le chiavi"; Lucchi, "La Santacroce"; Black, "Humanism and Education"; and Bagni, "Artes dictandi."

18. McGregor, "Ovid at School," 39–40.

But surely it is wrongheaded to favor this evidence, which yields lists of books in other than classroom contexts, over the records of books really used by grammar masters, however hard to count.

Conrad and the other medieval authors on curriculum present ideal courses of study conditioned by the resources of their local libraries and by their own ambitions to appear learned. All these authors wrote in the central Middle Ages, an era of system building deeply concerned with human psychology and with the techniques of learning and teaching. It was also an age of encyclopedism. One suspects them of including things they knew of but never read, or read but never taught. Such reading lists, as a result, are impossibly extensive and duplicative. They describe a choice of books ideally available to a model schoolmaster; they describe only the ambitions of the central Middle Ages.

Medieval library catalogues are even further removed from the schoolroom. They describe, usually very summarily, books owned at a given moment; they never tell us how recently copied, acquired, or read a given volume was. Like curricular compendia, they represent at best a range of possible choices, though with the advantage for the historian that they can be dated and localized. The medieval reader of a copy of Conrad of Hirsau could only dream of the library of grammar texts Conrad describes; the reader of a library catalogue was at least in the presence of the texts, to hand and in some sort of order.

*Libri manuales*, reading anthologies of poetic texts, are closer to the classroom. They are surviving books and can be individually described in terms of probable date, place of origin, and subsequent use. Some of the schoolbooks described later in this study are *libri manuales*. But if a scholar merely tabulates the contents of a broad sample of such anthologies, he or she abstracts too far from their concrete reality and obscures the actual use and nature of the texts included. *Liber manualis*, indeed, is a difficult term; it represents the kind of neat and orderly commonplace that often obscures the messy realities of medieval life. Eva Sanford's pioneering work on the subject, a compilation of four hundred such anthologies, has been cited to prove far more than she ever claimed for her inventory; she was well aware of the miscellaneous nature of the books both individually and as a group.[19] All too often the rest of us have treated the *liber manualis* as a true genre with a fixed meaning and intent. In fact, such anthologies could be assembled for a great variety of reasons. We know of examples designed as humble commonplace books for one or

19. Sanford, "Use of Classical Latin Authors," 190.

two users. Others were sturdy reference books for institutional reading, deluxe anthologies to grace a noblewoman's chamber, or schoolbooks. Only a few *libri manuales* were clearly and unambiguously used in schoolrooms; only those should be counted as evidence for schooling.[20]

Within studies of the curricula, too, our field has been bedeviled by an anachronistic search for order and by imprecise, shifting terminology. Scholars have tended to think that textbooks followed one or more set patterns across many centuries. Both the *Liber Catonianus*, proposed in 1914 by Boas, and the *Auctores octo*, invented it would seem as a marketing come-on by French printers of the fifteenth century, are misnomers when applied to medieval Italian teaching practice.[21] They represent attempts—one modern, one ancient—to find or impose a canon of elementary Latin readings. But, though such canons certainly existed among teachers and students of individual schools, cities, or regions, it merely confuses our view of the situation to assume that they did not much change over time. Nor can we assume that they changed in some orderly, organic fashion, so that a venerable *Liber Catonianus*, a collection centered on Cato, was gradually modified through addition and substitution, slowly and naturally becoming the *Auctores octo*.[22]

Above all, we must not believe that "teachers seem to have valued all *auctores* equally; all taught language and good morality."[23] The evidence we have shows the exact opposite. Long before the humanist critique of the medieval elementary curriculum grew hot, schoolmasters, abbots, even bishops had strong opinions about which authors to include or exclude. Their choices conditioned not only what students learned but also in large degree how they learned it. The great reforms of the fifteenth-century humanists concerned texts, to be sure, but also the context of learning. Although the techniques for inculcating elementary skills changed hardly at all across the period from 1300 to 1500, the early humanist educators quickly saw that the boarding school context could offer a level of control over the life of the student that reproduced in some ways the ideal of the monastic school.[24] This was so because educators of the Renaissance shared the medieval idea that grammar education was an education to the moral and spiritual life. As we see throughout this book,

---

20. An otherwise exemplary study that makes this error is Avesani, *Quattro miscellanee.*
21. Avesani, "Il primo ritmo," 475–78. Cf. Boas, "De librorum Catonianorum historia."
22. Grendler, *Schooling*, 114, presents this last notion, based on the work of Boas, Garin, and Avesani; it is echoed by Black, "Italian Renaissance Education," 328.
23. Grendler, *Schooling*, 114.
24. Ibid., 2–3, 131–32, 141.

the urban schoolmasters of the trecento also held this view; indeed, they bequeathed it to the humanist teachers of the quattrocento. But in their schools, amid the turbulent life of commercial towns, they could never achieve the degree of control over the students' behavior that boarding school masters had. The Tuscan masters seem to have compensated for this perceived instability by modifying and restricting the curriculum.

By now it will be clear that I believe that an important way to see how grammar teaching worked, and especially how it could have created a public for the new humanist authors, is to close in on a sufficiently well-defined segment of the highly varied Italian educational scene and examine its local usages and prejudices. Florence seemed the obvious choice to me, not only for the richness of its surviving sources and the eminence of its favorite sons, but also because, both in myth and in fact, it was the commercial and intellectual center of Tuscany. Tuscany is a region separated by tradition, language, and a high mountain range from the rest of northern and central Italy. Purely on the level of material culture, it is easier to isolate the products of Tuscan schools and bookmakers than those of any other region. It is easier to say what, if anything, distinguishes this one region from others. Then too, by the middle of the thirteenth century and for a good while thereafter, a precocious Tuscan vernacular literature created different conditions for the study of Latin south of the Apennines than obtained to the north. In the early years of the fourteenth century, Dante pictured the linguistic map of Italy with a sharp divide at the Apennines.[25] What we know of the earliest humanist scholarship confirms the Apennine boundary. The real birthplace of humanist classicizing style was in northern Padua, and it was many decades before Florentines wholeheartedly embraced the new movement.[26] In late medieval Tuscany the literary preeminence of Latin and the value of classicizing style were not taken for granted, and so the role of the Latin teacher could not be the same as in the north.

It would also seem that the grammar schools of Tuscany were less dominated by university masters than those of Emilia or Lombardy or the Veneto, where the universities of Bologna, Pavia, and Padua acted as centers of attraction and diffusion in literary affairs. The Tuscan universities of the trecento, by contrast, were weak and sometimes intermittent

25. *De vulgari eloquentia*, I.x.3–6.
26. Witt, "Origins," 96–103. For more on Florentine provincialism, see Lanza, *Polemiche*, 79–102, and Raith, *Florenz*, esp. 138.

centers of activity. The communal grammar schools in small towns, the modest upper schools at Pisa, Arezzo, and Siena, and the flourishing private or independent grammar masters of Florence were rather more on their own in matters of curriculum than more northerly schools, and less tied to a university-preparatory mold or to the pretensions of fashionable teachers of the great *studia* of the north. In short, Florence offers us a laboratory for studying a regional teaching tradition. It was not a typical trecento town, but it is isolatable; we can describe it in some detail.

The choice of the exact period for this study is somewhat more arbitrary than the focus on Florence, but it seems logical to consider the fourteenth century, broadly conceived as running from about 1260–70 to the 1390s, for several reasons. I have already alluded to the fact that the trecento is less studied by historians of education than the fifteenth or later centuries. If we add to it the last thirty or forty years of the thirteenth century, the period includes the active careers of the teachers of the great Florentine authors from Dante to Salutati and yet stops short of the first schoolmasters to have been influenced by the humanist critique of the medieval curriculum. In terms of great teaching personalities, we may want to think of the period as running from Brunetto Latini's generation to Francesco da Buti's.

Obviously, this definition of period is aimed at controlling the evidence. We need to focus on a period that can be considered as a unified whole, without having to worry that intervening changes in literary theory and philosophy will skew the descriptions we create of classroom practice. When I began to examine the surviving schoolbooks of the period, it also became clear that a new style of Latin reading book was designed and became common in Florence toward the end of the thirteenth century and became the standard in Florentine classrooms in the early trecento. This form of elementary reader continued in use into the fifteenth century.

There are parallels in other fields of social and cultural history that confirm this choice of period. In the non-Latin realm, 1250 marks the beginning of the first great Tuscan literary flowering, the *stil nuovo*, and contemporaneously the start of intense activity in translating Latin texts of all sorts into Tuscan prose of varying quality and literary pretension. There is evidence, too, that in the last third of the thirteenth century the Tuscan ecclesiastical establishment finally began to implement the educational decrees of the Lateran Council of 1215. This meant improved education of the ordinary clergy and the possibility that even relatively humble parish priests might take on teaching of reading and writing if not also of grammar.

Political and administrative developments also give us good reasons for picking up the story in the late thirteenth century. The first good records of municipal support for grammar schools in Tuscany date from about 1240. This situation directly reflects the improved quality of record keeping and thereby also a higher level of literacy and a political awareness of educational issues associated with the preservation of administrative records. The withdrawal of bishops from local political affairs in favor of the communes was largely complete by the mid-thirteenth century.[27] This development may have contributed directly to the communes' new sense of responsibility for grammar education, or it may merely signal the fact that a nonclerical class of record keepers was now essential for the maintenance of good and legitimate city government. In either case, it meant that grammar masters would be freer to depart from the traditional, clerical concerns of Latin education.

Last, the fourteenth century represents without a doubt the period of Italy's liberation from cultural models imported from northern Europe, especially France. The Hundred Years' War definitively ended French cultural hegemony in Europe even as, from the mid-thirteenth century on, the French language was spreading from poetic to nonpoetic contexts and becoming as much a legal and administrative language as a courtly and literary one. This development both provided models for nascent Italian vernaculars and dethroned French and Provençal as the poetic languages of preference among the Italian aristocracy. At the same time, the earliest attempts at classicism in Latin poetry, beginning about 1280, gave a very tentative birth to the movement we now call humanism.[28]

The end of our period coincides with the first maturity of Florentine civic humanism, in the generation after Salutati. As now-classic studies by Hans Baron have shown, this was also the first version of humanism to be concerned in significant part with a local readership. We may expect that it had a major effect on that local culture. The present book is limited as far as possible, therefore, to the period before the antihumanist polemic of the turn of the century, the better to isolate the point of departure of the civic humanists and the ideological divergence between them and their local critics.

The picture of Florence that results from the existing literature is incomplete, scattered, and uneven. It certainly does not tell us what was unique about Tuscany in the early Renaissance. I have therefore developed two new bodies of data to enhance our understanding of how children

27. Cf. Raith, *Florenz*, 140–41.
28. Cf. Witt, "Medieval Italian Culture," 51–54.

learned Latin in trecento Florence. First, I undertook a broad survey of the grammar and reading books that survive from the period and can be surely assigned Florentine or Tuscan provenance. In surveying the class-books, it became clear that a fixed and regular type of book was designed and made for the use of students in the grammar schools of Florence at the stage in which they were learning to read. Florentine teachers used these readers to teach Latin reading and study skills, much as modern teachers use graded readers. Such readers include many traditional texts used by earlier medieval teachers, but they do so selectively, in a way that seems to have been distinctive of Florence. Within the larger survey, I therefore developed a systematic census and codicological descriptions of the manu-script readers that fit this classroom format (see the Appendix). This approach allows us to describe in some detail the reading curriculum of trecento Florentine grammar schools. It is remarkable that a wide variety of ancient and medieval texts were available to the teachers of fourteenth-century Tuscany but that Florentine grammarians chose to use a highly restricted selection of only five or six basic books on a regular basis. Thus, the census offers us empirical evidence for describing and localizing the attitudes of one city's teachers. It also provides us with a map for further study of the meaning of grammar in Florentine society, in the form of a list of books we know were read more or less intensively in that city's gram-mar classrooms.

Armed with this map, then, I try to give each of the teaching texts a pedagogical and specifically fourteenth-century reading. The results of this second stage of investigation confirm the commonplace claims of grammar masters to provide a moral education along with an initiation into the useful and prestigious arts of the Latin language. This com-monplace has been a sticking point for many writers on elementary education, because it is not clear, except on the local-culture level, how teachers can use textbooks for more than rote memory teaching. Then too, the elementary commentary tradition does not go deeply into moral lessons; it is necessarily concerned with the essentials of getting the stu-dent through the texts linguistically. This is true at every period in the history of education: we can frequently recover the textbooks used, but we have far less to go on in describing the specific uses teachers made of those texts. As a result, medievalists have tended to accept uncritically the claim of grammarians to be teaching morals and to assume that some fairly elementary code of conduct was meant, based on Augustinian moral thought but either so vaguely defined or so universal in application as to defy localization and even description.

In fact, there were—and common sense tells us there must have been—

both local variations and temporal changes in what was taught. I think we can achieve a genuinely fourteenth-century reading of the school texts by attentively placing them in their social context and by reading them in the surviving manuscripts as well as with the aid of critical texts. The manuscripts are quite specific about context and use. Among other things, they provide us with the names of many of the students who owned them, their neighborhood and family affiliations, sometimes also the names of their grammar masters. Notes and *accessus* (formal, literary introductions) give us clues about the lessons sought in these venerated texts. Literary sources, even the vivid condemnations of the early humanists, also enrich our sense of the context of learning and teaching. Even the combinations of texts in individual manuscripts are evidence.

These two stages of the inquiry are presented in some detail in Chapters 2 through 7. They are preceded by a scene-setting chapter on the institutional structure of Latin education at Florence. The final chapter is an attempt to situate educational matters in the context of Florentine society more broadly. Throughout this work, I have tried to understand grammar as fourteenth-century women and men did, as an introduction to the meaning of Latin culture within a bilingual civilization. It is essential, then, to address the social meaning of Latin in a society increasingly dominated by non-Latin readers.[29] The grammar master was a moral interpreter and guide for his students. Although he owned only modest social standing in oligarchical Florence, he was a crucial figure in educating the literary public. Without "the slender flame of poesy in Italy," as Boccaccio called the grammar school authors, there would have been no public at all for the poetry of the early humanists.

In this context, the significance of Latin study in trecento Florence becomes clear. It was a conservative force harnessed to the political needs of the ruling elite. Latin study had by this time been so thoroughly inserted into a bilingual, oligarchical culture that traditional Latin grammarians necessarily resisted the newer, more classicizing grammar of the humanists, which was too little tied to the Guelf literary establishment of Florence. The traditionalists, moreover, were abetted by the immensely popular and influential mendicant preachers whose own learning was intimately connected with the older grammatical tradition.

By examining the educational situation of a single city and its region, I hope to have drawn a portrait of a local literary culture. In particular I have tried to describe a Latin readership with many levels of ambition,

29. Cf. Bäuml, "Varieties," 262–65.

accomplishment, and sophistication. The new, humanist taste makers in Italy did not write with the educational level of a broad literary public in mind. Much less did they think of their audience as consisting of a single city. But the Florentine public certainly was eager for latinity of all sorts, including classical and patristic texts, classics of medieval piety, classicizing romances and fiction, and translations in all these genres. Our portrait, therefore, embraces literary consumers of all sorts, among them the ones who supported early humanism.

# EDUCATIONAL
# STRUCTURES

Any discussion of education in fourteenth-century Florence must begin with Giovanni Villani's proud portrait of the schools of the city in the late 1330s. Although brief and sketchy, it is the only literary work of its time to attempt a characterization of a whole city's educational system: "We find that there are from eight to ten thousand boys and girls learning to read. Of boys studying *abbaco* and arithmetic, there are from 1000 to 1200 in six schools. And those studying Latin and logic in four large schools number from 550 to 600."[1]

Villani was not just a talented chronicler and promoter of Florentine civic pride; he was also the exponent of providential notions of political history and an eloquent apologist for the oligarchical political system of the Florence of his youth. The passage on schools is part of a four-chapter digression from his account of the War of Messer Mastino (1336–38), and it is expressly intended to illustrate how the wealth and power of Florence made it possible for the city to undertake an expensive foreign war. The chapter in which the schools are described has its own brief preface that tells the reader what to make of Villani's numbers in moral and political terms: "It seems to me that I should make mention of other great things of our city so that our successors in future times will understand her rising and falling fortunes. Thus the wise and powerful men who

---

1. The passage occurs in Book 11, chap. 94, here in the text of Villani's *Cronica*, ed. Gherardi Dragomanni, 3:324; all following *Cronica* citations are to this edition. On this passage, see Frugoni, "Giovanni Villani." Villani's nearest rival in describing schools is Bonvesin de la Riva, who gave four short items on the subject in his *Meraviglie di Milano* at the end of the thirteenth century; see the edition of Verga, 20–21.

rule her in the future will, with the example and record of this chronicle, be able to move the city forward and bring her to greater power."[2] What follows is an overview of all the numerable *grandi cose* Villani was able to assemble. Sometimes the reader is left puzzling as to his sources, but the rhetorical meaning of all these numbers is clear: this is the wealth and power of the city, diligently to be preserved.

What then do his remarks on schools really tell us? Leaving aside for a moment the reliability of Villani's numbers, we note immediately that several different kinds of schools are mentioned. Comparing his account with other sources for the period, we discover that these schools were typical of Florence but not of all Italian cities. Particularly striking is the immense number of boys and girls who were learning to read, apparently a matter of civic pride to Villani. Taken at face value, his claim gives trecento Florence the highest literacy rate in premodern Europe.[3]

A much smaller number, of boys only, were studying business arithmetic, or *abbaco*, in six schools. Villani assumes that these are separate from the reading and grammar schools, something that seems to have been a regular practice at Florence. This separation, however, was not the case elsewhere. It never characterized primary education at Genoa and seems to have been at most an occasional practice at Venice, the only comparably large, non-university towns about which we have good information. In smaller towns of Tuscany the Florentine pattern sometimes held, but not invariably.[4]

Last, a select group studied "Latin and logic in four large schools." Again, the case is singular because Latin (*grammatica* meant this) was not segregated from business arithmetic in most other big-city schools we know about, and because each of the four Florentine schools must have enrolled well over a hundred students and have had several teachers each for Villani's numbers to be even approximately correct.[5]

This overall pattern is unlike what we know of urban schools of the period in northern Italy and beyond the Alps. We do find a comparable segregation of the curriculum in some city-run schools elsewhere in Tuscany, but there is nothing to suggest that any of these specialized schools

2. *Cronica*, 3:323.
3. Graff, *Legacies*, 78–79; Grendler, *Schooling*, 71–74; Klapisch-Zuber, "Le chiavi," 774–75; Fiumi, "Ecomomia e vita privata," 249–51.
4. Petti Balbi, *L'insegnamento*, and Grendler, *Schooling*, discuss the Genoese and Venetian evidence, respectively. On the *abbaco* course as a broad training in literacy, see Melis, *L'economia fiorentina*, 194–96; Sapori, "La cultura," 60–68; Raith, *Florenz*, 149–52.
5. See note 16 below.

were as large as those Villani describes, nor did any other town count as large a number of students as a portion of its population.[6] Although *abbaco* was widely taught, it was something of a Tuscan monopoly in the specialized form Villani mentions.[7] This suggests several things. There may have been a Tuscan teaching tradition distinct from that of Venice, Milan, or Genoa, probably also from the rest of transapennine Italy. And Florence itself stands apart from the smaller Tuscan towns, both for the size and complexity of its schools and for its general lack of subsidies for public instruction.[8] In short, there seems to have been considerable local and regional variation in the teaching traditions of trecento Italy.[9]

It should be noted that most scholars have not reached this conclusion. The traditional historiography of education assumes a common medieval teaching tradition throughout Europe or at least throughout Italy.[10] But, as we see in the next chapter, there was a distinct Florentine curriculum for the Latin reading course. It seems highly likely that other regional variations also obtained. Certainly the pattern Villani describes was firmly established in Florence. Diarists, documents, and literary sources are quite specific that children studied either *abbaco* or *grammatica* after once learning to read, but that they never did both at the same time. Usually, they went to quite different masters and schools for training in the two skills, at least in Florence. In smaller Tuscan towns a single master might in fact teach all three courses or two of the three, but, even then, few if any students did both *abbaco* and *grammatica* at the same time.

There does not seem to have been a preferred order of study either; *abbaco* could precede, follow, or interrupt the Latin grammar course. Nor were there fixed ages for starting the various school courses, or fixed terms

6. Black, "Humanism and Education," 175–76; Barsanti, *Il pubblico insegnamento*, 54–57. Zanelli, *Del pubblico insegnamento*, 114–28, found no evidence of *abbaco* teachers at all in fourteenth-century Pistoia; this may mean that *abbaco* was taught there in the reading and writing schools, as at Venice and Genoa, or in separate schools that are not documented as well as the public grammar schools. Or, it may just mean that the sources are prejudiced against the *abbachista*; Bonvesin de la Riva describes eight grammarians, forty singing masters, and seventy elementary teachers but no *abbaco* masters in Milan.

7. Denley, "Governments," 101; Raith, *Florenz*, 151.

8. Denley, "Governments," 99–104, shows how differences in scale between cities resulted in curriculum and organizational variation.

9. On regional variation, see Frova, "Le scuole," 119–43, esp. 126; Petti Balbi, "Istituzioni," 25–26, 28; and Denley, "Governments," 99–104.

10. Frova, *Istruzione*, 102–3; Grendler, *Schooling*, 111–17; Garin, *Pensiero*, 91–93; Petti Balbi, "Istituzioni," 21–34. Raith, *Florenz*, 138, on the other hand, emphasizes as I do the distinct Florentine tradition.

of study.[11] We know most in this regard about the difficult and text-oriented grammar course, but *abbaco* too had a flexible program. Students seem to have started schooling of all sorts when they were able and their parents willing. They left off the course when they had passed a pertinent milestone set by their elders (reading the psalter, mastering the grammar book, finishing Aesop or the poetic anthology of Prosper of Aquitaine), or when necessity called them into the world of work, or when they failed and were sent home by their masters.[12]

Villani's schools and courses, then, were defined functionally in terms of tasks and not by expectations of age or according to developmental norms. This is consistent with what we know of late medieval educational theory more generally. Medieval pedagogy was founded on neoplatonic philosophical psychology, enlarged by Aristotelian notions of the action of the mind, and completed with an Augustinian theology of salvation. In brief, man was created and could be sanctified by the virtuous, informing power of God. Man's task was to return along the creative path by imitating virtues whose image was implicit in his own likeness to the creator. God's informing of the soul was answered by man's conforming to paths of virtue. At the same time, information of all sorts was organized by the individual mind and stored in the memory, from which it could be produced on demand for salutary effect. Ethical behavior was normally learned through the example of other good men, but it could also be studied in moral literature of all sorts.[13]

11. Grendler, *Schooling*, 308–9, implies that Villani says *abbaco* preceded *grammatica*; but there are individual cases in which this was clearly not the order of study, for example, Bartolomeo di Niccolò dei Valori, as evidenced in his diary (Firenze, BNC Panciatichi 134, fol. 1r), and Donato Velluti's son, on whom see Sapori, "La cultura," 71. Villani does list the two schools in the order *abbaco, grammatica* but does not say that students took these courses in any order. Petti Balbi's opinion, exactly the opposite of Grendler's, that *ovunque la grammatica precede l'abbaco* ("Istituzioni," 38), is also too doctrinaire; it seems grounded in the notion that the reading and writing course was a course in "grammatica," but Villani and many other contemporary sources do not use the term in this way, reserving it instead for the stage of latinizing (explained below).

12. Cf. Frova, *Istruzione*, 102–3, 115. For examples of such dropouts, see Klapisch-Zuber, "Le chiavi," 775–79; Sapori, "La cultura," 67–71.

13. Ducci, *Un saggio*, 29–35, 51–52; Carruthers, *Book of Memory*, 54–60; Klapisch-Zuber, "Le chiavi," 773–75. For Dante's view of grammar as a moral art, see Vance, "Differing Seed," 237–38, 252–55. Such neoplatonic notions of the moral end of all language arts manifest themselves in several ways. A particularly telling example is the need felt by the translator of the pseudo-Ciceronian treatise on the rhetorical colors edited by Scolari, "Un volgarizzamento," 246–47, to precede his purely technical manual with a disquisition on the four cardinal virtues.

In such a scheme, children had no distinct psychology. They were merely smaller and weaker than adults and had to be encouraged (or forced) to learn through the same sort of imitative behavior prescribed for the moral improvement of adults. They were given clearly defined tasks to master; and they were required to take as much time to master them as needed because, unless they conformed their minds well to the pattern implicit in the task, they had learned no lesson at all, or no virtuous one. This theory underlay the strong task orientation of all medieval education. Translated into the bilingual world of trecento Italy, it helps explain the relative exclusivity of the "grammar and logic" course Villani describes.

The segregation of the curriculum also depended on contemporary perceptions of the appropriateness of different subject matters for different kinds of student. Reading was a skill widely valued and relatively widely practiced in trecento Italy. It was, if not expected of all, certainly considered highly useful; it was appropriate even for girls to learn. *Abbaco*, or computation, was also a useful skill, but it pertained to the working world of commerce and industry, and then only on the administrative, managerial, and entrepreneurial levels. Many but not most boys would have had some use for it; girls would not. Latin, by contrast, was the skill of professionals, churchmen, and intellectuals. It was above all a public man's accomplishment, one that set men of certain political and cultural ambitions apart from their fellow citizens. The singularity of the segregated arithmetic course has struck scholars as a particular characteristic of Florentine schooling, but it is probably fairer to say that Florentines segregated Latin from the more mundane disciplines.[14] It was both less immediately useful—a prejudice universal among middle-class Florentine writers—and more prestigious in linking the student with a larger world of learning.[15]

Villani assumed that his readers had a certain familiarity with the three types of school he described and with their distinct functions. He would have expected his audience to know exactly how to assess the numbers he sprinkled so liberally through his chronicle. Modern readers, alas, have none of Villani's particular counting habits, and they disagree considerably on what the numbers mean. The great Florentine chronicler was certainly no statistician and, as with many premodern authors, the larger his numbers the less reliable they seem to be in modern terms.[16]

14. Cf. Sapori, "La cultura," 66–68; Melis, *Economia fiorentina*, 194–96.

15. Frova, "La scuola," 141–43; cf. Cardini, "Alfabetismo," esp. 508–11; Raith, *Florenz*, 116–21.

16. The most recent attempt to treat Villani's numbers as statistics is that of Grendler,

Villani was not a naif, however. He clearly indicated the vagueness of his first student population estimate, telling his reader only that he wanted to claim more literate citizens for Florence than any rival city could boast. He might as well have said five to six thousand instead of eight to ten; those numbers would obviously yield vastly different statistics, but they would have had the same rhetorical effect. By contrast, the other two numbers provided are given some precision. In particular, he adds the number of schools in each category by way of specifying his sources or methods of computation. In a casual walk about town, he could have visited these ten schools in a morning; even more likely, he gathered information by gossiping with friends and colleagues in the piazza about where their sons studied and how many schoolmates they had. He even seems to anticipate some protest about the numbers of grammar students when he specifies four *large* schools, larger perhaps than his reader might expect. Villani for some reason excludes from his prideful counts the numerous small schools run by masters teaching privately. Perhaps they did not seem significant enough or singular enough. Villani may have thought that their existence, like that of private tutors to the very rich, would be obvious. In any case, such small schools were surely beyond the ability of any fourteenth-century citizen to count, *da non potere stimare*, as Villani would have put it.[17]

There is no point in belaboring such numbers as hard statistics; they are not and cannot be taken as such. But Villani did expect us to believe him, and his choice of phrasing betrays the accounting mind of the Florentine merchant class. We can almost see the ledger page. Our finding is: item, reading students, eight to ten thousand; item, *abbaco* students, six schools, to a total of 1,000 to 1,200. We are to understand a large population of studious young people, a broad literacy rate, substantial specialized training in *abbaco* schools, and four large, proud Latin schools for well-selected sons of culturally ambitious Florentines. As the list goes on, the data become both prouder and more verifiable. The numbers are rhetorically

---

*Schooling,* 71–74; cf. especially, Graff, *Legacies,* 76–81, and Raith, *Florenz,* 136, 142. Villani's large numbers of grammar students are not as improbable as Grendler suggests, for even in northern Italy there were occasional very large schools of this sort with many *repetitores*. Frova, *Istruzione,* 111, cites Parma statutes that limit the number of students per *repetitor* to fifty. At Lucca the statutes limited one master to forty-five pupils; see Fumi, *Regesti,* 2:2.621. Villani's four large schools, therefore, would only have needed staffs of four or five people to achieve the numbers he claims.

17. *Cronica,* 3:325. My point about the rhetorical reading of all such numbers is also made by Raith, *Florenz,* 136.

arranged and intended to convince, not by their numerical accuracy or precise magnitude, but by their pomp and concreteness.

Much farther than this grand introduction to the material Villani cannot take us. But we can go considerably farther. Certainly there are plenty of questions to ask Villani, and answers to be found in an attentive reading of the documentary and codicological evidence. Who were the students Villani describes and who were their teachers? Some few of their names survive in contracts or letters of appointment and a few more in the margins of schoolbooks. How and why did they study or not study Latin? Schoolbooks again provide part of the answer, though we must supplement their data with reference to literary sources and especially to family diaries. Above all, what did they learn? Here, more than anywhere else, we are dependent on surviving textbooks, which we must attempt to read with fourteenth-century eyes—both children's and teachers' eyes. We must also somehow come to terms with the students who do not appear in Villani's remarks, those who learned Latin in the small private schools that seem to have been common, or with parish clergy, with mendicant tutors, in apprenticeships with notaries, or at home. After this brief look at Villani, then, we must turn to the educational philosophy and curriculum to see what was typical practice in Florence and how these usages compared with those outside the city.

Since the Jesuit educational reforms of the late sixteenth century, the study of Latin has concentrated rather single-mindedly on the cultivation of good style based on the authors of the Golden Age. The Jesuit program was strictly skills oriented and left issues other than latinity aside.[18] Before the Jesuit reforms, however, both medieval and humanist grammar masters had assumed that practical moral philosophy was learned through the study of the Latin school authors, and that these moral lessons were inseparable from the linguistic ones. I have already mentioned the neoplatonic psychology behind this curricular assumption. In the trecento, the moral import of Latin study was taken for granted, as part and parcel of Latin's unique place as a regulated and immutable language of philosophical discourse. Even in Dante's idiosyncratic view, which privileged the *volgare* as a poetic instrument because it is more natural and better

18. Cherchi, "Jacopo Facciolati," 46–61, offers a corrective on this point to the view expressed by Curtius, *European Literature*, 264. On the Jesuits, see Cherchi, "Jacopo Facciolati," 55–56.

embedded in history, Latin was the only perfect and certain instrument for attaining to the wisdom and moral probity of the ancients.[19]

Dante developed this view against a widespread medieval notion that only Latin literacy could have moral import. The monastic grammar curriculum assumed that Latin was the student's first read language, something no longer true in fourteenth-century Italy. From the eleventh to the fourteenth century, the Latin literary culture of the West had been joined by new vernacular literatures. New kinds of literacy emerged: first the dual literacy of those who read and wrote Latin and applied this skill to the vernaculars, and then literacy in the vernacular alone. By the fourteenth century the "old" literacy, in Latin alone, had begun to disappear. In the fifteenth century a child educated first to Latin and unable to read a Romance or Germanic dialect would have seemed a freak.[20]

Under these circumstances the cultural role of Latin literature changed too. Latin had always been the vehicle of the West's high culture and would remain the linguistic badge of the most highly educated until the early twentieth century. But with the appearance of learned poetry in the vernaculars and of translated Latin classics, Latin necessarily ceded its exclusive claim to represent Western high culture. Moreover, some of the everyday burden of record keeping and legal business was transferred to the vernaculars. Especially in Florence, vernacular dialects claimed an ever larger portion of the language of business, government, and even law.[21]

As the boundaries of the Latin field changed, the study of Latin increasingly became the approach to an exclusive realm. Its adepts reserved for themselves ancient memorial and rhetorical methods of teaching which had traditionally been the first step in learning to read and write. The vulgar tongues had always been taught through direct mimicry of spoken language; the written vernaculars, once established, were similarly learned. But Latin had been primarily a literary tongue since the fifth

19. *De vulgari eloquentia* I.ix.2. Cf. Grayson, *Cinque saggi*, 1–31; Folena, "Volgarizzare," 76–82; and Grassi, *Renaissance Humanism*, 5–11.

20. The fundamental studies on literacy are summarized in Graff, *Legacies*. See also Richter, "Kommunikationsprobleme"; Cardini, "Alfabetismo"; Paccagnella, "Plurilinguismo"; and Baldelli, "Le lingue."

21. For the outlines of this change in Italy, see Bruni, *L'italiano*, 5–38; Cardini, "Alfabetismo," 500–505; Cardini, "Intellectuals," 29–30; and Petrucci, "Il libro manoscritto," 506–8. Dante's notorious opinion about the superiority of *volgare* as a literary tongue could only have been possible after so much of the burden of everyday *written* culture had been transferred to the vernacular; cf. Tavoni, "Fifteenth-Century Controversy," 25.

century at least; it now claimed sole use of literary methods in the classroom, methods it had always employed but which now became its hallmarks by contrast to the new vernaculars. In Dante's day it was still possible for the great poet to claim superiority for the poetic potential of *volgare* because a certain degree of "synchronic equality" (the term is Folena's) had been achieved between the two languages; in distinct realms each tongue could claim a certain superiority. By the last quarter of the trecento, the Latin curriculum had become sufficiently exclusive, in response to the humanist reevaluation of the classics, to make such claims difficult and to discredit Dante as a linguistic theorist in humanist circles.[22] Even as the purely Latin realm shrank, the claims of Latin teachers for their art—and especially of those supreme masters of latinity, the first humanists—became more universalizing, shriller, and more deprecating toward the *volgare*.

For understanding the disjunction of Latin from the vernaculars in the later Middle Ages, the role of memory theory is crucial. It remained an important part of the training of learned Europeans well beyond the Renaissance. In a memorial system the physical book, the text recorded in written-out form, was merely an introduction to truth. A greater prestige and importance attached to the spiritually internalized, memorized text. The language of written record was primarily a tool, writing a mere technology; its content was information. The language of memory, by contrast, was a literary and philosophical ideal, within which writing and reading were language functions on a continuum with spoken and remembered language. The content of language in this sense was truth or wisdom. Latin education remained throughout the Renaissance a key to this latter kind of language, because Latin was learned with a formal mnemonic.[23]

Latin literary culture was memorial, then, as well as moral; it was in some sense "memorable" as the vernaculars were not. The vernacular languages, at least insofar as they did not aspire to classicizing literary status, were merely technical languages. Language of this sort was mere skill; it did not lead to anything beyond itself. Latin, by contrast, retained its mysterious and sacred character; it continued to embody language as a human tie to God via the acquisition of the wisdom inherent in the common literary tradition of the West. It merited, therefore, a special kind of education and, in the fourteenth century, a special kind of textbook.

22. Folena, "*Volgarizzare*," 96–100.

23. Paccagnella, "Plurilinguismo," 133; Frova, "Le scuole," 28–29; Carruthers, *Book of Memory*, esp. 154–55.

This separation of Latin and the vernaculars did not happen suddenly, clearly, or in the simple terms I have used in presenting it here. The vernaculars were not standing still while Latin changed. As vernacular literatures, and especially poetry, achieved literary and elite status, they too became "memorable." But on the level of elementary education, we can see clearly and concretely that Latin was making claims for its old privilege. Since vernacular high literature was not the basis for instruction in reading and writing (technical language was), Latin could press and win its claims at the literary entry point. For it was in the Latin course that young people left behind the purely practical skills; with Latin they embarked on reading poetic texts and began to employ age-old techniques of moral commentary and memorization.

We might expect the elementary Latin curriculum of the trecento to reflect the existence of the parallel, vernacular literacy, and it does. Indeed, the beginning course seems to have been structured to introduce children to the existence of the Latin realm as distinct from the more familiar vernacular one and to ease the transition they needed to make. Documentary sources—largely teachers' letters of appointment—offer much the best evidence we have for the curriculum at the elementary level.[24]

The notarial recorders of such appointments followed fee schedules traditional among grammar masters. They distinguish the grades of instruction we have already seen in Villani between the reading students who are learning the alphabet, the psalms, and "Donatus" or "Donadello" (the basic grammar book) and those farther along who are "latinizing." A third group of students are referred to in notarial records as *auctoristae* or *legentes auctores*, meaning that they have gone on to advanced study of Latin authors, chiefly Virgil, Statius, Horace, and Ovid. These sources, then, give us three classes of students: the non-latinizers, that is, beginners whom we should perhaps call not-yet-Latin students (*non latinantes* in some documents); the latinizers (*latinantes*) who could actually read and understand Latin texts; and authors students, who were preparing for university-level studies.

It is rather important that we understand clearly the differences between the first two groups, for the educational functions of the elementary

24. Many of these were published by Italian scholars in the last century, and a new, comprehensive collection of the Tuscan ones is in preparation by Robert Black, whose preliminary findings are reported in "Curriculum," esp. 139–44. Scholars also continue to study late medieval reading patterns by analyzing the sources of medieval writers. As such studies multiply they are giving us an alternate body of evidence, complementary to archival and codicological studies. See, e.g., Bruni, "Boncompagno da Signa," 79–83.

curriculum were divided in a way that was typical of medieval education but not of ancient or modern practice. In modern terms, we might be tempted to call the two groups prereaders and readers, because the *non latinantes* are so often described in the documents in terms of simple alphabetic skills. But we must take care in making such analogies. The first group were also presented with simple reading texts; and some sources, among them Villani, call these "students of reading and writing." In fourteenth-century Italy the transition from the first group to the second usually involved graduating from *volgare* to Latin, and this distinction is what calling language students after a certain point "latinizers" signified.[25] In earlier medieval schools, pre-Latin or reading and writing instruction was always *in* Latin and for the sake of learning Latin; only Latin was taught as a written tongue. In fourteenth- and fifteenth-century Florence, by contrast, it is clear that most students never learned Latin in any form. Thus, the first level of instruction described by the Tuscan documents could have two meanings: either the students studied the alphabet table and psalter in Latin as their predecessors had for centuries, or they could begin with Italianized versions of these texts and go on to Latin proper only with the Donatus.[26] In either case, they were not learning to understand Latin texts at the first stage but merely to sound out and recognize what they saw on the page.

The term *latinantes* was used in two ways. Substantively, *latinantes* can only mean readers or students of Latin, and this usage applied to the more advanced students as well the intermediate ones. There was a substantial lapse in time and skill, however, between the Donatus and "authors" in the advanced sense, and this is what is most often indicated by the descriptor "latinizing."[27] Very few students seem actually to have progressed to advanced authors, and those who did were probably destined for the universities.

Latinizers in the intermediate sense were set to mastering the Latin language as a practical instrument of communication and as a repository of history and philosophy. Such students had no other subject courses;

---

25. See Frova, "Le scuole," 129–31, and the contrary opinion of Black that reading was taught in Latin only, "Curriculum," 141–43.

26. See Novati, "Le serie alfabetiche," 391–97, on the use of clearly *volgare* alphabet tables and mnemonic verse from the fourteenth century onward.

27. Black, "Curriculum," 145–47, assumes a much more restricted sense of this term. He would have it mean "learning Latin grammatical rules," as distinct from reading or studying texts or *auctores*. What we have already seen about the holistic medieval approach to language study makes it clear, I think, that Black is wrong.

everything needed for their instruction to cultivated adult life and the professions was included in the Latin course. They studied Latin in this sense by reading texts chosen for their salutary content and because they could be parsed and memorized profitably. There is no evidence that these texts were rigidly graded or ordered, but they were intended to provide a continually growing vocabulary, repeated drills in regular and irregular forms, and experience with syntax in both prose and poetic word order. The books that included them were graded readers, then, in two ways, both in the modern sense of textbooks that were increasingly difficult linguistically and also in that they gradually introduced the student to a whole range of historical, mythological, geographical, philosophical, and moral concepts.

The distribution of graded texts between the younger *latinantes* and students reading authors is not very clear from the documents; but the surviving schoolbooks give us some hints (of which more in the next chapters). There would have been a fair amount of room for tailoring the study of more advanced students to their own needs and to the interests of their masters; on the elementary and intermediate levels the curriculum was more rigid and tradition bound. As we see in later chapters, the evidence is strong that every Latin school student first mastered the little books of Donatus and Pseudo-Cato and then went on (if he went on at all) to simple reading texts by Prosper of Aquitaine or Aesop.

The most elementary students were often further subdivided. A typical schedule of grammar master's fees, for example, from Colle di Valdelsa in 1380 gives five elementary grades or levels of study, and five fee levels:[28]

> *a legente cartam* [from the reader of the chart]
>
> *a legente quaternum seu salterium* [from the reader of the booklet or psalter]
>
> *a legente donatum testualiter* [from the reader of Donatus literally]
>
> *a legente donatum sensualiter* [from the reader of Donatus for sense or, perhaps, by memory]
>
> *a latinantibus* [from the latinizers]

This description is repeated with more or less detail and with minor variation everywhere in Tuscany. It assumes that the beginner first masters the alphabet table (*cartam*, the "chart" or "sheet," sometimes also called

---

28. Archivio di Stato di Siena, Comune di Colle di Valdelsa, 121, fol. 63v. This reference and those that follow are courtesy of Robert Black; see also his "Curriculum," 139–41. Numerous lively debates and letters exchanged with Professor Black over the years have conditioned and refined my reading of these documents considerably. I am immensely grateful to him.

*tabulam*, "table" or "slate," or *collum*, apparently from the grade of scrap parchment used). Then a primer based on prayers and the seven penetential psalms is studied (*quaternum* meaning merely "booklet," *salterium* meaning "prayer book"). Third, the student goes on to *donatus*, that is, to whatever set of elementary grammar rules the teacher chooses as textbook.[29] Only after this complex elementary stage do students merit the title latinizers, *latinantes*.

For understanding the content of the course described in our documentary sources for the Latin schools, and especially for understanding what was meant by "latinizing," we must keep in mind the increasingly bilingual nature of high culture in Tuscany. Scholars have tended to claim that the skills of reading and writing were universally taught on the basis of Latin texts and that to read and write meant to learn Latin.[30] This opinion is based on what we know of earlier medieval practice. In fourteenth-century Tuscany, however, and probably elsewhere in urban Italy from the thirteenth century at least, many readers never studied *grammatica*. They learned to read and write for commercial purposes and learned only what they needed to decipher account books, correspondence, and administrative and legal documents and to keep their own records. In the fourteenth century, Italians also had many new literary texts written in *volgar lingua* and many others translated from Latin. Increasingly there existed a literacy quite outside Latin. This was a true vernacular literacy, not only in the sense of being able to read, but also in the sense of participating in the written culture by reading texts composed in or translated into *volgare*.

The evidence that some schooling was entirely in the vernacular is sketchy but incontrovertible. Above all, there are the large numbers of girls and commercial school boys for whom Latin was beside the point, those who are described so proudly by Villani. Very occasionally, we also find clear evidence of single-language, *volgare* schooling, as in the case of the Buggiano statutes described by Witt. There, in 1372, the city fathers

29. For an illuminating discussion of these various elementary schoolbooks, see Lucchi, "La Santacroce," 598–612. See Black, "Curriculum," 140–41, and Grendler, *Schooling*, 173–76, on the various books called "Donatus"; and Alexandre-Bidon, "La lettre volée," 960 on psalms and prayers, and 961–71 on alphabet tables.
30. Migliorini, *Storia*, 201–2; Lucchi, "La Santacroce," 598; Rizzo, "Il latino," 394; Black, "Curriculum," 141–43. Cf. Grendler, *Schooling*, 160, 194–95, who correctly departs from this view and explains the two-track or two-stream Latin/vernacular schooling in some detail; Bresc, "Ecole et services," 5.

provided for a stipend of 50 lire for a schoolmaster who could teach *grammatica* and 25 lire if the only one available could not offer such instruction. Here, as always in fourteenth-century documents, the term *grammatica* means Latin. The master who could not teach *grammatica* but who could teach reading and writing was surely not teaching in Latin.[31]

Because there were many Tuscan readers who did not ever intend to study Latin, the term "non-latinizers" that occurs in the documents should be taken to include all beginning reading students, even those who would never study Latin. Some of these would have been directed to continue on with the Donatus, latinizing, and eventually "authors," whereas others, less apt or less interested, would have been diverted after learning to read and write alone. They would go on to study more practical things. Girls, for example, were sent to reading and writing masters and mistresses but almost never went on to grammar school. The reading and writing classes could be mixed ones of girls and boys, but grammar schools were the preserve of boys. In the rare cases when girls were allowed to learn Latin, they did so at home with private tutors, or learned from their parents or older brothers, or acquired this unusual skill in a convent.[32]

In looking at the most elementary level of study, it is also useful to distinguish between Florence and the smaller Tuscan cities. Most of the detailed information we have on curriculum comes from letters of appointment to municipal grammar masters, which survive exclusively in the archives of smaller towns. The city fathers of Florence did not appoint elementary grammar masters on the city payroll in the trecento, apparently because the city had great plenty of private teachers. One of the most remarkable things about Villani's account is the vast educational establishment completely without government subsidies he describes; it was truly a symptom of the city's wealth and size. By contrast, a list of beginning courses like that from Colle di Valdelsa examined above assumes a smallish school with all levels in the hands of one master paid by the city government and answerable to it. In Florence from the thirteenth century at least, there were separate schools for reading and writing with masters of relatively low educational and social status; these are the schools Villani characterizes with his claims of extremely large enroll-

31. Witt, *Hercules*, 30; see Black, "Curriculum," 139–40, on the small or absent Latin of reading and writing masters in the fifteenth century.

32. On gender differences, see Klapisch-Zuber, "Le chiavi," 775–84; Grendler, *Schooling*, 93–102.

ments. The vast majority of students who attended such schools learned alphabetic skills primarily for the sake of keeping records in *volgare*. We do not know whether the grammar masters in Florence repeated such elementary instruction once the students went on to the Latin course, but it seems highly unlikely that they did. The first task of a Latin master would have been to transfer existing alphabetic skills to Latin texts. At the same time, he would be instructing his students in the existence and meaning of a separate, elite language realm.

The distinction between basic language skills and *grammatica* was expressed in several ways by fourteenth-century writers. Villani remarks indirectly the stage at which girls dropped out of the elementary course when he contrasts "boys and girls learning to read" with "those boys studying Latin and logic."[33] One of the Colle di Valdelsa notaries seems to be struggling with this same distinction when he describes students in the communal school as receiving instruction *ad letturam scolasticam disciplinam tam in grammaticalibus quam in lettura seu doctrina donati libriccioli carte et alii* [in the study of school subjects, whether in Latin texts or in reading and studying the booklet of Donatus, the alphabet table, and other texts].[34]

The key position of the Donatus is clear: it was the last prelatinizing text and the first one that approached Latin as a subject. We look at this text more closely in Chapter 3. For now we should note how it marks the transition from reading and writing skills to the study of language in a systematic way, that is, the transition from alphabetic skills to Latin. In some documents the students are described in descending order from the most advanced to the least; in some others the order is reversed. None of these writers stops to explain that some students were learning reading of vernacular texts only and others would eventually read Latin as well, just as none of them defines such terms as *donatus* or *latinare*. These were commonplaces understood by all and defined for individual students by the grammar masters who were alone competent to judge who should follow which course of study.

At the end of our period, in 1406, a student such as Giannozzo Manetti was sent right from reading school to learn *abbaco*:

33. The text reads *fanciulli e fanciulle che stanno a leggere . . . quegli che stanno ad apprendere la grammatica e loica*.

34. Archivio di Stato di Siena, Comune di Colle di Valdelsa, 110, fol. 2v, citation and transcription courtesy of Robert Black.

His father Bernardo sent him to learn reading and writing when he was still quite young, as was the custom in the city [of Florence]. And in a short time he learned everything necessary to one who was to become a merchant, so he was moved on to learn *abbaco*. And in a few months he learned all there was to know of that science. At age ten he went to work in the bank.[35]

Manetti's father made the decisions in the matter of his early education, and he clearly thought that a limited time learning reading and writing was enough. To have continued would have led to Latin study. In the event, the bright young Manetti spent ten years in the workplace and then decided on his own to study literature, starting with Latin only in his mid-twenties. His was an unusual study pattern, but one that clearly displays the limited tolerance of the typical Florentine father for book learning. A much more typical school career, but one equally limited by the commercial vision of adults, was that of Pierotto di Paghino Ammanati. Pierotto was an orphan; his guardians provided for his education by sending him to a reading master and then to two additional teachers specifically to learn to write. We hear nothing of Donatus, so we may be sure no consideration at all was given to a Latin course for Pierotto, and we would not expect that there would be, for the boy was destined to become a blacksmith's apprentice.[36]

Both of these cases imply a rather strict segregation of vernacular and Latin forms of literacy in the minds of the parents and guardians who were making decisions about schooling. To this same point, Grendler provides an interesting new reading of the 1480 *catasto* statistics for students in Florence based on documents published by Armando Verde. Although the sources are very incomplete, it would seem that at most 12 percent of the student population in that year was studying Latin.[37] It is not possible to generalize from these late numbers back to the situation in fourteenth-century Florence, and even less to the preplague city, but it is remarkable

35. Vespasiano da Bisticci, quoted in Garin, *Pensiero*, 297.
36. Sapori, "Un bilancio," 354–55.
37. This figure results from Grendler, *Schooling*, 75, Table 3.1, as follows. Disregarding the students whose grade level or type of school is not specified in the *catasto* on which the table is based, those students described as studying in grammar schools and those called "clerics," meaning they were in other schools where the instruction was also in Latin, total 75 of 628 students listed. Twelve percent is thus the maximum figure for Latin students; the real figure was presumably lower, but it cannot be as low as the 2 percent Black too categorically claims in "Florence," 35; see Black, "Curriculum," 142, for his method of computation.

nonetheless that so few Florentine students of the later period went on to Latin studies beyond the stage described as *leggere e scrivere*. At both periods, only a small percentage of the students who learned to read were destined for Latin.[38]

What did the course Manetti completed as a young child consist of? What exactly was "everything necessary to one who was to become a merchant"? Almost surely this meant memorizing prayers, reading pious texts, and learning the rudiments of commercial record keeping, both reading and writing. There is no reason to think it included Latin at all. Latin versions of the commonly memorized prayers of the *salterio* had been used by Christians of all classes throughout the Middle Ages and continued to be known among lay people into modern times; but the flourishing lay piety of fourteenth-century Italy had also produced numerous vernacular versions of these popular prayers.[39] The penetential psalms in Tuscan *volgare*, for example, are known in many manuscripts and would be among the first popular products of Italian printing presses in the 1470s. Reading and writing masters would surely have thought it useful for beginners to learn to read such texts in the vernacular. For many, if not most, it was the only language they would ever learn to read.

The literacy of piety was not in any way distinct from that of commercial record keeping. The fruits of a strongly pious education to vernacular written culture can be seen in almost any piece of Florentine merchant's prose, perhaps most strikingly in the invocations that stand at the head of the many private and family account books that survive from fourteenth-century Florence.[40] To cite only one example, from an unpublished *ricordanze* at the Newberry Library, notice the completely un-Latin diction and piety of Pepo d'Antonio degli Albizzi as he opens a new secret account book in 1338:

38. Grendler, *Schooling*, 74–78, and the various studies cited there; the documents are in Verde, *Lo studio fiorentino*. Cf. Lucchi, "La Santacroce," 601.

39. An interesting little private prayer book from fourteenth-century Tuscany now at Lambeth Palace Library (MS 1504) contains psalms and litanies in both Italian and Latin; see Ker, *Medieval Manuscripts*, 1:101–2. In some cases, mixed-language texts of such prayers occur, for example, the *Confiteor* in Chicago, Newberry Library, MS 122. Lucchi, "La Santacroce," 601–2, describes the complaint of Boccaccio that the monks of Montecassino had mutilated many large, ancient manuscripts by cutting strips from the margins to use for *psalteriolos* to sell to boys, and for other small books to sell to women. In this case the psalters could have been in Latin or *volgare*, used for reading instruction or private devotions. The same is true of the many *salterii* cited by Black, "Curriculum," 140–41.

40. On merchant piety and merchant prose, see Cicchetti and Mordenti, "La scrittura"; Bec, *Les marchands*; and the introduction to Branca's *Mercanti scrittori*.

*In nome di Dio e de la Beata Vergine Madre Madonna Santa Maria e di tutti i*
*santi e sante di paradiso che mi deano bene a fare et bene a dire et che mi*
*deano guadagno chon salvamento de lanima et del corpo . . .*

[In the name of God, and of the Blessed Virgin Mother Our Lady Saint Mary,
and of all the saints male and female of Paradise, that they grant me good
deeds and good speech and profit with salvation of soul and body . . .][41]

Every phrase here comes from a formula of vernacular prayer or business
usage; what is more, the two spheres interpenetrate conceptually and
linguistically. Pepo, who went on to be a major political figure, mastered a
literacy that is thoroughly vernacular; there is not a single echo of Latin,
not even in the formulas of prayer. His combinations of commonplaces
are facile and personal but not latinate; his schooling was that offered by
vernacular reading and writing masters. Like the young Manetti a half-
century later, he had learned well what was needed for a commercial
career, but no more.

The two language realms remained essentially separate in conception
well into the fifteenth century. The graphic representation of the distance
between Latin and Italian is a hierarchy of scripts whereby even the great
trecento *volgare* poetry and all sorts of humbler writing not in Latin was
copied in *mercantesca*, the cursive script developed for use by merchants
in keeping accounts. Meanwhile, the higher cultural aspirations and more
learned texts of Latin writers were set down in versions of the gothic book
hands that had been used for several centuries.[42] The elementary notebooks of Sozomeno da Pistoia offer indirect evidence that writing was
taught hierarchically as well. As we see in the next chapter, elementary
reading books and alphabet tables were written in gothic *rotunda*, a
particularly clear and legible script easy for beginners which was related
to the hands used for most Latin books. Vernacular readers, however,
learned to write first in *mercantesca*, as Sozomeno's notebooks show. He
was set to copying out Latin reading texts and was apparently expected to
do so in gothic *rotunda*, but he found this so onerous and uncongenial a

41. Chicago, Newberry Library, MS +27, fol. 1r, as transcribed by Thomas Simpson,
who is preparing a critical text of the book and has graciously permitted me the use of his
draft.

42. There is a substantial literature on this matter of hierarchy of scripts throughout the
Middle Ages, for both Italy and the rest of Europe. On the Italian case, see the contributions
of Petrucci, "Il libro manoscritto," and Jed, *Chaste Thinking*. On the disappearance of
*mercantesca* under the influence of print culture, see Quondam, "Nascita della grammatica,"
564–65.

task that he completed some of them rapidly in the script he knew better, a gothic cursive with *mercantesca* elements. Exactly the same phenomenon may be observed in a nearly contemporary copy of a school reading text now at the Biblioteca Universitaria in Bologna. The student there began in an awkward imitation of a gothic *rotunda* and finished in *mercantesca*.[43] This hierarchy of scripts was rigidly observed in Tuscan schoolbooks, but not as regularly in books of a similar sort written north of the Apennines.[44] The real if not always rigid separation most fourteenth-century people observed between the language realms was bound to have an effect on the way Latin was taught and learned.[45]

Before tackling Virgil, Horace, Statius, Lucan, and Ovid—in the *auctores* course—latinizers were expected to learn to analyze texts grammatically and to study important lessons of natural and Christian moral philosophy on the basis of the school texts thought particularly appropriate for new Latinists. Petrarch clearly indicated the intermediate character of such books when in old age he "remembered," doubtless with some exaggeration, that he had skipped this stage altogether: "From my earliest youth, while all the others eagerly studied Prosper or Aesop, I was deeply absorbed in the books of Cicero."[46]

The documentary sources largely desert us in describing the grammar course once the students arrived at this intermediate level. This is because the fees charged to latinizers were substantial, to reflect the degree of care required of the master, and often only one further fee increment was envisioned, for the *auctoristae*, or advanced students. The content of the courses at this level was not specified in documents concerning appointments. At most they describe *latinus minor*, *latinus mediocris*, and *latinus maior*, terms without specific curricular meaning.[47] I rely in the chapters

43. Sozomeno's notebook is Pistoia, Biblioteca Forteguerriana, A.33; on which, see De La Mare, *Handwriting*, 91–105. The Bologna manuscript is Biblioteca Universitaria 1206, a fifteenth-century miscellany that contains a student copy of Henry of Settimello's *Elegia* on fols. 12–27. Black, "Curriculum," 140, presents evidence that many reading masters wrote only, or usually, in *mercantesca*.

44. None of the professionally written schoolbooks in our census is written in *mercantesca*, but I have seen several examples of these same texts written in the Veneto in fine, calligraphic *mercantesca*. See, e.g., the charming *Physiologus* and *Chartula* in Rovigo, Accademia dei Concordi, MS Silvestriana 310.

45. Cf. Baldelli, "Le lingue," 8.

46. *Senili* XV.1, cited in Garin, *Pensiero*, 91.

47. Black, "Curriculum," 145, shows that these terms were widespread in the fourteenth century, but he erroneously equates them with the course divisions marked in some manuscripts of the *Regulae grammaticales* of Francesco da Buti.

that follow on manuscript copies of the reading texts themselves to help in describing the intermediate course.

For the *auctores* level, we are even less informed. Few if any manuscripts designed expressly for use at the *auctores* level of study survive. Students this advanced were already reading as adults. They would have used books designed for adult reading, or they would have made copies for their own use of the texts under consideration in their schools. Occasionally we find useful ownership notes.[48] Sometimes we can also discern glosses or annotation that seem to indicate that a detailed but relatively elementary rhetorical analysis of the text was in progress. Such notes may imply that the owner of the book was studying with a grammar master or that the book belonged to a master who used them for teaching. But there is no separate genre of schoolbook at this level such as can be discerned for the latinizers. The *auctores* were read in books designed in the way poetry had been presented for centuries, either in professionally produced copies purchased from stationers or commissioned from trained scribes, or else in personal copies made rapidly and sloppily in paper notebooks, often in the course of reading the text for the first time in another manuscript.[49] These latter books offer promising information on personal reading habits, but they can rarely be assigned with certainty to a student at any particular level. Even students' notebooks or personal copies like the well-known set of school texts compiled by Sozomeno da Pistoia or the Cortona manuscript included in the census here are difficult to evaluate in pedagogical terms. Either they have no annotations beyond the base text at all, or they contain several sets of annotations made in the course of reading and rereading the important authors. Some of Sozomeno's notes seem to have been made many years after the copying of the text.[50]

48. Black, "Curriculum," 149–54, cites many examples but does not describe them or attempt a typology.

49. The rare examples known to me of books used by Tuscans at the *auctores* level in the fourteenth century are the following: Laurenziana, Acquisti e Doni, 208 (Virgil); Laurenziana, Conv. soppr. 546 (Virgil); Nazionale, Magliabecchi VII, 1063 (Statius, Virgil, *Ilias latina*). Some doubtful cases and fifteenth-century examples are mentioned in the Appendix, Part III. Possibly but not surely Tuscan are Bologna, Biblioteca Universitaria, MS 1206 (Virgil and Henry of Settimello), and Rome, Biblioteca Angelica, MS 1461 (Claudian). To these we may add the oversize schoolbooks (see Part II of the Appendix), which I discuss in the next chapter.

50. On the schoolbook reader of Sozomeno, see De La Mare, *Handwriting*, 98. The Cortona manuscript is no. I.1 in the Appendix. Contracts and letters of appointment sometimes specify authors to be studied at what we may think of as a university-preparatory level, but there is little consistency in these lists. Rossi, "Un grammatico," 28, cites one from

Another area we can only glimpse in the sources is the education of Latin students outside lay-run grammar schools. The conservatism of the discipline was such that the outline of the curriculum was much the same for a student studying at home, with a parish priest, or with a notary as for one who went out to study in the more public schools run by laymen. We know that private and clerical tuition was undertaken regularly, sometimes with parish clergy and sometimes under the aegis of a religious confraternity or monastery.[51] For some very bright or unruly students there would have been a distinct advantage in securing the intensive and flexible attentions of a personal tutor. The same would be true for students aiming single-mindedly at a notarial career. There was an oversupply of notaries in Florence as in smaller Italian towns, and such language professionals would have had time to take on students either as apprentice notaries or as elementary Latin scholars even if they did not have a clear intention of going on to become notaries. Certainly, it was not considered outlandish, inappropriate, or unusual for notaries to teach Latin.[52]

In some cases, it was also apparently possible for Florentine boys to study Latin in schools run by mendicant friars or monks. It is frequently said that the Italian church relinquished its educational mission to lay teachers beginning in the twelfth century; but this is a misapprehension of liberal historians, born of admiration for the many achievements of the commues, which included schools maintained at public expense and open to all. As Petti Balbi has rightly remarked, Italian churchmen did not so much abandon the education of laymen as retain an old-fashioned

---

late fourteenth-century Chioggia that specifies Seneca, Virgil, Lucan, Terence, "et similes poetas et auctores." See Grendler, *Schooling*, 205–12, on Cicero.

51. Giovanni Dominici criticizes clerical tuition as not up to the standards of his youth, making it seem a real and normal alternative to the lay schools even at the time of his writing in the 1390s; see Dominici, *Regola*, ed. Salvi, 134. At Florence there is also the well-documented case of a priest, Lapo Nuti, who taught reading and writing while serving as a chaplain of Santa Reparata between 1315 and 1339; see Debenedetti, "Sui più antichi doctores," 338n3. See Davidsohn, *Firenze*, 210–12, and below notes 53–56, on confraternity and monastic schools. We have to look beyond Florence, however, to find documents that illuminate the internal workings of parish and confraternity schools. One interesting case is that of Ser Cristofano di Gano di Guidino, who studied first at home and then with a teacher affiliated with a religious confraternity at Siena, that of the Misericordia; see Cherubini, *Signori, contadini*, 397–98. Lapo Nuti's case is parallel to the occasional examples of teaching clergymen cited by Bertanza for Venice, for example, *Documenti*, 191, where two clerics appear in separate documents of 1389. One of these was probably a full-time teacher with his own school at Venice who also held a clerical benefice at Treviso; the second was a parish priest who may have had just one student.

52. See Chapter 8 for a discussion of notaries as teachers.

notion that Latin grammar was primarily a preparation for a church career.[53] This traditionalism left them without a role in educating laymen to the newer forms of literacy, whether entirely in *volgare* as in the commercial course, or in the bilingual literacy of academic, legal, and political circles where Latin was an essential but nonreligious accomplishment.

Religious schools differed considerably in their openness to outsiders and in their curricula. Both the Franciscans and Dominicans actively discouraged teaching young boys and teaching grammar to anyone not clearly planning a career with their orders. The Dominicans were particularly rigid in this regard, and no grammar schools are attested for Dominican houses outside Spain, even though Dominicans in all provinces were allowed to specialize in arts at the university level. The Franciscans, by contrast, made provision for relatively elementary instruction of novices in a course termed *studia grammaticalia* but then required their students to abandon arts studies to go on to theology. In some places at least, *studia grammaticalia* may have embraced an elementary grammar course, but most often it seems to have been a wide-ranging introductory course in Scripture, logic, and moral philosophy analogous to the *auctores* level in secular schools. The Augustinians and Carmelites had schools of general studies that offered instruction in language skills equivalent to the entire grammar curriculum as well as more advanced studies.[54] In and near Florence there were schools of grammar run by the Vallombrosans in Passignano, the Cistercians at Settimo, and the Augustinians at the urban church of Santo Spirito.[55] Villani did not include these schools in his catalogue of civic accomplishments, but they must have enrolled substantial numbers of students to judge by their reputations.

Most detailed studies to date on grammar in the mendicant houses of Florence have relied on the incidence of grammatical texts in libraries we can reconstruct. These make it clear that some grammatical reference books and classical *auctores* existed in almost every mendicant library, but they are inconclusive as to the presence of formal grammatical study. They do not show much evidence of the presence of elementary Latin reading texts like those we examine in the next chapter; this would seem

53. Petti Balbi, "Istituzioni," 24–25.

54. The documentation for the existence of such schools is almost entirely in the form of provincial statutes and other occasional references in legal documents. These are cited by Maierù, "Tecniche di insegnamento," 314–20; and D'Alatri, "Panorama," 65–67.

55. Davidsohn, *Firenze,* 211–12. The Vallombrosans also brokered books for copying, including schoolbooks; see Brentano-Keller, "Il libretto," 149.

to argue against any very elementary study in these schools.[56] But the reconstructible Franciscan libraries all belonged to big-city houses, whereas the rare specific references we have to Franciscan grammar schools all come from smaller towns where students from several provinces studied.[57] This could mean that younger and less sophisticated students were sent to smaller centers to take elementary instruction well away from the distractions of Florence and then came to Santa Croce or other big-city schools for more advanced studies in theology. Or it may merely mean that the great theological *studia* at Florence were so prominent and impressive that flourishing elementary schools in their shadow simply did not attract the notice of record keepers. There were many learned friars at all levels of study at Santa Croce and Santa Maria Novella who could have tutored novices, or private students, "off the books."

In any case, we are at a distinct disadvantage in describing religious schools or any kind of private tuition not covered by a formal contract. In one trecento Venetian case, for example, we would have no reason to suspect that the Servites employed a layman as a grammar master in their monastery if it were not for the fact that a theft there involved some of the teacher's property so that he is recorded in the criminal records of the case.[58] Noncontractual educational arrangements simply do not turn up in the documents. This fact skews the evidence for the grammar schools in Florence. For the rest of Tuscany we can be sure that most Latin students learned from lay grammar masters who made their living by keeping schools subsidized by the communes. Often these masters were not natives of the cities where they taught, and the communes actually competed for their services, so that it was not at all unusual for a master to teach in several different towns in the course of a successful career. In Florence, lay masters were dependent on student fees paid by parents, and there is relatively little evidence that they came from distant parts of Tuscany. It is also certain that secular clergymen, friars, and notaries taught Latin to many elementary students in Florence.

---

56. Davis, "The Florentine *Studia*," 346–47, and "Early Collection," and Jones, "Franciscan Education," 443–44, conclude that grammar was taught by some Franciscan houses if not other mendicant ones; but it is only in such references as those cited by D'Alatri and Maierù (see note 54) that we can be sure such schools existed.

57. D'Alatri, "Panorama," 66.

58. Bertanza and Della Santa, *Documenti*, 200–201.

# SCHOOLBOYS' BOOKS

What kind of book did Florentine boys carry to class once the Latin course was well begun?[1] What could nine-year-old Bartolomeo di Niccolo dei Valori expect to read when, as he put it in his memoir for the year 1363, "I set myself to learn grammar in the school of master Manoello"?[2] We might answer by looking at a book written in Bartolomeo's childhood and in his family's possession at the end of the next century, the present-day codex Panciatichi 68 of the Biblioteca Nazionale Centrale in Florence.[3] It is in three distinct parts, each of them originally a separate booklet. Any or all of them could have been Bartolomeo's:

I. (5 gatherings)
   A vocabulary and grammar drillbook by Goro d'Arezzo
II. (5 gatherings)
   1. Prosper of Aquitaine, *Epigrammata*
   2. Aesop's *Fables* in the translation of Walter the Englishman
III. (3 gatherings)
   1. Prudentius, *Dittochaeon*
   2. Pseudo-Bernard of Clairvaux, *Chartula*
   3. *Physiologus*
   4. Vitalis of Blois (Pseudo-Terence), *Geta*

1. Some material in this chapter appeared in my article "Latin Readers." I thank the many who responded to that article with additions, corrections, and suggestions for clarifying the typology there developed, especially Robert Black, Giulio Orazio Bravi, Paul F. Grendler, and Ronald Witt.

2. Florence, Biblioteca Nazionale Centrale, Panciatichi 134, fol. 1r: *mi puosi a imparare gramatica ala schuola di maestro Manoello.*

3. See the Appendix, Part I, item I.20. Hereafter, manuscripts described in the Appendix are cited "Census I.20," "Census II.4," and so forth.

This is a fairly typical combination of school texts for the late Middle Ages. Note, however, that the grammatical manual in Part I of the Panciatichi miscellany was produced separately from the other texts. Each of the three component booklets of the manuscript is quite short; this is usual for school texts. Even more typical than the content is the format of these books. All three are small (21 cm in height) and each probably once existed as a set of loose gatherings without binding. Each of the parts is written in a different round gothic book hand with few abbreviations (for easy legibility), and plenty of space is left between the small number of lines per page for interlinear notes. But there is no room for marginal glosses; the text occupies almost the full measure of the page.

These features, with only the most minor variations, characterize all the books in the census of fourteenth-century Tuscan reading books found in Part I of the Appendix. Together they constitute a remarkably coherent body of books, even a class of manuscripts apart, which for lack of a better term I dub elementary Latin readers.[4] This usage emphasizes their functional character as books designed for learning to read and points to the fact that, in terms of audience, they were personal, not institutional, books. Their inclusiveness and level of ornamentation could be tailored to the needs and desires of individual owners. Many owners felt free to write notes, draw pictures, and add texts to the books they had bought.

The seventy-one such schoolbooks I identify in this work actually survive in modern collections as parts of forty-nine codices, described individually in the Appendix. The descriptions there attempt to treat each medieval schoolbook as a distinct entity, but they are quite summary. Only partial notes on those portions of existing codices not pertinent to this study are provided. On that account, a few general remarks are in order on the survival of schoolbooks of this sort before I examine them in detail.

The survival of these books, although affected by the usual chances that operate in such matters, is not entirely beside the point of their original use. Schoolbooks get used up. Designed as they are for repeated readings

---

4. In the article offered as a preliminary report of this study I called these books primers; but, as several readers of that essay have since remarked, the word "primer" can be ambiguous. In its broader sense of "elementary schoolbook" it surely applies to the readers at issue here, but it also has a narrower sense, meaning a simple grammar book with alphabet table and sets of basic grammatical rules for beginning readers. None of the books in the census conform to this more specialized notion. All were designed for teaching reading, however, so the English "reader" (despite *its* ambiguities) seems the better word for these books.

by inexpert and often unwilling readers, they are frequently abused. This generic history is evident in the surviving examples and may skew our sample in significant ways. It is not by chance that, of the sixty-one complete specimens, only three are written on paper. Among the fragments, only parchment leaves survive. By contrast, the proportion of paper copies of such books to survive from the fifteenth century is much higher, perhaps as many as half the books that exist today. There may have been a preference in the fourteenth century for parchment; but the relative fragility of paper also ensured that a far greater proportion of parchment manuscripts would survive their first decades of intensive use.

What is more, an untypically large percentage of the extant manuscript readers were deluxe products in the first instance. It seems likely that the humbler schoolbooks disappeared in larger numbers. Almost all the surviving books (sixty-six of seventy-one) were written by fully professional, expert scribes. None of the booklets in our sample are completely without decoration of the simple sort thought appropriate for children's books; but, whereas almost all the books were written by professional scribes, a rather large number of the decorations were added clumsily or inexpertly by readers. A few books (five) were also written by inexpert hands— uneven, tentative, and badly formed. These seem to have been products of Latin school students themselves. This latter mode of production must have been more important both as a pedagogical and as a scribal practice than the surviving numbers indicate, if only because an important career opportunity for the Latin student was as a professional scribe or secretary.

A well-known example of such a student-scribe is Sozomeno da Pistoia. Sozomeno was fifteen when he began to assemble a notebook in 1402, apparently having been encouraged to practice a clear, round gothic hand by copying just the reading texts so consistently used in Florentine classrooms across the previous century. It is unlikely that he was encountering these texts for the first time. He may have been writing in part from memory. The youth's impatience with the task is obvious; he several times completed the texts begun in gothic book hand in a rapid cursive. The results survive in a fascinating collection of scraps that seem to have remained unbound well into Sozomeno's maturity. They have been rebound several times since, most recently in the late 1960s; today they constitute codex A. 33 of the Forteguerriana Library at Pistoia. But the present order of the pages is disturbed and some sheets are missing; the disorder seems to date from very early in the history of these awkward, highly informal little booklets. Their survival was almost surely due to the subsequent fame of their maker, a distinguished scribe and translator of

Greek; even his disordered, adolescent notebooks would have been important collector's items after his death. Many another such collection of loosely folded sheets must have been thrown away or reused.[5]

Loose scraps is the form in which several of our manuscripts seem to have arrived in the hands of the fifteenth- and sixteenth-century readers and collectors to whom we owe their present existence. A significant number of copies of these elementary school texts stand today in one, two, or three gatherings that contain single texts and bear no evidence of having been intended to receive anything more elaborate than a paper or vellum wrapper. Others have two or three texts in five to seven fascicles. Some also survive in a fragmentary state that implies they were used without a sturdy binding and so lost inner leaves of their gatherings or wore out leaves that doubled as covers. This is the case with Sozomeno's notebooks. Still others, like Bartolomeo dei Valori's reader, appear in combinations of texts or groups of booklets which may have been assembled early but which were designed as distinct, pamphletlike books of a few fascicles each.

The typical elementary Latin reader, then, was a booklet of eight to forty leaves, stitched in gatherings of irregular size adjusted to the lengths of the texts included. When there was more than one gathering, these might have been sewn lightly together, or laid walletlike into a wrapper, or at most given a cover of limp vellum with one or two creases at the spine and a simple yapp edge. Several of the manuscripts in our group have remnants of original binding structures of this sort. Census I.37 comes closest to exemplifying the form. Its ancient wrapper, of heavyweight parchment quite different from that of the book itself, survives today in the form of front and back flyleaves long since disconnected from each other by subsequent binders but recognizably once part of the same sheet. Other examples of such wrappers survive in Census I.25 and I.9. A fragment in Census I.36 appears to be a spoiled sheet from one reading book used as a wrapper for another copy of the same text prepared in the same workshop.

No fourteenth-century Latin reader I know, however, retains its original binding or survives in anything quite like its original booklet form.[6] Instead, these little books have been given collectors bindings of greater or less elegance. Only in rare cases do these date from the fifteenth or

5. De La Mare, *Handwriting*, 91–105.

6. Milan, Biblioteca Trivulziana 629, is a mid-fifteenth-century example, the earliest known to me.

sixteenth century; but many of the later miscellanies in which our booklets survive have decoration, catchwords, or other markings that indicate
that at least parts of them are assemblies formed in that period. (Census
I.8, I.12, and I.15 are examples.) It would seem that such reading texts
were still deemed useful into the sixteenth century. Copies were resold to
new students or passed on within families or through teachers as long as
they were legible.

Other manuscript evidence corroborates this conclusion; right up to
and beyond the invention of printing, manuscript readers that included
some or all of the same texts in very nearly the same format as that devised
in the early to mid-fourteenth century continued to be produced. The
changes in pedagogy many historians have postulated for the early fifteenth century, in schools like those of Guarino Guarini and Vittorino da
Feltre, did not much affect the production of elementary readers. Even the
reform of curriculum about which Guarino and others boasted does not
seem to have affected the basic books from which Tuscans learned Latin.
The first application of printing to elementary Latin readers yielded books
that mimic closely the format designed for comparable texts in the previous century. Well into the sixteenth century, Italian printers who used
Roman types almost exclusively kept on hand a black-letter typeface
modeled on the legible Italian round gothic of our period, used largely for
printing primers and elementary readers.[7]

Heavy and continuous use across decades and even centuries was the
fate of the Latin reader, a broadly useful but rarely pretentious book. It is
amazing that so many survive. This result is probably due to the chance
that, just as these books became obsolete in the classroom, that is, just
when humanist ideals of latinity made late antique and medieval reading
texts unacceptable models (a development that did not become universal
until the sixteenth century), a rising tide of antiquarianism made these
humble manuscripts collector's items and heirlooms. That this was the
general case is borne out by the fact that so few early examples bear
evidence of monastic provenance.[8] Monastic schools retained conserva-

---

7. Dr. Ennio Sandal informs me that the Biblioteca Queriniana of Brescia owns a set of
early fifteenth-century manuscript readers that served as the printer's copy for the earliest
Latin readers printed at Brescia. Primer type fonts called "Donati" or "Da Donati" appear in
the shops of Italian printers until the end of the sixteenth century, e.g., Milan, ASM Notarile,
Pietro Maria q. Aloysii Crivelli, filz. 11801, 16 Apr. 1556. For this reference I thank Kevin
Stevens.

8. Only Census I.10, I.11, I.14, I.41, and possibly I.48 show any evidence of monastic
provenance.

tive teaching patterns longer than others, and so they continued to use, and use up, their Latin reading anthologies. Books of our group were not made for monasteries in the first instance. Their self-conscious simplicity and naivete was an address to young children, whereas monastic learners could be of any age and most often were older teenagers and adults. A child's book would have had no logic in an institutional setting where reading could be taught as it had been for centuries, from any large book that allowed of several students reading together.

Pride of personal ownership is an important characteristic of the developed Latin reading books from Florence. We might almost say that the child's sense of ownership was essential to the development of the type, for there is little point in creating a new form of book for children unless the children are ready, or can be taught, to want and value the books offered them. We may distinguish two distinct types of written expression of such pride of ownership. There are the simple marks of possession or use, usually in the form "This book is mine . . .," and there are colophons of the older type in which the scribe identifies himself.

In manuscript books of all periods, the owner who was also the scribe was likely to want to record some sense of satisfaction in this fact. Schoolchildren were, if anything, more likely to indulge in such vanities than others:

*Finito libro frangamus ossa magistro.*
*Explicit libellus de casu mundi.*
*Iste liber est Galeacii boni pueri.*
*Qui scripsit scribat semper cum domino vivat;*
*Viverat in celis Galeacius hoc fidelis.*
*Laus tibi sit Christe quem liber explicit iste.*
*Ego Galeacius filius domini Floriamontis judicis scripsi m° ccc° xxxv°, indictione tercia. Unde referrantur domino nostro Jesu Christo mille gracie. Benedicamus domino domino Gratias.* (Census I.1, fol. 46v)

[This book's done, now let's break teacher's bones! Here ends the book on the origins of the world. This book belongs to Galeazzo, a good boy. May he who has written write; may he live forever with God. May faithful Galeazzo live in heaven. Praise be to Christ, for this book's ended. I, Galeazzo, son of Lord Floriomonte the judge, wrote this in 1335, in the third indiction; for which may a thousand thanks be given to Jesus Christ. Bless the Lord, the Lord be thanked.]

This colophon, one of three Galeazzo entered as he copied a complex poetic miscellany, weaves conventional verses that occur in many student productions (lines 1, 4, 5, and 6) with his own self-advertisement, couched, as we might expect in the case of a youth, in terms of family pride.[9] Galeazzo was not above a bit of schoolboy falsification either. The second and subsequent gatherings in the manuscript contain an *Ilias latina* started in a different hand and continued by Galeazzo after about two pages of text had been put down by the first scribe. At the end of this section of the miscellany the boy exaggerates the usual wording of the colophon: "I Galeazzo wrote all of this work" (fol. 38). The pride of accomplishment here extended even to claiming for his own what he had merely taken over unfinished.

The other kind of ownership claim is simpler and more direct. Scribes, after all, had been taking the credit for writing books for many centuries without also actually claiming to own the manuscripts they wrote. In institutional and especially monastic settings the good manners of humility usually required that the scribe's claims be those of a prayerful laborer and not a prideful craftsman. In the thirteenth and fourteenth centuries, the ideal of apostolic poverty expounded by the mendicant orders produced readers' marks of the form "This book is assigned to the use of . . ." (e.g., Census I.11, fol. 46v). It is quite a different thing, and becomes typical only from the central Middle Ages onward, to add to a book written by someone else a claim of personal ownership. "This book is mine" reduces the sense of belonging to the possession of any object.

This merely possessive sense is not without cultural meaning, however; to a schoolchild it could have been a considerable source of pride. It is interesting to note that the most expansive form of the Florentine schoolboy's ownership mark also inserts him firmly into the setting of his school, his family, and his city (see Figure 1):

*Iste liber est mei Nicolai Francisci populi Sancte Felicitatis ultra Arnum manentis in scolis magistri Antonij* [This book belongs to Nicolo di Francesco of the quarter of Santa Felicità Oltrarno studying in the school of Master Anthony.] (Census II.6, fol. 50v).

---

9. The conventional phrases here belong to the schoolboy milieu of near literacy. They occur, in Latin, at the end of many fourteenth-century vernacular texts, e.g., that edited by Cherchi, *Andrea Cappellano*, 193, from a Newberry Library manuscript of the *ars arengandi.*

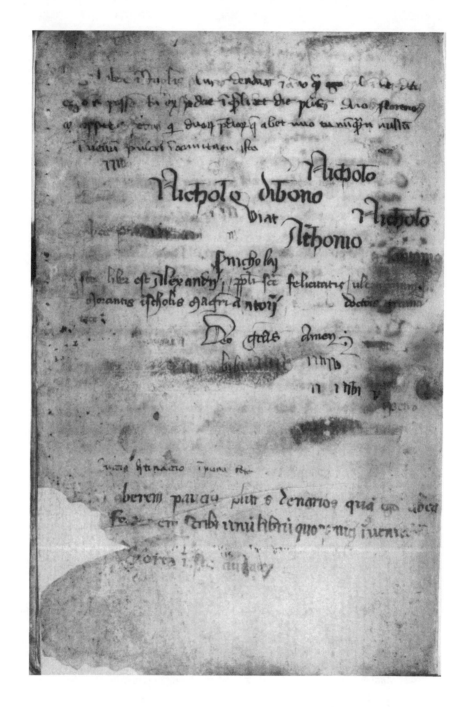

*Figure 1*. Florence. Biblioteca Riccardiana. MS 682 (Census II.6), fol. 50v.

The most likely case is that this inscription was suggested or dictated by Master Anthony, and the ownership of the book was explicitly connected to a scholastic setting. The inscription emphasizes the student's cultural place on the threshold of a Latin career along with his social and political credentials as a family member and resident of a quarter of the city.[10]

Many students' ownership marks were also exercises in handwriting. They tend to be traced in a formal round gothic that mimics the hands used in the texts themselves. They are often repeated several times in the same book word for word, and they sometimes have erasures and corrections that betray the mind of a student bent on getting the lesson right. Occasionally we can glimpse the very moment at which a student first takes possession of his new book, for a neat schoolmaster's hand writes the inscription in the student's name, and then just below a tentative child's hand traces the same ownership mark letter by letter.[11]

Not all students' marks, of course, were officially sanctioned. Indeed, one of the immediate side effects of private ownership is the sense of being at liberty to make personal additions to the book, even to deface it. Such graffiti have neither positive nor negative value in themselves for, although they were usually expressions of personal sentiment and creativity, they just as often represented pure malice or a simple destructive urge. To "break teacher's bones" was formulaic, the sort of bad boy's bad words repeated from generation to generation and harmless enough. Obscene drawings or doggerel are similarly unoriginal in most cases, and normal, not pathological. But however natural they are, such marks were also deliberate challenges to authority as vested in the teacher by society and parents. They are part of the child's self-discovery, but they are no less defacements for that: defacement is of the essence of the expression by which children define themselves against society. In light of what we know about the Latin grammar course as an initiation into high culture, reserved as it was for the elite in Florence, these defacing marks are doubly significant. They are not merely universal boyish pranks; they are also the very individual expressions of boys being forced to conform to high cultural norms and aspirations.[12]

10. On the formula *de populo de*, see Cohn, *Laboring Classes*, 43–47; on neighborhood loyalty, 57–62.

11. Census I.47 is an example. Many of the surviving ownership marks seem to have been written by teachers or parents; those that can be surely assigned to students are rather fewer. The most likely cases are in I.49 and I.21.

12. The initiatory quality of Latin is explicated by Ong, "Latin Language Study"; see Bec on the ideal of *socialitas*, in *Les marchands*, 282–84.

Drawings in schoolbooks have a particularly interesting role. In some cases they come close to illustrating the text with figures of characters or scenes, even short narratives. In other cases they represent visual word-play and "illustrate" no more than a single word. Still others are completely extraneous to the text. Rarely do these marks display any evidence of having been designed into the book, or of being systematically used (as other readers' marks often were in the period) to mark or label the text for pedagogical or memorial purposes. In this sense we should probably distinguish schoolchildren's own, spontaneous marks from those of other, more expert readers, and from marks entered into their schoolbooks at the prompting of their teachers. The childrens' own marks are proof that these books were used *by* children. Other, "adult" sort of readers' marks, especially those dictated by needs of the classroom, should be considered part of designing books *for* children.[13]

The grammar course was open-ended. There were favorite texts and commonly used methods, but few formal prescriptions to limit the teachers' and students' choice of texts. The elementary Latin reader was developed for the classes of latinizers, as an aid to their absorption of the first Latin texts they studied with the developed literary manner of analysis their teachers considered the hallmark of Latin as the universal mother tongue of the West. The students' first division of a text was doubtless simple and elementary, but the method of dividing, marking, and memorizing was the same used by careful readers of literature at all levels. It was the student's introduction to rigorous analysis of texts and more broadly to the whole intellectual life. As such, this method was an important step in the intellectual and moral formation of one who could eventually claim to be a member of the Latin elite.

What were the texts used at this early latinizing level of instruction? The seventy-one manuscripts in our census include 120 items: sixteen literary texts that occur more than once and seven additional texts that turn up only once:[14]

---

13. The "official" nature of some ownership marks is clear in cases where an inexpert writer copied his own name underneath a model handsomely written by a parent or teacher; see note 11. A particularly telling case of adult graffiti in a grammar book is to be found in University of Chicago Library, MS 99 of the *Regule grammaticales* of Francesco da Buti, where sophisticated verbal puns on the catchwords are included in scatological drawings made by an early owner. Similar puns are reported by Stolt, "Das Werk."

14. The standard editions of these texts are cited in the bibliography and in Garin, *Pensiero*, 91–104, where also many extracts are printed. Excluded from this list and the

| | |
|---|---|
| Prosper of Aquitaine, *Epigrammata* | 23 copies |
| Aesop, *Fables*, versified | 17 copies |
| Prudentius, *Dittochaeon* | 12 copies |
| *Physiologus* | 8 copies |
| Boethius, *Consolation of Philosophy* | 8 copies |
| *Disticha Catonis* | 7 copies |
| *Chartula* | 7 copies |
| Henry of Settimello, *Elegia* | 6 copies |
| Bonvesin de la Riva, *Vita scholastica* | 6 copies |
| Theodulus, *Ecloga* | 5 copies |
| *Ilias latina* | 3 copies |
| John the Abbot, *De septem virtutibus* | 3 copies |
| Vitalis of Blois, *Geta* | 2 copies |
| Pseudo-Boethius, *De disciplina scholastica* | 2 copies |
| *Facetus* (inc. *Moribus et vita*) | 2 copies |
| Pseudo-Jerome, *De contemptu mulierum* | 2 copies |
| Claudian, *De raptu Proserpinae* | 1 copy |
| *Doctrina rudium* | 1 copy |
| Anon. *De casu mundi* | 1 copy |
| Coluccio Salutati, *Elegia* | 1 copy |
| Coluccio Salutati, *Fabula* | 1 copy |
| Avianus, *Fabula* | 1 copy |
| Petrus de Riga, *Historia S. Susannae* | 1 copy |

At first glance this list seems a typical roster of medieval school authors. But the frequencies of occurrence are not what the existing literature on the Latin course would lead us to expect. Many school texts do not occur in our census at all, most notably neo-Ovidian and neo-Terentian poems composed in the twelfth century by Vitalis of Blois, Matthew of Vendôme, and other French clerics and such popular courtesy books as the *Facetus* (inc. *Cum nihil utilius*).[15] Our list is also remarkable for the rarity of such "standard" school texts as Claudian, Avianus, *Geta*, *Ilias Latina*, and *Facetus* (inc. *Moribus et vita*).[16]

---

totals are copies of texts made in the fifteenth century and bound in with fourteenth-century books, and copies of doubtful provenance which I have not been able to examine personally and judge to be Tuscan (see explanation in the Appendix). For example, two additional copies of the *Disticha Catonis* in the Escorial and Vienna codices are not included here. I have not been able to identify this *De casu mundi* (Census I.1).

15. This last text is not to be confused with the other *Facetus*, which does appear twice in the census. On the two, see Garin, *Pensiero*, 94–95.

16. All of them very popular in northern Europe. The case of the *Ilias latina* is particularly interesting, for it appears frequently in Tuscan readers I have seen, redacted in just the form

Most important of all, none of the Golden or Silver Age poets appear in these reading books. It would seem that the lyric Virgil, Horace, Ovid, and Terence—whose use was criticized in late fourteenth-century polemics against the humanist educational program—were not used at the latinizing level in Florence much before the time of that controversy. Nor do we find Appian or the epic poetry of Prudentius, Statius, Virgil, or Lucan. These authors seem to have been reserved for the later, *auctores* course. They would have been given only to older boys, and only to the few who went on to the university.[17]

It is clear, then, that many so-called school authors were not in fact much used in Tuscan schools before the end of the fourteenth century. The case of Terence, perhaps the most widely read school text of the fifteenth century and commonly used in northern European schools in the earlier Middle Ages as well, is particularly instructive. As G. Padoan has remarked, almost none of the learned early commentators on the *Divine Comedy* seem to have been familiar with Terence at all. Taking this into consideration along with our new evidence, it is obvious that Terence could not have been read in Tuscan schools and probably was not commonly used elsewhere in Italy either, certainly not at the elementary or intermediate level of Latin study.[18]

As for the other familiar school authors who do not occur in our list, we may be similarly suspicious. It is important to stress in this regard that no trace of a standardized curriculum or canon can be found in our sample. The Tuscan readers average fewer than two texts per book and so were not true anthologies at all, much less standardized ones. Although a relatively restricted number of possible reading texts were used in Florentine schools at the intermediate level, we find no trace of a set reading anthology, by apparent contrast to English and German schools of the same period.[19]

---

described in the census but of a somewhat later date, after the turn of the fifteenth century. Similarly, two of the three copies in our census are very late fourteenth or fifteenth century in date. Clearly, this was a text that, for all the poor quality of its Latin, gained in popularity with the advent of a taste for classical mythology.

17. Black, "Curriculum," 147–54, presents a list of manuscripts of ancient poets used in Tuscan schools in the fourteenth and fifteenth centuries. His descriptions seem to indicate that these authors were read only by advanced students.

18. Padoan, "Il *Liber Esopi*," 80. Billanovich, "Petrarca, Pietro da Moglio," 370–83, demonstrates that Terence was read at the university level north of the Apennines at least in the last half of the fourteenth century; he traces the humanist revival of Terence as a school text to the work of Petrarch's friend Pietro da Moglio.

19. Garin, *Pensiero*, 92, remarks that the curriculum of the Italian schools differed greatly from that in northern Europe in the late fifteenth century, but he assumes that this was due to

We can also draw a contrast between the curriculum in use in Tuscany and that in transapennine Italy. I have not undertaken a systematic survey of comparable texts in the north, but there are some striking differences in the occurrence of manuscripts of individual authors. The *Doctrina rudium*, for example, occurs in eight Italian manuscripts that can be dated before 1400; only two are Tuscan and only one of them is in reader form. The reverse is true of the very similar courtesy book of Bonvesin de la Riva, a Milanese master whom one might expect to find more frequently in the north than in Tuscany. In fact, of the eight Italian manuscripts datable to the fourteenth century, six are Tuscan.[20] In the matter of courtesy books, then, the Tuscan masters display a clear preference for Bonvesin over the closely similar but French-authored (and somewhat older) *Doctrina rudium*. This must have been a conscious choice, for both texts were available in Florence and other Tuscan towns, and the relative popularity of the two texts in medieval Europe overall would lead us to expect that the *Doctrina* would be more popular in Tuscany, just as it was everywhere else, even in Bonvesin's native Lombardy. Another favorite son, the Florentine Henry of Settimello, occurs in six Tuscan readers in our census, in several other Tuscan copies not formatted for school use, and in seven northern Italian school copies.[21] Here the Florentine masters were more in line with their colleagues in Lombardy, Emilia, and the Veneto. Clearly, Tuscan masters had a fair choice of curriculum materials and they expressed distinct preferences.

Along with the reading texts, there are also found scattered copies of manuals of grammar. There are two occurrences of the *Ianua*, the book referred to by Tuscan teachers as the Donatus or Donadello, three of the versified *Regulae grammaticales* of Master Tebaldo, and single copies of prose manuals by Bartolomeo da Lodi, Filippo di Naddo, two works by

---

the more advanced state of the humanist reform in the south. He implies that all of Europe had a medieval grammar curriculum *ormai consacrata, degli auctores octo* before the advent of humanism. This position was criticized as early as 1965 by Avesani, "Il primo ritmo," 475–86, but persists in the literature. The English curriculum is described by Bonaventure, "The Teaching of Latin"; the German one by Voight, "Das erste Lesebuch." Useful lists and descriptions of the common reading texts are also to be found in Grendler, *Schooling*, 111–14; Garin, *Pensiero*, 91–124; and Avesani, *Quattro miscellanee*. These highly inclusive lists of textbooks should be used carefully, however, because they do not distinguish between the texts common in Italian classrooms and those Italians could have found only in sizable libraries.

20. Vidmanovà-Schmidtovà, *Quinque claves*, 3, 39.

21. Cremaschi, ed., *Elegia*, 19–24; cf. Cremaschi, "Enrico," 206n2, for one manuscript not included in the edition.

Goro d'Arezzo, and two unidentified texts. It is worth noting how rarely the reading anthologies included grammar texts as such. There are only ten examples in our entire sample, of which four occur in just one manuscript (Census I.12). Three others are associated with the most elementary reading text, the *Disticha Catonis*, in two manuscripts (Census I.13 and I.15). Another way of putting the point of frequency is that only five of seventy-one surviving manuscript readers contained any grammatical text.

Thus, grammar rule books (usually in prose) were not normally put down in the same format as reading texts (usually in poetry); and grammars were much less likely to survive in the personal libraries of students who studied Latin than their readers were. The two types of texts merited different kinds of books; apparently they were read differently as well. Some grammatical paradigms were learned by rote before the stage at which the student read lengthy continuous texts; others were drilled while reading the poetry that was the mainstay of the latinizing stage. A written grammar book might have helped in the drills, but it may not have been essential even then. In any case, the grammar once learned was not intended to be read and reread in the way moralizing poetry was.

The relative popularity of the texts in our census is striking. Three texts show up more than eleven times each and together account for 43.3 percent of those that survive in the elementary readers. The next seven texts, which occur five to eight times each, account for an additional 39 percent of the total sample. Ten texts, then, represent over 80 percent of the reading material actually presented to fourteenth-century schoolboys in Florence and surrounding provinces at the early latinizing stage. The chances of survival mean that we cannot generalize too rigorously from these numbers, but some observations are clear. First, Tuscans showed strong preferences in choosing texts for their children from among the wide range of poetry available for school use. The large number of texts that occur only once or twice proves that much more could have been brought into the classroom than usually was. It seems that we are witnessing a deliberate restriction of the curriculum by the elementary Latin teachers of Florence. Moreover, the strong preference for a certain few texts suggests that these were the ones used at the most elementary level. Prosper, Prudentius, and Aesop were at the core of the curriculum. They were used more frequently and with more students than other, comparable texts.

The Florentine elementary reader was one of the artifacts of literary initiation; it marked the new man as a reader, as a Latin-literate adult, just as a schoolboy's first pen and blank notebook marked him as a writer. Such school implements were primarily if not exclusively aimed at boys, for they represented initiation to a professional culture not open to women. Moreover, the reading book had strictly limited aims; it was not intended to function as an introduction to the sophisticated and somewhat cynical pagan culture inherited from antiquity. That was matter for more advanced students, and so for the *auctores* course. Similarly, the grammar manuals, which were technical books and not readers, would not have been redacted in the same form as the basic texts. Neither the pagan poets, who were too advanced, nor the reference manuals, too strictly factual, were initiatory texts. But the anthologized moral poetry *was* initiatory in this sense; it was a wisdom literature, a courtesy literature, and for the most part a lay, male-oriented literature.[22]

It is interesting to note that there is a small body of Tuscan books redacted in reader form but somewhat larger in size which includes texts of the *ars dictaminis* or the *Graecismus* of Eberhard of Bethune. These texts were the staple of the university-level arts course at Bologna and other Italian universities. The examples of this sort of book known to me are listed in Part II of the census. Since the only distinguishing feature between these books and those is Part I is size, there is no hard and fast border between the two sorts of books. One *dictamen* treatise occurs as a stray in one of the elementary readers in the first part of the census, and one copy of Prosper of Aquitaine is found in the oversize category.[23] This latter group of books clearly descend from the same production or publishing tradition as the elementary readers, that is, they were sold by the same stationers that published the readers.

We might speculate that these books were aimed at pre-professional graduates of the Latin reading course or at the *auctores*-level course. The presence of several copies of Boethius's *Consolation of Philosophy* in this group confirms this hypothesis that they were intended for advanced grammar students. A small number of ordinary sized reader-form books also contain Boethius or other texts that seem rather advanced for beginners. An intriguing example of this latter sort is the anthology of Prudentius's *Psychomachia*, Virgil's *Bucolics*, and the *Physiologus* found in Riccardiana 418 of the very late fourteenth or early fifteenth century. This

22. Cf. Ong, "Latin Language Study," esp. 120–29, and Klapisch-Zuber, "Le chiavi," 778–80.

23. The untypically large Prosper is Census II.5, which belonged to a convent in the fourteenth century, as evidenced by ownership marks on fol. 22v. It also has many *volgare* glosses.

book appears to be the product of a single stationer's shop, but each of the texts occupies a separate gathering and is on a different lot of paper. As we have seen above, the only one of the texts here widely used as an elementary reader at Florence is the *Physiologus*. It may well have ended up in this anthology as a holdover from an earlier place in the curriculum. In any case, it is clear that there was no clear border between the curriculum labeled "latinizing" and that called *auctores*. The terms themselves are too inclusive in their common meanings to have been assigned a rigid curricular sense; and as students progressed through the grammar course, their programs were increasingly tailored to their individual interests and career needs.

We might well ask who determined the highly limited curriculum of the initiatory Latin reading course. On the surface it seems likely that teachers had the largest degree of control. Certainly, in the classroom they could opt to stress one text or part of a text and deemphasize another. On the other hand, small-town city councils often dictated curriculum in a way that makes it sound as if the parents had some say too. Paul Grendler cites, although admittedly for a much later period, a schoolteacher who confesses that he teaches children to read whatever books their parents send along with them.[24] We should also admit the possibility that booksellers, especially in large cities such as Florence, had an influence on the curriculum. Teachers with many students owning their own books would naturally have directed them toward purchasing the same or similar textbooks. The availability of these in stationers' shops would have influenced the teachers' choices, and a popular teacher with a large school might have been able to influence what stationers' offered. As I argue throughout this book, the restricted curriculum in Tuscany reflects the coincidence of the social conservatism of parents and the pedagogical conservatism of teachers. Their common interest arose precisely because the curriculum at this crucial level was seen as initiatory and not to be tampered with. The easiest changes would have been to drop too-frivolous, potentially controversial, or doubtfully moral texts. Meanwhile, new texts could be added only at the risk of unsettling the normal course of study. Such considerations were reinforced by the commercial interests of the stationers in encouraging a regular, predictable market for standardized goods.

The average number of texts in each medieval book within our sample is only 1.69. In this regard it is important to count medieval books as they were designed, not surviving books in the form of collections of the

---

24. Grendler, *Schooling*, 290.

fifteenth century or later. Most readers were designed to carry only a single text. This fact should be a warning against too much reliance on our modern notion of reading anthologies or miscellanies, for this description accepts as normal the composite codices in which they survive and the extensive miscellanies that became common in the fifteenth century.[25]

The question of how the manuscripts were produced is crucial. As we have already noted, two systems were used. Most of the surviving books are commercial products, that is, copied in sizable numbers by or for stationers who stocked them against a constant demand. A secondary mode of production, by student copyists, is considered below. The home-made book was always an option for students from poorer families, or in localities where commercially produced readers were harder to find, or in the case of students being trained as scribes.

Stationers most frequently sold reading books in the form of loose fascicles or lightly wrapped or sewn booklets. This is the way they are described in the surviving inventories of stationer's shops: *j. Donadello vecchio*, or 2 *Tres lei in coverta*, or again *Uno gramaticale Arrigheto Tres leo et Etiopo*.[26] Probate inventories also list, sometimes among more substantial codices, small books with titles we can identify from our lists: *j. Isopo in gramaticha* or *j. quaderno di Donatello*.[27] Some interesting lists of books donated to the Compagnia di Orsanmichele in the 1350s and 1360s use the inventory-style term, *1 pezzo d'Ovidio* or *1 pezzo di Luchano*, apparently for loose fascicles of books used in teaching *auctores*.[28] And a tariff roll at Perugia in 1379 refers to a typical *livero . . . de gramaticha picholo picholo*.[29] All these books are described with terms that refer to their diminutive size, but we should not confuse them with modern miniatures or with the octavo and duodecimo printed school-

25. On miscellanies, see Avesani, *Quattro miscellanee*, 20–21; Petrucci, "Il libro manoscritto," 509–11.

26. Carabellese, "La compagnia," 208–9; De La Mare, "The Shop," 247. This last usage is interesting because *gramaticale* seems to mean "Latin reader" in the sense I have developed it in this chapter.

27. Bec, *Les livres*, 150–65. The most interesting examples are those that specify combinations of texts familiar from our census, e.g., *j. Donadello con Prospero*, 152; or in formats like those we see repeatedly, e.g., *Esopus in duobus quaternis in pergameno*, in Rome, Archivio di Stato, Agostiniani in S. Agostino, Reg. 34, fol. 37. I am indebted to Katherine Gill for calling my attention to this interesting, unpublished list of grammar books.

28. Carabellese, "La compagnia," 268–69. Dolezalek, "La pecia," 210–12, is of the opinion that many if not most teachers' copies of textbooks were left unbound.

29. Migliorini, *Storia*, plate IX; cf. Petrucci, "Il libro manoscritto," 513–14.

books that became common in the sixteenth century. Medieval miniatures existed, but they were tiny because they were portable versions of long texts written out in hairline scripts. The Latin reader format is what we would call small quarto, usually six to eight inches in height, intended to carry short texts in large letters. The smallness of the Latin reader consisted in its small number of leaves and slight texts.

In short, these were booklets of one or more gatherings loosely wrapped or sewn together and recognizable to literate people by short-title references or with very generic labels. It seems likely that most elementary students bought and used books in this form without intending to bind them up. Even when they were bound together in the period, the descriptions sometimes make it clear that they were understood as separate entities. Thus the inventory of a Bolognese grammar master's books from early in the trecento describes "Item, one volume of books in grammar containing many books, which volume begins *Cum ego Cato* and ends *dira venena nocent.*"[30]

That such books were available in significant numbers, most often through the same stationers who arranged for their production, is also clear from Census I.26, in which no fewer than nine works were copied by the same scribe and decorated in identical fashion but have a pattern of catchwords that makes it clear they were designed to be used singly. Only at some later point were the additional catchwords added as instructions to the binder to assemble the collection in its present order. It would seem that the individual works in this manuscript were offered in fascicles by a stationer or scribe for combination as required by the customer or grammar master.[31] Other poetic texts, especially lyric poetry, were available in this format throughout the later Middle Ages and early Renaissance, and in this regard our Tuscan readers were typical of poetry manuscripts in general.[32]

A close reading of our census confirms the notion that the elementary Latin reader was essentially a booklet and not a formally bound, library-style book. The most frequent text, Prosper of Aquitaine, occurs twenty-three times. In over half these cases, however, it appears alone. These little Prospers typically occupy three or four gatherings. In another six cases the

---

30. Orlandelli, *Il libro a Bologna*, 87–88.

31. Manuscripts of this type, so clearly the product of a single workshop, are rare. Vatican Ottob. lat. 3325, described by Avesani, *Quattro miscellanee*, 16, 38–46, is an early fifteenth-century Tuscan example.

32. See, e.g., Filelfo's request for a Juvenal in "tre overo doi quaderni," cited by Billanovich, "Petrarca, Pietro da Moglio," 390–92.

poetry of Prosper is copied along with only one other text. The total number of gatherings, in these cases, is usually only four or five. Only twice does Prosper appear in books clearly designed as anthologies of more than two texts, as part, that is, of what we would call a full-size book. With this physical structure firmly in mind, let us consider the typical page layouts of such commercially made readers and explore their classroom use.

Since the content was poetry, usually in the short and consistent line lengths dictated by elegiac couplets or dactylic hexameters, the model for the Tuscan reader was the poetry book of the high Middle Ages, a type used widely all over Europe. In its most beautiful form, such books were relatively tall and narrow and displayed a single column of verse on each page in a long vertical rectangle. This form was emphasized by capitalizing or flourishing the initial letter of each line. In most cases these line initials were set slightly out into the left margin, creating a column of their own for which the page was ruled at the time the membrane was prepared. Such books have a simple, functional design much to our modern tastes, pleasingly graceful and somehow also monumental. Often, this model was also adapted for more modest and everyday books of verse, quite without pretensions to fine design, something that was most likely to happen when the poetry was contemporary, or didactic, or just not important enough to merit elaborate presentation. It is this latter version of the form, what we might call the informal poetry book, that provided the model for the Latin readers of Tuscany and the rest of trecento Italy.

We may choose almost any modest thirteenth-century book of poetry as an exhibit of the form. To hand as I write, for example, is Newberry Library MS 21.1, an English book of the late twelfth or early thirteenth century containing the *Anticlaudianus* of Alain de Lille, a work both relatively contemporary to the writing and didactic in nature (Figure 2).[33] Each page, of well-prepared but highly irregular parchment, is ruled in lead to receive thirty-eight lines of verse, and a marginal column is ruled at the left for a line of capital letters at the beginning of each line. Although the script is small, the spacing between lines creates a open general appearance and allows readers to interpolate interlinear glosses. The rigid left margin and the ragged right would have told any medieval reader at a glance that the work is poetry. But the margins are not sufficiently generous to accept an extensive commentary, so the reader is also cued to

33. Saenger, *Catalogue*, 37–38.

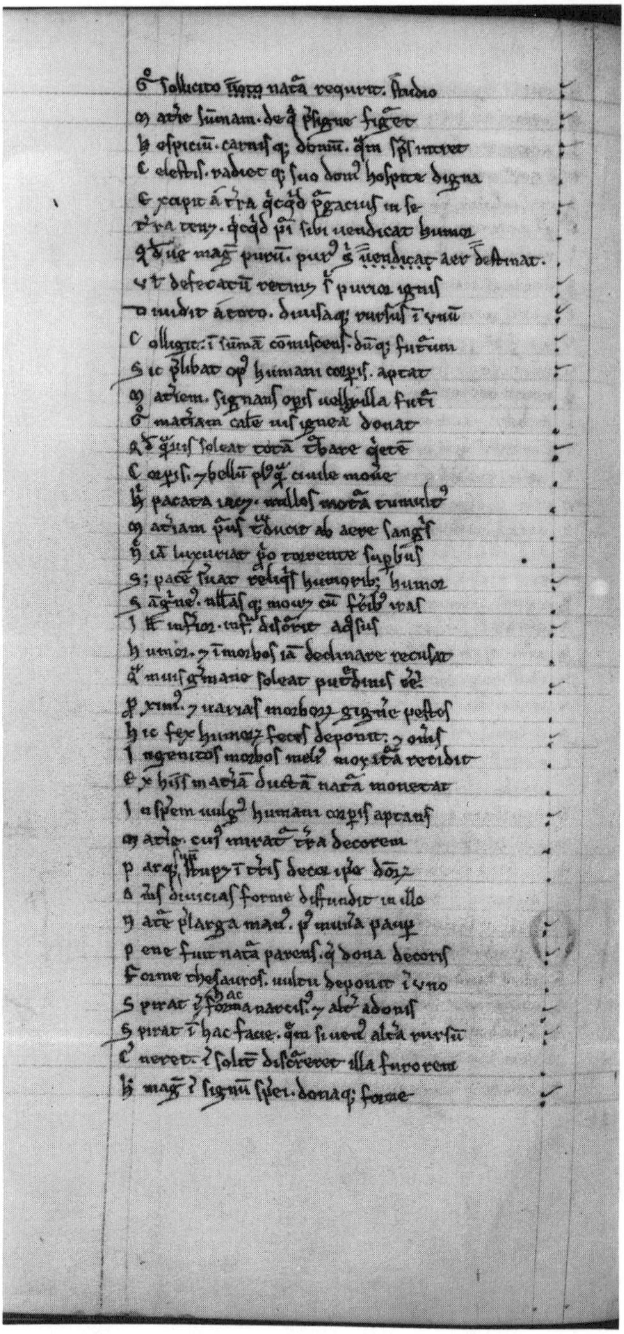

*Figure 2.* Chicago. Newberry Library. MS 21.1, fols. 23v–24.

c edit. q̃ nt̃a corp̃ pinguedine surgit
s; mag̃ ī mācō tendit. sic oīa iuste
p ossidₑ. ī alto decor e? claudicat. īmo
ꝟ el mai coffoc f̄ nata. tulō
ħ g̃ s̃ies. caut p̃cendit honore
q &c s̃ese possit vire cōmode laudi
ꝯ audie. laudem q; suo ideat ab hoste
ꝑ q̃ mariō narō dex̃t beario
v uted humanis diam goodra carni
f edit. y stabili cōuectu destana negri
l uncta renu gitt̃hi subriubₑ; ayt ii
c oposito simplex. hohen subribₑ. ligneg;
ꝑ ede cōplacito carni digna mayora
g noctis lueo cōnedor. y ciba cre
d iuisa remoꝝ pacor sio distona lucem
o oponunt ham. ū ea caro bella minuā
g pur cedens. s; no sq̃ mine ntoo
ħ et nā corpₑ uestē fasridor alhoz eras
g ff. hospicio ueli locat̃. ū umbra
c̃ non famag̃ ho. miseo inullo
g e vinc porullo ꝑtorens narā stupet q;
v ye og̃ xo. sui credens. qo focat ipa
a counitar dotel p̃nietas copia plono
l fundens corū. narō mūia, nullam
ꝓ enfure moₑa ꝑeruet. ī merde coneo
q corū qo utₐ suf inpacta, nulnos
e ꝟhausto mūu rant diffundir ī quo
g o p̃bar. y q̃at possit metti tillo
a coodit f̃ anos ī dotō. ue caina poₑ
ꝗ ūda ꝑfecdor ꝑdant gionni laudi
ħ as f̃ina g̃ fauer. donasti ū doua place
p ossiō.; ate p̃flanr tor mūia sanca
ꝗ gnus solear ūum coₑꝟe falso
ħ ic nesaꞇ ū ūa loc. moꝝsq; necusto
e ꝟut. y de se retinet sibi nota fame
ꝟ o ibi sive su ve. nō tux sū lauder suanq;
c ar ab ypoch laudem. res digna f̃inoce
ꝗ uua leraae largir g̃ta uieent

expect poetry of a sort that is to be read with only minor glosses. As if to emphasize the ragged right margin, the scribe has finished every line at the exact, ruled margin with a small dot and, between the dots, irregularly placed strokes or dashes. In a vertical row that balances the column of initial letters, these marks define the written space as ruled and provide the only decoration to the typical page.

This manuscript can be profitably compared with one in our sample, the important Magliabecchi codex of *Ianua* and other school authors (Census I.16), also of the thirteenth century. The Italian scribe has used parchment of a very scrappy and irregular sort, some of it ruled for other purposes and reruled for use in this book. The overall size is small and the page relatively narrow; indeed, in shape and size this piece is nearly the same as the Newberry manuscript. Like the English scribe, this one has followed the classic format for poetry. The script is small and there are many lines per page, but the spacing of the lines and the ragged right margin create visual openness. There is room for interlinear glosses, but almost none for marginalia. As in the Newberry book, the line initials form a clearly visible column of their own to the left of the written space. The Italian scribe has emphasized their distinctiveness by flourishing them with the same red ink used for rubrics. The rubrics, moreover, do not interrupt the unity of the column as designed, for they are placed out into the margin, almost as an afterthought. The English rubricator did much the same thing with subject index notes added to Alain de Lille's poem. In both books, the larger section initials indicate breaks in the text without really breaking the visual unity of the column.

In one significant way, however, the Magliabecchi codex is different from the English one and anticipates refinements of the Tuscan form of Latin school reader in the next century: the Italian scribe has been careful to abbreviate relatively rarely. This is a first step toward improving legibility, and it is applied here (as universally in books of this sort in the next century) to elementary texts formatted for reading by beginners. In this regard we may distinguish the Magliabecchi codex from a nearly contemporary Italian manuscript of Ovid and the neo-Ovidian *Pamphilus* now in Toledo. The format is almost identical to that of the Magliabecchi anthology, but the higher degree of abbreviation, the larger margins, and the lack of elementary glosses, as well as the Ovidian subject matter, make it likely that the Toledo book was intended for somewhat more advanced reading.[34]

34. See Bonilla y San Martin, "Una comedia latina," 427, for a plate of the Toledo codex, which is no. 102–11 in the collection of the cathedral of Toledo. Cf. *Pamphilus*, ed. Becker, 67–68.

In the fourteenth century, schoolbooks of this sort gradually moved away from the high medieval norms for books of poetry and developed a look of their own. The size of the script was enlarged, making the unabbreviated lines somewhat longer and the number of lines per page fewer. This required a broader text column, sometimes a slightly wider page as well, and further reduced the width of the margins as a proportion of the entire space. The result was a book with overall dimensions that vary only slightly around an average of 18 cm in height and 12 cm in width, and with an average of twenty-three to twenty-four lines per page.[35]

The Prudentius in Census I.12 (Figure 3) typifies the developed form. Twenty-two lines are generously fitted into a written space that occupies almost 13 cm in height. Rubrics are centered on lines left blank for them before each of the four-line poems, a practice which might seem rather prodigal of parchment but which gives the page a very open and rather childlike feel. This is a clear design choice in favor of juvenile readers and not a mere luxury, for the margins are not wide. There was no functional reason for them to be so.

In the case of the rubrics, however, the designer did have a reason for his choice; not only do the centered rubrics give the book a certain pleasant naivete, they also make it more legible and render the text easier to fix in the memory. Children, like their elders, were advised to memorize using the page layouts of a specific copy of the text. This advice extended to visualizing the layout of the whole page opening, and the centered rubrics would have helped in this process by creating an open, well-articulated page.[36] In readers designed for children, this practice would also have served to reinforce their sense of owning the book.

An example of mid-century design is Census I.49 (Figure 4), a copy of Prosper's *Epigrammata*. This text mixes verse and prose, and so it offers design problems slightly different from those faced by the scribe of simple poetic texts, but the solution is based on the poetry book model. The continuous left-hand column of line initials has broken down somewhat because the short lyrics and proses of the text demand frequent large initials. But the line initials are still flourished, to create a prominent if discontinuous column at the left margin. Similarly, the ragged right margin of the poetry is interrupted by short blocks of prose that run all the way to the ruled margin.

The Italian scribe has chosen to emphasize the ragged margin where it

35. Excluded from these averages are a few schoolbooks designed in a similar way but on a larger page. These I characterize as oversize schoolbooks. They include all the manuscripts in Part II of the Appendix and Census I.24 and I.47 (both borderline cases).

36. Carruthers, *Book of Memory*, 93–95.

de suspendio inde laqueo·

Ampus achaldemach sceleteris micede nefandi
Venditur exequas recipit tumulosq̄ humandas
Sanguinis hec p̄tiuz e v uidas eminus artat
Infelix laqueo collum p̄ emine tuto.

de domo inqua flagellat̄ e dn̄s

Impia blasfemy recidit dom̄ alta cayph
Inqua pulsata e facm xp̄i
hic pecator mam exitus obruta quor
Pena ruinosis tumul sine fine manebit.

de dn̄o ligato ad colupnā

Vinctus ibis dn̄s stetit edib) atq̄ colũnis
Auex tegmis redit ut siule fragell
P̄stat aduc teplus regit q̄ ueneranda colũna
Nos q̄dā citis imunes uiuare flagris.

de dn̄i nr̄i yh̄u xp̄i morte

Transfectis p utriusq̄ latus latioezq̄ cruore
Xp̄s agit sanguis uictoria tinsa lauacru
Tunc duo discedit crucib) hic ide latrones
Contiguus negat ille d3 fert i coronat.

de ascensioe xp̄i

Montis oliueti x̄ de uitice sursum

Anpantes rediit singnas uestigia ÷
ƒrodibz ethis pquus liqt uinor
Qui probat infusiuz tris & crismate donuz.

de morte sɋ stephani

Pkiʒ init stephaii mercedez saguinis ibze
Aflict lapiduz xpiiz tñ ille cruet
Int sassa rogat · ne sit lapidatio fraudis
Hostibz · o prime pietris misada corone.

de claudo que dñs liberauit

Porta maiz tepli spetiosa quas ucitat
Egregiuz salamonis opus ƒ magis illo
Xpi opus emicuit naz claud fuge uustus
Ore pet stupuit danatos cure gress.

de disco qd petrus sopniauit

Somniat dilaruz petrus abecte distui
Omnigenis gfectuz aialibz ille recusat
Mande. ƒ dñs iubet oia muida putare
Sugit & inuidas uicat admisteria getes.

de conersioe sɋ pauli

He lupus ate mpar uestut uelle molli
Saulu q fuerat fit adeto liue paulus

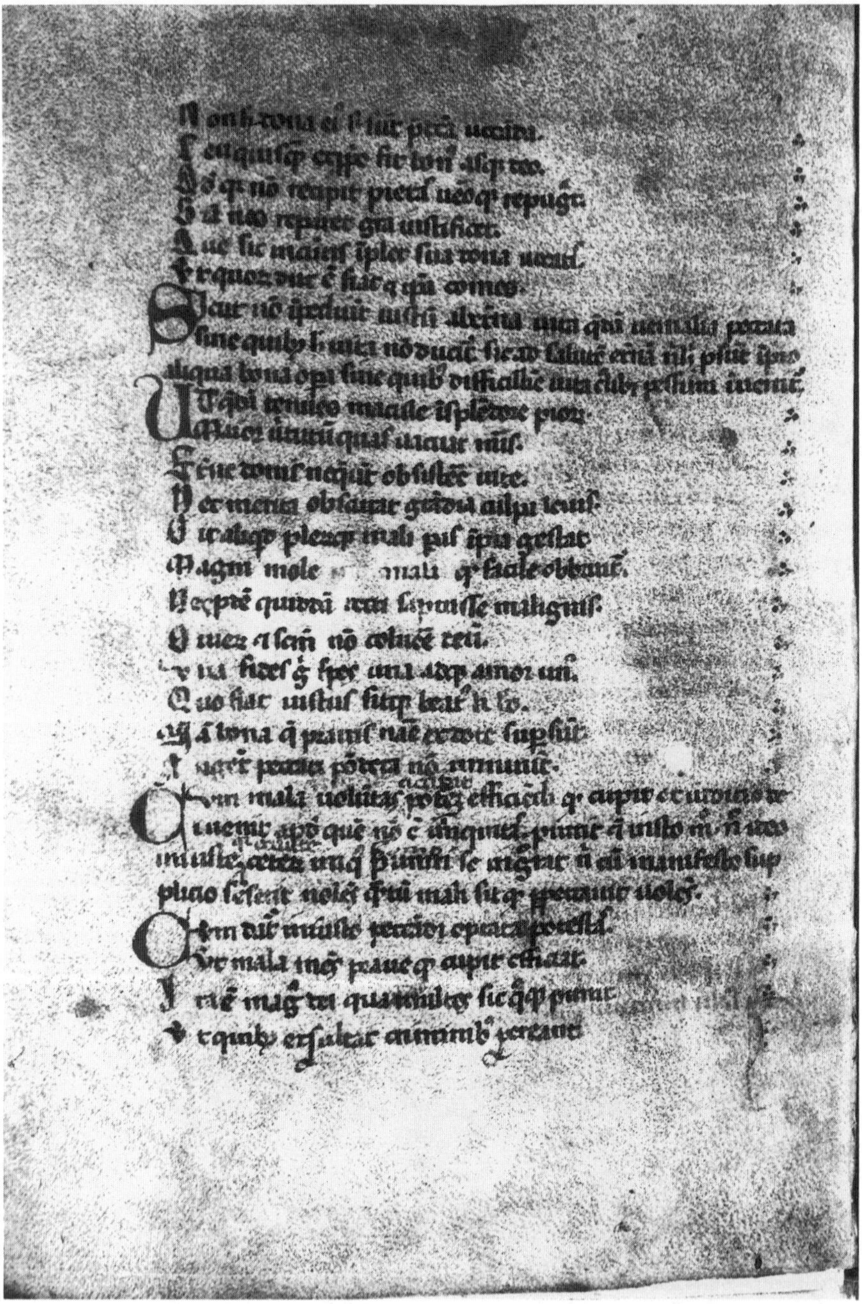

*Figure 4.* Volterra. Biblioteca Guarnacci. MS XLIX.33 (Census I.49), fols. 1v–2.

Tristis est occulte culpe pena reatus
Aut cui uultus suus nichil obstruit
Et magis errati ne parcit flagra timoris est
Qua ne non fiatque uoluisse nocet
Quia culpa in male factis tantum ualet sola superbia
nuditas factus euertat
Quin genus unitas ipso tria ualet actu
Et peccata sua quisque genus spes
Sola est omnium armata superbia tellus
Cui presunt cuncta et bene gula dare
Ne pluribus qual sit usu leui rex quod oramus ipse
cum rex quod omni acesse nam tibi temporalibus si tibi cuncta inter
nec uult frangit mani hoc si inter thebanate quod liberare nupsi
Si rebus mundi non ure est et cibus usus
Nec alia paribus cuncta sentir animus
In quam temas non blecta illent non aspera frangit
Et fiat inuicte gaudia uera uiuat
Terre de a semi leauit florens amatos
Seu caret opraens seu boni uult est
Alia mors puerta non est qua boni uita presserit non est sic
mali licuit non quod sequit morte non quod multa auxur
est sic acinur morituri ut morituri si morieris quod recogit
Tanta bonus presunt quibus et mors ipsi reatus
Efficiat ut sumat prima principii
Illeque sint malus et que pena sequet
Et quod spernit pena uolens erit
Ad quod ostrarnens lacrime cuncque laborer
Et notare perest qua signat mala
Tanta admirent corporis salueris mi mente si punta

does persist by resorting to the device used by the English scribe of Newberry 21.1, a pattern of dots at the right-hand margin of the poetic lines. The result is a design that enforces the visual sense of the piece as a *prosimetrum*. Despite the small size of the book and the irregular parchment, the page opening is made quite formal and enlivened with considerable use of color. This is surely no accident; the lively and charming yet formal page was an appeal to the child reader and also an encouragement to him to think of this as a grown-up, latinate book.

Toward the end of the fourteenth century, readers copied on paper became more common, or at any rate more paper readers of that period (and of the early fifteenth century) survive. Meanwhile, the layout of the page in parchment readers becomes more generous. It seems that ordinary copies of readers were increasingly made of paper while more expensive parchment schoolbooks became something of a luxury product. Census I.30 (Figure 5) exemplifies this development. This is a luxury schoolbook if we may ever speak of such a thing. It compares well with the Laurentian Prudentius we examined earlier. There are still just twenty-one lines per page, and the rubrics are still centered. The quality of the inks and parchment is however, the best, and the page is decorated in the restrained fashion favored at Florence for fine poetic manuscripts. Moreover, the margins are extremely wide for a small book like this; as a proportion of the written space they are of luxurious dimensions, comparable to those in the best books on the market. And yet it is still a child's book: naively charming, small in format, intended to be used unbound, and much marked up by its juvenile users over the years.

The second method by which elementary reading anthologies of the Florentine type were created was by assembly at the hands of a student or grammar master. We might call these personal anthologies or miscellanies, though as often as not more than one reader participated in the assembly of the whole. Then too, sometimes one part of such a personal reader, often the nucleus around which the rest of the book was assembled, was a stationer's reader. Thus when Galeazzo di Floriomonte de Brognolis, the student scribe we met in Census I.1, began his handsome little book of readings, he already had to hand two leaves of an *Ilias latina* written by a professional scribe. Young Galeazzo tried to obscure the distinction between this original kernel of the book and the portions he made himself by placing the acquired leaves in the middle of his book and adding colophons claiming the whole of the work as his own. He added his own decorations by way of personalizing the book further.

An even clearer case of such a growing miscellany is that owned by

Paolo di Morello dei Morelli in the fifteenth century (Census I.8). Like Galeazzo's book and other personal miscellanies of the period, this book was also decorated by its scribe or by an early reader with informal drawings in some margins, especially on catchword leaves. What is now the third gathering of the manuscript was once a separate book, probably written for a stationer in the last decade of the fourteenth century. It contains the *Physiologus*, the *Ecloga Theoduli*, and a fable by Colluccio Salutati. At some later moment, another scribe took up the work, either for himself or on commission, and added the present first, second, and fourth gatherings so that the miscellany now contained the *Ilias latina*, another small poem of Salutati, the *Chartula*, and a copy of Prudentius's *Dittochaeon* in addition to the original three texts. Thus far the book is a fairly typical late fourteenth- or early fifteenth-century reading anthology, its only unusual trait being the works by Salutati, which never came into wide use as school texts but which were certainly suitable as such and well known to Florentines in Salutati's own circle and beyond.[37] The anthology was further extended by the same scribe on different paper but in the same format and, we may assume, at a third moment, with four gatherings (5 through 8) that include rather more advanced reading texts by Prudentius, Statius, and Avianus as well as the *ars dictaminis* of Giovanni di Bonandrea. With this addition, the character of the miscellany was substantially changed, for these are texts appropriate to a student at the *auctores* level, and a fairly ambitious student at that. The further addition sometime in the fifteenth century of a copy of Claudian's *De raptu Proserpinae* probably represents joining yet another professionally written stationer's booklet to the anthology.

It is tempting to see Paolo di Morello dei Morelli's book as representing not an anthology acquired for pleasure but rather a course of study followed by the original owner of the book. Perhaps it dates from Morelli's own childhood in the first decade of the fifteenth century, a period when the Morelli family, in the person of his father Morello and his uncle Giovanni di Pagolo, were attempting to return to the Florentine political limelight following in the footsteps of their elder cousin Giano di Giovanni Morelli. The extensive cycle of *auctores* in the miscellany may represent, then, the family's hopes for the eldest son of the eldest son of the remote cadet Pagolo di Bartolomeo (ca. 1305–74), and thus the ambitious course of study set for a student in a family still struggling for a secure place in the political class. In any case, the book attests to the way school

---

37. Jenson and Bahr-Volk, "Fox and Crab," cited to Census I.8.

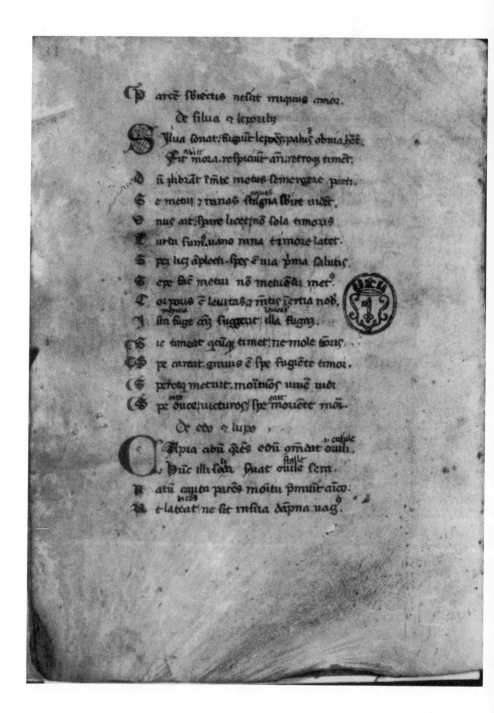

*Figure 5.* Florence. Biblioteca Riccardiana. MS 725 (Census I.30), fols. 10v–11.

Hic latet; ecce lupus mouet hostia uoce capellã.
Exprimit, ut pateãt hostia clausa petit.
Ita zoul agñ aut; capzas guctur̃ falso.
Cũ male capzeges, te zoul cñ uolo.
Quod mea sic mat̃ mitif ymago loqudi.
Ermula qua uideo te docet cñ lupũ.
Insita natoz cordi doct̃na parẽtuz
Cũ pariat fructũ spretu noc̃ solet.

### de angue et rustico

Rustica milia diu nutritũ noueãt anguẽ.
Humanaz potuit anguis amare manũ.
Vña lõga uiri sobita mutat̃ miraz.
Ira panguineũ dirigit arma capud.
Vulneris actor eget, se uuln̄ credit egeñs.
Angui pretria supplicat, anguis aitz.
Hoc ero securus dũ est sit tanta securis.
Cũ cutis hñ nouit uulnera scripta est.
Qui lesit me, reũ ledet, si ledere posset.
Expedit insito nõ iterare fidez.
Et si te piguit sceleris factũ ã remicto.
Nã gemitus ueniaz uuln̄ cordis emit.

anthologies grew along with their owners and a clear progression of studies from the simple school authors to the complex poetic readings of the advanced grammar course.

We can see some additional ways elementary Latin readers of both commercial and personal sorts were used in the classroom by examining the patterns of annotation within them. Whether copied by the student or purchased from a stationer, fourteenth-century Latin readers were designed to receive little annotation. The margins were usually relatively narrow, as noted above, but the spacing between lines permitted interlinear notes. Contemporary annotations in fourteenth-century readers are, without exception, of a very elementary sort. Proper names are glossed historically or mythologically; a few difficult words are given etymological or morphological explanations; and difficult or complicated syntax is sorted out with reference words or with small numbers or letters to guide the eye of the inexpert reader in finding the correct word order. Some texts used at the *auctores* level of instruction also have simple *accessus* or marginal observations on rhetorical structure or the use of figures of speech.

It is the strictly elementary character of the annotations in the Florentine readers that ultimately proves they were used at the latinizing level and not in more advanced courses. We might look, for example, at the glosses on Henry of Settimello's *Elegia* which appear in Census I.7. At the opening of his lament—it is the complaint of an academic who has lost his job—Henry invokes the ancient poets who should help him regain his position at the archbishop's court in Florence. The poets are identified in interlinear glosses. Over the author's *Maronis*, we can read *id est Vergili*. Even more simpleminded is glossing the genitive *Lucani* with the nominative *id est Lucanus*, telling the student that this proper name is a second-declension noun. Only the most elementary students needed glosses like these. And yet these are not just the notes of a single student or grammar master. They are written in the hand and ink of the text, and they were copied from an earlier manuscript along with the text, as proven by the occasional misplacement of notes, for example, on the same line as Lucanus where *Naso* is glossed *Ovidius* but the gloss is placed incorrectly over the word *commendant* and not over *Naso* where it belongs.

The same manuscript offers good examples of the use of syntactical markers. At the opening of the poem *De septem virtutibus* of John the Abbot, the complex syntax is sorted out with small letters from *a* to *n*, in this order: *k, n, b, a, c, d, f, h, e, g, i*. An even more frequent kind of syntax marker consists in adding reference words between the lines to make clear the relation of the word glossed to others in the sentence or to unexpressed subjects or objects. Thus, the copy of Henry of Settimello's *Elegia* in Census I.4 contains frequent glosses that supply *ego* for the various first-person verbs, especially for deponents. Syntax glosses could be used at any level of instruction and would also help readers outside the classroom. When they are the only glosses not of an elementary level in a given book, they were probably supplied as an aid to young readers.

Most of the annotation in the Florentine readers is in Latin. Occasionally, lexical equivalents are also given in the vernacular. Notes of this sort have a long history but, by contrast to the Florentine readers, classbooks that survive from the earlier Middle Ages are always teachers' copies.[38] This may also have been the case for the earliest examples in our census. Teachers, either as consultants to scribes or through the use of teacher's copies as models, decided what kind of commentary the students' books were to have.

The annotations in the Florentine readers concentrate at the beginning of each new text and tend to disappear after a few pages. This is normal practice in many medieval books, especially those used for intensive study. In elementary-level books, where the commentary that survives was often copied by the scribe and therefore an integral part of the design of the book, it implies that each new author required a bit of written orientation for the reader starting out. Once the style and diction of the author became familiar, fewer notes were needed. Students may even have been taught that this practice was the appropriate method for approaching a new author.

The well-used and much marked-up copies of reading texts that survive also evidence the expectations of their owners that schoolbooks would see many years of classroom use. The fourteenth-century preference for parchment over paper was part of this expectation. Patterns of repeated ownership marks make it clear that two brothers or a father and son often used the same reader. In still other cases, two students in the same school entered their names successively in the same book (Census I.11, I.19, I.24, I.25, and I.31).

This continuous reuse of elementary Latin readers was not mere thrift; it bespeaks as well the moral and pedagogical conservatism that obtained at entry level in the Latin course. Following Walter Ong and Christine Klapisch-Zuber, I have referred to this stage of study as initiatory. It is not

38. Cf. Wieland, "Glossed Manuscript."

stretching the point too far to add that the reading book itself was an initiatory object. Many symbolic moral lessons were embodied in the Florentine practice of giving readers to new latinizers. First of all, they would learn pride of ownership in a physical artifact of the Latin high culture of the West. The contents of the book were to be memorized but also to be owned in written form; and so, well before he was able to copy or buy books for himself, the Florentine child destined for Latin literacy could participate tangibly in the larger book culture. He could be a book owner; at least potentially he could be a book collector. We may even suspect the stationers of trying to make the child into a bibliophile by offering so charming and elegant a model to new readers.

In format these books offer a second lesson too. Although small in size and frequently left unbound, elementary Latin readers were modeled on larger, more formal books of Latin poetry and not on vernacular books. Their informality and calculated naivete did not extend to employing cursive scripts or other vernacular book usages. Nor were these readers allowed to become mere notebooks or overly miscellaneous, after the fashion of vernacular *zibaldoni*. These distinctions were important, for the physical structure of the books themselves served to set off the realm of Latin literacy from that of reading and writing in *volgare*. Thus, even in the case of students' own copies of school poetry, gothic book hand was the norm. And the student scribes labored mightily to reproduce other aspects of the look of their exemplars too, especially the open, uncrowded page and high degree of legibility. With a whole series of visual and physical cues, then, the Latin student was encouraged to aspire to literary maturity, and to a latinate cultural aristocracy.

Last, the content of the elementary reader was moralizing poetry and not mere language arts for a good reason. With a book of this sort the child was given something worth having to hand, rereading, and contemplating for the rest of his life. This seriousness of purpose may explain the extraordinarily high frequency with which Prosper of Aquitaine's *Epigrammata* appears in Tuscan schoolbooks. Prosper's were poems about the mature Christian life, not mere fables for children. Moreover, they were thoroughly Christian in content—untainted by pagan ideals of urbanity, for which there was plenty of room later in the *auctores* course.

The first Florentine books designed expressly for children were developed in the generation of Dante, indeed, almost exactly in his lifetime. They are an expression of the educational aspirations of just that period. Before the mid-thirteenth century, Florentine teachers, like those elsewhere in Europe, had apparently been content with schoolbooks of a monastic type, derived from the classic format for setting down all Latin poetry. With the growth of a self-conscious Tuscan vernacular literature and the spread of literacy more generally, Florentines and other Italians began to see new uses for the traditional Latin-style education. They therefore began to create books for the personal use of urban school-children with aspirations to Latin careers outside the church or within the new mission of the mendicant orders to minister to the populations of the great cities. We may justly see in this a reflection of the larger aspirations of the merchant elite of Florence to insert their own civic achievements into a universal culture that had for centuries been dominated by Latin literature and law.

This cultural movement was not yet a classicism in the humanist mold because, following the monastic grammatical tradition and the newer mendicant notions of spirituality, it looked to a unitary, Christian inheritance from the ancient world. As Ronald Witt has shown in recent studies of early humanism, the first stirrings of true classicism were isolated and sporadic and did not develop evenly in all parts of Italy. Florence remained rather behind transapennine Italy in the trecento; the splendor of the vernacular literary achievement of Tuscany in the thirteenth and fourteenth centuries retarded the introduction of neoclassicizing humanism. In my view, these same forces acted to affirm the older kind of grammatical study based on the Christian classics and indeed to put it on an even more sternly moralizing basis than elsewhere.[39]

Dante's universalism was merely the most ambitious and elevated version of a highly self-conscious civic culture based firmly on the inheritance of the ancient world as interpreted by the scholastics of the thirteenth century. These thinkers, among them Dante's teacher Brunetto Latini and many highly skilled and popular mendicant preachers, founded their thought in turn on the Christian classics. Latini, Dante, Francesco da Barberino, and others like them possessed a particularly earnest brand of moralism that stressed the responsibility of the owner of property to educate himself to virtue. This moralism took many forms. In the hands of some minor writers and teachers it amounted to little more than affirming the narrow-minded moralism of the urban merchant-oligarch. One small but important expression of the theme of responsibility to property was the production of books for children, books that gave the child setting out

39. I am indebted here to the interpretation of early humanism developed by Witt, most clearly stated in "Origins," 103–6.

on the study of Latin culture both a clear set of moral goals expressed in the form of school poems and also a tangible artifact of book culture, the Latin reader itself.

Bartolomeo da S. Concordio's advice, "Through all his life, a man should regulate himself according to the sayings of sages," expresses this bookish moralism perfectly.[40] The Christian returns again and again to the wise sayings of the church fathers for guidance in leading life. The urban, middle-class Christian needed this discipline especially, for he lived outside the well-regulated monastic community that had for centuries been the ideal of Christian perfection. The methods of the new, literate lay piety were based on the ancient practices of reading and memorization as these had evolved in monastic communities. We may deduce from the survival of the Latin readers of Florence that these traditional habits were reinforced by keeping a few well-loved, personally owned books close to hand.

Bartolomeo assembled his miscellany of patristic and classical opinions in two versions, Latin and vernacular. He stands in a Tuscan tradition that both popularized and set apart the ancient tradition of Latin literature: popularized it by making it available in translation, but set it apart by collecting its jewels in the original language, with the clear implication that the original was worth preserving and worth studying Latin for. The reading books used at Florence were similarly in between: they were doors through which young boys passed in traveling from the contemporary, largely *volgare* culture of their homes on their way to a distinct, Latin realm.

It is important for our evaluation of the Florentine teaching of Latin to be able to measure the degree to which Latin retained for the lay teachers of the fourteenth century the status as privileged vehicle of antique culture that it had held unchallenged in the monastic schools. This task is particularly urgent when we realize that the curriculum of the elementary Latin course consisted almost entirely of texts preselected by conservative teaching habit. Only one of the reading texts regularly used by Tuscan grammar masters in the trecento was composed after 1210; most had been classroom standbys in monastic schools at least a century before that. All these texts had a tradition of use in clerical contexts where Latin was not only a career necessity but also a bearer of sacred wisdom and the necessary vehicle of the ethical formation of the Christian.[41]

40. Bartolomeo de S. Concordio, *Ammaestramenti*, 69, my translation.

41. An astute discussion of the issues involved in such educational conservatism may be found in Frova, *Istruzione*, 102–4 and in her concluding note. See also Kohl, "Humanism and Education," 6–9.

In the trecento, to be sure, "Latin" careers were fewer than before as a proportion of an ambitious student's options. In Florence, in particular, the mercantile tradition of the oligarchy meant that numerous, more practical careers were open to young men. The precocious Florentine use of Tuscan *volgare* for business, political, and administrative records meant that many traditionally Latin professions in civil service and law were virtually bilingual. This quasi-bilingualism gave the circles of Petrarch and later Salutati much of their urbanity. Learned lawyers, notaries, and Latinists of other sorts mixed easily with well-born Florentine politicians who, though admiring all things classical, were not always very accomplished in Latin. A basic, working mastery of Latin was essential, but real achievement in Latin was no longer a prerequisite for professional success. Latin merely added prestige and polish, especially because it offered entrée to ancient philosophy and poetry. The success of humanism, especially as embodied in the early canonization of Petrarch and Boccaccio, lent an additional air of exclusive urbanity to the study of Latin in the new, humanist mode. Toward the end of the century this fashion would become increasingly influential. It would even alter the strongly commercial prejudices of Florentine fathers in favor of Latin study for their sons.

Meanwhile, lay piety too had found vernacular means of expression that obviated the exclusive claim of the lettered in Latin to the full Christian life. The mendicant orders in particular promoted a lively popular piety that took full advantage of the *volgare* both as a forceful, homely medium and as a vehicle of polished elegance. Such popularization by translation was essential to the mendicant mission of broadening the religious culture of the laity. Still, we can take a cue from the constitutions of the mendicants and assert categorically that Latin still owned its privilege in the sphere of religious culture; only friars with solid grammatical learning were allowed to frequent the theological lectures that prepared them to preach.[42]

It is fair to say, then, that the Latin student of the trecento was still studying, not for literary pleasure or out of philological interest, but for the sake of acquiring the key to Christian high culture. This was true whether or not the schoolchild (or parents) had a clerical or university career in mind. Even as a finishing course or as preparation for government service (notarial or merely scribal), or, as in the case of some noble

42. Davis, "Remigio de' Girolami," 304. See also the essay of Maierù, "Tecniche di insegnamento," 307–52. An important discussion of the role of the *volgare* in mendicant spirituality, with particular reference to the learned-but-popularizing tradition of the Dominicans in Tuscany, is Delcorno, "Predicazione volgare."

men and women, out of personal interest, Latin was seen first of all as a vehicle of access to the highest civilizational goal of Western culture, wisdom.

This attitude goes far toward explaining the choice of elementary texts, their limitation in terms of genre, and the dynamic of conservatism in the primary school classroom. The question of literary form is important both in terms of pedagogical technique and again on the plane of moral psychology. A wide variety of subjects were treated in elementary reading texts, but almost without exception beginning students were given moralizing poetry to read. This choice is usually explained in terms of the universal practice of learning by memorization. It is a simple and obvious fact that verse is easier to fix in the mind because its formal qualities provide an additional "hook" for the memory. Beyond this consideration (which was not merely mechanical but embraced also an entire memorial psychology as well as a concept of wisdom arranged by memory), other ethical and normative notions of language were at work.[43]

Poetry offered the schoolchild models of expressivity on a par with those of prose if not exceeding them. Expression in language, particularly the language of the ancient and modern sages, was seen as an essential part of the moral formation of the individual on at least two levels. First, Latin literature embodied the moral ideals and lessons of the ancients in the rhetorical forms that allowed the reader to internalize them most thoroughly. And second, mastery of literary usage gave the individual an opportunity to develop his own expressions of comparable lessons. Such compositions, whether they originated as meditations on received texts or were "invented" rhetorically by the student, were good and moral actions in themselves and led to other practices of virtue. Indeed, it is fair to say that the grammarians of the Middle Ages felt that language mastery was a form of self-mastery.[44] We see shortly how thoroughly this moral psychology, ultimately derived from Saint Augustine, was embedded in the works chosen for reading texts. For the moment I need only remark that, since poetry was seen as an essential form of language use—not a separate or esoteric but a normal usage—the schoolchild had to acquire facility in understanding poetic expression as well as prose usage.[45] Indeed, the (to us) rather mundane content and mediocre quality of much school poetry

43. Carruthers, *Book of Memory*, 162–70; Grendler, *Schooling*, 196–97; Stotz, "Dichten als Schulfach," 2–7.

44. Copeland, *Rhetoric, Hermeneutics*, explores the academic context of this kind of moral invention.

45. Stotz, "Dichten als Schulfach," 3–7, 15–16.

can be attributed to just this attitude, that it was an accomplished but not a special or mysterious use of language. School poetry was chosen to facilitate moral learning and not to provide lessons in mere language mastery. The formal qualities of poetry both facilitated memorization and made it easier to internalize the virtues there embodied.

# DONADELLO

## *Deciding to "Latinize"*

In this and the following chapters I examine in turn each of the poetic texts that were used for teaching Latin reading in Florentine schools. My method is strongly literary. I hope to tease out the many possible meanings these texts had for fourteenth-century readers at the pre-university level. At times this means going somewhat beyond what was probably taught in elementary classrooms. We have, in fact, relatively little concrete evidence about classroom approaches to these texts at any period before the invention of printing, and even afterward. Still, our census has given us a clear sense of the texts used, and we can certainly assess the underlying meaning and import of those school texts. Only if we examine this deeper level of meaning can we understand why these texts had such staying power within the curriculum. Conservatism, after all, is not a thoughtless or lifeless stance; often it is a dynamic approach informed by a sense of the positive value of traditional ways of doing things. Needless to say, I do not claim that every student or even most students could get as much out of the texts as they potentially contained. Even some trecento teachers would not have handled these texts in a very sophisticated way. But the medieval tradition of textual study was founded on the notion that there were many possible readings of every text, and that texts should be read repeatedly, even life long, in search of their deepest significance. Even the dullest grammar masters would have claimed this ideal as validation for studying literature with boys, however far short of it they and their charges fell. They would not make the modern mistake of separating off technical from moral meanings, or even of placing them side by side as partial explanations of a whole. For trecento readers, as for their medieval predecessors, the simpler meanings of any given text were embraced within the complex ones, and learning Latin was the key to reading on more than one level of meaning.

Most students of Latin had professional careers in mind. Still, the existence of a strong, highly pragmatic commercial class at Florence and the large number of teachers of all sorts available there ensured that by the end of the thirteenth century it was possible for parents and children to aim for a literacy that was purely vernacular. Students with this goal were most often aiming at business careers; they sought a literacy that was adequate to the needs of commerce. Sometimes the non-Latin literate also had ambitions as readers of *volgare* literature, perhaps even as authors of it. At least some members of this latter group wanted to acquire a smattering of Latin too.

The turning point in a Florentine boy's education came when his parents decided whether to send him to a Latin grammar school after he had mastered the basics of reading and writing. This decision could also be made after some training in *abbaco*. It was not an option open to girls. The moment of choice was symbolized in the curriculum by the basic grammar book called a "Donatus." Only after this book was mastered was the student normally said to be latinizing, that is, reading or studying Latin.

There were several elementary grammar texts available to medieval teachers and called "Donatus" after Aelius Donatus, the fifth-century author of one dialogue-form grammar book. Most of the texts that circulated under this name, however, were not by Donatus. In Tuscan usage the books were typically called by the diminutive "Donadello." The diminutive refers to the elementary nature of the text and probably also to the small size of the books, since the text usually occupied fewer than twenty leaves. In Latin documents this same diminutive sense was sometimes rendered with the phrase *donatum libriculum*. The appositive expression linking two nouns makes it clear that the name of the book, not of the author, was Donatus.[1]

1. On other such diminutives for schoolbooks, see Lucchi, "La Santacroce," 601. "Donatus" and its derivatives had currency as a general term for grammar book in Italy from the thirteenth century at least. For example, the first known vernacular grammar, composed about 1240 in Italy, was the *Donatz proensals* of Uc Faidit, also called *Donatus provincialis* (in the earliest manuscript) and *Donato prodensal*; see Marshall, *Donatz Proensals*, 61–63; Ising, *Herausbildung*, 30. For other such uses of "Donatus," see Alessio, "La grammatica speculativa," 74; Ising, *Herausbildung*, 29–30; Black, "Curriculum," 141n37.

The Donatus that circulated most widely in Italy was a dialogue with an introduction beginning *Ianua sum rudibus* (literally, "I am a door for the ignorant") and sometimes just called *Ianua*.[2] In fourteenth-century Italian documents the terms "Donatus" or "Donadello" almost always refer to the *Ianua*, whereas in northern Europe (and in the fifteenth and sixteenth centuries, everywhere) they more often refer to other basic grammar books. In this chapter I use the terms "Donatus," "Donadello," and *Ianua* interchangeably, reflecting the usage of trecento Tuscany. This first little grammar, in whichever form it took, was first sounded out syllable by syllable and memorized (*legere donatum testualiter*) and then studied a second time, more closely, for the sake of mastering its meaning (*sensualiter*).[3] The process was not easy, and it represented a major investment in time and energy for the student.

The decision to latinize was a commitment to second-language study. The *volgare* was widely assumed to have no rules of its own, so language-by-the-rules was already what we would call a second-language skill. From the thirteenth century onward in Italian towns and cities, Latin was no longer invariably studied, as it had been in the earlier Middle Ages, as a "second native language," one as fully mastered as a mother tongue.[4] Instead, it was acquired as a true second language, and its study was symbolized by the Donadello, a real *Ianua* or doorway in the sense of a liminal text that represents a rite of passage into a realm of wisdom.[5] In the trecento the Donatus was used almost exclusively as a propaedeutic to further Latin study. It was not given to students for whom the further Latin course was not planned.

So momentous a decision had to involve the common consent of student, parent, and teacher. The student would normally have had to demonstrate enough ability to make the master willing to take him on, and the parent would have had to consent to an extended and expensive course that was expressly not for everyone. Giannozzo Manetti, though eventually a distinguished humanist, had the decision *not* to study Latin made

2. Grendler, *Schooling*, 176, cites one case of this text being called by its incipit in the sixteenth century. In earlier manuscripts, the first word *Ianua* is prominent; this was the usual way of describing such texts more precisely than with a generic term like "Donadello."

3. Black, "Curriculum," 142–43, gives a different reading of these terms; see below.

4. The expression is Percival's, "Grammatical Tradition," 247.

5. The title *Ianua* echoes commonplace usage whereby any authoritative guide could be called a "doorway" to wisdom. Rhabanus Maurus had used the term "doorway and teacher" for God; Coluccio Salutati applied the same epithet to Ovid! See Ullmann, "Some Aspects," 39.

for him by his father when he was ten years old; the year was 1406.[6] In Siena around 1355, it was the decision of Ser Cristofano di Gano's grandfather, who had taught the boy "up to and including Donatus" at home, that he should go on to *grammatica* proper with a master when he was about ten.[7] Although nine or ten was a common age for setting out on the grammar course, there was no fixed age requirement. The documents evidence considerable variation in the ages of students at various levels. Giovanni Morelli boasted that his son had mastered the psalter at age six and the Donadello at age eight.[8]

A particularly striking case is that of Bartolomeo di Niccolo dei Valori, who put the decision, made by and for him when he was nine, in a class with his other autonomous career choices:

> When the plague receded in October of 1363, I Bartolomeo set myself to learn grammar at the school of Master Manoello; there I remained until the end of May 1367 and then in June I set myself to learn *abbaco* so as to know how to keep accounts, this with Master Tomaso di Davizzo de Corbuzzi. There I stayed until February of 1367 [i.e., 1368] when I put myself to work in the booth of Bernardo di Cino Bartolini, a banker in the New Market.[9]

The use of the first person here is the long scribal habit of a highly successful merchant writer, aged nearly sixty when he set down this reminiscence. It may also represent in retrospect the sense of accomplishment that completing the Latin course had given the self-made Valori boy. Certainly, Valori looked back on his Latin schooling as a useful cultural initiation or rite of passage. Apparently it helped him to decide for a commercial career and against a learned one. Given that he spent nearly four years at the grammar course, we may assume that he had ability as well as determination. He must have mastered the Donadello and begun to latinize in this time, but there is no evidence that he went on to study

6. Garin, *Pensiero*, 297.

7. Cherubini, *Signori, contadini*, 397.

8. Branca, *Mercanti scrittori*, 294.

9. Florence, Biblioteca Nazionale Centrale, Panciatichi 134, fol. 1r: *E lanno mccclxiij dottobre ristata la mortalità Io Bartolomeo mi puosi a imparare grammatica lì alla schuola di maestro Manoello. E stettivi sino al anno mccclxvij per tutto il mese di maggio e poi in giugno anno detto mi puosi a imparare albacho per sapere fare di ragione col maestro Tomaso di Davizzo de Corbuzzi. E stettivi in sino al febbraio anno 1367 e detto dì mi puosi alla tavola di Bernardo di Cino Bartolini banchiere in mercato nuovo.* For similarly autonomous career decisions at a young age, see Branca, *Mercanti scrittori*, 137.

advanced authors; certainly his prose style in the vernacular betrays no evidence of his Latin education. Instead, he turned his considerable intelligence toward succeeding as a merchant.

A book from the period of Bartolomeo's schooling survived in the Valori family for generations afterward, our Census I.20, described in the previous chapter. If it was young Bartolomeo Valori's book, he set about the Latin course with considerable ambition to achieve the literary and moral-analytical skills that were believed to accompany Latin reading. And his parents promoted this sort of ambition with the gift of a rather substantial little book for a nine-year-old.

Significantly, this anthology does not contain the Donatus itself but rather an intermediate grammar by Goro d'Arezzo. Bartolomeo would have mastered the Donadello *before* going on to the texts in the reader that survives. The book thus represents a token of his success in studying the Donatus. The extreme rarity of surviving copies of the Donatus may mean that Bartolomeo and others like him did so entirely by memory and without a personal copy of the text. Perhaps as likely, given the diagnostic nature of the text, the Valori boy used a copy of the Donadello that belonged to his grammar master. Such copies got repeated, heavy use by generations of schoolboys and do not survive in large numbers. Other sources leave no doubt that Bartolomeo and his schoolmaster read the Donadello twice, once *per litteram* (by letter) and a second time *sensualiter* (for the meaning), before going on to the texts in the reader that survives.

The practice of reading the Donadello twice may seem strange, but its logic becomes clearer if we look briefly at its contents and think of it as a first exercise in bilingualism. Its first meaning and function was to test the student's ability to memorize and to conceive of language in formal terms. Only thus could he start acquiring a second, morally normative sort of literacy. In a second moment the text could be used in a substantial and instrumental way as a means for acquiring some understanding of Latin grammar. Full mastery of grammatical terms and paradigms could not have been learned from the *Ianua* alone. For that, the student needed to work carefully through some of the Latin reading texts listed in Chapter 2.

With the Donatus the student was making a highly significant step. The most basic levels of study concerned reading in the sense of recognizing letters. This was accomplished by sounding them out on the page and copying them onto slates or tablets of wax. Beginning students were simply said to be learning *leggere et scrivere*, reading and writing. This is a meaningful phrase. This first level was distinct from latinizing, or *grammatica*, because alphabetic skills could be applied to either Latin or *volgare* texts. Only at a second level, after mastering the Donadello, was the student ready to start reading Latin itself, to latinize. The beginning texts were prayers and psalms, texts that would already have been familiar to children from their religious education at home and at church. The student's chore was to recognize on the page words he already knew that had meanings already clear to him. Reading the Donatus, however, was quite different. It had two stages because it was the student's first completely *new* text, the first one he had neither heard nor seen before and the first analytical or technical text he ever encountered.

This double process of learning depended on well-developed memorial techniques used universally in medieval classrooms. Students first learned the text syllable by syllable, by sounding it out from a text in front of them or by repeating after the teacher. Necessarily, the text was divided at this stage into short segments for memorization, in a process the memory theorists called *divisio*. Doubtless the young students would have recognized many individual Latin words and phrases in the process of memorization because these were cognates of *volgare* ones. They would also have noticed some differences between Latin and their native vernacular. But their first task was memorizing the ordered phrases of a text in a language they did not yet know. Once the Donatus was committed to memory, they would progress to reading it for sense, its content being the first rules for deciphering their new language. At this stage they would probably memorize the text again according to a content outline, arranging the brief *divisiones* in order under larger points following the arrangement of the text itself. They would pay particular attention to drilling paradigms of Latin inflectional forms for nouns and verbs, precisely the forms that made Latin so different from the *volgare*.

These two kinds of memorization were used by medieval students at all periods and in all stages of learning. In other words, this first contact with technical Latin embodied an integrated group of study habits that would remain with the student life long.[10] The process must have been torturous, and, given the way it was divided functionally and graded by task, it is clear why students were not said to be latinizing until they had mastered

---

10. Carruthers describes this double form of memorizing at length in *Book of Memory*, 80–121, esp. 86–91. See Lucchi, "La Santacroce," 600–601, on its application to the Donatus.

both the elements of reading and writing and the Donadello. Until they had learned to read in this close, analytical way, students could not be said to have passed over into latinate reading.

The two stages took their logic from classical educational philosophy. Ancient and medieval teachers believed in separating the act of reading for recognition of letters and sounds from the distinct act of reading for meaning. This distinction was clearly made by Augustine when he described the study of scripture in his *De doctrina Christiana*:

> In all these [canonical] books, those who fear God and are meek in their devotion may find the will of God. The first care of this endeavor, as I have said, is to know these books. Although we may not yet understand them, nevertheless, by reading them we can either memorize them or become somewhat acquainted with them. Then, those things that are clearly asserted in them as rules, governing either life or belief, should be studied more intelligently and attentively.[11]

Augustine distinguished two levels of reading and assigned them two different moral values. True mastery of a given text could be achieved only at the second level, by understanding and applying the rules it embodied. Medieval memory treatises employed this same notion and expanded on it, for they clearly differentiated between learning by rote with a primarily visual and aural, text-based memory, and memorizing by content, from a concept outline created in the act of reading.[12] Medieval theologians and philosophers of language also held this Augustinian and Platonic concept of language and struggled to Aristotelianize it. One reason they could not jettison it entirely was that it was so deeply imbedded in schoolbooks like the Donatus that everyone learned when first they set out on a latinate career.[13]

The Donadello usual in Italian schools, the *Ianua sum rudibus*, opens with a short prologue addressed directly to the new learner. It promises to teach him the ways of the world through study of the language of learning:

> I am the door for the ignorant desiring the first art; without me no one will become truly skilled. Because I teach gender and case, species and number,

---

11. Augustine, *De doctrina Christiana* II.9, trans. Gavigan, with my clarifications. My thanks to Mary Carruthers for pointing out the pertinence of this passage to the study of grammar.

12. Carruthers, *Book of Memory*, 86–91.

13. Cf. Kelly, "Medieval Philosophers," 217.

and formation in their parts which are inflected. I put method into the remaining parts of speech, explaining what agrees the best. And no use of the word remains that I do not teach. Therefore, unskilled beginner, read and dedicate yourself to study, because you can learn many things with rapid study.[14]

This is advertising verse, grammatically straightforward and uncomplicated. The surviving manuscripts, however, are few and this part of the text was rarely glossed or annotated, so we do not know how closely it was read. Possibly it was merely explained by the teacher and memorized by the student in the first reading of the text. It may or may not have been studied closely again in the second run-through *sensualiter*, but there would have been an advantage in doing so, for it presents several fundamental analytical terms (case, number, etc.) that come up again almost immediately in the next section.

We know from sources outside Italy just how such texts were gotten by memory in the later Middle Ages. Elementary memorization of categories in lists was accomplished by numbering the categories on the fingers of the left hand. If the student also had a written copy, he could hold his place in the written text with a finger of the right hand.[15] These techniques were intended to reinforce aurally acquired information, spoken and heard aloud, with two visual grids, that of the fingers and that of the written page, and with a numerical grid as well, one that was both visual and aural to begin with and would eventually be second nature to the reader. The student of the *Ianua* prologue would have memorized the list of the characteristics of Latin words in just this way at first, ticking the unfamiliar terms off on one hand while fixing them in mind, and reserving to a later moment an understanding of what they meant. Subsequent *divisiones* of the text would have been memorized in the same way.

It should be said that we do not have any fourteenth-century Italian descriptions of the process of learning the Donadello. There is some evidence, presented in recent articles by Robert Black, that the *Ianua* was used exclusively in written form, not memorized, in the mid- to late fifteenth century. After 1470 it was widely available in printed editions too, often bilingual ones. Black has further shown that the printed versions of the text differ from one another and from fifteenth-century manu-

---

14. Grendler, *Schooling*, 176, where also the Latin. Cf. Schmitt, "Ianua," 56–57.
15. Stolt, "Das Werk," 315–18, describes this process on the basis of a fourteenth-century German manuscript.

script ones, and that there was probably some evolution of the manuscript form from the earliest known copies of the thirteenth century to those produced in the fifteenth. All this suggests that the way the text was used also changed. But the evidence is sketchy, especially for the earlier period, because so few manuscript copies survive.[16]

Only two copies of this fundamental text survive from thirteenth- and fourteenth-century Florence, and they are not at all similar. The *Ianua* in Census I.13 is so heavily abbreviated that it can only have been a teacher's copy, that is, a classroom prompt; it could be read and used only by someone who already had the text by memory. By contrast, Census I.15 contains a little-abbreviated version of the text, one that could have been used by teachers or students. The latter codex is also one of the oldest known copies of the *Ianua* and contains more examples and fuller descriptions of doctrine than the text represented by fourteenth-century manuscripts. Black believes that it represents the original, "fulsome text of *Ianua*," designed for instruction in Latin grammar, and that later, abbreviated versions were used merely as reading texts, for decipherment or sounding-out exercises but not for the study of Latin itself.[17] But the other fourteenth-century copies recorded are not Tuscan, so it is hard to say whether the differing texts represent change across time or merely regional variation.

Even if we had more manuscripts to go on, however, it is hard to see how the *Ianua* could have been used in the fourteenth century as a mere reading and sounding-out text. At the early reading stage represented by the Donatus, the student should have gotten both an oral-aural drill and a visual one, just as he had when reading the alphabet table. In the fourteenth century especially, when medieval memorial techniques and the neoplatonic approach to language study they embodied were still strong, such drills almost surely involved memorizing the text too. In schools with more than a few students studying together, such multiple-level drills were essential. Obviously, the student would not have been understanding much Latin grammatical information at this stage, but his ability to do so later would depend on his having the basic text by memory.

We can see as we look more closely into the *Ianua* and other extremely elementary texts how this memorial approach worked. It had another important function too, for the Donadello was used as a diagnostic tool. Whether or not it was memorized, it could be used to assess the student's

---

16. Black, "Curriculum," 142–44, presents the conclusions of his study to date. He describes the manuscript evidence and some early editions in "Unknown."
17. Black, "Curriculum," 144.

ability to conceptualize a second language and go on successfully to Latin study. It was a predictor of success precisely because it was so foreign conceptually and so difficult. Its hortatory prologue well expresses this diagnostic use. The student is encouraged to do well on this piece so he can go on to the next.

The *Ianua* introduction is followed by a dialogue-form analysis of the Latin noun, starting with the first declension. Students who had never read anything but the prayers of the psalter could hardly have made much of this to start with:

> *Poeta*, what part [of speech] is it? A noun. Why [a noun]? Because it signifies substance and quality either properly [of an individual] or in common [i.e., generically] through case. How many are its qualities? Five. What are they? Species, gender, number, figure and case. What is [a] species? Primitive. Why [is it so]? Because it derives from no other [word]. What is [another] species? Derivative, as when [*poeta*] is derived from *poesis*. What is its gender? Masculine. Why [do you know that]? Because the pronoun that precedes it [i.e., in declining] is *hic*. What is another gender? Feminine. Why [do you recognize it]? Because the pronoun preceding it [in declining] is *hec*.[18]

My translation here is rather clearer than the highly telescopic Latin original. But even expanded and explained, this series of concepts must have been near gibberish to a new reader. With careful, slow explanation the schoolchild could only have grasped a few words, preferably the key terms, and fixed them in memory. The full meaning of even these first few lines of text would have become clear only after the question-and-answer pattern was repeated many times in the context of reading literary texts. Repetition and memorization are integral to the course of study envisioned by the *Ianua*.

Another regular feature of the *Ianua* also emerges from this brief open-

---

18. Translation mine; the Latin in Census I.15 reads: *Poeta que pars est? Nomen est. Quare? Quia significat substantiam vel qualitatem propriam vel communem cum casu. Nomini quid accidunt? Quinque: species, genus, numerus, figura et casus. Cuius speciei? Primitivae. Quare? Quia a nullo derivatur. Cuius speciei? Derivitivae, cum derivatur a poesis. Cuius generis? Masculini. Quare? Quia preponitur ei pronomen hic. Cuius generis? Feminini. Quare? Quia preponitur ei pronomen hec.* This thirteenth-century manuscript contains the form of the text most widely used in the trecento classroom, though the *Ianua* was of its very nature a fluid text. Some of the parenthetical explanations I have included in my translation are added in later versions of the text, e.g., in the one reproduced in plate 7 of Grendler's *Schooling*, 177, or the edited version of Schmitt, "Ianua," 74, which is based on a 1481 imprint. Census I.13 (ca. 1300) contains only one of these insertions. For descriptions of the ways the extant printed and manuscript versions vary, see Schmitt, "Ianua," 50–56, 67–69, and Black, "Curriculum," 143–44.

ing passage: the student was not permitted to concentrate merely on a single paradigmatic word, in this case the noun *poeta*. Instead he was immediately required to recognize that there are two "species," both the "derivative," of which *poeta* is an example, and the "primitive," of which it is not. Similarly in the continuation of this drill, he memorized definitions of seven genders, two numbers, and three "figures"; but only one of each of these categories could be applied to the sample word *poeta*. This overload of rules, largely without reference to concrete facts of Latin usage, was set out at the very start of studying grammar. It reflected the teachers' integrated, neoplatonic concept of language and language study. In such a view, grammar is not merely a descriptive or instrumental discipline; it is a normative one. *Poeta* is quickly lost in a consideration of how nouns signify. Only later does the student return to the model word and inflect it through all its forms. This pattern is repeated over and over in the *Ianua*. A word is used as a memory hook for starting a discussion of its general properties. Then the discussion is turned back to a detailed description of the paradigmatic word.

Wolfgang Schmitt points to another characteristic of the *Ianua*, the fact that many versions of it omit the sample words altogether after the first few examples for each declension or conjugation. The manuscripts consulted by Schmitt show amazing variation in the number of sample words listed for each inflectional paradigm, varying in one case (the third declension) from three to ninety-eight. Obviously individual grammar masters could choose any model words they wanted beyond, say, *poeta* for the first declension and *dominus* for the second, to suit their own class needs.[19] Thus, if he could foresee his students' using a given irregular noun or proper name in an early reading text, the teacher could include that word in early drills. Or he might choose to run his brightest students through the series of definitions quickly and then proceed directly to reading simple texts with them, returning to the drills of the *Ianua* in the context of real Latin poetic diction.

The Donatus or *Ianua* merely provided a framework for understanding Latin; it was learned by rote, then repeated with examples that gave descriptive meaning to the abstract notions it set forth. But even after a second reading of it, the student had not mastered Latin; he had merely acquired a plan of attack for approaching the Latin texts to follow. Part of the *Ianua*'s popularity must have resided in the pedagogical flexibility that results from so thoroughly schematic a structure. In the classroom, we

---

19. Schmitt, "Ianua," 55, 59; Black, "Unknown," 106–8, expands on this observation of Schmitt's.

must assume that every teacher chose to drill what seemed appropriate and repeated the drills as often as his charges needed.

It must have been believed, then, that a certain amount of "Latin" could be absorbed mechanically. This concept is radically different from some modern theories of second-language acquisition. It accords in a way with the total-immersion techniques developed in our own century for teaching conversational language skills. But Latin, we must remember, was largely a written language throughout the Middle Ages. Even if students did learn to speak it eventually, they started by learning to read it, and the oral-aural drills were aimed at mastery of written texts. Latin study was a child's first introduction to written, organized, and regulated language. In bilingual Italy, Latin remained life long a literary tool or a professional one.

After the Donadello was studied for the second time—*sensualiter*, or *per senno*—the student started reading other Latin texts. The *Ianua* or Donadello gave only very elementary rules, really just the inflectional paradigms and some lists of irregular words. So every new text read by the latinizer would be parsed word for word, on the model of the way the Donatus had been learned the second time through. The student and master would work out the structure of each sentence in detail. Real, practical mastery of inflectional paradigms and most other grammatical notions were acquired at this stage, by applying the rules learned in the study of the Donadello to practical reading situations.

The distichs of Pseudo-Cato were typically the first texts used after the Donatus or with it. They begin, in the most common version, *Deo supplica. Parentes ama . . .* [Pray to God. Love thy parents . . .]. So the youth began his life as a Latin reader with second- and third-declension nouns, first-conjugation verbs, the imperative mood, God, parents, affection, and obedience. It would be a mistake to think that the functional concepts here, what we call grammar, were distinct in the minds of the teachers or students from the moral ones. The very idea of a linguistic norm was charged with moral meaning. Preceded as it was by prayers and psalms and followed by the moralizing *Disticha Catonis*, the Donadello was seen as a moralizing text too. The child was not expected to make a full transition from mechanical recognition of words to morally beneficial reading in the course of learning these first Latin texts. But the model of a two-step reading process that would stay with students for all their reading lives was explicit even at this early stage.

The methods of trecento grammar masters presupposed that many Latin words sounded familiar to Italian *volgare*-speaking children. Students could be invited to get involved in the new language by breaking the code that made it different from their mother tongue. Learning Latin by direct translation and paraphrase, linking the students' new, codified language with their old, natural one, was a regular practice in the classrooms of Italy from the twelfth century onward, or so we judge from the intermediate grammar books composed for use there.[20] This sort of study fell considerably short of really comparing the two languages, but it presupposed that Latin was learned through the medium of the *volgare*. The vernacular was probably used for this purpose as soon as the student was presented with literary texts.

With the *Disticha Catonis*, or even before them, the teacher might take his young charges back through the prayers of the psalter, declining and conjugating in Latin and paraphrasing in Italian as they went. The latinizer would have been invited at this point to notice that *Ave Maria, gratia plena, dominus tecum . . .* was Latin, subject to the rules of a formal language system called grammar, and not merely a strange and archaic form of *volgare*. The lesson would proceed thus: *gratia*, noun of the first declension, declined *gratia, gratiae . . .* , here ablative as governed by *plena*, adjective declined . . . Next, *Tecum* not *teco* or *con te* as in *volgare* but a compound of pronoun *te*, accusative, declined *tu tui tibi te te*, combined with a preposition *cum* meaning "with," governing the accusative. And so forth.

Word-for-word analysis was the task of the latinizer through all the beginning and intermediate stages of learning. Even if beginners were reading texts they had already rehearsed in the pre-Latin stage, they did so in a different way, for this kind of parsing through was not attempted at the level of *legente salterium*. At that earlier point the skill in question was recognizing syllables and words on the page, not reading for sense, analyzing according to rules, or working to internalize the moral value of the text. As we have seen before, the heavy cognitive load in the elementary classrooms of the trecento was directly dependent on the notion that linguistic and moral rules alike were the province of Latin study. Gradualism was not an ideal of the curriculum; students were burdened from the beginning with complex and sophisticated ideas.

Still, we can discern three distinct stages in the presentation of written language to new readers. At the very start they were taught to recognize simple, familiar texts. At a second stage they memorized a new, never-before-seen text by rote. They read in a fully meaningful and understanding way only in a third moment, when they could combine the rather

20. Percival, "Grammatical Tradition," 237–38.

abstract lessons of the *Ianua* with concrete experience of reading Latin poetry. This approach assumed a psychology of learning first by eye and ear and then by mental internalization which had very ancient roots. Later in a student's career as a reader these three functions became more closely integrated in time and were superimposed intellectually. But there is good reason to think that even experienced readers of the late Middle Ages approached serious texts in stages: first by glossing, parsing, and memorizing each phrase; and then by rereading for sense, to memorize the conceptual framework and larger meanings of a text and to internalize it and make it thoroughly their own.[21]

There was no prejudice at any point in such a system against repetition. Students might be led through the same texts several times. Each student repeated his assigned text until he had mastered it, as many times as was necessary to satisfy the instructor that he was ready to go on to the next. The texts were chosen for their moral merit and were believed to be worth lifelong rereading. In the classroom, as long as there was a pedagogical reason for repeating a text the teacher would do so without hesitation; it could not possibly harm students to reread the seven penitential psalms or to memorize them in Latin even if they already knew them in a *volgare* version. At the elementary stage there was good reason to stress the differences between the versions and to rehearse the ordered structure of the grammatical, Latin text by contrast to the vernacular one. In the case of their first fully Latin text, once pupils had learned the Latin Donadello first by rote, syllable by syllable, it would be beneficial, even morally necessary, for them to repeat the exercise more intelligently and analytically.

Despite the large dose of rules at the very beginning of learning Latin, not everything a student needed to understand Latin texts was included in the *Ianua* or other beginning grammar books. The *Ianua* offers a basic outline of the five parts of speech, definitions of them, and the pertinent inflectional paradigms; the book also provides examples of irregular nouns and verbs. The text does not extend to the study of syntax, and we do not know of any other, more systematic grammar book used by early latinizers in trecento Italy. Nor was any one of the many available manuals on syntax (called *constructio*) used to supplement the *Ianua* at this early stage.

These omissions in the first stage of Latin study reflect the way scholastic grammarians divided the realm of language into letters, syllables,

---

21. Carruthers, *Book of Memory*, 158–62.

words, and sentences.[22] Apparently it was felt that the morphology of the Latin word had to be absorbed thoroughly before the student could go on to study the fundamental unit of continuous discourse, the sentence. Similarly, the understanding of letters and syllables preceded the study of words. Here we see the real meaning of the three-stage approach to reading noted above. In the prereading stage, students learned the alphabetic skills needed to allow them to sound out letters and syllables and thereby recognize the words and phrases of familiar prayers. By the trecento this was no longer, strictly speaking, a Latin skill, since sounding out could be applied to vernacular texts as well as to Latin ones. The first Latin text, the Donatus, embodied rules of morphology; its primary subject was the inflected, Latin word. Although such rules had begun in the thirteenth century to be applied to vernacular languages learned as second languages, the only inflectional model available to medieval Westerners was the Latin one.[23] Word-form study was an essentially Latin discipline. In the case of Latin as a second language, then, the rules were also learned *in Latin*. First, the Donatus was learned by rote, like the prereading texts; then it was given a properly Latin reading, with emphasis on the sense of the rules in it. This double process was a step toward the morally normative reading to follow. But until the third stage, when students began to read continuous texts, they did not progress to a full grammar, one that provided a key to the meanings embodied in Latin *sententiae*. Not incidentally, the texts they read first were moralizing poems. At this level the two meanings of *sententia* come together. It means both "sentence" (fully meaningful grammatical unit) and "idea," "opinion," "maxim," or "theme" (morally meaningful unit).

It was further believed that the rarer words and unfamiliar aspects of Latin syntax could best be learned in the course of reading poetic texts and parsing through them in a detailed fashion.[24] Irregular forms could also be dealt with by studying lexica and drilling from compendia of rules. But medieval pedagogues thought that these forms were best absorbed by requiring students to stop and drill new words (and old ones) as these turned up in their reading texts. On this account a variety of reading texts with a broad range of vocabulary were used in the latinizing stage. Such

22. This distinction is found in Priscian; see Percival, "On Priscian's Syntactic Theory," 67. It is also stated in the prologues to intermediate grammar books written in late medieval Italy; see, e.g., Fierville, *Un grammaire*, 7–8.
23. See Law, "Originality," 51–52, on the Provençal grammars that faced this problem.
24. Law, "Panorama," 138–41.

poetic texts could be read through by students with a knowledge of the Donatus, but only with the supervision of a teacher. As the students got further into the study of Latin, and especially when they turned to Latin composition, they would have to look for further guidance in matters of vocabulary and syntax.

Syntax is taken up in the intermediate grammar treatises that sometimes occur in the Latin readers from Tuscany. These texts represent a genre of Latin grammar, the *liber de constructione*, which did not exist in the ancient world and developed in the high Middle Ages as an aid to students learning to read in a bilingual context. The doctrine was a development of the rudimentary syntactical rules contained in the last two books of Priscian's *Institutio de arte grammatica*, mixed with a variety of observations on other grammatical points.[25] W. Keith Percival has traced the earliest examples to the schools of northern Italy in the early thirteenth century.[26] In our period, judging from the relative rarity of these works redacted in a form for children, it would seem that most of them were aimed at the students of composition, perhaps largely for university-preparatory training. The same is true of the *Doctrinale* of Alexander of Villa Dei, the *Graecismus* of Eberhard of Bethune, and the *Poetria Nova* of Geoffrey of Vinsauf, which survive in a few Tuscan copies that seem aimed at intermediate or advanced grammar students. In the rare cases in which we have clear evidence of classroom use, it is at a relatively advanced level, for young adults, or at the university level.[27]

The Italian syntax treatises share a common terminology and most include vernacular phrases that presuppose the use of *volgare* in the Latin classroom. But none of them offers a comprehensive Latin grammar, so they must have been used to supplement more basic books like the *Ianua*.[28] It is more difficult to say at exactly what stage they were brought into the classroom. Intermediate and advanced grammars of this type served to help the student of Latin grasp the important differences in construction between Latin and the Italian vernaculars. This issue can arise in the course of reading Latin literary texts, especially those with poetic word order, but it is a more urgent issue in teaching composition.

25. Percival, "On Priscian's Syntactic Theory," 65–72; Law, "Panorama," 141–44.

26. Percival, "Grammatical Tradition," 233–38. Our census records copies of such manuals by Bartolomeo da Lodi, Goro d'Arezzo, Filippo di Naddo, and Petrus de Isolella; see Census I.11, I.16, and I.24.

27. Schiaffini, "Esercizi," 1–3; Law, "Panorama," 131–32.

28. Percival, "Grammatical Tradition," 233–38; see Percival, "Hitherto Unpublished," for an example of the genre that does not use *volgare*.

Thus, at the reading stage, syntax glosses in manuscript readers point to the relations between words widely separated or merely understood in poetic sentences. Teachers sometimes required students to paraphrase at length in *volgare* from the texts they were reading together in Latin. In such a case, they could not fail to notice how different the Latin constructions were from those in Tuscan. Comparisons made in the course of reading, however, would not have been intended to provide a comparative sense of grammar, or even a series of general rules. At best they could merely get the student inside the Latin mode of expression embodied in the reading texts to hand.

It is significant, I think, that the *Ianua* manuscripts do not contain vernacular glosses or insertions of the sort that occur in the intermediate grammars, or at least that the *Ianua* did not acquire such insertions until the fifteenth century. After bilingual alphabetic skills were taught, students were presented with the Donatus as an entirely Latin text. This was part of its newness. Teachers might have explained the book in part in *volgare*, but until students progressed to the third stage, of reading literary texts, they were invited to concentrate on the strictly Latin forms of the Donatus. This segregation by language might have been intended to help elementary students conceptualize the radical difference between weakly inflected *volgare* words and highly inflected Latin ones. The task of the student of the Donatus, we must remember, was mastery of inflected word forms.

Once continuous discourse in the form of literary texts was presented, however, vernacular paraphrase was a logical practice, and one we can glimpse, if only imperfectly, in the manuscript reading books. Fourteenth-century readers from the latinizing stage only occasionally have vernacular glosses, and when they do these tend to be word-for-word vocabulary equivalents. *Volgare* is seldom if ever used for syntactical glosses. The Prosper in Census I.12, for example, has both Latin and vernacular glosses; but, whereas the Latin ones commonly point to syntactical relations and explicate unfamiliar vocabulary as well, the *volgare* ones merely give the single-word equivalents required for in-class translation.[29] The logic of this distinction is that syntactical advice in glosses was intended to

29. See fol. 47v, where *extolitur* is glossed *e superbia* to explain the concrete meaning of the verb within the larger discourse, with fols. 45v–46, where a series of Latin and vernacular glosses give simple equivalents, *occidit* for *intervenit*, *sottomessi* for *subdatur*, *di fuore* for *exterior*. This is not an isolated phenomenon; in the *Physiologus* in Census I.8 only five of the over eighty glosses are in the vernacular and all of these give lexical equivalents. See Census I.18 and II.5 for the same phenomenon.

point out relations *within* the text at hand, so these remained in Latin, whereas vernacular equivalents could allow the student to create a second text by translating or paraphrasing *out* of Latin.[30] Composition students, of course, also needed to translate *into* Latin.

Most of the evidence for the use of translation in the trecento classroom comes from northern Italy, not Tuscany; but the practice was widespread. Some scholars have connected it specifically with the training of notaries.[31] Among the books in our sample, only one gives clear evidence of in-class paraphrase: Census I.30 contains three separate books, the first of them with an important set of vernacular glosses. These are largely elementary and lexical, as in the Census I.12 Prosper. The Aesop in Census I.30, however, got an early reading by a student or teacher who felt the need to write his *volgare* paraphrases between the lines of Latin, beginning a few folia into reading the fables. At first these vernacular glosses merely bring together a few words into phrases. These phrases are not always fully parallel to the Latin, though they work in the direction of true paraphrase. The reader is struggling not with finding the internal meaning of the Latin phrases but with enunciating vernacular equivalents. Then on fol. 8r the annotator gives a full interlinear paraphrase for an entire fable, one of the shorter ones, *De accipitre et milvio*. The result is an interlinear crib that brings to life the classroom practice of vernacular paraphrase at the latinizing stage.

The need for an analytical treatment of syntax of the sort attempted in the Italian treatises on construction was (and is) more urgent in teaching Latin composition than in reading. The vernacular insertions in the intermediate grammars seem to be aimed at the student who has enunciated a notion in *volgare* and wants to put it into Latin.[32] Composition, called *dictamen* in Italian sources of the period, was primarily a task for advanced latinizers, especially those who were going on to university or to become notaries. At the university level, *dicatmen* was taught as a branch of rhetoric aimed particularly at the letter-writing needs of municipal, royal, or ecclesiastical bureaucracies. But grammarians claimed the field too, on behalf of their students who would not go on to advanced study. Many of the intermediate-level grammars contain advice on *dictamen*, which must therefore have been treated in the grammar course. For a

30. On syntax glosses, see Wieland, *Latin Glosses*, esp. 61–77, 98–143.

31. Schiaffini, "Esercizi," 2–8. Other evidence for this practice is summarized by Copeland, "Vernacular Translation," 144–47; a good basic description of the process is that of Murphy, "Teaching of Latin," 163–68.

32. Percival, "Grammatical Tradition," 237–38.

merely literary reader with no pretensions to Latin writing, or for redacting simple business documents in formulaic Latin, even for some notarial tasks, more complex study of Latin composition was not necessary. The presence in many of the intermediate works of advice on orthography points in this same direction, that they were used for teaching writing.

Still, it must be said that we do not understand very well how the treatises *de constructione* were used. They are not systematic works, even in the field of syntax, and they usually include highly miscellaneous bits of advice on many other subjects. By contrast to the simple, concrete advice on syntactical relations given in the glosses to reading books, the grammar manuals multiply rules and provide complicated and arcane examples. In all probability the intermediate manuals that occur in elementary readers were studied and memorized just as were the Donatus and the literary texts in the curriculum. A less likely scenario is that they were included in the elementary readers primarily as reference works to be consulted rather than memorized. Even as reference books, however, these treatises assume that their readers would memorize some sections. Typically each brief point of doctrine is followed by a list of words that exemplify the rule. Often these lists are versified, a practice that has no logic whatsoever unless it is meant to help in memorizing them.[33] They can be referred to in their written form, but if a student were really aiming at mastering Latin usage he would have to memorize at least the words that occur frequently.

It is also worth noting that, whatever their similarities in doctrine and method, the various Italian syntax treatises differ considerably from one another in physical structure, length, and level of sophistication. It would be misleading to compare too closely the little books by Goro d'Arezzo or Petrus de Isolella with a weighty tome like Francesco da Buti's *Regulae grammaticales* or the lengthy grammar that introduces Giovanni Balbi's *Catholicon*. These latter are clearly reference books. Such books might well have served as the texts for a university-level course in grammar but

---

33. The extant treatises vary in their use of this device: in some it is common; others include only a few examples. Moreover, in a long treatise such as that of Francesco da Buti only some points of doctrine have mnemonic verses; others were not considered susceptible to this device, which was useful primarily for memorizing lists of words. Manuscripts (and later printed versions of similar grammars) were also designed to facilitate the task of memorization. Thus, in the manuscript of Francesco da Buti's *Regulae grammaticales* at the University of Chicago (MS 99), each mnemonic verse is introduced by a formula such as *unde versus* or *ut dicit versus*, and the lines of the verses themselves are underlined in red and blue to make them stand out from the page. That this Chicago manuscript was not intended to be memorized in full, however, is proven by the presence of another set of scribal notes that refer the reader forward and back by leaf number.

could not have been offered to students much before the *auctores* level.[34] None of the many surviving manuscripts of them contain elementary reading texts of the sort present in our Florentine census; they either stand alone, or are appended to lengthy lexica, or occur in collections of grammatical and philosophical texts.

There is some doubt (to my mind, at least) as to the direct classroom applicability of even the small intermediate grammars that appear in Florentine Latin reading books. We will never know exactly how they were used until critical texts are available. Only that of Petrus de Isolella has been edited. He wrote sometime in the thirteenth century, probably in Lombardy or the Veneto. Some parts of his little grammar are written with a clear mnemonic intention and could have been used for drills. Other, long stretches repeat information on morphology already covered in the *Ianua*, but in a different form and somewhat less systematically. Whereas the *Ianua* provides parsing paradigms for nouns, for example, the treatise of Petrus teaches rules for recognizing the gender of nouns from their endings in various cases. Obviously, this latter is aimed at helping the reader recognize agreement between nouns and adjectives and helping the composition student write correct sentences. Even though the arrangement is by noun morphology, the import is to teach the relations between words in sentences. It is assumed that, if he wished, a student could parse through the entire paradigm for a given word in a text, as he had learned to do in studying the *Ianua*. Petrus gives new rules that offer a shortcut,

---

34. The clearest example is the *Regulae grammaticales* of Francesco da Buti. Some manuscripts have rubrics in the first section that refer to the graded benches in a classroom. So, some rules are first-bench rules, others second-, third-, or fourth-bench. After the fourth bench, however, these indications lapse, and the rubric indicates that the "minor Latin" course has ended with its consideration of "general rules," and that the next part of the treatise concerns "middle Latin" and "special rules." A third major division is "major" or "advanced Latin," including the doctrine of conjunctions and that of figures of speech. The arrangement is a reminder that da Buti taught both in a private, elementary grammar school and at the Pisan university. Up to the end of the "minor Latin" section, his book has the character of a review grammar and may have been intended for students who had completed an elementary course and were now going on. In later sections, the number of rules multiplies and the doctrine becomes so complicated that the book seems largely intended for reference or study by advanced students. Black, "Curriculum," 145–46, presents this work as if it contained the comprehensive outline of a pre-university grammar curriculum. This cannot be the case, since the *Regulae* do not repeat doctrine covered in the *Ianua* and include a great deal of highly advanced material in reference form. The only late medieval treatise that seems to me to include a whole and rounded curriculum for the pre-university grammar course is the *Doctrinale novum* of Sion of Vercelli, described by Capello, "Maestro Manfredo e Maestro Sion," 62–69.

helping the student recognize a noun's gender and number immediately in relation to adjectives and verbs that surround it. The subject is syntax, the level intermediate, and, if the rules were to be memorized, this was done only after the Donatus paradigms were well learned and had been practiced on reading texts. Our best single evidence as to how these small grammars might have been used is in the fact that they survive in some of the reading books alongside school authors. This seems to imply that they were used in the latinizing stage by way of solidifying the drills done with literary texts.[35]

The syntax treatises concern the complexities of Latin usage, especially composition, and not the deciphering of texts at a basic level. Insofar as they reflect university-level studies, they also concern grammar in a nearly modern sense, that is, functional linguistic analysis largely without reference to philosophical or moral issues. As we have seen, however, beginning Latin in the late Middle Ages was as much about morals as about language. The transition in progress at the early latinizing stage in the curriculum was not merely from one language to another; it was a movement from technical, vernacular language use to morally normative, latinate usage.

To some degree all study had moral value for medieval people. Every teacher of small children was required to guide them in the acquisition of good manners; and, as vernacular literacy became the norm, the vernacular languages borrowed from language theory more generally the power to reform the mind and conform the individual to God's will. But Latin study was uniquely charged with conforming the individual to the largest cultural norms and highest aspirations of Christianity. Merely the most extreme form of this claim is Dante's statement in the *Convivio* that Latin is the means to moral perfection.[36]

Grammar and morals are constantly linked in teachers' contracts for this same reason, because Latin was seen as the introduction to a new, moral way of thought. At Volterra in 1368, for example, both the learning and the righteousness of the teacher are at the disposition of the students, "to teach all the students who wish to learn Latin and every other liberal art in which you are yourself learned, so that they may likewise be

35. Percival, "On Priscian's Syntactic Theory," 65–67; Law, "Originality," 51.

36. *Convivio* I.xiii.5 and I.ix.7–8. In the *De vulgari eloquentia*, Dante would also propound a vernacular grammar possessed of the same morally and socially transforming power; see Scaglione, "Dante and the *Ars Grammatica*," 307–8, 311–15.

instructed in good morals."[37] At Macerata in 1391 the master is expected "to teach, instruct, advise, correct, and castigate all those who come to hear and learn grammar and authors in the said city and to do so in a teacherly and paternal way."[38]

This insistence on moral instruction was not incidental to grammar. Grammar *included* morality. Teachers chose Latin texts of moral merit and taught good behavior along with good Latin. All who wished to learn were to be given the opportunity, for the manifest good of the city-state, which needed leaders of unambiguous moral probity. And students with the will and talent to do so were to be able through grammar study to have access to every other liberal art, for which grammar provided models of both linguistic and moral rectitude. The roots of this moralizing trecento model of Latin study lay deep in the monastic teaching tradition, based in turn on Augustinian and Ciceronian moral rhetoric. In Florence, the study of grammar and rhetoric had also acquired a profoundly political meaning with the teaching of Brunetto Latini. Latini classified grammar and the other disciplines of the trivium as the verbal sciences pertaining to politics, one of the practical branches of philosophy. This political view of grammar explains why, even in secularizing Florence, so heavy a burden of moral decision making rested on grammar, where rightness and wrongness have mostly to do with linguistic forms.[39]

The critical transition from vernacular to Latin ways of thinking and reading was the task of the student of the Donadello. We might think of it as a personal translation too. For, instead of receiving the wisdom of Western culture in vernacular translation, the Latin student was invited to translate himself, or at least his active intelligence, into a second language, that is, into the original language of the great inherited texts. Once he was ready to latinize, he was also able to conceive of an intellectual world with more than one compartment. Latin offered a separate realm for study and

37. Volterra, Biblioteca Guarnacci, MSS Documenti istorici . . . spettanti a Volterra, Filza 38, no. 14; Battistini, ed., *Il pubblico insegnamento*, 87–88: *grammaticham et omnem aliam scientiam liberalem de qua instructus essetis docere scolares discere volentes, ipsos ad bonos mores pariter instruendos.*

38. Commission of 3 October 1391, Colini Baldeschi, ed., "L'insegnamento pubblico a Macerata," 23: *in dicta civitate legere grammaticam et auctores consuetos omnibus venire discere et audire volentibus, et ipsos instruere, docere, monere, corrigere et casticare scolastice et paterne.*

39. Cf. Brunetto Latini, *Rettorica*, 30–35. The fundamental work on the question of ethics in language study is Carruthers's chapter "Memory and the Ethics of Reading," in *Book of Memory*, 156–88. Black, "Curriculum," 137–38, offers pertinent examples of the rhetoric of contracts, public debates, and letters of appointment and acceptance.

self-improvement. The case of Giannozzo Manetti is instructive. Some-time around 1416 he realized that life in his father's bank had little moral value, but that there was a remedy for this in making a crossover to a different status: "He began to think within himself what [little] point there was in possessions or fame or glory, either to himself or to his family, and on the contrary how there was no means to anything better except through the study of letters."[40]

The merchant-diarist Giovanni Morelli described the two language realms with eloquence equal to that of Manetti's biographer and depicted an almost idyllic longing for a secret life of creative leisure separated physically from the hubbub and humdrum of business and commerce:

> As far as you are able, make sure that every day for an hour at least you study Virgil, Boethius, Seneca, or other authors such as are read in the schools. From this practice you will derive great strength of comprehension. You will understand, from study of the teachings of the authorities, what you need to do in this present life for the sake of your soul's welfare as well as for the honor of the body. . . . You will have at your beck and call all the great men of history. You will be able to closet yourself in your study with Virgil for as long as you like, and he will never put you off and he will answer whatever you ask him, and he will give you good counsel and instruct you without any charge in money or in kind. He will distract your melancholy mind, lift worry from your brain, and give you solace and pleasure.[41]

The texts Morelli recommends in this passage are those of the *auctores* course, with a particular emphasis on the civic philosophers favored by Florentine rhetoricians since Brunetto Latini's day.[42] Intermediate reading texts of the sort we examine in depth in the next chapters were also thought to have permanent study value.

Of particular use to us in evaluating the Latin course is Morelli's repeated insistence on daily reading of the authors, "such as are read in the schools." The goal he offers for this habit is moral consolation. His

---

40. Garin, *Pensiero*, 297.

41. Branca, *Mercanti scrittori*, 199–200; cf. Trexler, *Public Life*, 160. For more on this writer, see Pandimiglio, "Giovanni di Pagolo."

42. An interesting parallel to this passage occurs in the letter of Bernardo di Lapo da Castiglionchio to his father, replying to a small treatise on nobility that Lapo had sent to the young Bernardo, then studying at Bologna. Bernardo dropped his usual course of study, he claims, to spend many days in the examination of his father's piece. His elegantly deferential reply echoes Morelli's description of a private study cluttered with books and cites Boethius and Seneca to reassure his father that he had properly internalized the moral lessons of the latter's treatise. See Lapo da Castiglionchio, *Epistola*, 133–35.

*Ricordi* goes on from this passage to suggest acquiring and cultivating good friends and faithful servants for the same purpose. He draws a parallel between the friends the good paterfamilias consults for advice in the bosom of the family and those he consults daily at his reading stand, chosen from a well-selected and well-thumbed shelf of good books. By way of emphasizing the parallel, Morelli ends his section on the choice of friends and intimates with a quotation from an elementary school author on study:

> But above all, if you want to have good friends and relatives, try not to need them. . . . Keep in mind these verses taught by the authorities for our instruction, such as you will find in study (in the Notable Sayings of Aesop, if I am not mistaken): "In good times many are happy to be called your friends, but when Fortune fails, then will no friend be found." And there are many other genuine teachings of the sort to be found in study which, by God, you should never abandon. Rather, keep at study until your dying day for you will derive much pleasure, profit, and good advice from it.[43]

Just as the key to managing a family is the hard work of studying and testing one's familiars, so also the key to ancient wisdom is the study of Latin *auctores*. Morelli thus helps us explain why the texts chosen for use at the intermediate and *auctores* level were so important, and how it might have come about that Florence, as we have already seen, had its own distinct curriculum of a sort designed to promote moral education on pious, conservative lines. It was in the stage of latinizing that the study habits of a lifetime were formed, along with the habit of seeking moral guidance in study.

The latinizing stage is the subject of much of the rest of this book. We look closely at the texts chosen by Florentine masters and try to say how and why they were used. It becomes clear that, just as the *leggere et scrivere* level of study could be propaedeutic to Latin study or serve as a terminal course for less-promising students, so also the latinizing course was both self-contained and open-ended. A rather small proportion of the beginning reading students went on to study *grammatica*, and a smaller number still continued their studies to include composition and classical *auctores*. The grammar masters designed their courses accordingly, on the assumption that each textual unit should contain solid and permanently useful moral lessons, almost as if at the end of each unit the student might

---

43. Branca, *Mercanti scrittori*, 203.

drop out of school, something that certainly happened to a goodly number of students. Facility in Latin, the merely linguistic skill, was acquired only slowly and gradually; it might never amount for many students to more than a finishing school accomplishment. But the substantial lessons of moral rhetoric could be absorbed at every level and were intended to last, even if the students' facility in reading and writing Latin faded quickly away for lack of regular use.

This model of Latin study was not new to the fourteenth century, nor was it a concession to the needs of urban students, though it could certainly be excused in their case as valuable to the political education of upper-class boys. The model was, however, a monastic one. Many who learned to read in medieval monasteries did so primarily for the sake of making their sacred rounds of prayer more meaningful in a moral sense, quite without intending to go on to learn to write in Latin or to read advanced texts. A similar, limited or indirect effect of Latin study was posited for urban students in the trecento. We explore just how this indirect pedagogy worked in later chapters. Judged by classical norms or by those of the university culture of the Middle Ages, this type of moralizing study of Latin seems a poor thing. But in terms of a broad-based Christian social mission on the lines propounded by the mendicants, and for the sake of educating a reading public to civic virtue, it had a sure and thoroughgoing logic of its own.

*Grammatica* in this sense was not aimed primarily at the mastery of language skills but rather at the transformation of the inner man. It aimed at providing a reading skill that was morally normative, with rules of behavior mirrored in those of language. Such moral lessons began with the Donadello, the little Donatus. The dual reading given to it contained the fundamental lesson that study of Latin involved close reading and analysis of texts that were essentially, necessarily normative. Latin texts could be *normalized* too, that is, they could be discerned to operate according to linguistic rules. But it was much more important to teachers and parents that they contained lessons worth internalizing through memory and keeping life long. Latin study—Latin itself—was the first and most basic moral art.

# READING TEXTS
## *The Pagan Classics*

The distichs of Pseudo-Cato almost always followed directly on the Donadello in the Latin course, but we have little evidence of the order in which other texts in the latinizing stage were taught. In the chapters that follow I consider the reading texts identified in Chapter 2 in groups based on thematic similarities. This chapter concerns the only non-Christian authors, Aesop and Pseudo-Cato.

The *Disticha Catonis* and Aesop's *Fables* are eminently poetic in a purely formal sense. They are highly memorable and easily memorizable; they offer commonplace truths in forms that would have intrigued children by their novelty; and they are in verse with a predictable rhythm. Admittedly, no modern critic or teacher would offer either the versified Aesop or the *Disticha Catonis* as models of good style. But both have a quality of telescopic brevity that offered definite pedagogical advantages. They could be learned in succinct units of two to twenty lines, almost every word of which could be opened out into a grammatical lesson through glossing—either syntactical, etymological, or moral, and often all three at once.[1]

From the first moment of literary, Latin reading, therefore, students were introduced to the notion that texts have multiple meanings and that their authority resides in their moral import. Such a lesson was urgent in the case of these pagan authors. Multilevel reading implied the potential for both good and bad meanings, moral and immoral applications of

---

1. Wieland, "Glossed Manuscript," 155, develops the typology of elementary glosses I use here.

a given text; but it precluded amorality in reading, for every text had to be read with a moral end.[2]

Pagan authors had always represented a problem for Christian readers, and the whole question of the meaning of the classical inheritance was reopened anew by the early humanists. August Buck describes a concept of authorship that was new with Petrarch but still impossible to the generation of Dante. Petrarch repeatedly expressed a longing to have lived in the world of the great Latin authors. He built on this longing to create an artificial, literary, but also real and deeply felt friendship with such great writers as Virgil and especially Cicero. Buck follows Giuseppe Billanovich in seeing this novel literary relationship as one of the driving forces in Petrarch's attempt to recover a clearer and more accurate text of the works of his beloved Cicero. Petrarch's intensely felt friendships for the great writers of antiquity were highly personal creations, never quite reproduced by later humanists, but the idea quickly became a commonplace. Humanist scholars and pedagogues claimed the ideal for their own and created a new kind of philologically critical biography and historiography on it.[3]

It took a long time for such notions to reach the Latin schools, however, and in the classrooms of the period we are studying it is fair to say that authors were approached in a much more traditional way. That is, the author and the text to hand were virtually identified, and little attempt was made to individualize the writer or to contextualize his work. Even the medieval *accessus*, which provided a few biographical details and described the intention or value of the work, is largely absent from the Tuscan school readers. Teachers may have relied on glosses or the various *accessus* available, but students seem to have approached texts without benefit of a written historical or philosophical introduction. It was up to the teacher to add biographical information as needed, and there is little evidence for our period that they supplied anything of the sort. Authority resided in the text itself. The text was to be mastered through memorization, and its themes appropriated so thoroughly that they belonged to the student. The authority of such a text was henceforth internal, engraved on the memory for life.[4]

2. This theme of multiple meanings recurs throughout this book as a fundamental characteristic of latinate reading. By the end of the Renaissance it had become the standard of all learned reading; see Grafton and Jardine, " 'Studied for Action'," 30–32, 76–78.

3. Buck, *Rezeption*, 14–17; Billanovich, *I primi umanisti*, 57–66; Lorch, "Petrarch, Cicero," 73–76.

4. Carruthers, *Book of Memory*, 211–20.

Nowhere is this approach clearer than in the study of the two pagan authors who appear in the elementary school curriculum. The distichs of Cato and Aesop's *Fables* were not single-author texts to begin with. In both cases the more or less standard medieval versions had gone through many authorial interventions: textual accretions of various sorts, translations, and in the case of Aesop a versification. Neither text was completely stable even in the fourteenth century, since their anthological character allowed scribes to omit or add on easily. Anthologies also permitted teachers to skim over or skip what seemed least useful and to concentrate on the most important lessons.

It would have been useless to attempt a careful biographical or historical approach to such texts. "Cato"—variously identified in the trecento as Cato the Elder, Cato the Younger, or a later, homonymous author—was merely a word for sage. He was the speaker of epigrammatic moral virtue. In some manuscripts, for example, he is little more than a gloss to the opening lines of the poem. The preface consists of an eight-line address to the reader that begins, "When I noticed how very many go seriously wrong in their manner of living, I decided that they must be helped and counseled so they might live gloriously and achieve honor."[5] This passage was often written with the gloss identifying the speaker included right in the text: *Cum ego Cato animadverterem vidi quam plurimos homines* [When I —Cato— noticed —saw— how very many —men— go seriously wrong]. Here *ego Cato* and *vidi* and *homines* were once glosses over the words that precede them but have been thoroughly incorporated into the text.[6] The reader, whether teacher or student, would be given an author's name at the very start, but this *ego Cato*, originally supplied to explain the verb to neophyte readers, had no historical context; he is merely the moral-reforming poet.

"Esopo" was an even more shadowy figure. The author of the most sophisticated and compendious encyclopedia of literary biography composed in the trecento can only say "Aesop was a Greek" before going on to specify that the text used in the schools was a translation, not only into Latin but also from prose to verse. He did not know the name of the versifier, only that of the mythical translator, Romulus, probably because the only *accessus* available to him was to the prose version. Walter the

<hr />

5. *Cum animadverterem quam plurimos graviter in via morum errare, succurrendum eorum opinioni et consulendum famae existimaui maxime ut gloriose viverent et honorem contingerent*; *Disticha Catonis*, ed. Boas, 4, my translation.

6. My transcription from Vat. Ottob. lat. 1967, fol. 1r. The same glosses occur in Census I.15.

Englishman's verses never had their own *accessus* and none of the Tuscan schoolbooks identifies Walter at all. The substance of the encyclopedist's piece on Aesop, which surely refers to the verse version since no other was common in the Italian schools, can be summarized in just two phrases: "[Aesop] presents birds, snakes, trees, and beasts as speaking. . . . But I have thought it useless to add more about these fables because they are known to almost everyone."[7]

This wide but nonspecific reputation was typical in one degree or another of all the elementary school authors. They were so well known, via memorization of the school texts themselves, that no further explanation or citation of them was necessary, even when they were paraphrased closely or quoted directly in an original work. Aesop and Pseudo-Cato were commonplace texts par excellence. A reader who found one of their phrases quoted in a letter, oration, or treatise would recognize it as his own, as common intellectual property, rather than think of it as a quotation from an individualizable author. Giovanni Morelli's citation of an unidentifiable passage, "such as you will find in study (in the Notable Sayings of Aesop, if I am not mistaken)" is exactly of this sort. *Lo istudio* was Morelli's course of study and his personal library, stored in his memory as well as in the study room or secret closet he describes elsewhere in his memoir.[8]

To some degree this sort of authorial anonymity is true of all the reading texts in our census of Tuscan school manuscripts. We may use its relative anonymity as a test of how truly elementary a given text was. At the advanced end of the curriculum, where Latin grammar became the study of *auctores*, not only were the writers treated as historical figures but their individual works were also distinguished as having separate identities, forms, and purposes. Aesop, however, and Prosper or *Pauper Henricus* (Henry of Settimello) were merely the shorthand titles of well-known texts. Most other school texts were treated even more anonymously, called by their opening words or incipits, *Chartula* or *Tres leo* or *Ethiops.*

---

7. *Vitae philosophorum*, in Florence, Biblioteca Nazionale Centrale, Conv. Soppr. G.4.1111, fol. 44r: *Esopus natione grecus. . . . Inducit autem aves serpentes arbores et bestias loquentes quas quidem fabulas prosaico sermone translatas quidam poetico more ad versus vertit que etiam hodie a pueris leguntur in scolis. . . . Has autem fabulas inferre superfluum duxi maxime cum sint quasi omnibus note.*

8. Branca, *Mercanti scrittori*, 203. The modern editors of Morelli treat this passage as a general reference to a good book. To me it reads like a citation of a specific book in Morelli's private study room.

This was true even when the author was a great literary figure, as when the *Dittochaeon* of Prudentius was called merely *Eva columba*. Some of the ambiguity in references to schoolbooks in inventories and literary sources can be traced to this sort of authorial reference. "Donatus" meant simply "elementary grammar manual," always referring to a specific manual, but not always to the same one. Even "Boethius" could be unclear as a title for a specific work, although the educated reader would easily recognize him as an author of great prestige.

No comparable prestige could have attached to either Aesop or the *Disticha Catonis* in fourteenth-century Florence. They were recognizable writers primarily, perhaps only, because everyone knew the texts that bore their names. The two pagan authors had another quality in common, intimately tied to their commonplace nature. We have already noted that of the school texts only Prosper of Aquitaine regularly had an *accessus*. Aesop and Pseudo-Cato rarely did (never in our Tuscan readers), but the redactors of the common versions of these texts provided each of them with a little verse prologue addressed directly to the child reader. The *Ianua sum rudibus* catechism also has a prologue of this sort, and so do some courtesy books used in northern European schools. These direct address introductions are unique because, alone of the reading texts used in Florence, Aesop and Pseudo-Cato were compiled and composed specifically for children. We see later the consequences of using adult texts for teaching reading; here the question arises as to what qualities these books written for children had that others in the curriculum did not.

The most obvious thing, of course, is that they are designedly elementary. As nearly as we can tell from the literary, documentary, and manuscript evidence, the *Disticha Catonis* was read immediately after the primer had been mastered. Aesop had a less clearly defined position in the curriculum but probably was used next, along with Prosper of Aquitaine and Prudentius, the other texts that occur most frequently in our census and are most easily adaptable to an elementary course in morals. Given the frequency of occurrence, it is clear that many if not most Latin students never went beyond these few texts.

The two pagan sages, Pseudo-Cato and Aesop, were made to address their readers directly with avuncular advice about the value of their respective books. Pseudo-Cato is quite explicit about the moral value of reading and the rhetorical value of moral improvement: "Now I will teach thee, dearest son, how thou mayest fashion a rule for thy life. Therefore, so read my precepts that thou mayest understand them, for to read them and not to understand is negligence, not reading at all."[9] The use of the verb *componere* (fashion), a standard rhetorical term for writing up, is interesting, for what the child "writes" in this case are the rules or habits of moral behavior (*mores*). The locus of this writing is his own mind, as emphasized by a word play in the last clause (*legere / intellegere / neglegere*). This writing in the mind is memorization in the meditative sense of thoroughgoing internalization of a text. The subject is moral virtue, and the method is virtuous in itself. The final, much-quoted saw puts a construction of duty on the whole endeavor of reading: To read without understanding is negligence.

The introduction to Walter the Englishman's Aesop is similar but more playful:

> The present page strives to please and profit. Serious things in jests depicted will sweetly please. This garden bears fruit and flower together; and both the fruit and the flowers can be of profit. One is showy, the other tasty. So if the fruit pleases more than the flower, select the fruit. Or choose the flower if you'd rather. Take both if both please you. . . . A light weight of words bears an honest burden of morals just as a dry hull hides a good kernel.[10]

From the start the student reader is asked to take what he pleases from the anthology, on the assumption made explicit in the final couplet—that, however charming the verbal dress, there are serious and salutary lessons to be learned at every turn. There is always more than one such lesson in a good poem; the more one works at them, the more these poetic fables yield.

The prologues to both these children's books claim universal applicability for the lessons they contain, a claim no one seems to have disputed, even though the authors were pagans. Everyone knew Cato and Aesop, or at least every educated person did. Or did they? The survival rates for Cato manuscripts may give us pause in this regard; only seven copies of

---

9. *Disticha Catonis*, ed. Boas, 4: *Nunc te, fili carissime, docebo quo pacto morem animi tui conponas. Igitur praecepta mea ita legito ut intelligas. Legere enim et non intellegere neglegere est*; *Distichs of Cato*, trans. Chase, 13. I have usually translated the distichs myself in this chapter. In this and some other cases, however, I use Chase's translation, despite its archaisms, because trecento children reading Cato for the first time must have considered it a quaint and musty way of saying commonplace things, marked by unorthodox poetic syntax, just as we do in reading Chase. Where the sense is seriously altered by Chase, I have modified his readings freely. Here I have altered his version of the last line to better represent the important wordplay.

10. Hervieux, *Les fabulistes latins*, 2:316. My translation, here as elsewhere when not otherwise noted.

the *Disticha Catonis* survive in reading books datable to fourteenth-century Florence. This is only one-third the rate of survival of Aesop or Prosper in comparable manuscripts and may at first glance suggest that Cato was less known or less frequently used.

The apparent anomaly is surely only apparent. It has to do with the nature of the text and of the manuscripts that once included it, and with the way the text was taught. The circumstances are sufficiently interesting to our understanding of the place of the *Disticha Catonis* in the curriculum, however, to warrant some closer examination. Moreover, they can lead us to conclude that survival evidence, although affected by chance, is solid and reliable evidence nonetheless. In part the relative rarity of Pseudo-Cato manuscripts may be due to the brevity of the text. It could easily be copied onto a single gathering of eight leaves or even six. Indeed, it survives in just this form in four of the seven examples in our census. Where it occurs on a separate gathering in this way, it is usually first in the anthology as bound. So, we might speculate that many copies were lost from their vulnerable position at the head of a miscellany, or because they were heavily used separates.

All three of the counterexamples are in manuscripts that vary somewhat from the norm of the Florentine reading book. Census I.15 and I.13 are the earliest manuscripts in our census. In both cases Pseudo-Cato is appended directly to the *Ianua*, which seems to have been a common practice at many times and places and which clearly indicates the extremely elementary nature of Pseudo-Cato by comparison with the other reading texts. Many other manuscripts survive, especially from the fifteenth century, which are just such booklets containing *only* the *Disticha Catonis* and the *Ianua*.[11] This was the original format of the first part of Census I.15 as well; indeed, this manuscript is both the earliest example of the two-text combination and the earliest surviving manuscripts of the *Ianua*. In the first age of printing Pseudo-Cato also accompanied the *Ianua*. The implication of all these bits of evidence is that Cato was read immediately after, perhaps even along with, the *Ianua* and was considered a basic text like it.

The third counterexample is Census I.17, in which Pseudo-Cato occurs at the beginning of a large collection assembled at one time. But this manuscript is relatively late, possibly even fifteenth century, and untypical in another way, for it contains a highly miscellaneous collection that

11. See, e.g., the several examples in Part III of the Appendix at Modena, Vienna, and El Escorial.

includes such uncommon texts as the misogynist tract of Pseudo-Jerome and the *Ilias latina*. Its compiler seems to have had no single theme or group of themes in mind; he or she was assembling a collection of everything elementary that came to hand.

Survival evidence is difficult to assess, and in the case of the *Disticha Catonis* we are in a particular quandary, because this text was also short enough to have been memorized easily without recourse to a written copy. The distich form was devised originally for memorization, and there is extensive literary evidence that the book was in fact memorized at all periods.[12] Latin students and their teachers knew the distichs by rote and new students learned by repeating after their teachers. Such students may never have seen a written copy, and if they had one it may simply have been in the form of reusable wax tablets. Copies that did exist may not have seemed much worth saving because of the thoroughness with which the text was memorized and the relative ease of making or getting another copy.

We can achieve some control on the data in our census, however, even when they seem to have been confused by accidents of survival, by comparing survival rates for the same texts in other parts of Europe and at other periods. For example, there are far more English and French manuscript copies of Pseudo-Cato at every period than there are Italian ones. This suggests that the low figures for fourteenth-century Florence are not completely anomalous and that the text really was used more rarely—or differently—in Italy than elsewhere.[13]

Medieval texts also survive through the medium of print, and again there is a strong differential for Pseudo-Cato's distichs on regional lines. The repertories of early printing attest to twenty-eight pre-1500 editions of the *Disticha Catonis* as a separate text without commentary, thirty-six with commentary, and twenty-nine in collections or anthologies under the rubric *Auctores octo*. Only six of these ninety-three editions were produced in Italy. What is more, none of the six were done in Tuscany, and only one was printed anywhere north of Rome.[14]

12. Roos, *Sentenza e proverbio*; cf. Schmitt, "Ianua," 57; Carruthers, *Book of Memory*, 80.

13. Boas lists the manuscripts in *Disticha Catonis*, lix–lxii.

14. See *Gesamtkatalog der Wiegendrucke* 6250–6384 and 2776–2805 for the editions in general; cf. Avesani, *Quattro miscellanee*, 21–22, 89–92. Comparable differences in the number of early editions of Donatus, Aesop, and Prosper of Aquitaine suggest strongly that the Italian market for schoolbooks in the late fifteenth century differed radically from that of northern Europe.

It seems then that Pseudo-Cato was either not as important in Florentine and other Italian schools as elsewhere in Europe, or that the text was used in a different way that did not require as many written copies of the text or did not conduce to their survival in reading books of the sort we have isolated in our census. I have already hinted that my guess, based on the way the *Disticha Catonis* is linked with Donadello (another author who does not survive in many Italian manuscripts and printed books) in legal documents, literary sources, and the rare surviving manuscripts, is that Pseudo-Cato was learned by rote, orally and not necessarily from a written copy. We must imagine the students repeating the distichs after their teachers, perhaps with the aid of a dictation exercise copied onto wax tablets. And we must assume that the teachers themselves sometimes taught the "book" of Cato like the *Ianua*, from memory. They may well have done this without copies in hand, or they may have relied on teacher's copies like ones that survive for many texts of the grammar course in the earlier Middle Ages.[15] In either case, they must often have taught by dictation to students who did not have personal copies of their own.

Since the publication of Mary Carruthers's *Book of Memory*, we can assert with confidence that this difficult teaching method was possible, even common, in the fourteenth century. She has shown that it was applied to texts at all levels, whether or not the reader owned the book in question. The Florentine Pseudo-Cato and Donadello are particularly likely cases of the survival of this technique even in trecento Italy, where students were beginning to own their own books relatively early in the grammar course. Donatus and Pseudo-Cato were neither readers nor primers in the traditional sense but elementary foreign-language texts for memorization. Learning them only partly depended on lessons in reading. If a child was also given a copy of the *Disticha Catonis* to read, he or she would have looked at it as if it were a psalter or other prayer book, containing a text already familiar, now to be puzzled out in this novel, written-down way.

It is worth noting in this regard that *salterii*, true primers or hornbooks, which contained the alphabet and a few prayers on a single sheet, also do not survive from our period, although they are mentioned in legal texts and depicted in art works.[16] Again, part of their nonsurvival is to be explained by their small format. But they were also fugitive because they contained material so easily memorized that it was unnecessary to provide

---

15. Wieland, *Latin Glosses*, 196–97.
16. Grendler, *Schooling*, 142–54.

a copy to every student. Moreover, the text was so slight that it could easily be written out; there was little incentive to save any given copy once it was worn.

Psalters, Donadellos, and Catos belonged to a class of transitional texts. They were steps on the way to learning to read Latin; they were used in ways similar to the alphabet and prayers of the primer but different from more advanced reading texts. None of these texts survives in large numbers because their place in the curriculum did not link them with other, more difficult and less commonplace reading texts. In particular, they do not often take the form of the readers described in Chapter 2, a form designed for the latinizing stage of study and designed to be kept, not discarded.

Because they were also among the fundamental texts of contemporary high culture—unlike modern reading texts that serve only to teach reading and do not have the status of classics—the first Latin texts were also memory texts. They were taught and studied in a double way, as truths to be internalized through memory and as the first texts to be puzzled out on the page. Reading, memorization, and second-language skills were studied simultaneously. As I have remarked above, the educational philosophy behind this heavy cognitive load was neoplatonic. Then current pedagogical theory assumed many notions associated with the need for memorization, among them the intellectual-spiritual wholeness of the individual, the oneness of the community of learning, and the unity of truth.

In practical terms, students who could not accomplish complex and richly layered thinking were winnowed out of the Latin course from the beginning, and students were encouraged to think that no one reading of a given text could exhaust its many meanings. Important texts were texts for continual rereading and contemplation. Even at the most elementary level, while students struggled with grammar and vocabulary, moral lessons with many possible layers were set before them.

Let us look more closely at the lessons a Florentine schoolchild might learn from Pseudo-Cato, this shadowy pagan author of an often unseen book. The medieval commentaries on the *Disticha Catonis* were strongly allegorical and Christianizing.[17] In particular, the proverbs were referred to moral maxims in canonical Christian literature, especially the wisdom

---

17. Hazelton, "Christianization," 162–72; additional bibliography in Roos, *Sentenza e proverbio*, esp. 228–44.

literature of the Old Testament.[18] A similar approach, stressing the moral improvement of the individual within the community, is taken by one of the few extensive fourteenth-century Italian commentaries to come down to us, in a Ravenna codex that comes from a university grammar course like that at Bologna or Pisa.[19] Much of the thematic material would have been familiar to young students from sermons heard in church. It could be presented to them as a recollection of the truths already embedded deeply in the unitary moral culture of Western Christendom.

In turn, Pseudo-Cato's major themes, and often the distichs themselves, occur frequently in the collections of *volgare* proverbs so popular in Tuscany. Above all, we find expressions of the vicissitudes of Fortune, exhortations to wage virtue as war in manly fashion, and proverbs about idleness, garrulity, and the unstable friendships of women. In earlier medieval schools most of these themes were turned to the praise of monastic virtues: obedience and humility, silence and chastity. These remained ideals of behavior for young schoolchildren (and for women of all ages, as Christine Klapisch-Zuber has remarked) in trecento Florence.[20] In grammar schools for young boys they also had to be linked with political and civic virtues. The sometimes warlike vocabulary of Pseudo-Cato and his praise of such rhetorical virtues as quick thinking and distrust of appearances were well adapted for teaching such lessons.

Even the traditional monastic virtues were presented by Pseudo-Cato in a civic context. Keeping silence is a positive good in itself: "Believe me, the first of virtues is to rule the tongue: Godlike is he who knows how to keep silence by reason."[21] Thus, at least, the late version of the text in use in the Florentine schools; this particular proverb does not occur in the earliest versions of the collection. It is part of the Christianized Cato that developed by accretion in the monastic schools, but the last phrase, *qui scit*

18. Cf. Hazelton, "Christianization," 164nn30–32. That the *Disticha* was read this way is also proven by the frequent imitations and echoes of the distichs in the courtesy books also used by elementary Latin readers, especially Bonvesin de la Riva, Henry of Settimello, and Pseudo-Boethius.

19. Ravenna, Biblioteca Classense, Cod. 358; cf. Mazzatinti, *Inventarii*, 4:223–24. This manuscript contains detailed moralizing commentaries on several of the most popular works in the Italian elementary curriculum. Those on Prosper, Cato, and Prudentius contain almost no strictly grammatical or linguistic analysis, suggesting that this was no longer the point of reading these texts at the university level. Instead, grammar masters in the making were invited to analyze them in philosophical and theological detail.

20. Klapisch-Zuber, "Le chiavi," 775–78.

21. *Disticha Catonis*, I.3, ed. Boas, 36.

*ratione tacere*, would have meant something very different to a Florentine with some sense of Ciceronian civic virtue than to a monastic reader of the earlier Middle Ages. Still, silence for Pseudo-Cato is not so much a personal good as an appropriate response to the excesses of others:

§ Try not with words the talker to outdo; On all is speech bestowed: good sense on few.
§ Spread not vain talk lest thou be thought its spring; silence ne'er harms but speech may trouble bring.
§ On others' promise do not base thine own; talk doth abound: good faith is rarely shown.
§ When praised, thou of thyself the judge must be; accept no praise not spoken truthfully.[22]

As in the distich about keeping silence by reason, this is not an exhortation to absolute silence but to careful discourse; one must consider well both what others say and what answers to hazard. Above all, little faith is to be given to mere words or even to the appearance of meekness and silence. However comparable some of these ideas are to monastic notions about language, they ended up being altogether more worldly and skeptical when studied outside the monastic context of radical humility and strict obedience.

There is little room in Pseudo-Cato's world for simplicity. One must expect that others will dissemble their true feelings and motives, and a good measure of the same sort of concealment is advised for every man, whether in business or friendship:

§ Beware of soft, cajoling speech. Truth's reputation is for simplicity, that of storytelling is deceit.
§ He who pretends is a faithful friend only in word not in his heart. In his own coin repay him, with art for art.
§ Do not trust in men's too-flattering speech; for sweet sounds the fowler's pipe to lure the prey.[23]

The virtues of Stoic acceptance and patience were among the counsels of Pseudo-Cato easiest to reconcile with Christian notions of patience, simplicity, and long-suffering. But there were further sophistications that

22. Ibid., I.10, 12–14, ed. Boas, 42–47; *Distichs*, trans. Chase, 17–19. Cf. Roos, *Sentenza e proverbio*, 221.
23. *Disticha Catonis*, III.4 and I.26–27, ed. Boas, 156 and 63–65. Again, I have followed some of Chase's wordings, *Distichs*, trans. Chase, 21, for the sake of the piquant metaphors.

an urban schoolmaster might choose to develop for students aiming at a business career:

§ Remember always well the value of Fortune's gifts. A good reputation gives fewer gifts than good morals.
§ When fortune's favor seems not thine, take thought of him to whom Dame Fortune hath less brought.
§ Begin what thou to finish canst not fail; safer near shore than on the deep to sail.
§ When wealth takes wings thou shouldst not then repine; rejoice more that anything is thine.[24]

Perhaps the proverbs that endeared the *Disticha Catonis* most to teachers at all periods were those that concern the high purposes and values of study. These appealed to the studious monks of the earlier Middle Ages, but they took on new meaning in the era of such supremely learned laymen as Dante, Petrarch, and Boccaccio. From the mid-fourteenth century onward they were increasingly identifiable with the humanist endeavor of study for its own sake. The preface that universally accompanies the *Disticha Catonis* in Florentine and most other medieval manuscripts is insistent on the value of studying the written word. We have already looked at its coda, which is variously put in the surviving manuscripts, probably as a result of the frequency with which it was cited and copied from memory. All the versions, however, contain the play on words that links reading, comprehension, and duty, a combination that was bound to be dear to the schoolmaster's heart.[25]

The grammarian's mission as a teacher of morals, implicit in the very use of proverbs for teaching Latin, was made all the more clear in the proverbs on study itself:

§ Learn only of the learned: teach the untaught; the teaching of good things must be carried on.
§ If thou wishest to lead a life free from cares, cling not to faults which injure character. Remember that you must always maintain [or, frequently reread] these precepts. With them for a guide, you will be able to avoid bad things.[26]

---

24. *Disticha Catonis*, III.1a and IV.32–36, ed. Boas, 152 and 235–40; *Distichs*, trans. Chase, 41.
25. Roos, *Sentenza e proverbio*, 213.
26. *Disticha Catonis* IV.23 and IV.Preface, ed. Boas, 219 and 190; cf. *Distichs*, trans. Chase, 39 and 35.

According to the last lines, the precepts themselves, carried in the memory or reread repeatedly, become a teacher and guide for the student in future life.[27]

As I remark again and again in what follows, the classroom use of centuries-old texts tends toward conservatism in both moral philosophy and educational practice. But no text prescribes its own application; it merely circumscribes the options available to the bright and talented teacher. The more flexible the text structurally, the greater the freedom for the individual teacher. And nothing could be much more flexible than a collection of two-line proverbs.

We can never quite know what individual teachers made of the sage opinions of Pseudo-Cato, but we can find some telling echoes in the popular literature, especially the *volgare* courtesy literature of trecento Tuscany. Proverbial expressions are often thought of as popular in origin, but such citations in popular texts represent rather high-culture pretensions. The proverbs we find most often reflect identifiable literary sources, and there are correspondingly few instances of proverbial usages that seem entirely without literary source.[28]

In trecento Tuscany, moreover, proverbs seem to have been linked with the latinate pretensions of vernacular authors. Long stretches of Paolo da Certaldo's *Libro di Buoni Costumi*, for example, are nothing more than collections of unrelated proverbs drawn from a variety of sources and put down, on the model of the biblical Book of Proverbs, as a wisdom or courtesy book tailored to the needs of trecento urban life. The Latin analogies for this are to be found in Henry of Settimello or Bonvesin de la Riva, whose books I describe in Chapter 7, rather than in the pagan school authors.

When Giovanni Morelli interrupts a political narrative or the descrip-

---

27. This last quatrain, the preface to Book IV, is somewhat problematic. I have translated as best I can from the Latin version that occurs in all the Italian manuscripts and early Italian editions I have seen: *Securam quicumque cupis perducere vitam nec vitiis haerere animo, quae moribus obsint, Haec praecepta tibi semper retinenda [or legenda] memento: invenies aliquid quod te vitare magistro.* Chase translates from one of the reconstructed versions of the last line, reading *utare* for *vitare*: "Thou wilt find them a teacher through whom thou wilt be able to transform thyself" (35). But, though the version in the Italian editions made no sense to Boas either, it was certainly used and taught for centuries and I find no glosses to suggest that it was even a problem for schoolmasters in Italy. My special thanks to Alan Leopold for puzzling though this and other passages with me.

28. Ageno, "Tradizione favolistica"; on the problem of sources for proverbs, see Novati, "Le serie alfabetiche," 337–38, 349–50.

tion of his own uncomfortable orphanhood to moralize sententiously, we may fairly look for a Latin model in Cato or Aesop.[29] For example, his description of the intense politicking behind his attempt to return to public life in the election *scrutinio* of 1404 is characterized by a bit of political philosophizing that rapidly wanders off into proverbial thinking:

> Morello and I made every repeated request we could, in order to carry our candidacy forward, and we spared no trouble and were careful to make every honest representation possible. Whether this had effect or not I do not know. The results make one think it did work for the better and offended no one, for ingratitude is conquered by humility, by courtesy, and by working to please those who seem to wish ill to you. Moreover, this is a method that gives you honor.[30]

Morelli speaks here in specific terms about the rhetorical problems he faced in winning an election, but he quickly puts his specific predicament into a context of universal morality and honor. Before the tale is done, his personal history has become philosophical advice to the readers of his book. One wonders how many of those readers would also have quoted back to him Cato's good political advice: "Revive not memories of former strife; 'Tis shame to bring old hatreds back to life"; or "Though thou canst win, yield sometimes to thy friend; thus yielding, strength to friendship thou will lend"; or perhaps the very next proverb, "Do not hesitate, in quest of great things, to spend a little."[31] Just as Morelli's account of his own political crisis in 1404 is proverbialized, one of the bitterest of his childhood memories is characterized with a moral straight from Aesop. His helplessness as an orphan under the guardianship of others is described with a translation of the proverb in Aesop on the plight of lambs who lack a guardian.[32]

I have already remarked the freedom enjoyed by teachers using an anthology of short texts with pointed lessons that could be dwelt on or passed over as the students in a given class seemed to need. The converse of this characteristic is that the distich form allowed for little real development of theme, even if two or three proverbs relating to each other were

---

29. On the political import of Aesop, see Branca, *Esopo toscano*, 9; Filosa, *La favola*, 56–58.

30. Branca, *Mercanti scrittori*, 280, my translation.

31. *Disticha*, II.15 and I.34, 35, ed. Boas, 117 and 75–77; *Distichs*, trans. Chase, 27 and 23. Cf. Roos, *Sentenza e proverbio*, 223.

32. Branca, *Mercanti scrittori*, 174, citing closely the wolf and lamb story examined below.

juxtaposed. The student was constantly and fairly quickly moved from one commonplace to the next. This may have seemed an advantage to elementary teachers, especially if the students were sometimes memorizing the distichs without written copies in front of them. It may also have contributed in a negative way to the perennial popularity of the antique sage in Christian Europe; not even the dourest Florentine churchman or the most narrowly pious parent could worry that a pagan worldview so limited in depth or development would undermine the essential Christian values of trecento society. As we see in the next chapter, the most universally used school text was a profoundly Augustinian corrective to Cato's skeptical stoicism.

At Florence, there seems to have been little worry about reading Aesop, for the verse version by Walter the Englishman was as widely known as any school text in the curriculum. As with Cato, Aesop was unlikely to seem too pagan to parents or teachers; and the text, particularly in its versified form, offered some distinct pedagogical advantages for beginning students.

Like Cato, Walter's Aesopian fables are highly telescopic.[33] To modern readers this makes them seem more difficult, but ancient pedagogy relied heavily on techniques of puzzling out. Language at all levels had an esoteric dimension; the reader's chore was to unlock the ornate but tightly closed lid presented by the text and spill out the contents of the literary treasure chest. In the case of Aesop, the morals of the tales were relatively unsophisticated. Most often they simply advised carefulness, thoughtfulness toward others, and the advantages of quick thinking and ready command of language. But these morals were expressed in all the fable collections available to medieval teachers. Walter's translation, which seems to have driven the others from the classrooms of Italy, was popular because it was useful for teaching.

Walter, an English priest at the Norman court of Sicily, ended his career as archbishop of Palermo. He is supposed to have prepared his version of Aesop about 1175 in his capacity as tutor to the young William II. It is a versification of the prose translation attributed to "Romulus" in many medieval manuscripts.[34] A comparison of the two versions highlights the

33. On Walter's style, see Filosa, *La favola*, 5–6.
34. See Hervieux, *Les fabulistes latins*, 1:490–91, on Walter's authorship of the versification; some dissent on this attribution was voiced by Mauro, *Francesco del Tuppo*, 114–15, and developed at some length by Filosa, *La favola*, 6–13. Branca thinks that their arguments merit further attention; *Esopo toscano*, 48. Throughout this discussion I speak of Walter in generic terms as the author of this particular versification, as is usual in the literature. At

classroom values at the root of Walter's project to versify these well-known fables.

Often we can see just which grammatical lessons Walter had in mind. The popular fable of the wolf and the lamb, of which many versions are known, stands early in Walter's collection as in many others. In the prose version it began with a simple setting of scene: *Agnus et Lupus sitientes ad rivum e diverso venerunt. Sursum bibit Lupus, longeque inferior Agnus* [A thirsty lamb and a thirsty wolf came to a river from different sides. The wolf drank upriver, the lamb much farther down].[35] In itself this was already a good pair of simple declarative sentences with a variety of adverbial expressions on which to rehearse a beginning reader. Walter put it into verse and both simplified and complicated the grammar by rewriting to include a lesson on demonstrative pronouns: *Est Lupus, est Agnus: sitit hic sitit ille; fluenti Limite non uno, quaerit uterque viam. In summo bibit amne Lupus, bibit Agnus in imo* [There was a wolf; there was a lamb. The former was thirsty, the latter too. They came to a riverbank not by the same path but each from a different side. Upstream drank the wolf, the lamb drank below]. Walter also spelled out an important psychological detail: "When the wolf spoke, the other creature was assailed by fear."[36]

Thereafter, the prose version merely described the action of the fable and moralized in a minimal way: "The wolf, pretending that the water was muddied by the lamb and listening to no contrary reasoning, claimed that the lamb's father had offered the same insult to him, and so attacked and killed the lamb. Thus he snatched life from an innocent one."[37] Walter elaborated considerably, creating a dramatic dialogue both charming and unsettling:

---

Florence, the collection usually included sixty-one of the sixty-two tales edited by Hervieux as the vulgate version, 2:316–51, on the basis of Paris, BN lat. 14381. The missing tale is no. 48, *De viro et uxore*, sometimes added at the end of non-Tuscan manuscripts I have seen (e.g., British Library Add. 27,625). The order of the tales varies slightly and many surviving copies are fragmentary, so it would be difficult to say categorically that the sixty-one-tale redaction that survives was invariable. Branca, *Esopo toscano*, edits a popular *volgare* version prepared in Tuscany in the late fourteenth century based on Walter's anthology with all sixty-two tales, so the fuller version must have been available even if it does not usually occur in the Latin readers. Whether we accept Walter the Englishman as author or not, the intent of the piece is didactic and elementary, and not, as Mandruzzato would have it, a learned work separate from the classroom Aesop; "L'apologo," 157.

35. Hervieux, *Les fabulistes latins*, 2:365.

36. Ibid., 2:386. Here as elsewhere I sometimes translate the present-tense verbs as narrative pasts.

37. Ibid., 2:365.

"You have befouled my drink and disturbed the beauty of this riverbank." The lamb denies it, defending himself by reason, "I've harmed neither you nor the riverbank, for water never flows upward, and this stream sparkles aplenty." Then the wolf bellowed a second time, "Do you threaten me?" "Not a bit," replied the lamb. To which the wolf came back, "Yes you do. In fact your father did the same thing six months back. Since you have imitated your father so well, you will die for his misdeed." Then the lamb said, "But I wasn't even alive then, you bully!" Came the resounding reply, "How can you even claim it, liar!" And with that the wolf ate him up.[38]

The action has been complicated by the violent and erratic words assigned to the wolf, whose verbal attack turns quickly into naked violence. The versified version also stresses the moralizing sentiments of the translator in a closing couplet that was intended to be memorized and to recall to mind the whole of the fable: *Sic nocet innocuo nocuus, causamque nocendi invenit. Hii regnant qualibet urbe lupi* [Thus the harmful harm the harmless and invent a reason for doing harm. Wolves like these reign in every city!]. In Florentine schoolbooks and others intended for children, these two-line maxims at the end of each tale are often set off with paragraph marks to make them easier to find and memorize. And harder to miss in the first place.[39]

The prose original already owned the notion that the violent do not listen to reason in their dealings with the weak or innocent. Walter embroidered on this theme to show how an individual bent on doing evil invents his own reasons and expresses them, with wordplay and legalistic trappings, to justify what he intends to enforce through sheer violence anyway. The tale ends with a stern warning that there are sinister wolves of this sort in every town; they come with urban culture.

The self-justifying power of language, even for evil ends, thus became a lesson—alongside mastery of demonstrative and relative pronouns—in classrooms that used the tale of the wolf and the lamb. Language study

38. Ibid.
39. The memorial force of these couplets is also clear in the way they were used by the translator of the *Esopo toscano* edited by Branca. There, every tale is much expanded by the addition of two explicit morals, one for those in religious communities and one for lay people, but every tale also ends with the *Latin* distich from Walter's version. It is as if these Latin distichs crystallize and reify the discursive lessons of the tale; this is a memorial device. Cf. Carruthers, *Book of Memory*, 242–44. A good example of how this sort of memorial practice of learning Aesop worked itself out in the writing of original literature is in Padoan's illuminating reading of the two Aesopian citations in Dante's *Inferno*, "Liber Esopi," esp. 98–101.

involved not only grammar and idiom but also the uses to which language can be put. In almost every case, Walter elaborated the prose fables in this same way, to build moral lessons more deeply into the text. He spelled out the dialogue and motivation implicit in the sketchy prose fables, and he developed a dynamic psychology of language. The student was encouraged to think that his lessons would give him power, both to avoid falling victim to language misused by others and to achieve his own ends rhetorically.

Once schoolboys progressed to the stage of composing their own Latin, they would have ready a store of vivid exempla, attached to morals and ready made for any compositional need:

The Wolf and His Offspring:
*Tempore non omni, non omnibus omnia credes*
*Qui miscere credit, creditur esse miser.*

[Do not always believe all things of all people; whoever thinks himself miserable will be thought so.]

The Viper and the File:
*Fortem Fortis amat, nam fortem fortior angit*
*Majori metuat obvius ire minor.*

[The strong love the strong, for the stronger worry the merely strong, while a lesser being fears to meet up with one greater.][40]

It is obvious from these examples that Walter's version of Aesop was also much taken up with wordplay, and in particular with the rhetorical figure known as *derivatio*, in which words with a single root are repeated in close proximity, usually with only slight variation of inflectional or derivational form. There are two distinct lessons here: young readers were drilled in recognizing grammatical forms on sight in context; they were also urged to see that the power of language resides in wordplay of a subtle and sometimes treacherous sort. The students' mastery of language included the ability to decipher multiple meanings, for enjoyment of course, but also so that they would not be left behind in the word game that is civilized discourse.

Many of the fables carry the puzzling-out aspect of language study to an

40. Hervieux, *Les fabulistes latins*, 2:328, 343.

extreme. Toward the end of the collection we meet wolves and sheep again. Needless to say, the sheep still get the bad end of every bargain:

> *Pugna Lupis opponit Oues, Ouiumque satelles*
> *Est canis, est Aries; hac ope fidit Ouis.*
> *Palma diu dormit, desperat turba Luporum.*
> *Et, simulans fedus, federe tentat Ouem.*
> *Fedus utrumque fides iurato numine fulcit;*
> *Id Lupus, id simplex obside firmat Ouis;*
> *Datque Lupis male sana Canem, recipitque Luporum*
> *Pignora, nec metuit, nec sua dampna uidet.*
> *Cum natura iubet natos ululare lupinos,*
> *Turba lupina furit, federa rupta querens.*
> *Ergo pecus tutoris egens in uiscera mergit;*
> *Preside nuda suo sic tumulatur Ouis.*
> *Tutorem retinere suum tutissima res est*
> *Nam si tutor abest, hostis obesse potest.*

[A contest is joined between wolf and sheep; the sheep's attendant is a dog. There is also a ram whose power the sheep trust: while he sleeps beneath a tree, the pack of wolves despairs. So, simulating a treaty, the pack attempts to discredit the sheep. With a holy oath faith upholds a mutual pact; the wolf and silly sheep confirm it with hostages given: the sheep unwisely hand over to the wolves their dog and receive wolf cubs. They do not fear nor even see their downfall. When nature calls the baby wolves to howl, the wolf pack rages, claiming the treaty is broken. Therefore, the flock, lacking a protector, swim in their own bloody vitals. Naked of protection the sheep are entombed. Moral: It is safest to guard well one's own guardian; if the guard is gone the enemy can do harm.][41]

This poem is singularly obscure. The pretentious wordplay abstracts the concrete events of the story into a mere outline. Only the maxim is straightforward, and even then there is wordplay. Because this poem occurs near the end of the collection, the student may have been expected to cope better than earlier on with Walter's convoluted style. Still, there are many words and expressions that would have needed explaining by the master. The wordplay *fidit / foedus / foedere / foedus / fides / foedera* must have confused many students, especially since the contemporary orthography for the dipthong *oe* was simply *e*.

The theme of the tale is promises made and promises broken. The

41. Ibid., 2:343.

wordplay on good faith and deception could have been powerful, once it was explained properly. But the young scholar would have had to work very hard indeed to decipher it in the course of a reading that would have included parsing almost every word in the poem. The grisly images at the end, of the flock naked of protection, swimming in their own guts and finally entombed, would have taken less deciphering. The shuddering schoolboy might then be expected to welcome the moral. But the moral was not easily arrived at; only by a close reading can the piece be made to say anything at all.

It may seem strange that this kind of stylistic obscurity should be presented to schoolboys so early in their Latin careers. Stranger still that such a notion of linguistic *urbanitas*, rooted in the stylistic excesses of the eleventh and twelfth centuries, should survive not only into the fourteenth century but also well into the Ciceronian age of fifteenth- and even sixteenth-century Italy. Walter's tortured verses remained in school anthologies well after humanist scholars had prepared new translations of the Greek Aesop, and after humanist pedagogues had eliminated the unclassical but sober and virile Latin of Prosper of Aquitaine from the curriculum.

The key to understanding this seeming anomaly, I think, lies in the nature of wordplay itself. Wordplay survived the stylistic reforms of the Ciceronians because pedagogues, and pedants, love puns and etymologies. Moreover, for elementary students wordplay has a psychological value we have already partly explored. If language is an instrument of power, for both good and evil, through moral rhetoric or deceit, then its essential ambiguity on the moral plane must be mastered early. The study of Latin, considered equivalent to the study of sophisticated language use itself, was based on this sobering lesson. *Urbanitas* was the facile and elegant use of language that characterized the cultured man; it involved as well the sadly realistic knowledge that language both creates civilized discourse and enforces the power of one individual or group over others. If the sons of merchants learned nothing else in Latin school, this was a sufficient lesson to justify their fees and time. Whether or not they chose to pursue Latin, these boys went out into a world where Latin was an empowerment to certain professional and cultural goals. If they learned only what its power was, they could use that knowledge even if they never or rarely used Latin as such.

Social and civic lessons were attached to Aesop too. The stylistic wordplay of Walter's Aesop was reinforced by the genre itself; in fable, all these sobering lessons were put in the mouths of talking animals. The power of fables for schoolchildren resided in their combination of charming rural settings and urbane play of language. Moreover, they were the only straightforwardly narrative texts in the Florentine elementary curriculum. Not until their teachers thought they were ready for *auctores* such as Statius or the *Aeneid* would the Florentine Latin student again meet a narrative text, and then the generic context was radically different, the extended narrative of epic poetry. As we see repeatedly, these careful restrictions and gradings of the reading of young children, self-consciously imposed by grammar masters who had a wealth of other material available, existed because the teachers and parents of Florence felt a need to control the content of a grammar course inherited from the monastic schools but now being applied to urban contexts.

Late medieval educational writers almost universally posited a child psychology based directly on that of adults. They attributed the young child's short attention span and volatile emotions to her or his lack of firmly rooted moral habit (*habitus*).[42] These educators were realistic enough to see that a text such as Aesop had sufficient charm and variety in its short animal stories to engage a child's attention. They were not about to let such an opportunity pass without using it to drum in moral ideas. Walter's version, with its easily memorized moral couplets, recommended itself on just these grounds. Memorization was held to be the intellectual equivalent and partner of moral habit, so the child would both internalize a moral idea and develop a good habit of thought with each Aesopian tale.

In Florence and other trecento Italian towns, these lessons were absorbed piecemeal by students who left the relatively closed circle of the grammar school daily and returned to houses where the principal preoccupations were business and family. The masters could not assume a continuing context of good moral habit, and certainly not the monochromatic moralism or consistent textuality of a monastic house. Even when the household was a sober and pious one, it was typically supervised by a woman. Her grasp of real morality was suspect in late medieval thought just because she was a woman and therefore morally and intellectually inferior as a role model. Moreover, women were notorious among male Latinists for exactly the kind of flightiness and inconstancy that moral-grammatical education was designed to counteract. It was all very well to entrust very small children to the care of a child-woman, but the

---

42. See the critical comments in Ducci's edition of Pseudo-Boethius, *Un saggio*, 51–53.

factual break with maternal care represented by sending boys out to the grammar school was also a symbolic break with the tutelage of women.[43]

Aesop was not heavily weighted with misogynist lessons, but it was an easily capsulized and easily controlled vehicle for teaching morals, and at the same time an initiation into classical culture. Its initiatory quality would have made Walter's Aesop a particularly good text for the early part of the course. Neither the documentary sources nor the manuscripts regularly link it with Cato or Donatus, but it occurs so frequently in our census that it is logical to consider it with Prosper of Aquitaine and Prudentius among the texts used soon after students started latinizing. Moreover, it is clear from the sources that Aesop was not thought of as appropriate to the *auctores* course, for it was considered a child's text.[44] It is remarkable that the only pagan texts to appear in the elementary and intermediate curriculum at Florence were near the beginning of the course. There they could symbolize the break with merely female and merely popular culture in an initiatory sense for young boys. There they could also be carefully isolated and controlled, surrounded by large doses of Christian poetry in the form of Prosper and Prudentius.

Women, interestingly enough, appear in Walter's version of Aesop only three times, invariably with a moral on the lines of *Femineum non bene finit opus* (Nothing involving women ends well).[45] The widely diffused story "Thais and the Youth" is virtually the only one to include a woman in anything approaching a speaking role. Thais is offered as a universal figure of women's idle and evil speech; she is a prostitute who pretends to love her clients. The youth meanwhile is Everyman or, rather, Everyboy; he is the picture of conventional immaturity, but he does not have a name.[46] In this story as elsewhere, Walter dwells on the use of language in a realistic way, using a dialogue that students might expect to hear on the street except that it is in Latin, presumably not the usual medium of exchange between trecento prostitutes and their clients, even if they were

43. Klapisch-Zuber, 772–74. See also my discussion in Chapter 8 of the *Regola* of Giovanni Dominici.

44. E.g., in Petrarch's remark linking Aesop with Prosper; *Senili* XV.1, cited by Garin, *Pensiero*, 91.

45. Hervieux, *Les fabulistes latins*, 2:341.

46. Hervieux prints this fable with a rubric from a French manuscript that names the young man Damasus, but the fable itself just calls him *iuuenes* and all the Florentine schoolbooks rubricate the tale *De Thaida et iuuene* as if to emphasize his anonymity. In the Tuscan version edited by Branca, even the prostitute is nameless. A valuable discussion of this text is Padoan, "*Liber Esopi*," 86–89.

Latin school boys. The Latin translates the dialogue into a realm of fable as effectively as if the speakers were the more usual animals; Latin universalizes the story's message.

Walter does seem to have set out to provide a lovers' dialogue realistic enough that it would convince young students to distrust even their own words in such a situation:

> *Sim tua, sisque meus, cupio: plus omnibus unum*
> *Te uolo, sed nolo munus habere tuum.*
> . . . . . . . . . . . . . . . . . . . . . . . . . . . .
> *Sis mea, sumque tuus, nos decet equus amor;*
> *Uiuere non uellem, nisi mecum uiuere uelles;*
> *Tu mihi sola salus, tu mihi sola quies.*

> ["I wish to be yours and you to be mine. I want you more than anyone else, but I don't want your gift." . . . "You should be mine, I yours; an equal love becomes us. I wouldn't want to live unless you would want to live with me; you are my only refuge, my only peace."][47]

In the process, the students rehearsed the subjunctive of volition, the forms and uses of "to want," and so on, even as they absorbed the lesson that language is an instrument of deceit. The youth goes on to express doubts about the sincerity of Thais's protestations of love. He does so by citing an animal fable, as if to say that his school lessons stand him in good stead: "But I am afraid of being deceived . . . for a bird avoids the yew tree that he has tested by tasting." The moralizing couplet at the end reinforces the point that a spoken "you" most likely means "your money" when the context is sex: "Whoever loves Thais, let him understand that he is beloved for his goods and not for himself. Thais is lacking in love; she loves but the lover's gifts."[48]

Human characters, even males, are relatively rare in the Aesopian collection current at Florence, appearing in only eleven of the sixty or so fables. For the most part these characters are not well developed. Usually they are just the rustics accessory to an animal fable: woodsmen, ploughmen, hunters, or vaguely designated peasants. "The Father and The Son," for example, turns out to be a father telling a son a story about an ox and a veal calf; the only speaker is a ploughman.

Only two fables, paired near the end of the collection, concern human

47. Hervieux, *Les fabulistes latins,* 2:341.
48. Ibid., 2:342.

social relationships presented as such. "The Jew and the Royal Cup-bearer" and "The Burgher and the Knight" both have to do with the pretensions of noblemen. These tales, it seems, were original to Walter's version of Aesop. If they are untypical in including realistic human charac-ters, they are nonetheless highly important to our understanding of the collection, because they appear regularly in the Florentine manuscripts and almost surely reflect the reasons this version of Aesop was popular in Italy while others were not. Insofar as they have real social content, of course, these fables cannot have meant the same thing to the teachers and children of trecento Florence that they meant to Walter and his royal pupil a century and more earlier. But their lessons about the nobility of virtue could be well taken in both contexts. "Right overcomes might," begins the moral of the latter tale, "and bitter chance reveals a true friend. Goodness bears more fruit than hatred, good faith more than deceit."[49]

The tale of the knight and the burgher is not told well, has not even the slight poetic merit of some of the other verses, and offers no new lessons on grammatical forms. It must have been thought an apt way to end the collection by way of a transition from the mores of animals to the habits of human society. It is certainly realistic in at least one way, in that it portrays unequal social relationships of a sort that must have been constantly on the minds of boys growing up in an oligarchical, republican Florence not yet completely free of the violent pretensions of feudal magnates.

The characters are sketched in Walter's usual thumping rhythms and recall immediately the wolf and lamb: "A burgher and a knight flourished under the rule of a king; the knight fought for the king and the other man dispensed his riches; the first of them was an old man, the other young."[50] As the tale develops, the burgher is slandered by the knight, but the rich commoner is eventually vindicated by a ploughman from his own estates who stands for him in a duel. Later still, the merchant leaves a large bequest to the farmer. For Walter's student princeling, this story would have been a lesson in royal justice and injustice, for the whole story takes its departure from the king's inclination to believe the slandering knight rather than his longtime confidant and treasurer.[51] Florentine schoolboys would necessarily have read the signs differently, to show how defenseless a merchant can be before arbitrary exercise of aristocratic power.

49. Ibid., 2:350.

50. Ibid., 2:347.

51. Obviously I am here assuming the authorship of Walter the Englishman and not of the Bernard of Faenza posited by Filosa, *La favola*, 7–13.

Although we must be careful not to create socially and politically anachronistic readings of the Florentine Aesop, we are justified, I think, in asking ourselves why it was popular and to what use it was put in the classroom. Whatever realistic elements there are in the stories, all of them retain a strongly exemplary character and so an air of being composed to the moral rather than drawn from life. This may not have been obvious to schoolboys, but grammar teachers and the adult public for such tales would have understood the distinction between the lessons of life and those of artistically composed narrative.[52]

As Vittore Branca has repeatedly demonstrated, Boccaccio was acutely aware of such distinctions. So was the post-Boccaccio translator of the *Esopo toscano*, who transformed the fables under the influence of mendicant preaching by dressing the animals in specific trecento clothes and giving them more than one concrete, social application.[53] But Walter's readers were not invited to reflect much on realistic human characters. Even more than other available versions of Aesop, the Latin version used at Florence concerns animals that talk; their language is the highly telescopic verse that was traditional for new Latin readers because it demanded attention and concentration from the reader. These limitations of style, theme, and character are related to limitations we discover in the next text we consider, Prosper of Aquitaine's *Epigrammata*. Aesop represented a break from the popular Christian culture of home and parish; it was an initiation into Latin culture, the schoolboy's declaration of independence from his mother. It stood in contrast to other, strictly Christian texts of the curriculum as well. These texts also worked to differentiate the Latin student from the popular Christian piety of preachers, aimed at the non-Latin literate, especially at women. The boy student at this stage was invited to leave behind all the childish things of his mother's religiosity and set out on an exploration of Christian high culture, a man's world.

Since the point of grammar was the teaching of morals, we may fairly posit a certain moral hierarchy of texts in the curriculum. Cato and Aesop

52. On the adult public for such fables, see Pelaez, "Un compendio"; on their permanent impact on popular speech, see Ageno, "Tradizione favolistica." It is clear from literary reworkings and from the *volgarizzamenti* of Aesop that specific, concrete lessons, often political ones, were drawn from the fables by teachers and students in fourteenth-century Florence; Padoan, "*Liber Esopi*," 98–102, and Filosa, *La favola*, 56–58; cf. Delcorno, *Exemplum*, esp. 268 and n116.

53. First edited by Branca as *Esopo toscano*. On the moralizing undertaken by the author, see 15–19.

represented, albeit on an elementary level, the wisdom of the ancient pagans. Historically, this was considered pre-Christian philosophy; morally, it was natural insight by contrast to supernatural or revealed truth. From the study of mere philosophy, the student progressed to a study of the greater moral truths of Augustinian Christianity, digested and versified by the great popularizer Prosper. That Aesop and Cato held a limited and circumscribed place within the standard curriculum was a symbol of the limits of the child's perceived ability to deal with the moral ambiguities of pagan thought. Aesop's animals were on some level pagans. There were lessons to be learned from them, lessons of natural law and commonplace morality. Higher, Christian morality came next on the educational agenda. Only after the supernatural, revealed truths of Christian thought and its basic symbols and myths were well and thoroughly mastered would the student move on to the great pagan *auctores*, cautiously selected for their positive moral impact.

We see this preoccupation with lessons graded on a moral rather than linguistic plane again and again in the Florentine curriculum. Its logic is to be sought in the schoolmaster's belief that the student progressed in moral habit though a gradual and carefully controlled process of reading, memorization, and internalization of moral lessons embodied in texts. Once the student had mastered the primer and the Donadello, he was considered a latinizer. With Cato and a few other simple texts under his belt he was considered able to read; that is, he could understand and absorb texts composed in extended poetic periods, and he had come to understand many basic grammatical forms. The themes he rehearsed in Aesop were like those of Cato, concerned with natural law and civic virtue. He was ready to go on to stronger stuff, in the form of Christian authors who were also read in the latinizing stage of instruction.

In terms of the linguistic skills needed, Aesop was no more elementary a text than some of the Christian school poetry, although, as I have noted, the verse Aesop was composed for children whereas all of the Christian "school poetry" was originally written for adults. The curriculum was not rigorously ordered and we should not imagine that Aesop was always read before Prosper. But the chief preoccupation of Florentine teachers, as evidenced in our census, was to present Christian wisdom literature. Historically as well as in moral terms, Christian poetry followed and fulfilled pagan lore.

The documentation offered by teaching contracts and letters of appointment deserts us at this point in the curriculum, for it assumes a functional division between the beginners and the latinizers without describing any clear divisions with the latininizing stage. Usually the latinizers are lumped together as one group or described simply as belonging to lower and upper groups. That there was a moral distinction within the latinizers' curriculum we can infer from other evidence, particularly the manuscript readers, but also by the existence of the third level of grammatical instruction, the *auctores* course, which isolated the major pagan lyric poets in the final stage of instruction. It is highly likely that the latinizing stage was considered a time to concentrate on Christian poetry between studying pagan Cato and the more sophisticated pagans, Horace, Virgil, and Ovid. The widespread use of Prosper of Aquitaine, whose school poems we examine in some detail in the next chapter, was not dictated by language-teaching needs but by the logic of studying a Christian moral poet in some depth at the transitional stage. With Prosper, the Latin student could consolidate his command of grammatical forms and usages and conform his increasingly curious and active mind to the classical norms of Christian moral behavior. A rather stern sense of the importance of Christian reading as a lifelong study, then, combined at Florence with distrust of the teacher's ability to control the moral progress of his young charges outside the classroom to prescribe a strong dose of patristic medicine for the souls of latinizers.

# READING TEXTS
## *The Christian Classics*

Twentieth-century critics often look for large-scale themes in approaching literary works. But synthesis was not a common medieval approach to texts. The Latin grammar course enforced a different approach altogether, what A. Vitale-Brovarone has justly called a "near-sighted reading" of texts. The premodern reader examined each line and section of a literary work closely, seeking the practical moral and spiritual lessons therein. In so doing he or she often ignored the larger meanings of literary works or was content to acquire them unconsciously by means of the cumulative effect of small-scale readings.[1]

In such a world, readers rarely attempted interpretations of the collected works of a single author, nor yet did they attempt to recover the meanings of whole texts. The only possible large-scale, synthetic readings were those that attempted to conform the text to hand to the broad context of Christian literary culture understood in terms of moral commonplaces. Thus, Aesop's worldly wisdom and Cato's frequent cynicism were no danger to even small children because the lessons of these pagans were both highly episodic and easily inserted into a Christian worldview that preceded these lessons at home, accompanied them in the classroom, and subsumed them into a unitary truth. Moreover, they were followed up or accompanied by important Christian Latin readings.

Of the texts most popular in the Tuscan classroom of Petrarch's day, three clearly fall into a category we might call Christian classics: Prudentius's *Dittochaeon*, Prosper of Aquitaine's *Epigrammata*, and the *Conso-*

---

1. Vitale-Brovarone, "Testo e attitudini," 685.

*lation of Philosophy* of Boethius. These texts carried a major doctrinal component, albeit in the highly accessible form of verse, and represented for teachers of the fourteenth century the Christian ideals of the patristic age. They are in content considerably less tied to the clerical establishment of the late Middle Ages than the medieval products also used in the trecento classroom.

Still, though I treat them apart in this chapter, these patristic works should not be considered entirely separate from later texts. Fourteenth-century readers appreciated and respected the authority of the early fathers, but they read them through eyes well accustomed to the institutions of their own centralized, hierarchical church. Prosper, for example, was presented in the *accessus* that usually accompanied his minor works as a cleric of considerable, but sacred, erudition: "This Prosper was an Aquitanian, a citizen of Toulon, who, having renounced the world, dedicated himself wholly to matters divine and, selecting certain things from the opinions of Saint Augustine, put this book together."[2] Much the same portrait, in which any schoolboy destined for an ecclesiastical career could recognize himself, was given for Prudentius and Boethius, notwithstanding the fact that neither of these erudites was actually a cleric. All these texts included the topos of leaving (or losing) a political career for the sake of wisdom.

Fourteenth-century schoolmasters would not have made fine distinctions between the fourth-century pious context of Prudentius, the fifth-century polemical one of Prosper, and the neoclassical Christianity of Boethius's day. All three were assumed to have lived in a moral world much like that of Dante or Boccaccio or Villani, where everyday life was thoroughly corrupt, where princes were ready to disrupt Christian peace as a matter of course, and where the path of true wisdom led straight away from the concerns of this world. We may assume that, amid the fourteenth-century controversies over the true nature of apostolic life, the authors in question were also believed to have lived in a day when the church was less corrupt and closer to primitive ideals. But even this was not a historical insight, certainly not one that differentiated the fifth century from the fourteenth. Both, for women and men of the latter day, were periods on the way to the eschaton, and both were characterized by pernicious heresies and prepotent secular lords. The rhetorical oppor-

2. *Patrologiae latina* (PL) 51:425. The translations from Prosper in this chapter are my own. For the text of Prosper of Aquitaine's *Epigrammata*, we must still rely on PL 51:497–532.

tunities and the reasons for studying Latin were the same: to reform the individual and society through right use of language.

Let us look closely at each of the three texts, beginning with the *Epigrammata ex sententiis S. Augustini* (Epigrams after the Sayings of Saint Augustine) of Prosper of Aquitaine.[3] This work appears in our census more frequently than any other, and it is most like the pagan texts already examined in that it provides a series of short, relatively self-contained *sententiae*, or wise sayings. Self-containment may seem a largely formal quality, but like the use of verse it is a form with important implications for teachers of any period. It facilitates memorization outside the classroom and at the same time allows in-class digressions tailored to the needs of individual students or groups of students. In any age, teachers value this kind of open-endedness. In the Middle Ages, such nuggets of wisdom were particularly valued as an elementary tool because they were believed to help train the mind for memorizing larger and larger amounts of knowledge under commonplace rubrics. *Sententiae* were also the chief stylistic device for much occasional prose and almost all oratory. So, besides beginning with something short and sweet, the elementary student was provided with a repertoire of pretty and recognizable ideas to use in his own compositions.[4]

Prosper's compilation is, by any modern standards, a rather bizarre undertaking. Important opinions were first extracted from the works of Augustine. These extracts formed a popular work in their own right, which circulated widely. In a second moment, however, the extracts were further selected and reduced to verse, in this case perfectly competent classical elegiac distichs that also have a regular rhythmic scheme. Thus they can be scanned either metrically, in the classical manner, or rhythmically, on the principles that were normal for most medieval verse compositions. As models of prosody, they were doubly valuable to medieval teachers.[5]

The verses, already twice removed from their Augustinian origins, were then provided with prose arguments or paraphrases that repeat Augustine's basic idea in words not Augustine's. The resulting book seems strange to modern eyes, since the schoolboy was presented with a text

---

3. This discussion is based on Gehl, "Augustinian Catechism," q.v. for a more extensive reading of this text.
4. Cf. Schmitt, "Ianua," 57.
5. Lassandro, "Note," 119.

"after the sayings of Saint Augustine" that contains almost none of Augustine's own words. Instead, the reading text is a double paraphrase of key Augustinian moral notions, translated, as it were, from Augustine's high-flown Latin prose into didactic Latin verse and then translated again into simple Latin prose. Translated here means transposed, of course, since the ideas never leave Latin, but it may well be that this quality of double paraphrase or double translation made Prosper's anthology seem particularly apt for elementary students. At all periods, Latin students were expected to paraphrase texts. In medieval Italy, there was also the practice of bilingual paraphrase. The result of such a system is that rhetorical ideas become "a dynamic commodity transmissible between languages."[6]

Prosper's compilation was in this sense already predigested. It embodied the process of paraphrase and its results. It also provided a set of texts well adapted to being paraphrased again and yet again, not only as an exercise for one day's class, but also as a continuing part of the moral-rhetorical development of the educated Christian. All the school texts in the Florentine curriculum have some of this sense of commonplace about them. The *Epigrammata* of Prosper was doubtless particularly valued as a source of commonplaces from the supremely authoritative Augustine.

Versifications of great prose classics, not excluding the Bible, were common in the Middle Ages and continued to be produced right down to the eighteenth century. In Prosper's case, the reasons were clearly pedagogical, and unpretentiously so: "Since it is pleasant to exercise the mind on holy sayings, and rejoices the soul to feed on heavenly bread, it has pleased me to pluck some flowers from the field and to weave them into ordered little verses, so that each epigram may sing of its own theme and every section may be suited to its heading."[7]

Several important themes are sounded in these opening lines of the preface. First of all, it is pleasing to exercise the mind on sacred sayings. Whereas latter-day teachers and students usually assume that poetic diction and syntax are harder for elementary students of a foreign language to grasp, our medieval counterparts thought that they were easier and more useful because the variety of vocabulary and metaphor pleased the mind. Poetry exercises the student on new vocabulary and on strange, wonderful ideas. Poetry is a puzzle. Second, we also find in the preface an explanation of the procedure of versifying perfectly good, existing prose.

---

6. Norton, *Ideology*, 28; see also Percival, "Grammatical Tradition," 235.
7. *Epigrammata*, PL 51:498.

It serves to create individual epigrams each of which "sings of its own theme." This self-containment had pedagogical ends. A short poem is to be read, memorized, and opened out through commentary and discussion in the classroom. Some sense of the author's poetic method of composition is to be mastered in the course of reading; and the whole process serves to nourish the soul.

Prosper's book is a fairly elementary catechism; it covers a broad range of Christian doctrine in basic, highly concrete terms. Still, its readers do not begin with simple concepts. The very first epigram, "On true innocence," gives them a notion well chosen psychologically as an introduction to the Christian life and to the contradictions between Christian and commonsense morality. The poem presents the concept that the Christian should consider well the consequences of every action. Consideration as an internal process (in intellect) leads naturally to cultivating good intentions (a disposition of the will), so that one not only does no harm but also wills none. Already the elementary reader is in a world radically removed from the violence and sophistries of Aesop's wolves or Cato's calculated friendships.

The next epigram takes this process another step along, by considering the same virtue of innocence more abstractly under the rubric of charity, by which we may hate the deeds of others but never the individuals who do evil. This double moral movement represents a highly pragmatic approach to teaching virtue. The student is invited to think first in concrete and self-centered ways and then more abstractly. Prosper distrusted the potential of merely rote memorization to instruct in morals. He sought a way to internalize commonplace wisdom by appealing to real consideration of the truths involved. As is usual in early Christian moral thought, the individual is held to rigid, external standards of conduct. The moral-educational process is radically integrative. Conceptualization, intention, act of will, and deed exist in a single ethical moment crystallized in self-contained maxims.

Prosper's emphasis on self-containment does not mean that there are no larger unities within the collection. Indeed, the preface rather overstates the self-containment of the verses, for there are many pairings and minor progressions within the collection. One recurring theme is the individual Christian's quest for God and God's personal response. The Augustinian theory of grace is reduced to a series of opportunities offered. Trinitarian and Christological notions are kept in the realm of mysteries the tacit and utter acceptance of which is part of the individual's adherence to a community of belief. As befits an elementary work aimed at lay folk, there is no invitation to speculation. The ethic of habitual virtue here presented assumes a practical adherence to norms embodied in Christian tradition. This fundamental lesson was to be learned gradually through the memorization of many concrete epigrams. Another theme of considerable power is distrust of the world and its rewards, considered under such rubrics as "On hatred of the world" and "On the impunity of sinners."[8] Like other special themes, it also has a subsection of its own, where an extended consideration of evil turns the soul toward virtuous acts.

Most manuscripts of Prosper's *Epigrammata* are furnished with prose arguments for each verse. The Tuscan schoolbooks also follow this practice. These arguments contain just the kind of prose paraphrase exercises that students might have been required to do for themselves. The Tuscan manuscripts also have lexical glosses concentrating on words with irregularities of inflection and on points of grammar in the text. Such lexical glosses are sometimes vernacular and sometimes Latin. When they are in *volgare*, we can be sure they were a help to paraphrase exercises; but lexical glosses in Latin could also serve this purpose because they could point the student in the direction of rephrasing in Latin.

The same end is served by syntactical markers that indicate the proper word order in the heavily chiastic sentences favored by Prosper. Most annotated Prosper manuscripts have such syntactical glosses, either in the form of words that point to others in the verse sentences or, more rarely, in letters of the alphabet that sort out the word order. One surviving copy contains marks of this latter sort on over half the lines, indicating that at least one student or reader felt the need to put the words into prose order as a serious exercise (Census I.40). The text itself precluded the other common sort of gloss, on historical or mythological characters, since the collection has none.

The structural characteristics of the text and the evidence provided by the schoolroom manuscripts, then, suggest that the *Epigrammata* was used as the basis for drills in vocabulary and inflection, that is, as the most elementary sort of reading text. The frequency with which it occurs in our census and elsewhere in Italian libraries argues further that Prosper's *Epigrammata* was, along with Aesop, an almost universal text for teaching reading. These two are perhaps the only texts that do not show significant regional variation in frequency of use.[9]

8. On this theme, see Bultot, *La doctrine.*

9. This, at least, is my impression from examining manuscript catalogues and surviving copies of these texts from all over northern and central Italy; see Part III of the Appendix. One formal commentary on Prosper by a trecento grammar master is known to have been

Prosper may have been read as a deliberate balance to the rather cynical, worldly wisdom of Pseudo-Cato and Aesop. Tuscan grammar masters wanted to present the Augustinian core of the Christian inheritance in an encapsulated form to even the most elementary students so that they could internalize its lessons along with those received from the texts of the other ancient store of wisdom, the pagan classics. The fact that Ovid and Virgil were read only after the Christian classics were mastered points in the same direction. Students could have been taught to read from the Golden Age lyricists, but the moral lessons of these pagan poets could be better absorbed if they had already exercised their minds on a Christian moral system.

Christian maxims such as Prosper's, moreover, embodied an anti-sophistical rhetoric; they complemented the advice of the pagan fables and dicta in the school curriculum. The pagan texts praise the abilities of quick thinking and fast talking to win the day. Prosper takes a stance against such sophistries; he idealizes a psychology in which motives extend through words to actions. The Gaulish father is realistic to the degree that he warns his readers not to expect rewards in this world for their simplicity and integrity. In doing so he is at one with the Christian moralizers of pagan fables: "Wolves like these reign in every city," as the translator of Aesop has it.

Prosper, however, proposes a much more radically Christian approach to both life and literature than could be achieved by glossing ancient wisdom texts. His is a powerful, positive Christian rhetoric that begins with guilelessness and tranquility of spirit: "The simple mind, free of falsehood and evil, loves nothing unjust and would do no ungentle thing."[10] The next moral-rhetorical step is to frame one's every thought and action with the measuring rod of sacred Scripture. From Scripture, in turn, the individual proceeds to convert the mind to action, through prayer and through the imitation of Christ in word and deed. This is an active, primary rhetoric of an Augustinian sort whereby the Christian— constant in self-reflection and continually exhorted to virtue by personal prayer, liturgy, and preaching—achieves a fruitful habit of virtue.

Prosper seems to have designed his collection at least in part to provide increasingly longer and more discursive poems toward the end. As they became accustomed to his style, young readers could begin to follow

---

made by Giovanni Travesio (ca. 1348–1418); see Federici Vescovini, "Due commenti," 394–96, and Rossi, "Un grammatico," 37–39. To my knowledge, the text is lost.

10. *Epigrammata*, PL 51:519.

longer arguments in poetic form. Also toward the end of the collection, several of the poems have doublets, that is, two poems rather than one treat the same theme. Grammar students could thus discover how pervasive the classical and medieval art of paraphrase really was. Paraphrase was not merely an exercise used in class; it was fundamental to composition at every level. The multiplicity of rhetorical expressions of unitary truth was a culturally unifying phenomenon. Recognizing commonplace truths in a variety of handsome guises provided the individual with access both to the everyday wisdom of the community and to the divine wisdom that lies outside history.

The last of the maxims in the collection is an invitation to perseverance. Perseverance in faith against all adversity is also the major theme of the poem which invariably follows immediately in the manuscript readers and which the medieval audience considered part of the same collection: the 122-line *Poema coniugis ad uxorem*, an address by a Christian husband to his wife. The survival of a poem expressly concerned with a Christian marital relationship in a school curriculum that for centuries applied only to monks, nuns, and secular clerics may well be due to the vigor with which it sounds the monastic theme of fortitude. The brief mentions of husband and wife were referred in the usual monastic fashion to the relationship of the soul to God or Christ. In the trecento, however, the original meaning of the poem, a meditation on Christian marriage, re-emerged. In the last part of the poem especially, the poet husband expounds a notion of Christian citizenship which is the proper context of all individual efforts at salvation. The wife does not have a completely independent role, but she can have a fully Christian life. This ideal was suitable too for that other sort of Christian who attained salvation only through obedient humility, the monk.

The ideals of the monk and the wife were closely related because of the long tradition of describing religious women and men as brides. The continuing popularity of this work in the lay schools of thirteenth- and fourteenth-century Italy may have derived from this ability to offer so widely applicable a model of Christian piety. Its communitarian ideals, though entirely monastic in application in the earlier Middle Ages, were meant by Prosper to apply to lay people. In the fourteenth century it could thus quite easily revert to its original scope and be explicated in a family sense, and in a political one, in the way the last few fables in the Aesopian collection used at Florence were interpreted.[11]

11. The parallels are not just casual. In the final section of the *Poema coniugis* the husband exhorts the wife, *Custos esto tui custodis* [Be the guardian of your guardian]. This echoes the

Prosper composed his *Epigrammata* as a meditative text and it was used as such throughout the Middle Ages. Indeed, as we have already seen, meditation was the notion of reading that underlay the educational psychology of all medieval and early Renaissance educators. Commonplaces, developed for meditation, were used as memory devices and internalized through memorization as standards of personal conduct. Texts of all sorts, but especially sacred and proverbial wisdom texts, offered moral measuring rods to readers at all literary levels of sophistication. Much of the "intertextuality" of the culture of the late Middle Ages resides in this sort of moral mnemonic. There was much more than mere playfulness, and much more sincerity than sophistry in late medieval rhetoric, because piquant epigrams were intended not only to please but also to be memorized and internalized for lifelong use.

The second Christian classic of the trecento Tuscan classroom was even more telescopic in form than Prosper's maxims. Prudentius's *Dittochaeon*, mysteriously titled, consists of forty-eight quatrains each of which describes a different Old or New Testament scene. Apparently these little poems were composed to caption the painted or mosaic program of decoration for a church but were early and completely detached from their pictures and used as mnemonic verses for teaching Bible history.[12]

It is hard to say just why this happened, especially since the manuscript tradition of Prudentius's other poetry is rich in illustrated manuscripts. The iconic poems of the *Dittochaeon*, each of which describes a real picture, seem to have become examples of literary picture making of a special sort—so vivid an exercise of the imagination, indeed, that they were never supplied with illustrations. Reading them gave the elementary student a series of scenes from the historical books of the Bible. Most students would have known church art of the sort Prudentius describes, but they would have known these stories even better in the extended narrative form of preaching. The *Dittochaeon* verses could not be used to

---

lesson of the final Aesopian wolf-and-sheep story. Walter the Englishman may well have been thinking of it when he penned *Tutorem retinere . . . res tutissima est*. Both maxims can concern political and familial matters as well as purely spiritual ones.

12. The *Dittochaeon*, for all that it was probably Prudentius's most widely read poem, is not as frequently analyzed as others of that poet's works. See the highly perceptive remarks of Smith, *Prudentius' Psychomachia*, 121–22, 172–73, 232, and the essential article of Davis-Weyer, "Komposition und Szenenwahl." Several critical editions are available. In this discussion I have reproduced the text of Thomson for the Loeb series with my own, minor changes to his translations. I have also taken account of the edition of Lavarenne and of a useful commentary by Pillinger, *Die Tituli*. For additional bibliography, see Davis-Weyer, "Komposition und Szenenwahl."

teach sustained poetry making, but they do rather well illustrate the rhetorical figure and mnemonic device of presenting vivid, static pictures in few words. This may also explain why they were disassociated from the rest of Prudentius's prolific output of sacred poetry in the manuscript tradition. They were not usually part of medieval collected editions of Prudentius, and in our sample of school manuscripts they almost always appear without attribution, called merely by their incipit, *Eva columba*. No *accessus* ever attached to them. It was probably more for their utility than for the value of their author's name that they were so widely used.[13]

The *Eva columba* provided a storehouse of biblical proper names for explication by the grammar master. It may be that it was also considered a good complement to the more abstract theological approach of Prosper. The extreme simplicity of the quatrains and their largely descriptive nature might suggest that these verses were used before Prosper in the elementary course. But a caution is in order here, as for all the texts in our census. There is no external evidence to support either of these suppositions about the place of the *Dittochaeon* in the curriculum. In surviving manuscripts designed to carry more than one text, the *Dittochaeon* usually appears in first or second place, more often with Aesop or the *Physiologus* than with Prosper. In one case, however, the Bible verses of Prudentius were intended to stand after a copy of a very advanced text, Boethius's *Consolation*; and in another, the *Eva columba* follows Prosper. It seems fair on the basis of the manuscript evidence to put the *Dittochaeon* firmly in the early latinizing stage, but we cannot go farther. The schoolbooks that survive display design elements and patterns of use that make it clear that they were intended to be used both selectively and freely. There was no single, fixed place in the curriculum for the *Eva columba* or for any other text after the *Disticha Catonis*.

What, then, was the role assigned to this minor poem in the Christian education of trecento schoolchildren? We have already seen that the first reading text was usually the psalter. This book also served as an introduction to the concept of Scripture as a special repository of wisdom, to communitarian ideals of prayer, and, in a limited way, to biblical style and vocabulary. Somewhere along the line, probably earlier rather than later, Prosper and Prudentius were also read. Prosper's epigrams offered many new concepts, especially moral-rhetorical notions of virtue. We might

13. One of the few contemporary sources that explicitly assigns the *Dittochaeon* to Prudentius is the university-level commentary in Ravenna, Biblioteca Classense MS 358. Its author was aware of both the apparently slight nature and the high degree of utility of the work; see his introductory remarks, fol. 18r.

expect some of these ideals to be presented again in the study of Prudentius's poems, and they are. As in reading the psalter but not in studying
Prosper, the direct inspiration of biblical authority could be claimed for
the content of the *Dittochaeon* verses even if no particular emphasis was
placed on their eminent author. In particular, these little verses provided
an introduction to the Bible understood as a Christian canon, that is, as an
authoritative body of texts that relate the story of Jesus as fulfillment of
the promise of the Old Testament.

The question of authority is of particular importance in the case of
Prudentius. In general, some orientation to the authority of texts was part
of their right reading. The authority of Latin texts was also fundamental
to the claims of the Latin language to be a privileged, high-culture medium. The psalter was a special case among school texts because it was
thought to have been authored by one of the Old Testament heros, David,
under direct divine inspiration. Prosper's epigrams were a more usual
medieval case, with layers of borrowed and transferred authority: from
Scripture, through Augustine and Prosper, to the teacher and student.
Prudentius's text, however, embodies a different authoritative transfer, so
different that the manuscripts do not usually cite Prudentius as a mediator
of the moral-textual authority.

In the *Dittochaeon*, Scripture is not a source of discursive moralizing
but a narrative source. And the narrative, independent of the text, carries
the authority. The scenes are not directly related to scriptural texts; they
derive from paintings. It is not possible to read them as retellings of
scriptural texts, because they introduce details not in the Bible stories and
because they constantly refer to their source icons with such phrases as
"Here see . . ." or "Witness that . . ." Although he was the author of the
iconic text, Prudentius nearly drops out of sight; the real human author or
inventor was the painter. Behind the painter stood the biblical authors,
but they are not cited by Prudentius or mentioned in any of the surviving
glosses. Much more present, and the presumed source of the authority of
the picture text, are the biblical characters, starting with Eve in the incipit
*Eva columba* and continuing through the whole historical narrative sequence.

It would be hard to overstate the narrative power of these poems as
pedagogical devices. Each quatrain gives one or two moments of a story as
envisioned for the picture cycle they describe in a highly compressed form.
The result is strongly emblematic but frequently does not carry any significant reference beyond the story itself. Fully fourteen of the verses have no
explicit moral or theological content at all. They are purely narrative.

Another thirteen stanzas are directly moralized, usually by reference to a single vice or virtue. The Cain and Abel story, for example, illustrates envy; that of the martyrdom of Saint Stephen describes firm faith. Some of the moralizations are occasioned by a minor detail in the story and do not represent a departure from the primarily narrative frame. Thus, the Noah tale is described entirely in terms of the moment the two birds are released to test the waters: "Messenger of the flood already waning, the dove returns to the ark with a budding branch of olive in its beak. The raven meanwhile, captive to its own gluttony for the rotting corpses, tarried away. The dove carries back the joyous news of peace granted."[14] Here there would have been room for teachers to rehearse the larger story of Noah, its lessons of faith, and all the dramatic details that would have been familiar from sermons and liturgical representations of the story.

But Prudentius and the painter he followed point to a single narrative moment, that of Noah's salvation as revealed through the natural vices and virtues of animals. The raven is vividly portrayed in terms of the gluttony that detains him over the corpses of the flood victims, while the dove, symbolizing only vaguely some such virtue as constancy or obedience, is the messenger of peace. Prudentius or his pictorial source may already have been reflecting the widespread ancient tradition of the moralizing animal fable. In the trecento classroom these narratives would certainly have been seen in parallel to the Aesopian tales. They would also have carried a strong sense of the marvelous and revelatory power of Scripture itself, in which the working of God and the virtues of men are shown to all. If we remember the deep distrust for the world displayed in Prosper, it becomes clear that Prudentius could be used in similar fashion to explain how in literature, but not in life, the truth will out. Textual life is truer than real life.

This distrustful lesson, so strange to modern eyes, was fundamental to the coherence of text-based communities of the early medieval, monastic type. It served to reinforce the cultural elitism of literate men and women in religious communities and to define their world over against that of the secular powers they dealt with daily but did not ultimately serve. In the trecento it may seem to us a holdover of a religious culture no longer in universal esteem, but the reverse is true. By the time of Dante, the communitarian meaning of authoritative texts had been reinstitutionalized in the form of mendicant spirituality and offered as an ideal to a much wider

14. *Dittochaeon*, ed. Thomson, 2:348, my translation.

audience. In the mendicant reworking of this theme, mastery of literary forms and the ability to explicate sacred texts was a skill used for instructing a mass audience in the way to salvation. Literacy in Latin was a tool of the preacher, who defined himself not against the lay world but in a leadership role in reforming it. Mastery of narrative, fabulistic, and iconic rhetoric was one of the goals of studying Latin.

Still, only a minority of Prudentius's verses are directly moralizing. I have mentioned the fourteen purely narrative pieces. Another eighteen refer directly to Christological or ecclesiological concepts, which constitute the underlying meaning of the collection as a whole.[15] Again, we are justified in comparing this lesson, largely that of the meaning of the historical Christ and of Christ in history, to the lessons of Prosper. The two works, each highly condensed formally, provide complementary lessons of cosmic importance. Prosper concentrated on the personal path of virtue. He offered his readers an authoritative model of the interior life as it can develop in good works done in contemporary time. Prudentius started with the good works of individuals and put them in a historical sequence that begins with Adam and Eve and ends with the faith of the Christian church. It is significant in this regard that the last stanzas in the work relate New Testament events well beyond the ascension of Christ; the last one of all presents a vision of heaven drawn from the Book of Revelation. By analogy, the entire endeavor of Christian virtue in present time is included in this historical vision. The student of the poem could create a place for himself in sacred history.

Prudentius indulges in the pictorial artist's conceit of presenting historical action as occurring in modern landscapes. Thus the Beautiful Gate miracle whereby Peter repeats one of the healing acts of Christ (Acts 3:2–7) takes place in *Dittochaeon* 45 at the "gate which survives from the Temple," that is, in the ruins of the temple where Peter actually worked. This sort of historical telescoping does not weaken the sweeping vision of sacred history offered by the work. Just as modern dress versions of any classic may be intended to improve its accessibility, so anachronism can work to teach a notion of history that is synchronic. The whole thrust of the *Dittochaeon* as used in the late medieval classroom is in this direction,

---

15. Cf. Smith, *Prudentius' Psychomachia*, 121, and Davis-Weyer, "Kompostion und Szenenwahl," 19–21, 27–31. The latter scholar has proved decisively that the whole collection is a carefully arranged and callibrated Christology, even when the parallels are not immediately obvious.

of developing a specifically Christian notion of history in which modern virtue has both a traditional value and a cosmic significance.[16]

In the case of Prosper, and earlier in discussing Aesop, we saw how certain formal characteristics of the verse, in particular its extreme compression of thought, carried lessons that could refer to the moral plane as well. The same thorough interpenetration of stylistic device and pedagogical intent holds in the *Dittochaeon*, which is certainly one of the most extreme examples of narrative compression in Western literature. Since all the verses are identical in length, we can choose an example almost at random to illustrate this phenomenon. One biblical narrative, however, that of Samson, is actually given two quatrains, and its exceptionality invites us to look closer just at that point in the whole.

The Samson story represents the whole Book of Judges in Prudentius's scheme, just as the two emblems of David that follow stand for the whole of Samuel, Kings, Psalms, and Proverbs. But David is at least presented in two distinct narrative moments in a long career, first as the slayer of Goliath and then as a triumphant king. Samson receives a curiously monochromatic treatment, at what, we must remind ourselves, is twice the usual length for narratives in this work:

> 17. Samson: A lion tries to rend Samson, whose hair makes him invincible. He slays the wild beast, but from the lion's mouth flow streams of honey; the jawbone of an ass spontaneously pours forth water. Foolishness overflows with water, strength with sweetness.
> 18. Samson: Samson catches three hundred foxes and arms them with fire; he ties firebrands to their tails and lets them loose. He burns up the Philistines' corn. Just so nowadays the cunning fox of heresy scatters flames of sin over the fields.[17]

As so often happens in approaching medieval texts, we are struck first by what is not here, namely, Samson's repeated confrontations with the Philistines, his passion for Delilah, and his humiliation and then triumph, first as prisoner and then as destroyer of the temple of the pagan god. Instead, verse 17 gives us telescopic accounts of two of the miracles wrought by God on Samson's behalf. The hero kills a lion and honey flows from the mouth of the dead animal; later (fully a chapter afterward in the

---

16. Smith, *Prudentius' Psychomachia*, 169–75, shows how this moralizing mission characterizes all of Prudentius's poetry in one degree or another. Mannelli, "La personalità," 109–12, offers some examples of moralistic readings of specific quatrains.

17. *Dittochaeon*, ed. and trans. Thomson, 2:354–55, with my modifications.

Vulgate story) the jawbone of an ass, with which Samson slayed an entire Philistine host, proves to be the source of a new spring. Prudentius omits all reference to the narrative context of the Philistine wars and Samson's marriage negotiations.

The attack of the lion and Samson's slaying of it is the only narrative event here, but the forty-seven word biblical tale receives only ten words in Prudentius's version. Moreover, the lion slaying is a self-contained act of heroism in which the context of larger historical events or personal motivation are not even much missed. The poet refers the strength of Samson to his hairstyle and not, as regularly in the Book of Judges, to the indwelling spirit of God. In fact, one of the most swashbuckling narratives of the Bible is crystallized in an absolutely static emblem of martial courage rewarded not by natural consequences but by marvelous signs of God's favor. Just as in an emblem, there is a moral tag line here too: "Foolishness overflows with water, strength with sweetness," refers the lion and the ass to moral virtues essentially unconnected with Samson. This comes close to animal fable indeed.

The second quatrain is less crowded but even more strikingly emblematic. Here Samson's cunning act of vengeance against his father-in-law is narrated in two and a half rapid lines that describe only the act and not the hero's reasons for it or its ultimate consequences. The deed loses *all* motivational logic. This was thin enough in the biblical story, but there at least it had overtones of sexual energy and personal vendetta. In the *Dittochaeon*, the hero's exploit is pure vandalism. Prudentius's reasoning becomes clear in the second pair of lines. Samson's foxes are represented as heretics, and their rapid, uncontrolled course of destruction is taken as a warning for the church.

The history of the colorful folk hero Samson is reduced in these two little poems to a merely implicit narrative framework within which the poet tells three animal fables. It might be more accurate to say that he constructs three animal emblems of Christ, for these are not Aesopian fables. The animals do not act on their own. Instead, like the raven and dove in the Noah story, the animals are made into agents of God's historical action and, even more, agents of God's revelation to man. They are narrative devices employed for the explication of truth—employed by God himself in history as well as by the Christian rhetorician in telling the story and the Christian grammar master in explicating it.

The emblematic force of the stories can be understood only if they are given this thorough, moral-grammatical reading. Unlike discursive or purely didactic verse, which carries the reader along on a train of thought that must at least at first be read on a single level, emblematic verse constantly pushes the reader forward and then stops him short. It takes the student by the hand but sets him in a single spot in order to display a telescopic vision of reality that requires the eye to move through many layers into a distant realm of meaning. Students must explicate word by word and image by image, must tell and retell the parts of the narrative not included in the text itself, must look for the distant meaning in every phrase if they are to achieve the poet's own vision. More perhaps than in any other kind of text, the iconic lyric requires an activist reader; without the construing of the pupil or master, the poem has almost no meaning, certainly no moral meaning beyond the ink on the page or the colors on the painted surface.

It is tempting to think that the classroom popularity of this text (and of Aesop) was a function of the perennial fascination of children for animals. Certainly the presence of animals with all their obvious charms is strong in both works. But both authors merely use animals as a way of getting readers into their work; both had more serious, even radical points to make than to entertain or even to teach the mechanics of reading Latin. We would be selling trecento teachers short to suggest that they did not see and appreciate the deeper meanings of these texts, or to claim that they saw those themes as irrelevant to their classroom use of these texts.

The case of the *Dittochaeon* is particularly telling in this regard, since its animals are highly symbolic and tend to stand outside the biblical narrative. Prudentius (or the painter he followed) was so concerned with animal symbols that he inserted them where they do not occur or belong in Scripture. Noah's raven and dove reappear quite without precedent in the description of Paul's conversion on the road to Damascus. We read that the converted apostle became a preacher of great force, "having power with his lips to change ravens into doves." What is more amazing, Prudentius plays on the scriptural (and Aesopian) wolf in sheep's clothing by saying that Paul was reclothed: "One who was formerly a ravening wolf is clothed in a soft fleece."[18] This image is astounding, for Paul's metaphorical cross-dressing is not deceptive, as in all the possible precedents for the image; Paul was genuinely transformed from persecutor to Christian. The fourteenth-century schoolmasters could not have missed such a point. But they could have used these animal figures for contrast to those that appear in Aesop—and do so with authority that derived, if not from Scripture

18. Ibid., 2:368–69. For patristic parallels for the wolf and sheep, see Pillinger, *Die Tituli*, 114.

itself, then from sacred art. The iconographic requirements for symbolism and the rhetorical ones for vividness of expression become authoritative in their own right, almost without reference to scriptural sources or authorial intervention. The emblem's ability to impress a vivid moral on the memory is authoritative in that it constitutes a permanent part of the new Latinist's intellectual repertoire.

One last example, this time without animals, serves to sum up this discussion of Prudentius's poetic emblems. Perhaps the most static of all his pictures is this one of King David enthroned:

> 20. The Kingship of David: The marvelous David's royal emblems shine bright—scepter, oil, horn, diadem, purple robe and altar. They all befit Christ, the robe and crown, the rod of power, the horn of the cross, the altar, the olive.[19]

The didactic message is straightforward. David enthroned with his attributes represents Christ with the symbols of his passion and resurrection. The previous four lines, also on David, had given us the shepherd boy called to play his harp for Saul and then in the act of slaying Goliath. Here we see that narrative David transformed into statuelike majesty. The further transformation of King David into Christ the King extends the cosmic truth of the narrative, through one icon and into another.[20] Further still, in Christ enthroned we are reminded to look back into narrative where the passion and, implicitly, the boyhood and preaching of Jesus mirror the exploits of the boy David. A good teacher would have his schoolboys seeing themselves in young David. He might also hope to have them model their moral life on the passion of Jesus or their careers on Jesus's preaching. But most important of all, the students would have acquired a memory image, a multilayered icon of David to recall in all of its richness whenever they heard David invoked in hymn or sermon.[21]

19. *Dittochaeon*, ed. and trans. Thomson, 2:356–57.

20. Cf. Mannelli, "La personalità," 110–11, and Davis-Weyer, "Komposition und Szenenwahl," 22.

21. Davis-Weyer, "Komposition und Szenenwahl," 27–31, shows that each of the scenes in the poem has another interpretive dimension built in because it is paired with a second scene in the other half of the poem. Thus, all the Old Testament scenes, even those that have no obvious Christological reference, are paired with the directly corresponding scenes in the second half of the poem which provide a second interpretive level. In the close readings given the poem in medieval classrooms, these parallels may not have been drawn by every teacher, but their very existence is a confirmation of the multilevel reading Latin education aimed at.

At the start of the *Consolation of Philosophy*, the third of our classic Christian reading texts, the sixth-century courtier Boethius describes just such a rich, emblematic figure, Philosophia herself, who appears to him, or rather to his character Boethius, in the depths of despair:

> While I was thinking these thoughts to myself in silence, and set my pen to record this tearful complaint, there seemed to stand above my head a woman. Her look filled me with awe; her burning eyes penetrated more deeply than those of ordinary men; her complexion was fresh with an ever-lively bloom, yet she seemed so ancient that none would think her of our time. . . . Her dress was made of very fine, imperishable thread, of delicate workmanship. . . . But violent hands had ripped this dress and torn away what bits they could. In her right hand she carried a book, and in her left, a scepter.[22]

Boethius's character Boethius is an aged philosopher with decades of experience in dealing both with real people and with emblematic figures in his professional life as rhetorician, politician, and theologian-philosopher. His appreciation of this apparition cannot be compared to that of a schoolboy just beginning to read. Or can it? The character Boethius, after all, does not recognize his old companion Philosophia at first: "I myself, since my sight was so dimmed with tears that I could not clearly see who this woman was of such commanding authority, was struck dumb, my eyes cast down; and I went on waiting in silence to see what she would do next."[23] This degree of silent, obedient attention is a schoolmaster's dream. Philosophia responds first with a schoolmarmish complaint, then in a poem that offers an ideal of intellectual life that still resounded in the ears of early humanists like Petrarch and Boccaccio. After this, she rather matter-of-factly sets about looking for a remedy for her student's depression. That remedy is another poem, the beautiful sunrise verse, *Tunc me discussa*.

Medieval readers of this passage at the opening of the *Consolation* would have recognized the moral and educational psychology that stands behind it as the one expounded by their old grammar masters. Rhetorical remedies are applied to moral maladies because all the soul's moral powers are exercised rhetorically. Coluccio Salutati's teacher Pietro da Moglio, who made his reputation as a grammar master but taught rhetoric as well in Bologna and Padova, read this very emblem as an exhortation to unitary study of the trivium:

22. Boethius, *The Consolation of Philosophy* I, trans. Tester, 133–35.
23. Ibid., 135.

[Boethius] now describes [Philosophia's] clothing from a certain circumstance [its rents and tears], which is to say that there are some who go into the scholarly disciplines, and each one takes from them as much as he can. On that account these men lash out [at the fabric of Philosophia's clothing], saying "that one is a grammarian and no logician" or a logician and no grammarian, . . . and so forth. But since the disciplines are interwoven and any one of them is partially or wholly null without reference to the others, it is clear that any one alone is worth little, because that one alone is nothing or is incomplete for the purpose of posing a question [or proving a proposition]. Therefore, a mere grammarian is worth nothing without logic, rhetoric, and philosophy.[24]

The implications of this passage are developed elsewhere in the commentary, for Pietro treated Boethius in a thoroughly trecento manner, as a grammatical text for moralizing study. Grammar was not merely propaedeutic to the other disciplines; it was part of them and depended on them. The consolation of which Boethius wrote was accessible to every serious student of the text.[25]

As in the case of Prosper and Prudentius, the formal qualities of the *Consolation* offer clues to its pedagogical application. And as in the earlier cases, the peculiar traits of the manuscripts used in the schoolroom confirm the insights formal analysis can provide. The central formal fact of the *Consolation* is that it mixes prose and poetry, a combination with a long history before and since Boethius, and one that even elementary students knew because it was also the form of Prosper's *Epigrammata*. Almost every modern critic of the work has noted this form, and some have called it important. But there has been rather too much willingness to take seriously Boethius's jocular reference to the poetry as relief from tedious prose.[26] At the conclusion of the longest single prose in the book (IV.6), it is true, Philosophia remarks, "But I see that you are long since burdened with the weight of this enquiry and tired by the length of the

---

24. Federici Vescovini, "Due commenti," 408, translation mine: *Modo describit vestem a quodam accidenti, et est dicere quod sunt quidam qui vadunt ad scientias et unusquisque capit de ipsis scientiis quantum potest, et ideo modo lacerant eas quia unus est gramaticus et non logicus, alter logicus et non gramaticus, alter gramaticus et non retoricus etc. Sed quia scientie sunt intricate et sine ipsis simul in totum autem aliqua simul in partem nichil est quasi dicere quod una sola modicum valet quia una sola nulla est aut imperfecta ad propositum. Ergo simplex gramaticus nichil valet idest sine logica rettorica et philosophia.*

25. Ibid., 391–93.

26. Chadwick, *Boethius*, 223–24; Gruber, *Kommentar*, 16–18. Recent readings treat the piece as a unitary philosophical undertaking; see Glei, "Dichtung und Philosophie," esp. 226–28, 236–38, and Mueller-Goldingen, "Stellung der Dichtung."

argument, and waiting for some sweetness in verse; therefore take a draught, that, you may be refreshed by it and go more firmly on."[27] The prose in question, we should note, concerns the problem of evil, the central argument of the whole work, characterized by the author as "a matter the greatest of all in the seeking, and such that no discourse, however exhaustive, is sufficient for it."[28] It is framed by the apparently disparaging words about poetry we have already seen and by Philosophia's opening remark to the same effect: "But if the delights of music and song please you, for a little while you must postpone that pleasure, while I weave arguments for you bound to each other in due order."[29] The key to understanding the relation between prose and poetry in the *Consolation* is in this last phrase: the prose arguments are *nexas sibi ordine*, bound to each other in the ordered way any poetic argument can be made to be if the deliberately artificial word order and figurative use of language are unraveled and the ideas are laid out in prose with "normal" word order. This is the paraphrasing procedure we have noted several times; it was aided by the syntactical markers so typical of grammar students' reading books.

But prose is not just a better or clearer way of making a point. Much of the technical thrust of the *prosa* at hand revolves around the question of the philosopher's ability to discern the order of providence in the world.[30] The due order of the universe is, for a Platonic thinker such as Boethius, directly reflected in the good order of grammatical discourse. As Pietro da Moglio says in the passage cited above, the various disciplines of the trivium are also related in a necessary order. In this context, Philosophia's claim to resort to poetry when the philosopher's mind is exhausted by prose is, though ironic, more than slighting. Some truths can be approximated only by leaving behind prose reasoning and employing verse. As if to emphasize this point, she picks up the argument after meter VI with the ironic but real expectation that the poem will have explained everything: " 'And now do you see what follows from all these things we have been saying?' 'What?' I asked. 'That every kind of fortune,' she replied, 'is good.' " She is of course deluded, for Boethius replies exasperatedly, "But

27. *Consolation*, ed. and trans. Tester, 371.
28. Ibid.; cf. Lerer, *Boethius and Dialogue*, 204–16.
29. *Quod si te musici carminis oblectamenta delectant, hanc oportet paulisper differas uoluptatem, dum nexas sibi ordine contexo rationes*; ed. and trans. Tester, 357. Cf. Lerer's remarks on this passage, *Boethius and Dialogue*, 207; Mueller-Goldingen, "Stellung der Dichtung," 375, 379.
30. Lerer, *Boethius and Dialogue*, 210–12.

how can that be?"[31] Still, the point has been made that, whether rightly or not, readers of Boethius's day expected poetry to clarify, resolve, and illuminate prose argument, not just relieve it.

The structure of the prosimetric miscellany as Boethius crafted it assumes this sort of relation between verse and prose. From the very start of Book I, he placed the meters within the dialogue that gives the book its form. The meters are not add-ons, interludes, elaborations, or formal exercises. They are essential to the action of the dialogue, especially at the start of Book I where they carry much of the drama, but also later where the dialogue has become highly philosophical. The meters do not play off the proses, as if the proses were the dialogue and the verse inserted into it. If anything, it is the proses that were the less independent component of the mixed-genre miscellany to the medieval eye.[32] Every reader of the *Consolation* would have been familiar with the notion of poetry collections. Some of Boethius's verses circulated separately in just such poetry anthologies for sophisticated readers. Even in the elementary classroom, schoolchildren would have discovered early that prose was used to explain poetry, not poetry to illustrate or embellish a poorer sister form.

In the *Consolation*, moreover, each of the meters is put into the mouth of one of the partners to the dialogue. In full accord with the expectations of his audience, the narrator himself opens the book with a lament in verse. No medieval reader, and least of all a schoolchild, would be surprised to begin thus, with a well-crafted poem. Tuscan children might already have known the similar lament of Henry of Settimello, which, as we see in a later chapter, was an imitation of Boethius used in many schools. Throughout Boethius's book the poems are commented on and taken up by the proses, but there is no case of a verse referring directly to the prose discussions that precede or follow it and no poem that really needs a commentary in prose to succeed as a poem. This lends an air of independence to the poems seen within the work as a whole.

It is probably incorrect, however, to assume that any medieval reader would have felt the same degree of difference most moderns do between the meters and proses. We need only think of Dante's *Vita nova*, which depends heavily on Boethius for its formal inspiration, to realize how little integrated a work can seem to modern eyes that its contemporaries saw as a fully congruent whole with a necessary internal logic that did not permit of breaking it apart. Joachim Gruber has noted how Boethius rather

31. *Consolation*, ed. and trans. Tester, 375.
32. Cf. Mueller-Goldingen, "Stellung der Dichtung," 376–81.

closely parallels short proses and short poems, long verses and long prose sections, and how the work as a whole takes its structure from the arrangement of the poems in a single architectural pattern.[33] The careful integration of the proses into this preexisting scheme merely emphasizes the unity of the whole. A single voice, or rather a single pair of voices (as required by the dialogue form), creates a tightly woven composition around the poems and including them.

This digression on the internal structure of the *Consolation* should make clear why the poems were not extracted from the work as a whole for use in the Tuscan schools. Grammar masters were more than willing to tamper with the original form of a work if their editing would serve a pedagogical end. But even their radical prejudice in favor of poetry in the primary classroom, almost to the exclusion of prose, did not bring them to jettison Boethius's prose sections. This almost surely reflects their appreciation of the tight rhetorical unity of the whole and of the formal value of the *prosimetrum* for teaching moral rhetoric.

It is difficult to say just how Florentine grammar masters used Boethius in their classrooms. What external evidence we have for its use as a grammatical text comes from northern Italy and from settings related to university-level instruction.[34] The surviving manuscripts in Tuscan reader form are relatively few, although numerous copies survive that are laid out for monastic use or for study at a relatively more sophisticated level. There are also copies not in reader form which were clearly used by students in grammar schools, presumably at the *auctores* level. The *Consolation* could not have been a regular part of the early latinizing curriculum, then, but it was certainly read widely. It must have been seen as an advanced or special-case text, appropriate for the best and most promising students.

We may also hypothesize that it was read selectively. The master could choose passages most useful for his students to rehearse in class and leave the rest of the book for their private reading. Tuscan reading book copies of the *Consolation* contain elementary glosses and notes, but mostly on the verses, not on the proses, suggesting that the verses were considered

33. Gruber, *Kommentar*, 19.

34. Federici Vescovini, "Due commenti," gives a good description of the commentaries by Pietro da Moglio and Giovanni Travesio, who taught elementary as well as university students. Other commentaries from the period are described by Courcelle, "Etude critique," 116–17. One of the few truly basic commentaries is in Ravenna, Biblioteca Classense MS 206; it contains lexical and syntactical glosses of the simplest kind. This sort of annotation is also found in a few of the copies in our census, notably I.10 and I.22 but less systematically than in the Ravenna codex.

different, perhaps harder than the proses. Still, the text was not edited down or anthologized for the schoolbook versions, probably because of its status as a classic, a near-perfect example of *prosimetrum* with as authoritative an author as one could imagine in the trecento. If one were going to give such a text to a child, it would be with the expectation that he would want eventually to read the whole of this classic, perhaps repeatedly, in the course of his intellectual life.[35]

Then too, the glosses to the verses I have seen concentrate on unraveling the poetic word order and do not address other points. They provide, that is, a guide to paraphrasing the verses closely into prose word order (*nexas sibi ordine!*) and leave the rest to the reader. This suggests that in the grammar classroom, at least, certain of the verses were separated out for construction by teacher and students. At this level, the whole piece may have been presented to the student, but, because of its length, complexity, and difficulty, it may have been taught only very selectively. We should, however, posit this sort of reading for Boethius only in full realization that there is no evidence that other texts in the curriculum were taught selectively in this way. Selective annotation was given to all sorts of texts and does not mean that they were read only partially. Prosper could easily have been excerpted; and the brevity of his *sententiae* meant that teachers could skip around too. But other school texts such as Prudentius's highly architectural compilation of poems make sense only if read all the way through.

Just as surely as in the case of the other Christian classics, teachers valued Boethius's great work as a collection of moral commonplaces. Its grandiose neoplatonic cosmos, its idealization of the scholar's life as against the sordid business of this world, its complicated personifications, its detailed arguments were rich food, to be sure. As in the other texts we have been examining, the *Consolation* was chosen precisely because it was rich and open-ended and intoxicating fare. It was intended to fill the minds of the students who worked through it with memory pictures that had both poetic vividness and prose fullness. Its double form provided a model of the moral-intellectual relations of texts to one another, and of the ways different expressions of one idea could be linked. The *prosimetrum* was particularly well adapted to this task because there was no confusing one form of expression with the other, and because alternating

35. See Federici Vescovini, "Due commenti," 405–6nn, on the continuing influence of the text outside the university; cf. Rossi, "Un grammatico," 36–37.

them demonstrated the relative powers of each of the forms for forwarding a particular argument.[36]

These may seem rather sophisticated concepts to present to schoolchildren; but, as we saw in the case of Prosper, the pedagogy of the fourteenth century (and earlier) was nothing if not ambitious. There was a clear sense that it was appropriate to give children complex and even extremely difficult texts so that they could take from them exactly as much as they were ready and able to absorb, never less than the grammar master was able to give his best students, and at least in some cases rather more than the teacher might see as the immediate lesson to hand. There was no expectation in late medieval culture that any reader at any level would understand all the meanings of any text on any one reading. Since children were being offered a model of reading and rereading the same texts life long, it was important for them to be given rich and sophisticated models from the start.

36. Federici Vescovini, "Due commenti," 387–96, cites evidence for this sort of reading; on the difficulties of the *prosimetrum* for medieval translators of Boethius, see Copeland, *Rhetoric, Hermeneutics*, 127–50.

# READING TEXTS
## *The Monastic Heritage*

A long with the complex lessons of Prosper and other patristic writers, some Florentine schoolboys also read medieval Christian works. These works were also in verse. They offered notions of Christian perfectionism heavily colored by the religious and educational experience of the monastic communities from which so much of the conventional grammar curriculum and so many of the moral commonplaces embedded in it derived. Two of the texts in our census were products of the great flowering of medieval monastic culture between the ninth and eleventh centuries, the anonymous *Chartula* and the pseudonymous *Ecloga Theoduli.*[1] They appear respectively seven and five times in our Florentine census, making them only moderately popular, certainly far less so than the Christian and pagan classics we have examined thus far. But both had a long tradition of school use and both are frequently mentioned in Italian literary sources for the grammar school curriculum. If they were not great favorites of the Florentine grammar masters, they were at least well enough known to make us suspect that their relative unpopularity was the result of deliberate choice and not chance.

Grammar is a highly conservative discipline in terms of the texts used for teaching, and above all in terms of the reasons for using these texts. We need only recall how ardently the Christian leaders of late antiquity

---

1. The *Chartula* is most easily consulted among the works of Saint Bernard, Patrologiae latina (PL) 184:1307–14. Theodulus is edited in the uncommon critical text of Osternacher, *Theoduli Eclogam*, now easily consulted in Huygens, *Bernard d'Utrecht*, 9–18, from which I cite. The manuscript tradition of Theodulus is described by Quinn, "Ps. Theodolus," and Osternacher, "Die Ueberlieferung."

advocated the substitution of Scripture for pagan literature, and how slowly the elementary curriculum changed, to understand that this was so. No wonder then that, once established, Christian classics such as Prosper and Prudentius retained their places in the grammar school course until the invention of printing.[2] Another simple demonstration of the textual conservatism of the discipline is that only one of the texts that occur more than once in our census of trecento Florentine reading books was composed after 1210.[3] And yet the society for which the schoolboy of 1350 was being educated was vastly different from that of 1200, especially in heavily mercantile, highly literate Florence.

The *Chartula* and the *Ecloga Theoduli* present two different but profoundly monastic concepts of language use. They offer, in fact, the most thoroughgoing mystical paradigms available on an elementary level to late medieval people. In them, language is presented as the immediate and powerful tool by which the Christian sloughs off the concerns of this world, discovers an inner self that can be directed to God, and finally attains a salvation beyond even language. We cannot know how much of this implicit program any given teacher or pupil would absorb via the parsing and construing of these texts, but we cannot doubt that the program was there, or that the detail-oriented, open-ended medieval approach to texts left room for its comprehension and internalization.

The contrast between the career prospects of urban, lay schoolboys and the highly monastic coloring of many of their school texts is nowhere more evident than in the *Chartula*, a twelfth-century poem on renunciation of the world which during much of the later Middle Ages was attributed to Saint Bernard of Clairvaux. Bright boys destined for trading, notarial, or university careers thus spent a great deal of time memorizing thumping rhymes like these:

*Vox divina sonat, quod nemo spem sibi ponat*
*In rebus mundi, quae causam dant pereundi.*

---

2. The fate of these two texts in the age of printing is an interesting index of the penetration of humanist latinity into the schools. Each received several early editions in Lombardy and Piedmont, in Germany, and in the Low Countries, but they were not printed at Venice, Bologna, or south of the Apennines. The virtually nonexistent Italian market was almost surely due to the disdain of humanists for the quality of their Latin; cf. Grendler, *Schooling*, 235–37. On the other hand, Vives recommends both Prudentius and Prosper as late as 1523; see Cherchi, "Jacopo Facciolati," 51–52.

3. I.e., Bonvesin de la Riva's courtesy book, which I examine in Chapter 7. Grendler, *Schooling*, is insistent, indeed eloquent, on this matter of educational conservatism; see esp. 102–5, 110, 116–17.

*Quisquis amat Christum mundum non diligat istum.*

[A heavenly voice resounds that no one should place his hopes in things of this world, which are the cause of perdition. Whoever loves Christ ought not love this world.][4]

The argument of the piece is straightforward. It is addressed by a senior monk to a young man who has apparently just joined a monastic community, and it is intended to strengthen him in his resolve to lead the monastic life of Christian perfection. Scholars have rightly placed the piece in a common genre concerned with *contemptus mundi*, but little has been written about the way it fit into the grammar curriculum.[5]

We do know that by the late twelfth century the poem was popular as a school text; its rigorous, somewhat repetitive sounding of a single Christian theme no doubt contributed to its broad use. Indeed, it was a fine model of how to develop a complex theme through division, paraphrase, amplification, and abbreviation. These were the standard compositional exercises of the classical rhetorical curriculum, ones the grammar school boys would eventually go on to once they began to study composition, or *ars dictaminis*. The heavy-handed rhymes and rhythms would have made for easy memorization; and the self-contained, proverbial quality of many of the distichs presented the reader with examples of that favorite medieval stylistic device, sententiousness. In short, the piece was a good formal model for schoolchildren, even as it expounded the ascetic ideals of famous spiritual thinkers as no other text available to young readers did. Its durability into and throughout an age of considerably more secular culture, then, is probably to be explained by a combination of motives: general conservatism among teachers, formal appropriateness to classroom methods still in use in the trecento, and a sense that its theme was venerable.

It may be that the attribution to Bernard of Clairvaux added to the prestige of the work in some quarters. Bernard's sermons were certainly highly popular in Italy, particularly in mendicant circles and among women. Themes thought appropriate and edifying for women could be the same ones considered fitting for schoolboys. Bernard was also early and often translated into the *volgare*. The expectation that his name helped bring the *Chartula* to the Tuscan classroom, however, is not borne out by the evidence of the manuscript reading books, which never at-

---

4. *Chartula*, PL 184:1307; translations of this text throughout this chapter are mine.
5. Bultot, "La *Chartula*," 803–12. On the question of how the medieval curriculum suited the trecento schools, see Frova, "La scuola," 131–32, and Raith, *Florenz*, 153–56.

tribute the poem to him and rarely include any sort of *accessus* at all. When they do provide an introduction, it identifies the author merely as a monk and remarks that the addressee, Rainaldus, was a youth (*puer* or *adolescens*) and younger brother (in the religious sense) of the writer. This last information was probably aimed at increasing the immediacy of the piece for the young reader. It certainly stresses the formal character of the poem as an *epistola*, a genre widely understood to have certain conventions of direct, personal appeal even if highly rhetorical in construction.

In the case of the *Chartula*, this personal stance was not easy to maintain. The letter form is merely a framework around a series of compact, often rather abstract miniature essays (ten to twenty-five lines each). These are studded with even shorter two- or three-line *sententiae*. This loose structure would have been familiar to a student who had already learned his Prosper. The epistolary frame is developed only at the beginning, where the salutation mitigates the artificiality of the singsong verse:

> Our page carries greetings to you, Rainaldus; you will find many things here if you do not refuse these gifts. Sweet are the comforts of the soul I send you, but they will do you little good if you do not put them into action. Do not toss to the winds what my words advise you; let them sound in your heart and remember to retain them so that our admonitions might work great good in you and bring you through God's grace to the heavenly kingdom. These words can please a true heart. They show the way; they encourage; they do not reprove.[6]

This second-person address is frequently taken up again during the course of the 374-line poem, though rarely as successfully as in the salutation. The Latin in this passage, for example, is very compressed and unlovely:

> *Jam satis audisti, frater, quod gratia Christi*
> *Sic nos salvavit, nostrumque genus renovavit.*
> *Si sapis, hoc credis, nec ab hac ratione recedis.*

> [Now you have heard enough, my brother, of how Christ's grace has saved us and redeemed our race. If you know, then believe; shrink not from the concept.][7]

The stiffness of the final line is entirely typical; the writer had difficulty

---

6. *Chartula*, PL 184:1307.
7. Ibid., PL 184:1312.

escaping from his aphoristic manner long enough to effect any real personalization of the theme. Only at the very end of the poem does the warmth of the salutation return. The poet seems almost to realize that he has been too stern:

> Perhaps I send this sermon in vain to a boy like you, since you do not understand its logic. But may the boundless Father give you complete understanding, strengthen your youth, and give you at the same time integrity. May the Son of God himself, the hope of our children, author of honesty, and perpetual source of goodness grant you the flowers of virtue and good habits.[8]

The poem does not have a tight outline or clearly discernible overall structure but proceeds episodically according to a pattern by now familiar to us. Neither the lyric seven psalms, the narrative Aesop, nor the sententious Pseudo-Cato and Prosper possess a clear overall outline. Their effect, like that of the *Chartula*, is produced by sounding themes which, as they are repeated, become familiar and increasingly assume the character of variations on a limited number of commonplace ideas. In monastery schools this effect was consciously modeled on the repetitive psalm cycles and minutely varying liturgical round of monastic piety. By the trecento it represented less a direct imitation of liturgical and psalmodic language than an echo of it. But it was an echo that could easily be heard by city children because it had long since been absorbed into mendicant and lay piety. We hear it, for example, in the pious invocations that open and interrupt Florentine account books, legal documents, and personal memoirs (*ricordanze*).

The *Chartula* is even more single-minded than most theme pieces of the period, since its heart throb is the incessant repetition of exhortations to distrust, suspect, and devalue the things of this world. But the author does not resort to using some striking but difficult-to-develop themes common in treatises *de contemptu mundi*. There is no attempt, for example, to describe a past golden age from which our present moral state is a decadence.[9] Instead, the author chose a more present-minded contrast between the calm of a life directed away from this world and the turbulence and transience of everything world centered.

Over and over, this contrast is compressed into two- to four-line bons

8. Ibid., PL 184:1314.
9. Bultot, "La *Chartula*," 806.

mots. The pair wealth and poverty, a traditional monastic and quintessentially mendicant theme, is constantly evoked to this effect:

> What is a mass of treasure or gold to you when sinners are sent to the bottom
> recesses of hell, to suffer dark and fire forever without any hope of escape? He
> who is handed over to such punishments is tearful and sad; he would prefer
> to have lived a pauper all his life rather than to have had riches. . . . How
> wretched is he—and will be—who seeks after worldly things. He is truly rich
> who does not care to have any of it. . . . The gentle and venerable poor man is
> blessed; the useless and miserable rich one is damned.[10]

In such a context the straight and narrow leads through a perilous forest.
To stray from it invites sudden, catastrophic moral disorder, exactly the
usual state of the world outside the monastery.

One of the stable things that counteract the variability of the everyday
world for the *Chartula* author is the written word. He is insistent on the
continuing value of his own poem to its young addressee:

> Those who hold onto what I say know that it is wholly useful. Brother, listen:
> many useful things will come to you if you wish to hold onto them, for thus
> will you be faithful. Through this virtue [faithfulness] you will be able to
> attain salvation and you will be blessed if you do good works. Therefore
> remember always my words; let your mind's attention be always on these
> pages.[11]

This passage consciously echoes the Benedictine *Rule*. The student is
urged to *listen* to the *spoken* advice of the *writer* of these pages, that is, he
is to read the poem aloud attentively or listen as the teacher dictates. Next,
he is to hold onto (*retinere*, memorize) the contents of the text. The
consequence of his faithfulness is that he will also attain (*retinere* again)
salvation through good works, which include the acts of studying and
memorizing the text. The doublet *Quod loquor . . . retinere / retinere
salutem* (hold onto what I say / attain salvation) makes it absolutely clear
that the author proposes a radical interpenetration of study and moral
action. There is no value in the study of texts except moral value; and
moral progress is achieved directly through the virtuous action of studying
Christian literature well. Moreover, we are left in no doubt that this very
text is meant to be read and profited from in this way.

The title of the poem is significant in this regard, for the text is univer-

---

10. *Chartula*, PL 184:1310–11.
11. Ibid., PL 184:1312.

sally referred to by its first word *Chartula*, or "parchment" sheet. This is its incipit, the typical method of identifying common, especially anonymous texts. At the same time, the term *Chartula* is a substantive of paramount importance to the beginning reader. It is the concrete instrument of reading, the written page, as well as a common metaphor for learning, the mental page. A diminutive, it fits the child reader's world and contrasts with the adult sphere of monumental and formal legal writing. And yet *Chartula* is the title of a text that exhorts its reader to distrust the merely visible and temporal.

Presumably, exception is made for texts that provide a direct link to the salvific Word beyond the page. In the schoolroom context, this exception would extend to the whole study of Latin—would be, indeed, one of the sources of its claims to universality. The *Chartula* author also recommends study of Scripture:

> Everything that I show, you yourself can make out with some guidance. With the help of Scripture you can know many things. To the one who seeks eternal life, holy reading shows the mind a way. Receive as well the memorial of my writings. May you see—not with a heavy heart but with a gentle mind— what I have shown you, what I have sweetly introduced.[12]

The imagery here is highly visual, this because reading is a visual activity but also because memorization, the internalization of the text, is mastered through visualization techniques. Study leads to salvation through the radical internalization of Scripture; one guide or starting point on this visual quest is the *Chartula* itself. *Sacra lectio*, whether of the Scripture or other salutary texts, provides the mind with a clearly readable path, one securely directed toward God under the careful guidance and control of the grammar master.

All these lessons are strongly monastic in origin and flavor. The Florentine manuscripts of the *Chartula* do not give us license to say exactly how such lessons were absorbed in secular schools. As with most of the texts in the second rank of popularity in our census, the *Chartula* appears mostly in the larger anthologies and not in single copies. It may, then, have been an elective text or extra exercise, perhaps one to be dipped into if time allowed or the needs of a particular pupil required it.

A second product of the monastic Middle Ages used at Florence may

---

12. Ibid., PL 184:1314.

also have been used electively. The *Ecologa Theoduli*, sometimes attributed to Gottschalk of Ogier, dates from the ninth or tenth century and takes the form of a singing contest between a shepherd, Pseustis (or Falsehood), who relates tales from pagan mythology, and a shepherdess, Alithia (Truth), who replies with stories drawn from the Bible.[13] It was regularly used as a school text from the late eleventh century onward, apparently because it combined Christian doctrine with pastoral eclogue. The fact that it is a pastiche of direct quotations and echoes from the most popular classical and Christian poets probably also contributed to its popularity as a school text.[14] It was a bridge between such truly elementary texts as Cato and the more advanced *Bucolics* of Virgil, or so at least it seemed to the twelfth-century curriculum writer who advised that the student "might move from the eclogue of Theodulus to the eclogues of Virgil."[15]

Some scholars have opined that Theodulus was never popular in Italy, and it is true that by far the vast majority of surviving manuscripts are of northern European origin.[16] Still, Italian literary sources occasionally cite the piece, and we know that it occurred in Italy in both moral miscellanies and grammatical collections.[17] There are six examples in our census, redacted in the usual reading book form. In two cases Theodulus and the *Chartula* occur together in the same trecento anthology (Census I.15 and I.26), and in a third these two appear in an assembly of fourteenth-century books put together in the fifteenth (Census I.8). In all three cases the *Physiologus* is also present in close conjunction with Theodulus. This may mean that these three strongly spiritualizing texts were related in teachers' minds. There are also two examples of Theodulus as a separate (Census I.30 and I.39), and one in which it was written into blank pages left at the end of a copy of Boethius (Census I.37). This manuscript history suggests that by the fourteenth century this northern European "best seller" was merely an extra or elective text, perhaps in the process of losing what scant popularity it ever had in Italy. Certainly it was out of vogue there by the mid-fifteenth century. Although it was repeatedly printed in France, England, and the Low Countries between 1450 and 1550, there is no early

---

13. Questions of authorship and date are debated, though a growing consensus favors an early tenth-century date; see Quinn, "Ps. Theodolus," 383–84nn; Clogan, "Literary Genres," 202–3; Green, "Genesis," 49, 106; and Vredeveld, "Pagan and Christian," 113.

14. See Green, "Genesis," and Vredeveld, "Pagan and Christian," on the sources.

15. Hamilton, "Theodulus," 175–77.

16. Ibid., 180.

17. Avesani, *Quattro miscellanee*, 37n2.

Italian edition of the text, so we may be sure that it was not in demand in humanist schools.[18]

Like the *Chartula*, the *Ecloga Theoduli* presents a radical, monastic notion of language as a vehicle of salvation. A more direct confrontation of the pagan and Christian literary inheritances cannot be imagined. Strophe for strophe, line for line, and epithet for epithet, the aggressively virile heroics of Greek myth are contrasted with more feminine Christian virtues of meekness and obedience to the will of God. The Christian myths are often just as violent as the Greek ones, but the blood is that of passion, of those who suffer nobly the vicissitudes of Christian history. The shepherd Pseustis is given the quintessentially male role, bragging about plunder and conquest, while the *virgo decora* Alithia elaborates the figure of the sufferer. For monastic writers, suffering was the proper, feminine stance of the soul, spouse of the Lord, before her many detractors.

These roles are laid out in the prologue. The jeering Pseustis tries to bully Alithia into an unequal contest; she sighs that unless they secure a third-person judge the shepherd would never admit it even if he were roundly defeated. Apparently she knows the fellow all too well. Once they begin singing, with Mater Fronesis for their judge, the contrasts between them become linguistic and literary as well as personal. Pseustis gives us Saturn exulting in the propagation of a new race; Alithia replies with the sin of Adam and Eve, who suffer for having generated sickness and death. Jupiter cruelly dethrones his father; Adam and Eve are expelled from Eden. And so on, with Alithia constantly providing a meek and humble foil to the boastful, sexually aggressive deeds sung by Pseustis.

Before long it becomes clear that Alithia, for all her meekness and that of her heroes, has the upper hand in the contest. Her episodes accumulate to form a sacred history aimed at a salvation community, while the stories of Pseustis remain isolated cases of human or divine folly, whim, and frustration.[19] At most, the pagan myths explain some natural phenomenon. The Christian stories, meanwhile, witness God's intervention in history. Alithia constructs a series of natural monuments and human institutions that mark off the stages of her narrative. The rainbow, Mount Ararat, the multitude of languages, the Levite priesthood, eventually even the Bible itself, all attest to God's work and the human responses to it. As the poem progresses, the symbols of God's presence are more frequently embodied in human language. But language is never just human. It is also

18. Osternacher, "Die Ueberlieferung," 353–54.
19. Cf. Green, "Genesis," 63–68.

God's revelation; and so speech is the basis for building a human relation-ship with God. This is a powerful symbolic statement of the value of grammar study. The text was surely valued for its expression of Christian neoplatonic psychology and theory of history as well as for propounding a particularly crucial role for language study.

A turning point in the poem is reached exactly halfway through, when Alithia comes to the end of the historical books of the Old Testament and relates the story of Samson. As in Prudentius, the emphasis is on Samson the trickster and manipulator. This Hebrew hero comes closer to the Greek heroes of Pseustis than any other figure cited by the Christian poetess. As in Prudentius, the Theodulus author omits all reference to the destruction of the Philistine temple; Alithia ends her story with Delilah's betrayal of the hairy hero. Pseustis, however, apparently already knows the destructive end of the story, for he responds not to Samson and Delilah but to the affront to the pagan gods of ancient Palestine. He replies by praising the names of the deities in the pantheon and calls on them to defend their appointed poet. He is beginning to realize that he can no longer control the linguistic contest, and so he calls on powers beyond his own for help. Alithia responds with a placid, rock-solid hymn. The hymn apparently represents the Book of Psalms, but in her version it is a Trinitarian poem of praise, to the one God in three persons who is so vastly superior to the pagan pantheon:

> PSEUSTIS: O names of a thousand gods, defend thy poet. O you who inhabit hell and the starry heavens, every part of earth and the lake of the resound-ing abyss, O names of a thousand gods, defend thy poet!
>
> ALITHIA: One and the same God, majesty and glory and every power that is and was and will be praise you and serve you, who have three persons and three names. O one without end or beginning, bid us now triumph over falsehood.[20]

Just when pagan Pseustis falters in his own human powers and has to seek multiple divine reinforcement, Alithia turns her prayer to the one infinite God and asks for help in defeating the pagan's many falsehoods. The battle of words is already over, because the upper hand belongs to the shepherdess with her unitary history, single community of belief, and one transcendent deity. Pseustis, by now desperate, replies with his greatest weapon, the shepherd-poet Orpheus, in a version in which Orpheus

20. Lines 181–88, ed. Huygens, 14. On this crucial passage, see also Green, "Genesis," 54–55, 66.

rescues Eurydice. But Alithia responds with David. The battle is truly one of poets; the battlefield is language itself.

Through most of the rest of the book, language is an explicit theme. Alithia first relates the stories of the prophets and then abandons her Old Testament itinerary to evangelize openly, indeed to rail against the absurdities of Greek myth. In the end, Pseustis attempts to extricate himself, as Alithia predicted he would, by claiming that the hour is late and time short; but to a final, furious citation of the four evangelists by Alithia he admits defeat. Fronesis proclaims the winner and describes the sunset. In some manuscripts from the thirteenth century onward, an additional stanza ends the poem with Alithia singing yet another Trinitarian hymn in the gathering dusk.

I have belabored this curious text at a length not justified by its frequency in our census for several reasons. Like the *Chartula* it was immensely popular north of the Alps, and if we are to understand the limits of its popularity in Italian classrooms we must first understand how it could have been used to teach concepts of language use. Then again, both the pastoral letter *Chartula* and the pastoral poem of Theodulus expound themes sounded elsewhere in the corpus of texts that *were* popular. Distrust of the world was an important theme in Prosper. Many of the Old Testament stories in Theodulus are also to be found in the *Dittochaeon* of Prudentius. Moreover, each of the two poems represents a genre that was important to the early humanists. The admonitory letter on the life of study or on the vanity of the world had many trecento exponents, and pastoral poetry was, in the form of Virgil and the Greek lyricists, essential to the whole classical revival. Petrarch thought highly enough of the idea of the pastoral contest to imitate the themes of Theodulus in the epistolary prologue to his own collection of Latin eclogues.[21] We must ask ourselves, then, what limited the popularity of the *Chartula* and Theodulus. Why were they not more widely used? And perhaps more important still, why do they appear occasionally when other popular northern European texts (e.g., the *Tobit* of Matthew of Vendôme or the courtesy book *Facetus*) do not occur at all?

The case of the *Chartula* is perhaps the easier one to understand. It had the authority of conservatism both pedagogically and thematically. It is an extended development through multiple paraphrase of a theme venerable by antiquity, by claims to Christian elitism, and by general theological conservatism. Moreover, it picked up and expanded on a notion impor-

---

21. Cf. Bernardo, "Petrarch, Dante," 120–22.

tant in the universally used Prosper. This gave teachers a pedagogical reason for employing the *Chartula*, one that would make it a good model for composition later in the course. The chief devices of medieval compositional training were elaboration, paraphrase, expansion, and abbreviation of set themes. The *Chartula* presented these processes both by itself and in clear relation to another common school text; so it had a certain, if limited logic as a supplementary or elective reading. The *Chartula* was also an unpretentious piece, certainly less so than Theodulus. Its singsong was monotonous and not terribly elegant, but it was useful for memorization; and there was none of Theodulus's poor, imitative pastoralism to offend the increasingly sensitive ears of fourteenth-century neoclassicists. In this regard it is interesting that Guarino put the *Chartula* in a class with Prosper and Prudentius when criticizing the style of the traditional school authors. These three texts survived in the Italian schools up to the middle of the fifteenth century as Theodulus apparently did not. Guarino did not know or think Theodulus worth criticizing, perhaps because it was just not common enough in the second decade of the fifteenth century to worry over.[22]

The limited use Florentine masters made of Theodulus at first seems less easy to explain on thematic grounds than on rhetorical and stylistic ones. Its stylistic limitations are obvious; certainly it would not have impressed teachers who knew Virgil very well, and those who could recognize its character as a patchwork of quotations from earlier poetry might not think it particularly original. But it would be overly optimistic to think that most trecento grammar masters were truly well versed in Virgil or well enough read to recognize all the echoes modern students have found in the work. Style may have counted against Theodulus, but I suspect that the content was an even greater problem. To understand how this was so, we must look more closely at the way the biblical stories were presented elsewhere in the elementary curriculum.

We might expect, for example, that teachers would seek to tie Theodulus's Bible stories to those of Prudentius; but this could only happen if the teacher was willing to work very hard at it, and to ignore radical differences in genre between the two poems. Of the twenty-four Old Testament episodes or figures expounded by Prudentius, Theodulus's Alithia refers to only ten in the thirty-one strophes she dedicates to the same section of the Bible. The differences of emphasis derive from the differing fundamental structures. Every Old Testament scene in Prudentius has a

---

22. Guarino's critique is quoted by Garin, *Pensiero*, 91.

Christological analogue in the New Testament section of his iconic, narrative anthology. There is no such correspondence in Theodulus. The individual poems in Theodulus are not iconic or narrative at all but epideictic. They aim at creating a portrait of a historically aware and self-consciously developing Old Testament community. The New Testament is treated even more directly symbolically, in the tetragrammaton that symbolizes the four evangelists in Alithia's final argument. The endpoint of the theology is Christological, but only indirectly; and the historical process is not presented in a narrative. It is, rather, aimed at expounding the inheritance of the Christian community. As a result the two works take quite a different view of the canon. Alithia is compelled by her creator to follow the order of the canonical books closely, and so, for example, to deal with the prophets almost one by one. By contrast, Prudentius's iconographic source did not picture the prophets, so his Old Testament history altogether omits them. For the fourth-century poet, it was the potential emblematic impact that counted, not the representation of a unitary canon.[23]

Its almost total lack of iconic force is the most striking way the *Ecloga Theoduli* differs from Prudentius's *Dittochaeon*; this difference would have precluded the medieval reader from seeing the two poems as being about the same thing. Whereas Prudentius's poems function in symbolic terms, the verses of Alithia are discursive. The two poems would therefore have had to be presented differently in the classroom if they were to be more than mere reading exercises. To fourteenth-century Florentine masters, concerned with potential heterodox tendencies among an increasingly self-conscious and self-assertive laity, the verses of Theodulus might even have seemed dangerous reading for the uninitiated. Theodulus does not provide a single, primary set of symbols with an unambiguously orthodox, elementary meaning. There are few built-in controls on how the poem is to be read. Particularly the portions that concern the prophets and the confused polemical section at the end walk on the tricky ground of theological interpretation beyond the safe field of one-to-one Christological analogies. A grammar master who wanted to convey neoplatonic lessons about the embodiment of revelation in language would have to tread carefully if his base text were Theodulus. He would have to lift the poem out of the elementary classroom and teach it in a sophisticated way. Prudentius would have offered no such pedagogical difficulties because it

23. On the rhetorical strategies of these two works, see Smith, *Prudentius' Psychomachia*, 172–73, and Green, "Genesis," 61–65.

presented straightforward examples of allegory, each emblem representing Christ in a different but direct way.

There may also have been some lingering distrust among the Florentine masters about putting the thoroughgoing Greek mythologies of Pseustis into children's hands. The conservative Giovanni Dominici did not object to the *Ecloga Theoduli*, indeed he recommended it, but he did worry about Ovid and other mythographers. As the surviving elementary readers prove, Ovid, Horace, and Virgil were safely relegated in the grammar schools of Florence to the more advanced *auctores* level, where students could be expected to see that pagan myths were not in any way equivalent to the great Christian mythos. With the *Ecloga Theoduli*, by contrast, the two systems could seem too parallel. Even though Pseustis loses and loses soundly in the contest with Alithia, for long stretches the pagan poet is comfortably, strenuously sure of his own ground. His verses would have required an elaborate commentary both to make them comprehensible and to ensure that they remained in the realm of fiction. They early got such a gloss, by Bernard of Utrecht, who furnished the poem with extensive notes in the twelfth century, exactly the period at which it was being widely adapted in monastic schools. But the reading books of Florence were designed to be used without glosses, so the safeguard they provided was not to hand. It is also possible that the final hymn of Alithia was added to the poem to counteract the poor effect of giving the last word in the original version to Pseustis. If this is so, it would mean that already in the thirteenth century questions were raised about the healthiness of giving such heavy doses of paganism to boys.[24]

Whenever we observe a departure in the Italian schools from widespread usage of northern European or monastic curricula, we should suspect that it was made in response to the needs of urban education.[25] Urban schoolmasters, we must remember, had far less control over their students' reading than did the monk-teachers for whom the *Ecloga Theoduli* or *Chartula* were written. In a religious house, Latin beginners could be of any age; they were not boys at all in many communities. Often, the grammar master was also the novice master and thus lived with the students and supervised every aspect of their religious and intellectual

24. Quinn, "Ps. Theodolus," 384n4. The gloss of Bernard is included in the edition of Huygens.

25. Some valuable methodological observations along these lines are offered by Frova, "La scuola," 124–27.

development. There was plenty of opportunity to keep a close eye on the individual's reading and guide it along morally and doctrinally correct paths. In a closed community it was possible to read such complex and potentially dangerous texts as Theodulus, and even racy and morally ambiguous poetry such as that of Ovid or the medieval Ovidians, without endangering the upbringing of the student. Amusing but carefully circumscribed secular literature could be tolerated as a recreation from the endless round of monastic duties and the earnest dedication to Latin prayer.[26] Even the mendicants, who accepted students only after they had finished an elementary course, could correct heterodox ideas early on, because they required novices to undergo a strict education in a setting of common life.

No such degree of control was possible for the urban grammar master. Although he spent long hours with his seven- to twelve-year-old charges every day, the boys also left his supervision daily. The rare, bright student who studied on his own after school hours would have been beyond expert supervision and capable of going off on unproductive, erroneous, even unorthodox paths. Moreover, Latin school students lived in a world aflood with secular texts in the vernacular, many of them not salutary in the conventional Latin or mendicant sense. Nor would the rest of their day have had the careful structure of the monastic community life; it could be filled with bad companions and bad books alike.

For city youths, the Latin school was not part of everyday, family-centered experience but set apart from it. It was, as we have seen repeatedly, an initiation into a realm of elitist and esoteric high culture. Since the context of Latin study did not allow for the continual supervision of the students' reading, there was an urgent need for the grammar masters to establish particularly tight control over the moral content of the works used for teaching: both parents and religious authorities would have been alarmed if any other situation obtained.

In the *Regola del governo di cura familiare*, written about 1401 for the advice of Bartolomea degli Olbizzi, a noblewoman constrained to raise

26. Grendler notes a similar contrast in late sixteenth-century Venice, where closely supervised church school students were permitted to read Plautus, a text not thought suitable for students in the lay schools of the day. He elsewhere remarks the strong preference of the early humanist grammar masters Barzizza, Guarino, and Vittorino da Feltre for boarding schools, precisely for the sake of ensuring close control over the intellectual and moral development of their young students. This again mirrors the practice of the medieval monastic schools, but not of the urban ones of the trecento. See Grendler, *Schooling*, 52, 57, 130.

her sons in the absence of her exiled husband, the Dominican preacher Giovanni Dominici expressed just such concerns about the chaotic state of urban elementary schools. He assumed that the only real locus of moral control was the home and that sending children out to school was a dangerous practice, at least in his own day:

> And since I have already touched upon the matter of writing, you must without fail set your boys to learn to read as virtuously as possible. With the world as it is, you will put the boy in danger if you send him to study with monks or clerics; they are all much alike, and he will learn little. In the old days good boys learned well from clerics and became good men; now everything is overturned and the situation amounts to mixing the horses' hay with fire, or worse. If you send the boy to the common school—where there collects a great crowd of children who are uncontrolled, miserable, given over to evil and resistant to good—I fear he will merely lose within one year what he has struggled to achieve in seven.[27]

Dominici probably accomplished little more with this tirade than to discourage his poor friend; but the sharp contrast of home and school environments is interesting. It tells us that mendicant preachers of a conservative mold like Dominici, and with them their many spiritual followers, distrusted the existing schools. These included schools run by priests and monks, who could not be trusted as once upon a time, and also the chaotic lay schools, where the masters had license to teach what they would and maintained little control over the behavior of the students.

Dominici was more worried about the bad environment than about specific texts. He goes on to recommend some traditional readings, including *un poco di poetizzata Scrittura santa nello Aethiopum terras*, as he calls Theodulus after its incipit. This phrase, "a bit of versified Scripture," may also imply that Dominici felt this text should be excerpted and not read in full, or merely that his recollection of it was dim. In any case, he was recommending the texts of the good old days which were studied with a regularity (and, we might suspect, a lack of imagination) that seemed laudable to him. He obviously did not see any theoretical danger in the *Ecloga Theoduli* itself; but like any other text he thought it needed to be taught in a carefully policed and controlled context. Dominici wrote partly in reaction to the ideas of the humanists, who proposed broader

27. *Regola*, ed. Salvi, 133.

study of classical authors, even for young children. But he also reflected Florentine ideas about public morality and pedagogy that were much older.

Dominici's truculent opinions are a reminder that every urban schoolmaster in the trecento had to deal with parents who had learned public morality from mendicant preachers. The friars consistently refused to get into the business of teaching elementary reading and writing or Latin grammar themselves, but their sermons provided elementary education of a sort that reached a much larger public than any formal schools did. The parents of Latin school students might not themselves know Latin, but they had a broad vernacular culture and a sense of morality that was mendicant in spirit. This mendicant worldview included familiarity with many biblical stories and saints' tales, devotion to the Blessed Virgin and ideals of family life associated with her cult, and sometimes very puritanical notions about public morality in such areas as dress, manners, political duty, sexuality, and keeping the peace.

The urban grammar master had to satisfy the constant demands of paying parents for both orthodoxy and good order. Parents not only insisted on good academic performance, they also expected that their sons would be kept hard at work and away from unhealthy influences. Certainly the parents did not want to think their children might stray from Christian orthodoxy, and not a few might have questioned putting a book filled with pagan stories into the hands of a young boy. No such stigma would have attached to charming Aesop or staid Cato. But Theodulus, like Ovid and the neo-Ovidians, might have worried the less imaginative parents, especially those who themselves had little or no Latin and could understand only enough of their child's schoolbooks to know that the subject was pagan mythology or sexual farce. Early on in the *Ecloga Theoduli*, for example, Pseustis eagerly recounts the bloodthirsty patricide committed by Jupiter. This was not a theme even a liberal-minded and classically trained paterfamilias would welcome, much less the merchant father who was sending his sons to Latin school for the first time in his family's history.

Grammar masters of the fourteenth century inherited much more from the monastic schools than individual texts, and more from the mendicants than puritanical ideas of public behavior and a distrust of heterodoxy. They also inherited a strong sense of the value of small-scale, text-based intellectual communities. Such communities functioned in terms of commonplaces embedded in texts with widely held moral values. Every intellectual act was text based. The primary lesson of early Latin training was in the correct reading of commonplaces in texts chosen specifically for this purpose. This method required a high level of control at the early stages. The open-endedness of rhetorically construed texts meant that they were, by design, subject to multiple readings, so that the student had first to be taught to test his own reading against the moral commonplaces of the community and then, guided by orthodox, common wisdom, to construct new, more personal moral meanings. We find in the next chapter that this standard had much to do with the inclusion or exclusion of school texts, and with the ways they were used in the classroom. Service to the textual community was the norm by which all such judgments were made.

In Florence, some grammar masters thought that the *Chartula* and *Ecloga Theoduli* were of limited service to the Latin worldview they were developing for sons of the urban oligarchy. We cannot be sure if their objections were principally stylistic or moral. Both objections could be raised, and, given what we know about the rest of the curriculum at Florence before the advent of humanism, moral reasons would certainly seem to have provided the stronger motive.[28] In either case, the grammar masters felt that the additional labor of teaching texts so closely designed for use in monastic situations did not always repay the effort.

Does the relatively small emphasis laid on monastic texts such as the *Chartula* and Theodulus also betray a humanistic or prehumanistic approach to the elementary Latin curriculum at Florence? Probably not. Humanism was growing influential in the mid-fourteenth century, but it was still confined to a few sophisticated writers and university men. The earliest humanists criticized the medieval pedagogy they had suffered, but they did not develop a program distinct from what they had inherited. When they did begin to criticize medieval practices at the end of the century, the humanists attacked Prosper and Prudentius as well as Theodulus and *Chartula*, while traditionalists defended the whole of the older system indiscriminately.

The limitation of the use of these monastic texts at Florence can almost surely be explained in large part by their limited applicability to urban contexts. Indeed, it is remarkable that they retained as much prestige as they did. This is testimony to the essential conservatism of the discipline. Still, the Florentine grammar masters were no fools; everything we have

---

28. The humanists, by contrast, objected almost entirely on stylistic grounds; see Garin, *Pensiero*, 91–92.

seen of their work so far tells us that they were resourceful and above all pragmatic. They could find better moral applications for their beloved Prosper and Aesop than for some of the other texts, so the former remained the backbone of the curriculum while the less easily used texts became elective.

# READING TEXTS
## *Medieval Ovidians*

Among the texts that appear in our census of Tuscan reading books of the fourteenth century, the most popular were clearly pagan Aesop on the one hand and Christian Prosper and Prudentius on the other. Beyond these favorites, the preferences of teachers of the period are less clear. We have looked at the way they may have treated the monastic themes of the *Chartula* and *Ecloga Theoduli*, two books that, though popular elsewhere, were never favorites in Italy. The remaining texts on the list are also medieval products, and most could be classed loosely as courtesy books. But the constant moralizing given to the school authors effectively rendered them all courtesy books; all school texts were read with the aim of inculcating moral habits of behavior.

A rather more impressive unity in the remaining group emerges if we look closely at their dates of composition. The verse *Physiologus* is assignable to ca. 1080 but was used widely in the schools only from the early twelfth century. The comedic poetry of Vitalis of Blois was written sometime between 1120 and 1150. The *Elegia* of Henry of Settimello dates quite securely to the early 1190s. Also from the twelfth century is the *Doctrina rudium*, a classroom etiquette book of the "five keys of wisdom" sort from which the two later courtesy books on our list derive. Virtually all the remaining texts, then, are products of thee twelfth-century Renaissance in France or imitate such works. In literary terms, they are of the *aetas Ovidiana.*[1]

---

1. On twelfth-century Ovidianism, see Knoespel, *Narcissus*, and McGregor, "Ovid at School." Editions used for the texts discussed in this chapter are Cremaschi, ed., *Enrico da Settimello*; Eden, ed., *Theobaldi Physiologus*; Vitalis of Blois, *Geta*, ed. Bertini; and

Ovidianism, indeed, is almost the only thing these texts have in common. Significantly, I think, it is not an Ovidianism of theme but one concerned with verse forms, vocabulary, and poetic diction. Certainly there is little thematic unity between the allegorizing bestiary *Physiologus*, the bombastic Henry of Settimello, the earnest etiquette book maxims, and the irreverent ironies and blatant obscenities of the *Geta*. In the matter of diction and verse form, however, these works have much in common and are related as well to Walter the Englishman's twelfth-century Aesop. Over and above a continuing practice in grammatical forms and vocabulary, offered by all the texts in the curriculum, there were several important lessons to be learned from the medieval Ovidians: economy and piquancy of expression, especially in the rhymed distichs and leonine hexameters that were favored for sententious moralizing; the ability to use well-chosen words to penetrate psychological realities; and the value of language mastery for expounding truth and exposing falsehood.[2]

These pedagogical aims accord well with what we have already seen was a widespread medieval approach to pagan and patristic texts, still very much in evidence in trecento Tuscany. Language use and language mastery were not ends in themselves but clearly subservient to moral aims. Language, even in the form of urbane and elegant Ovidian stylistics, was not to be mastered for any but Christian moral ends; and true mastery of language necessarily involved both self-control and selfless devotion to the good of others. The Ovidian style as developed in twelfth-century France was exuberant and extrovert. It could contribute powerfully to a communitarian moral rhetoric if carefully aimed and well regulated. Above all, the ability of the neo-Ovidians to observe and describe human emotional life was admired; this too could be turned to moral ends.

It should be noted, however, that neo-Ovidian texts occur considerably less frequently in Tuscan schoolbooks than do Aesop, Prosper, and Prudentius, and less frequently in Italy than in northern Europe. This must mean that, whereas every schoolboy was expected to master the latter authors, there was less agreement on how important the Ovidian imitations were. In particular, the risqué comedies by Vitalis of Blois, Matthew of Vendôme, and others, although widely popular outside Tuscany, seem

---

Vidmanová-Schmidtová, ed. *Quinque claves sapientiae*, for Bonvesin de la Riva's *Vita scholastica* and the anonymous *Doctrina rudium*. Essential for the manuscript tradition of Vitalis of Blois is *Der "Geta"*, ed. Paeske, on which Bertini's text is based.

2. Cf. Garin, *Pensiero*, 58–63; McGregor, "Ovid at School," 30–31.

to have been suspect in the eyes of Florentine schoolmasters. By any purely literary standard, the *Geta* or the *Pamphilus* are vastly superior to the limping verses of Henry of Settimello; but Henry's *Elegia* survives in more Florentine school copies than all the medieval comedies combined. The *Physiologus*, meanwhile, the most cryptic and grammatically obscure of these Ovidian pieces, was the most popular in the classroom, a reminder that simplicity was not a criterion in the choice of reading texts. The occurrence of these texts in Florentine schools also differs from the overall survival rates of these same texts in Italy. In Tuscany at least, Henry's work and the *Physiologus* seem to have been valued largely as school texts, whereas the *Geta* and other poems like it were popular only in anthologies for readers of other sorts.[3]

Henry of Settimello is a special case in that he is the only Florentine author on the list. His popularity at Florence may reflect a certain favorite son status. It certainly could not have hurt that the *Elegia* is directed to an unnamed bishop of Florence and that it is roundly critical of abuses in the hierarchical church. This last is a perennial theme in medieval Ovidian verse, but the specific references to Florence might have made this piece seem applicable to the controversies between Florentine politicians and churchmen of the mid-1300s.[4]

Henry is open and even self-advertising about his sources, calling on the principal ones at the start of the poem: "If Ovid, if Virgil's muse, if the sounding horn of Lucan commend me, then my fortune will be just barely assured."[5] So much of the poem reflects the diction of just these authors— Ovid, Lucan, and the lyric Virgil—that Henry must have seen himself, and been considered by schoolmasters later, as introducing classical lyric usage to contemporary themes.

---

3. Cf. Velli, "Petrarca, Bocaccio," 243–54, esp. 242–43, 249–50. For surviving manuscripts of *Geta*, see Bertini, 160–64; Paeske, 8–66; Avesani, *Quattro miscellanee*, 83–88. For Henry of Settimello, the manuscript lists of Cremaschi, *Elegia*, 19–22, and "Enrico," 177–206, although limited, are the most recent ones to be found. Viscardi presents a rather different view of the place of Henry in the curriculum, arguing that in monastic schools he was used in the same way as ancient and patristic texts; see "Lettura degli *auctores* moderni," 867–73. As we have seen, the Tuscan manuscripts suggest a different pattern of use in the urban schools.

4. In particular there are references to the papacy, academic politics, and the secular clergy in III.191–250, and IV.31–40; *Elegia*, ed. Cremaschi, 74–78, 80; cf. Cremaschi, "Enrico," 195. For more on the significance of Henry, see Witt, "Medieval Italian Culture," 49.

5. *Elegia*, I.17–18, ed. Cremaschi, 26.

Henry's themes are straightforward and clearly presented in short, often exclamatory sentences. He rarely carries a thought or grammatical construction beyond two distichs; when possible he attempts to fit his ideas into a single pair of verses. There are relatively few difficult or obscure passages, but a wealth of rather academically applied figures of speech stud the poem. All of this made the piece useful for teaching; as Filippo Villani remarked, it is "highly appropriate for those learning the first art."[6]

Henry is fond of using different forms derived from the same root for rhetorical effect, a figure common to all the medieval Ovidians and one we have observed above in reference to the verse Aesop. This style provided classroom readers with drills in miniature: *Nocte gemo, gemino gemitus cumulusque dolorum / crescit* [By night I weep and redouble my weeping; the crowd of my woes grows].[7] A similarly drill-like passage is this:

> *Cur michi, seve, noces? Cur? Cur? Dic.*
> *Nescio. Nescis?*
> *Ergo quid innocuo, Juppiter alte, noces?*
> . . . . . . . . . . . . . . . . . . . . . . . . . . . . .
> *qui nocet innocuo quique nocere cupit.*

[Why, o cruel one, do you harm me? Why? Why? Speak! I do not know why. You don't know why? Why then, high Jupiter, do you harm a harmless one. . . . He who harms the harmless, he truly sets out to harm.][8]

Glosses in the surviving school manuscripts call attention to just these features of the text and to others that could be developed to good effect in the elementary classroom. Mythological characters are frequent, as when Henry compares his sufferings rather indiscriminately to those of Tantalus, Niobe, Job, Cadmus, and Tristan, all within six lines.[9] These names gave the glossator plenty to annotate and teachers presumably went well

6. Cremaschi, "Enrico," 204; *Elegia*, ed. Marigo, 25: *primam discentibus artem aptissimus.*
7. *Elegia*, I.181–82, ed. Cremaschi, 40; my translations throughout this chapter. Bianchini, "Arrigo," 861–62, shows that some of these wordplays are direct translations from Henry's Ovidian sources.
8. *Elegia*, I.51–58, ed. Cremaschi, 30.
9. *Elegia*, I.93–98, ed. Cremaschi, 32–34. The invocation of Tristan here is echoed elsewhere and joined to frequent references to Arthur and other Arthurian figures. Henry's sources for this are in the French romances he seems to have known directly and well, according to Bianchini, "Arrigo," esp. 862–63. This is the only poem used in the Florentine schools to include any significant mention of courtly literature.

beyond what the manuscripts attest, for whenever the students clearly needed help with an unfamiliar word they would have gotten it.

Occasional neologisms also required comment, so *neronizant* (literally, "they play Nero") is glossed in one manuscript as *crudeles sunt uelut Nero* [they are cruel, like Nero].[10] The manuscripts, however, do not tell us if the teachers approved of such obscurity, only that they realized it needed explanation. Reader response to Henry's bizarre style can also be tested by reference to the translations of the poem, known as the *Arrighetto*. One translator despaired of the metaphor in *neronizant*, but we know he got the point (with the help of a gloss?) for he wrote *incrudeliscono* [they grow cruel].[11]

The great popularity of the *Arrighetto* tells us that the themes of the poem were widely appreciated. So it was not merely a model of style but also a work that evoked real pleasure or seemed genuinely useful. What were the themes that seemed so valuable? We can make a start at answering this question by noting that the *volgare* version was called by a diminutive, *Arrighetto*. This title, "Little Harry" we would say in modern English, appears in manuscripts of the *volgare* text, in literary references to it, and in numerous inventories of books. It was also used to describe the Latin text: witness Boccaccio, who lumps it together with other school authors in a Latin letter referring to the Latin curriculum.[12] Henry and his work are also sometimes referred to as *Henrigettus* and *Pauper Henricus*, by way of relatinizing the *volgare* diminutive. Poor Henry or Little Harry was both the author and the book, just as the latter-day Poor Richard stands for Franklin's character and his almanac. The diminutive reflects the elementary nature of the text, Henry's hard-luck story, his attempts to cope with his career setbacks philosophically, and perhaps even the short proverbs embedded in and frequently extracted from the text.

Henry is visited and consoled by Lady Philosophy and, like Boethius in the same difficulty, he is portrayed as Poor Henry in need of considerable help. The help he gets is moral-rhetorical. His lamentations in the first books of the *Elegia* are set pieces of complaint and invective against Fortune, personified in Book II as a complacent old woman. These tirades vent his ill feelings and exhaust him, so that the rhetorical ministrations of Philosophy will serve to reconstruct his character and render him ready to return to an active, rhetorically productive life. Philosophy's first speech is

10. Census I.30, fol. 41r; cf. *Elegia*, ed. Cremaschi, 28.
11. Ibid., 29.
12. Corazzini, ed., *Le lettere*, 194.

explicit about this. Henry, she says, has been blinded by the fury of his own self pity and has forgotten everything he learned at school.[13] He thinks himself wiser than Cato and other philosophers; he is unwilling to continue to work at the attainment of wisdom.[14] Philosophy is scolding Henry, reminding him of those most elementary lessons of grammar, sober hard work and humility before the authors of the past. She complains against the more academic pretensions of Bologna-trained Henry too, for she sees these as a betrayal of the fundamental, communitarian aims of philosophical study.

Eventually, Philosophy's consolation turns into a miniature courtesy book containing eighty-one distichs' worth of advice, followed by a brief reading list (almost all pagan moral authors) and some vague but edifying counsel about setting out again into the world armed with virtue and self-knowledge.[15] Nowadays, we would call this last phase making Henry "marketable" again; and we would not be far off the mark, for in the last pages of his long work the poet dedicates it to the bishop of Florence, exactly the man whose sacking of Poor Henry had caused the despairing lament with which the piece began.

Necessarily, we do not know the end of the story, for the essence of the epistolary form used is that there is no reply, and the point of the consolation is that worldly honors are not worth striving for. The poem's near circularity, however, moving as it does from Henry's firing to his bid for rehire, offers several concrete lessons in effective writing. In the course of his lament Henry manages to criticize his detractors, excuse the actions that apparently got him fired, demonstrate his learning and mastery of style, philosophize a bit about the intellectual life, and provide his readers with a small courtesy book. All this is extrovert, primary rhetoric. It has practical ends both in terms of career enhancement and for the sake of self-knowledge, the rhetorical key to self-improvement. In the classroom, the open-endedness of the exercise could be turned to good use in encouraging students to see the double value of persuasive writing: first the articulation of a moral stand, and only then the achievement of some practical end.

On a deeper level, however, Henry of Settimello remains Poor Henry. He stands for the unavoidable misery of the human condition, not in a pessimistic sense but in a fatalistic Christian one. Henry is twice cited by

---

13. *Elegia*, III.17–18, ed. Cremaschi, 62.
14. *Elegia*, III.85–100, ed. Cremaschi, 66–68.
15. *Elegia*, IV.41–211, ed. Cremaschi, 79–90.

the great Florentine Dominican preacher, Jacopo Passavanti, to the point of the vicissitudes of fortune and the misery of human life generally.[16] The only true remedy for misfortune is moral rhetoric, and the models for this are exactly those Henry cites: the elegiac Ovid of exile, the partisan but strict Lucan, and by implication (one his fourteenth-century readers understood well) the great consoler Boethius.

If Henry were not quite so earnest we would suspect him of parodying Boethius. After all, Henry had merely lost his benefice, whereas Boethius had already faced political disgrace and was under threat of death when his *Consolation* was composed. Rather than a parody of Boethius, however, Henry actually gives his reader an honest imitation of the sixth-century sage (and of the late Ovid) in the form of a self-parody, though not a very funny one. In Book I, Henry is self-consciously pathetic and exaggeratedly, absurdly self-pitying. In Book II, he makes himself out to be nearly a madman. The excuse is that Fortune has appeared and argues that Henry deserved no better than he got because no one deserves better; indeed, no one should expect anything but change from Fortune. Henry replies with insults, but no constructive phrase making.

At this point Henry's readers are expected to recognize his real poverty, that of an educated man and talented verse maker whose prodigious literary effort is misdirected. For two books they have listened to Henry's emotional crisis in personal, self-directed terms. This is a magnificent demonstration of bad rhetoric, that is, technically brilliant but immoral language use. Henry has failed to realize that the only constructive use of rhetoric is to direct it outward, to the reform of the individual in the context of a community. In Book III, with the appearance of Dame Philosophy, Henry at last sits still and listens. Listening, he learns, is the essence of wisdom, because it provides a social context in which to measure personal experience. The rest of the book contains an exhortation to humility and a catalogue of virtues; these are the rhetorical exercises that produce true moral reform and so serve society.

The pedagogical point of studying Henry was akin to that of studying Boethius, namely, to learn that patience rewards the effort not only in objective distress but also in the classroom, which mimics life by requiring hard work without immediate hope of reward. Rhetorical consolation involves the exploration of sentiment, emotion, and loss in the larger context of social discourse. On the merely emotional level it can be

16. Kaeppeli, "Opere latine," 152n. The glosses cited by Marigo in his edition of the *Elegia* are also to this point.

calming and reassuring, but its true aim is long term, gradual, and communitarian, not just personal. The individual's morally constructive rhetorical act is to express his personal ideas in terms of civilizational commonplaces and thereby to reassert his place as a Christian citizen worthy of salvation. I noted a similar notion of Christian citizenship in the last section of Prosper's anthology.

Henry of Settimello's *Elegia* differs from the more ancient and more popular texts in the Florentine school canon in terms of its manuscript tradition. Almost without exception the Tuscan manuscripts that contain the Latin *Arrighetto* contain no other work, by contrast to the larger manuscript tradition in which Henry is most frequently found in anthologies.[17] When there is a second or additional works, these are in a different hand and written on gatherings completely separate from those that contain Henry's *Elegia*. Of itself this pattern is not unusual. Many other surviving Tuscan readers have single texts, and most were designed to circulate as small, pamphletlike booklets. Many of the "anthologies" that survive were assembled later from such booklets or from groups of them that had already been partially assembled. But no other text in our census appears alone with the absolute regularity of Henry. Another curiosity of the tradition is that two of the three copies of the small monastic courtesy book called *Johannes abbas de septem virtutibus* found in our census are associated with Henry's work, in both cases bound in with the *Arrighetto* but designed and written separately (Census I.41 and I.7).

It is not clear whether these two singularities of the tradition are related. Certainly the fact that Henry's work stands alone argues for the possibility that these manuscripts, though written in perfectly standardized Florentine reader form, may have had other than schoolboy uses. Prosper of Aquitaine's epigrams eventually came to be used outside the classroom as a marriage gift book.[18] It is entirely possible that favorite son Henry had an audience beyond the grammar schools too. His work was well known in its vernacular form, and the Latin was used by the secular poets of the fourteenth century. Its themes would have appealed to the large, literate clergy. In any case, the manuscripts are a warning that the texts of the school canon had other uses. Henry's work was, in modern terms, an elective in a curriculum where Prosper and Aesop were required courses.

---

17. Cremaschi, "Enrico," 204.

18. Gehl, "Augustinian Catechism," 108; see also Bec, *Les livres*, 25; Klapisch-Zuber, "Le chiavi," 776; and Ciapelli, "Libri e letture," 280–81.

Given its stylistic dependence on pagan lyricists and the degree to which it addresses rhetorical issues, the *Arrighetto* may have been a transitional text too, that is, one studied late in the latinizing stage, or even as one of the *auctores* in the next class level. Three of the six copies of Henry's work in our census contain a gloss that supports this hypothesis. The most developed version of it is in a late fourteenth-century book (Census I.5). This commentary explicates at some length the rhetorical strategies used by Henry at various points of the text. Its skeleton is a series of rhetorical *divisiones* that also occur in earlier manuscripts of the *Arrighetto*, including one of the other two in our sample. Commentaries like this one which concentrate on naming and defining rhetorical devices make sense as guides for students working on Latin composition. A clue as to the pedagogical import of this sort of commentary may be found in yet another copy of it, in MS 1206 of the Biblioteca Universitaria at Bologna. This book is a miscellany clearly intended for *auctores*-level study: Henry's work keeps company with Virgilian lyric poetry, a staple of those who really want to master Latin usage for literary and not just professional purposes.

What, then, of John the Abbot? The work itself is an unremarkable and traditional guide to the seven cardinal sins and their corresponding virtues. As its authorial tag would have indicated to fourteenth-century readers, it presupposes the monastic path as the most perfect form of Christian life; but there is both catechetical and memorial value in this sort of schematic diagram of moral virtue. No other Florentine schoolbook is so simply organized in categorical moral terms. This is doubtless the logic of its occasional appearance at Florence. The version of the text current in Italy is shorter than that used north of the Alps, omitting, curiously, a section on avarice and almsgiving and one on gluttony and sobriety. The omission makes the piece particularly monastic in flavor and seems particularly ill adapted to urban school use, although it should be said that the author did consciously attempt to expound moral situations not directly concerned with monastic life. Still, the moral code espoused is strongly traditional and monastic in feel: humility, obedience, meekness, and silence are the principal themes.

The poem does have a beautiful preface that propounds ethical harmony achieved through language, a theme we have seen before:

*Ethica dulcisonis uerba notabo modis.*
*Verba nocent, aptis si non moderentur habenis;*

*Turbat et armonicam dissona corda lyram.*
*A nostris igitur fugiat transgressio uerbis;*
*Transgrediens gladius ledere sepe solet.*

[I will express moral words in sweet-sounding measures. Words harm if they are not reined in rightly; a dissonant chord untunes even the harmonious harp. Let wrong use flee, then, from our words; the wrong-wielded sword often does great harm.][19]

The wordplay here is unusual only in its thoroughgoing use of musical metaphors, which effectively make the point that language is rightly used only if it is strictly measured and in tune with the ethical good of both author and audience. In contrast to the sweet harmonies of right language stands the uncontrolled sword of ill-used speech, a violent metaphor indeed.

Although there is no manuscript or literary evidence to demonstrate the point, we might speculate that John the Abbot's poem was well adapted to mendicant teaching and preaching at Florence. Its association with Henry, who attacked the corrupt secular clergy, would accord with this hypothesis; and the text itself is of a sort common in preaching manuals. The text also contains a considerable amount of moralizing animal imagery of a popular sort that was common in preaching sourcebooks. This would have added to its charm and utility in the classroom. The section on envy and love is particularly rich in such images and in citations of Old Testament figures as well. The constant measuring rod of vice is its embodiment of animal values and the corresponding mark of virtue is the way it conduces to harmony among humans.

The relation of preaching to elementary teaching is one that, as far as I know, has never been systematically explored for any part of the Middle Ages or Renaissance.[20] To some degree this lack reflects a distinction made in the period itself, for professionals segregated the *ars predicandi* in separate treatises and formulated elaborate rules for it. Common sense tells us, however, that every schoolboy's education could have been consolidated by comparisons he could make between his classroom lessons

---

19. Klein, "Johannis abbatis," 205.

20. Filosa, *La favola*, 23–31, and more recently Delcorno, *Exemplum*, address the relation of sermon rhetoric, and especially of collections of sermon exempla, to fable literature, a staple of classroom practice. Other aspects of the problematic relation between mendicant preachers and secular teachers are explored in my "Preachers, Teachers, and Translators: The Social Meaning of Latin Study in Trecento Florence," forthcoming in *Viator* 25 (1994).

and the sermons that were a universal form of devotion, education, and entertainment in the trecento. Moreover, every schoolmaster could assume a certain familiarity among his students with prayers, Bible stories, religious images, and other commonplaces of preaching. Among the most common of such commonplaces were the animal fables of Aesop and the animal symbols of the bestiary. We must turn next to the best-known school bestiary of the fourteenth century.[21]

The *Physiologus* of "Theobald" (his identity is disputed) was one of the earliest fruits of the so-called twelfth-century Renaissance. In fact, it was written before 1080 but saw its first wide dissemination in the early twelfth century. Like Walter the Englishman's Aesop, it is a versification of a Greek text widely known in the West in earlier prose translations. From the thirteenth century onward, *Physiologus* was by far the most popular bestiary. A distinct group of manuscripts of the thirteenth and fourteenth centuries attest to an Italian vulgate version of the text, presumably because of its wide use in the schools. Again like Walter's Aesop, the leonine hexameters of Theobald eventually drove most other translations from the field, especially, it would seem, in Italy south of the Apennines. There is some evidence that the early diffusion of the text in southern and central Italy was due to the influence of the school of Montecassino, just as the continuing popularity of the text into the fifteenth century can be attributed to the interest of monastic readers and copyists.[22]

The reasons for monastic interest in the text are not hard to find. Each of the thirteen poems treats of a single animal, referring it directly and immediately to an allegorical meaning, almost always Christological, although there are sometimes also everyday moral lessons. In the end the bestiary becomes an imitation of Christ, and Theobald gives it an epigram that directs the rhetorical exercise itself to the savior: "Now that this poem is done, praise and glory to Christ, whom I hope these verses of Theobald please, even if they please no one else."[23] The opening words of this couplet became a standard pious formula transcribed by generations of students into their readers.

The iconic value of the poem no doubt contributed to its continuing popularity both inside the monasteries and outside. Almost every one of

21. On the bestiary genre, see Filosa, *La favola*, 33–34; on its use as a mnemonic text, see Carruthers, *Book of Memory*, 126–29.

22. Eden, *Theobaldi*, 15; cf. Henkel, *Studien zum Physiologus*, 36–38.

23. Eden, *Theobaldi*, 72, my translation.

the animals in *Physiologus* could be seen in the mosaic cycles of the Florence baptistery, for example. Every schoolchild in the city would have known that writhing mass of human, animal, and fantastic figures. Bright and observant ones could have adduced other examples, more familiar still, from their neighborhood churches.[24] Some of the allegories on these very images would have been presented to them in sermons by preachers who in their own schooldays had memorized the *Physiologus*. As Mary Carruthers has remarked, moreover, the bestiaries were particularly well adapted to memory training because of the vivid word pictures they contain. Once learned, these could serve as visual markers for a wide variety of moral precepts arranged on any sort of memory grid.[25]

When it came time for schoolboys to memorize the text for themselves, they would recognize it as their own initiation into some of the most widely known commonplaces of Christian high culture. This pedagogy of recognition operated with several of the school texts. The students' wish to learn the material was reinforced by the whole social structure of preaching. Even a small child would have been able to realize the power of the skilled preacher and the admiration with which he was regarded. By school age he would have recognized some of the deeper structural messages in the act of preaching as well: how, for example, the pulpit segregated and elevated the cleric, and how it symbolized his existence in a separate world of learning that merely touched on the everyday world in the moment of the sermon. Soon enough it would also become clear to the young boy that church careers were, more than most others, open to individuals of all social classes who were smart and diligent and conformist. Above all, the church was open to those who could manipulate the commonplaces of Latin thought through memory and eloquence.

Although the animal symbols of the *Physiologus* were commonplace, they owned a certain esotericism too, because the allegories were frankly mystical. They could also be complicated:

XIII. THE TURTLE-DOVE. The turtle-dove does not know how to love idly; for once married to one husband she will always proceed in his company and remain by his side night and day, and no one will see her apart from her husband. But if she is widowed and deprived of him, even so she will not afterwards marry a friend: she will fly alone and sit alone, and will hold him

24. Giovanni Dominici specifically advised mothers to have religious images at home or, if that was not feasible, to take small children to the churches to see the examples of virtue present in the decorations there; see *Regola*, 132–33.

25. Carruthers, *Book of Memory*, 126.

in her heart as if alive, and in patient waiting she will remain chaste. So each faithful soul is made happy by union with a man, for Christ is married to her when he fills her heart full of himself; and living virtuously she always clings to him, and seeks no other friend though death has taken him. She believes that he survives in heaven, and looks to him to appear unchanged from there to judge the whole microcosm.[26]

For a monk, an image like this one would sooner or later merge into the broad stream of monastic preaching on the Song of Songs. An urban schoolboy might well eventually discover this body of literature, particularly through mendicant preaching; but the doorway to mystical theology it opened might be rather more an opportunity offered than taken. We need not doubt, however, that, traveled or not, the mystical road would have been recognized for what it was considered, the supreme inheritance of ancient Christianity.

It was, moreover, a rhetorical inheritance, one as intimately bound up with language study as the more familiar political and sermon rhetoric of trecento Florence. The study of Prosper opened up Augustinian moral philosophy to the literary initiate. In the *Physiologus*, the new Latin reader would get a first written taste of allegorical reading of symbols. The process would have been familiar from preaching, but here the invitation to the Latin student is to study the process in written form for himself under the guidance of the schoolmaster. In the way of all initiatory experiences, this one was also an invitation. It opened the door to an intellectual tradition of many centuries' duration and great prestige.

Of all the texts in the school canon, the hardest to explain in moral-rhetorical terms is the *Geta* of Vitalis of Blois, a twelfth-century cleric who based his work loosely on Plautus's *Amphitruo*. It is a cautionary satire on school learning, to be sure, but the dubiously moral plot is constructed around the confrontation of a gullible husband who has been absent studying at Athens and his wife who has meanwhile been seduced by Jupiter. The dialogue is full of sexual innuendo and double meaning and much of it is blatantly, offensively vulgar. Worse, the resolution of the plot depends on cynical, amoral self-delusion. All the characters have reason to doubt the wife's final explanation of her actions, but all agree happily to it because each of them gains some personal advantage from it.

The principal characters of the twelfth-century play are not the husband

---

26. Eden, *Theobaldi*, 69, where also this translation.

and wife but two cartoon character slaves, Birria, a glutton who stays home with the wife and slothfully neglects his duties, and the title figure Geta, who travels to Athens and there picks up a parodic version of the philosophy his master is studying. In a famous and much quoted set piece at the middle of the poem, Geta proves conclusively to himself that he does not exist, using the powerful but confusing tool of philosophical dialectic. The moral problems the text provides are not at all disguised. Vitalis of Blois's introduction states the plot baldly:

> Amphitrion, completely dedicated to a long study of Greek science, remained far from home in the company of Geta. Jupiter in false clothing came to Alcmena accompanied by Archas. She believed him to be her husband. When Amphitrion finally returns he sends Geta on ahead, but the slave, confused by Archas, convinces himself that he does not exist. It pains him not to exist and, further battered by Archas, he retreats and tells his master what he has seen. The latter is pained in turn, and arms himself. Jupiter, well satisfied, leaves with Archas. The others search for the adulterer. They find no one; they rejoice; the argument is dropped; anger subsides.[27]

All mitigating circumstances, and not a few essential details of the plot, are omitted in this summary, and the morally ambiguous complicity with which the play will end is clearly alluded to. We are not, then, to expect any justification, or any justice.

The poet goes on from here to a second prologue in which a further injustice, the writer's lot, is expounded:

> The poet has written some verses and wishes to please, but he is deceived for they please not. The fable fails because no one wants comedy; they are all after serious things, all out to make money. . . . It would be better to remain silent than write verse. The author makes no money, his poem wins no renown. Anyone who enjoys this job is only writing for himself; only he thinks the results are good; only he loves the poem.[28]

The Latin here as elsewhere in the poem is telescopic and proverbial in flavor, and some of these very phrases became commonplace in later writers' laments.

The poem was not originally intended for schoolchildren. It earned great popularity almost immediately as an adult, neo-Ovidian satirical

---

27. *Geta*, ed. Bertini, 182; my translations here and below owe much to the fine Italian version provided by Bertini.

28. Ibid., 184.

piece, appreciated for its deft, comic language. This is why it also came to be read as a school text soon after its appearance. By contrast to its frequent appearance in northern European school anthologies, however, relatively few Italian copies are known. Only sixteen of the surviving sixty-seven manuscripts are of Italian origin, and only two of these appear in our census of Florentine readers, indicating that the poem, though well known, was not widely considered a reading text for school use in Italy, certainly not in Florence.

The reasons are not hard to seek. The cynicism and vulgarity of the *Geta* simply cannot be explained away. One fourteenth-century Italian commentator put the problem thus:

> In this comedy Amphitrion is an old man, Almena a matron, Mercury a pimp, Jupiter an adulterer, and Geta and also Birria are slaves. . . . This good man [Amphitrion] intends to make the [other] five characters speak. The piece is useful for giving pleasure and somewhat for instruction in morals. The book therefore is to be considered one in ethics, somewhat; and I say "somewhat" advisedly, for it doesn't teach about morals very well.[29]

This scribe's ambivalence is telling. Schoolbooks were supposed to be moralizing. Even when they were not much good for inculcating good behavior or promoting fruitful reflection, they were subsumed under the category of ethics because that was the only one available for legitimate teaching texts.

The *Geta* continued to be admired as a comic piece well into the fifteenth century. Given the doubts expressed even by those who copied it, however, we may surmise that it was given to older boys—or sought out *by* them—primarily for its salacious interest and for the vivid comic language. It was known and used by Boccaccio, even copied by him when he was an adolescent.[30] But the future author of the *Decameron* was not a typical schoolboy; he was one of those unusual students who deliberately went looking for texts straight-laced schoolteachers might not intentionally have put in his way.

When the *Geta* was freely translated into Tuscan *volgare* at the turn of

---

29. Naples, Biblioteca Nazionale, Cod. IV.F.12, as cited in Avesani, *Quattro miscellanee,* 15–16: *in hac comedia Amphitrion est senex, Almena matrona, Mercurius leno, Iuppiter adulter, Geta servus et etiam Birria. . . . Intendit enim iste bonus homo inducere istas quinque personas ad loquendum. Utilitas est delectatio et qualis qualis morum informatio. Supponitur hic liber ethice quali quali, et dico quali quali quia non multum bene de moribus tractat.* The manuscript also contains another advanced school text of doubtful moral application, a version of Ovid's *De remedio amoris.*

30. Florence, Biblioteca Medicea-Laurenziana, Plut. 33, 31.

the fifteenth century, its plot was adapted as a satire against the pretensions of Florentine university teachers. This version was self-standing and did not rely on its audience knowing the Latin of Vitalis, though of course those who did would have been amused by the specific application to Florentine personalities.[31] This might seem to argue for a wide familiarity of the *Geta*, but the Latin version of the poem simply does not occur in schoolbook form often. It certainly never had the status of a standard text in trecento Florentine schools.

A similar broad fortune outside the schools is attested for other comedies, especially the anonymous *Pamphilus*. It survives in numerous northern European manuscripts, and it was known in Italy to Henry of Settimello, Albertano da Brescia, Pier della Vigne, and Brunetto Latini. Even such strict religious writers as Paul of Camaldoli quoted it, and it was translated into Venetian in the mid-twelfth century within twenty years of its composition. The editor of the Venetian version believed that it might be the work of a student, but again, the evidence of our census suggests that by the fourteenth century this text was not given to Italian grammar school boys. No copies at all survive in the form used at Florence for readers in the fourteenth century and only one manuscript I know of could possibly be considered a Tuscan schoolbook.[32]

Three other works, of relatively minor interest for our study, remain to be discussed. These are the *Vita scholastica* of Bonvesin de la Riva (ca. 1250–1313/15), which appears five times in our census; a Pseudo-Boethian prose piece with the title *De disciplina scolarium* (written in France ca. 1250), which appears twice; and the so-called *Doctrina rudium* (also northern, ca. 1200), which appears once. All are collections of maxims on good behavior. The first and last were aimed specifically at student audiences and frequently occur together in non-Italian manuscript sources. The Pseudo-Boethian text covers much the same ground thematically, but it was aimed at prospective teachers rather than at young students.[33]

---

31. Lanza, *Polemiche e berte*, 235–66; Spagnesi, *Utiliter edoceri*, 94–95.

32. In his edition of *Pamphilus*, Pittaluga describes the fortune of this text (41–44). His list of manuscripts is the most complete, but fuller descriptions of some of them are to be found in the edition of Becker. The only Italian manuscript that might be considered a schoolbook is Toledo, cod. 102–11, of the thirteenth century. It is very similar in both script and format to Census I.15, but it contains no elementary glosses; it is an anthology of Ovidian texts, none of which occur elsewhere in our census. On this manuscript, see *Pamphilus*, ed. Becker, 67–68, and Bonilla y San Martín, "Una comedia," 427 (with plate).

33. Edited in *Patrologiae latina* 64:1223–38; and critically by Weijers. Weijers provides the best text available of this mid-thirteenth-century work, probably written at Paris, but her

In only one case, a late one, does any of these three courtesy booklets appear with any other of them in a Florentine schoolbook (Census I.17). Nor do any of them occur in the same school anthology as Henry of Settimello, whose fourth book includes a comparable courtesy treatise. The isolated occurrences of all these little courtesy books are just that, isolated. They were not a systematic part of the grammar school course. Each occurs as an add-on to a book with one other, more important text, or in varied anthologies such as Census I.26, in which Bonvesin's poem appears with Cato, Theodulus, Prudentius, the *Chartula*, the *Physiologus*, Prosper, and Aesop. Their presence in elementary readers is easily understandable, but no one of them achieved, or merited, very wide use.

A student would hardly seem to have needed two of them in any case, since each provides a summary of classroom etiquette accompanied by some general observations on virtues and vices in proverbial form. All the advice is pretty much the same. We cannot dismiss them entirely, for they offer some insights into the classroom situation, but as evidence for teacher-student relationships their value is limited because they offer patterns for all schools everywhere and not particularly for the Italian situation. Together the eight occurrences of the three texts can be counted with six copies of the last book of Henry of Settimello, and two of the *Facetus*, inc. *Moribus et vita*, to give us sixteen examples of courtesy books of this sort in Florentine readers. Apparently grammar masters or parents wanted schoolchildren to study some straightforward guide to good manners, but there was no particular consensus among teachers in favor of any one or two texts. None of them had any substantial authority. All of them make for dull reading today, and if fourteenth-century schoolmasters thought otherwise it was not for any literary merit of the text but because the advice was practical and aimed at inculcating obedience. Only that of Poor Henry is even relieved by competent versification, and only Henry and Bonvesin de la Riva (the only Italian authors of such books) had any name recognition. Indeed, to the degree that there is a clear preference among our Florentine schoolmasters, it is for one of these Italian masters and against the imported, northern European or monastic equivalents.

Let us look at Bonvesin, then, who can stand for the lot. (He reproduces much of the *Doctrina rudium* verbatim, in any case.) Bonvesin de la Riva

---

introduction is singularly unhelpful. Ducci, ed., *Un saggio*, provides a text based on incunable editions that may be closer to the trecento Italian tradition and adds an astute essay on medieval educational psychology. The scant literature on Pseudo-Boethius is cited by Avesani, *Quattro miscellanee*, 19n5, and by Weijers.

was a prominent Milanese grammar master and an important *volgare* author. He is the only lay author to appear on our list of common texts and the only one who could be said to have had a school experience close to that of the Florentine masters of the trecento. Bonvesin introduces his book by expounding the notion that grammar, well mastered, leads to wisdom. This latter ideal is then used to organize the rest of the treatise around five *claves sapientiae*, or keys to wisdom. In Bonvesin's scheme these are (1) fear of God and avoidance of vice, (2) respect for one's teacher, (3) careful reading, (4) posing of thoughtful questions, and (5) diligent memorization. The five keys are not given equal treatment. The third, fourth, and fifth in particular are passed over lightly in a mere thirty, eighteen, and ten lines, respectively. From the point of view of the modern scholar trying to reconstruct pedagogical practice, this is unfortunate, for it is just in these sections that study habits and attitudes are described. The first two sections, by contrast, are lengthy and elaborately subdivided. The important lessons are everyday matters of how to behave. There are five distinct ways to honor one's teacher, for example, and a rather elaborate list of vices to be avoided.[34]

The essential notion of wisdom as a goal in studying Latin is never lost sight of, even amid the otherwise heavy-handed advice. How, we may well ask, does the grammar master Bonvesin expect language study to effect moral behavior? Principally, it seems, through a process of socialization that emphasizes community effort in the search for knowledge. The brief treatment of posing questions, to be encouraged whatever the subject, is almost eloquent about this ideal:

> The fourth key of wisdom advises us to ask frequent questions about doubtful things, for every road is laid open to one who asks directions often. Interrogate your teacher, your companions, and the learned constantly, and even lesser persons if in some way you can learn from them. Do not disdain to learn from the humble. So that you may be raised up safely, seek out the lowly and condemn the haughty. Disdain is foolish for it makes the disdainful unworthy of a noble art.[35]

The social power of language is immense: "Wisely manage your tongue with fine-tuned speech; the tongue, though soft, can shatter hard things."[36]

34. On Bonvesin and the five-keys tradition, see Avesani, "Leggesi"; Bonvesin, *Volgari scelti*, trans. Diehl and Stefanini; and Pecchiai, "Documenti."
35. Vidmanovà-Schmidtovà, *Quinque claves*, 88; my translation here and below.
36. Ibid., 44.

Many of the virtues to be cultivated and vices to be avoided have to do directly with the classroom situation. This is particularly evident in the portion of the poem dealing with respect for the master, but it is present elsewhere too. Since the structure of the school was hierarchical, many of the pertinent virtues are treated in terms taken over directly from the high medieval monastic literature on vices and virtues. A great premium is placed on silence and obedience, for example, and the sins to be avoided include contentiousness, sloth, and *amor turpis, sed plus Sodomitica sordes* [sinful love, and most of all the Sodomite vice], which merits fully fourteen lines.[37] These monastic sounding admonitions are interesting, coming as they do from the thoroughly urban Bonvesin. Although fears of pedophilia and concerns about noisy, even violent fighting between students were voiced in earlier monastic treatises on education, the community life of the monks also provided built-in controls on such behavior that some urbanites thought were not equally well exercised in lay schools. Bonvesin would not have repeated these strictures if they were completely outdated, and there is some reason to think that they were a particular concern in urban settings, not just a holdover from contemplative, monastic treatises.[38]

The rhetorical ideal expounded by Bonvesin was an extrovert one, pragmatically aimed at success in social relationships through the effective use of language in a moral fashion. This is clear in the section on asking questions quoted above; a similar stance is taken in the closing peroration. There we find a thorough example of the interpenetration of good deeds and good study habits, for the passage includes advice to pray, read and write often and carefully, give alms, and treat students and teachers with Christian charity, all in the service of a successful career.[39] These are lay ideals, or at least could be. A set of prose fables that accompany many of the manuscripts of Bonvesin's *Vita scholastica* are similarly secular in subject, concerning the virtues of soldiers, sailors, and farmers as well as individuals identified only in terms of family roles: mother, father, son. It is not clear, in fact, whether the Latin version of these fables is from Bonvesin's pen, but *volgare* versions of them are securely attributed to him and accord with what else we know of his urban, lay outlook.[40]

---

37. Ibid., 49–50.

38. Ducci, ed., *Un saggio*, 34–35, points out that these concerns are voiced in all books on classroom morals, so we cannot assume anything about local usages from their inclusion. Still, sexual abuse of boys seems to have been a particular Florentine worry; cf. Lanza, *Polemiche e berte*, 226–34.

39. Vidmanovà-Schmidtovà, *Quinque claves*, 98–100.

40. Cf. Manzi, "L'exemplum," 1–27.

Perhaps the most telling aspect of Bonvesin's treatise, well adapted as it seems to urban culture, is that it was not more popular in Tuscany. Of the eight trecento Italian manuscripts known to its editor, it is true, fully five saw use in Tuscan grammar schools, making the text more popular in Tuscany than in the north of Italy. But Florentine schoolmasters used the venerable Prosper and Poor Henry's versified advice, both infinitely more old-fashioned, more often than Bonvesin's.

All the thirteenth-century school-manners treatises emphasize wisdom as a goal in studying grammar. This theme was a significant addition to the sort of general advice offered by earlier Christian writers. We may be sure such "modern" Christian presuppositions were employed in studying all the reading texts favored at Florence. Edvige Ducci has correctly re-marked how the pattern of virtues advised by these treatises is based on a Christian neoplatonic psychology of learning.[41] The possibility of moral education exists, in this view, because of the ability of each individual to recreate by imitation the moral-ontological unity of all creation. The direct means for this recreative form of study is imitation, and the medium in the classroom is the affectionate but strictly hierarchical relationship of master and student.

The practical advice in the courtesy books derives directly from this well-developed psychology of learning. Docility, obedience, and attentive-ness are essential attributes of the student, not out of mere deference to the master but because they mimic the correct attitude of the creature toward his creator. Similarly, reciprocal affection between master and student mirrors the relationship of God to man, especially that mediated by the God-man Jesus. This essential relationship of affection accompanied by a hierarchy of power also explains the severity and extreme length of the advice against *luxuria*, especially as that might tend to sexual abuse. The powerful, authoritarian schoolmasters are advised even more strongly on this point than the schoolboys themselves, because only the master was really in a position to police the situation.

Wisdom in this context is the ability to make moral decisions in every-day life, and to do so by analyzing situations in terms of moral categories absorbed through reading and study, that is, Latin study. Only with experience in textual analysis could an individual make moral judgments fully in harmony with community norms. So Latin maintained its privilege as the medium of high culture in part by monopolizing the gateway to sophisticated reading and moral decision making. Well before the human-ist movement was established enough to have an effect on elementary

41. The following summarizes Ducci, ed., *Un saggio*, esp. 17–25, 65–75.

education, we can discern this privileging of Latin in urban Italy. I do not mean to imply by this that Florentine parents of the commercial class favored Latin educations for their children; indeed, the evidence we examine in Chapter 8 suggests the contrary. But medieval prejudices in favor of the power of Latin, so well expressed in Dante's remarks about its utility for science and philosophy,[42] still informed the elementary curriculum, even at the level where the sons of merchants were receiving their first initiation into the universal high culture of the West. This preference for Latin was not yet divorced from its monastic roots, but it was not quite the same either. Mendicant preachers had made Latin over into a tool for the moral education of a nonmonastic public, and their constant resort to Latin sources supported the popular perception that Latin literature was still the repository of high culture and wisdom.

The Pseudo-Boethian *De disciplina scolarium*, which appears twice in our census, is a little-known footnote in the progress of humanist education. It was widely read and commented on by northern European scholastics, but it merits no particular attention from us for its content, since it follows the pattern of the *Doctrina rudium* and Bonvesin rather closely. It is unlikely to have been used in elementary classrooms, because it is aimed at prospective teachers, not students. The attribution to Boethius is interesting, however, because it may explain a passage in Giovanni Dominici's *Regola del governo di cura familiare* (ca. 1401) in which he recommends that students be given the good old books of the ancient Florentines:

> I must say that our forefathers saw things in a clear light when it came to instructing children, while our contemporaries are blind, raising their little ones quite outside the faith. The first thing they used to teach was the psalter and prayers, and if they pushed their children at all beyond that they had the moral sayings of Cato, the fables of Aesop, the teaching of Boethius, the good study of Prosper after Saint Augustine, the philosophy of Prudentius or the "Physiologus," together with a bit of versified Scripture in the "Eclogue" of Theodulus, and other books of the like, from which no bad behavior is to be learned.[43]

The reference to Boethius has caused considerable comment because it seems to contradict such other evidence as Dante's remark in *Convivio* II.12.2–3 that Boethius was not much known among his contemporaries.

---

42. On Dante's notion of Latin, see esp. Scaglione, "Dante and the *Ars Grammatica*."
43. *Regola*, ed. Salvi, 134–35, my translation.

Some scholars have suggested that Dominici is referring to Henry of Settimello.[44] Although Henry was certainly seen as an imitator of Boethius, it seems unlikely that any Florentine would confuse them, especially since manuscripts of Henry's work regularly and accurately attribute it to him. The phrase "teaching of Boethius," however, rather strongly suggests the title of the Pseudo-Boethian text, always attributed in the Italian manuscripts.[45] It could have been telescoped as well with the real Boethian *Consolation*, which does occur in reading book form. In manuscripts designed for institutional or advanced use, the two works often occur together, as they will again in the early printed editions. Both works are unquestioningly attributed to Boethius by the author of the trecento *Vitae philosophorum*.[46] I remarked in Chapter 4 how a phrase such as *dottrina di Boezio* refers to both text and author or, rather, refers to the authority of the writer as much as to the author himself or to his text. Whatever text Dominici had in mind, he intended to associate it with the impeccable authority of Boethius.

Dominici's list is a fitting place to close our consideration of the Florentine school canon—or, rather, of the collection of texts we can be sure were used in classrooms in fourteenth-century Florence, for it is clear that there was no firm and universally adopted curriculum. Dominici claimed to be describing a standard, time-tested curriculum, that of the "forefathers"; but in fact his list comes closer to describing the loose and anticanonical results of our census. The passage reads like the fond remembrance of one educated in the good old days looking back over his bookshelf and remembering the lessons learned from each work.[47] But it is not strictly prescriptive; it offers a list of options and electives rather like the ones our census suggests were in use.

44. Avesani, "Il primo ritmo," 456. But the glosses to Henry of Settimello's work almost always describe the author as a modern character and frequently also refer to Boethius as a separate individual, e.g., Riccardiana MS 725, fols. 41r, 54r. Similarly, Jacopo Passavanti knew them apart and cites them separately and accurately in the 1350s; see his *Specchio*, ed. Polidori, 225–26, and his Latin sermons, cited by Kaeppeli, "Opere latine," 152. Lanza, *Polemiche e berte*, 95, suggests that the phrase of Dominici means the Pseudo-Boethian confession of faith.

45. This usage is paralleled elsewhere. Giovanni da Ravenna cites an elementary text for memorization, called simply "Boezio," which would have been used in his own schooldays at Ravenna in the 1350s; see Sabbadini, *Giovanni*, 132. Paolino Minorita, *Trattato*, 87, specifies *Boetio de disciplina de li scolari* as an authoritative work on treatment of students, not as a school text; he wrote in Venice ca. 1315.

46. Florence, Biblioteca Nazionale Centrale, B.R.50, on which see Garfagnini, "Da Seneca a Giovanni di Salisbury."

47. Cf. Grendler's astute reading, *Schooling*, 116, and Lanza's, *Polemiche e berte*, 95–97.

Indeed, Dominici tells us elsewhere (in the *Lucula noctis* written about five years after the *Regola*) that he himself never studied grammar with a master but was entirely self-taught:

> I confess in good conscience, witness the Holy Spirit, not only that am I no rhetorician, but that I have never studied grammar under a master. I read no grammatical rules; I did not study Donatus; I am utterly ignorant of the distinctions of nouns and verbs, and the forms I know by experience alone. A mimic, I recite, following those masters pagan and Catholic, ancient and modern, verse and prose, whom I studied as best I could by myself.[48]

Dominici exaggerates his ignorance in this passage, but it does seem to indicate that he did not study Latin reading in a grammar school of the Tuscan type. Still, in the *Lucula* he claims to have missed only formal study of grammatical rules; he did study the moral prose and poetry that was the mainstay of the Latin reading course. In the *Regola* he recommends works he could have read on his own by the testimony of his later claim. As the *Regola* list of readings goes on, Dominici's thoughts grow fonder, so the *Eva columba* and *Physiologus* are claimed rather grandly for "philosophy," and the *Ecloga Theoduli* is "a bit of versified Scripture." A self-taught character like this is just the sort to remember each of the texts he mastered as a personal triumph, and just the sort to suspect that other boys could not succeed as well except with close supervision.

What is more remarkable, the list in the *Regola* contains almost exactly the same books our census reveals were most popular fifty years before its writing; it leaves out the less popular works, some morally doubtful cases, elective texts such as Henry of Settimello, and other, relatively more modern courtesy books. Dominici was the declared foe of the humanists in recommending strongly against allowing children to read pagan authors; in the *Regola* he singled out Ovid and Virgil as particularly pernicious, either because they were the most used or because the lyric Virgil and Ovid both treat explicitly sexual themes.[49] But his commendation of the older-fashioned texts was not just an antihumanist stance. It also reflected other prejudices of old-time Florentines: against the immorality and irreverence of Ovidian comedies like the *Geta*, against too strictly monastic texts like the *Chartula*, against too many courtesy texts, and against too many texts at all. Dominici seems to have opposed reading

---

48. *Lucula noctis*, ed. Hunt, 355.
49. *Regola*, ed. Salvi, 135.

broadly at the elementary and intermediate levels; his is exactly the mentality that would have given Florentine grammar masters license to limit the curriculum to a few standard texts and a few electives.

Dominici, then, recommended leaving off grammatical studies after some very basic texts and going on from there to study Christian literature in a serious way. This was not just an antihumanist stance (the way Dominici is traditionally read); it was a Dominican program also expressed fifty years earlier by Jacopo Passavanti.[50] It excluded frivolous or difficult-to-apply works and included only those "from which no bad behavior is to be learned." Above all, it supposed that a little (carefully modulated and thoroughly religious) learning was good but that advanced studies should be professional or, on the mendicant model, undertaken in the context of religious life.

It is always dangerous to give too much credence to ill-humored social criticism by conservative middle-aged men writing about their old school days. But there is no doubt that Dominici's querulous complaints about giving pagan authors to young boys did reflect a pervasive, high-toned bourgeois moralism that existed in Florence well before the classicizing humanist manifestos of the 1380s and 1390s, which are usually cited as the occasion for Dominici's commentary.[51] Florentine booklists and books survive from earlier in the century to tell us, if we read them aright, that Dominici was accurate in describing what mid-trecento Florentines read in their Latin schools. It seems to me that he also describes the moral tone and moralizing reasons behind such choices accurately and forcefully.

---

50. Passavanti makes a clear distinction between learned and lay readers at several places in his *Specchio di vera penitenza*, esp. 223 on the impropriety of using Ovid; cf. Kaeppeli, "Opere latine," 155.

51. Most recently Lanza, *Polemiche e berte*, 94–96. As long ago as 1940, however, Hunt made the point that Dominici's antihumanist polemic was not tied to his ideas on the education of children, but rather that Salutati tried to turn the traditionalists' arguments to this end, suggesting that they meant to say that only the young and inexperienced should not read the classics. But Dominici's objections to the study of the classics were in his own mind valid for all Christian readers at all levels. See Dominici, *Lucula noctis*, xvin26.

# LINGUISTIC AND
# SOCIAL HIERARCHIES
## *The Grammarian's Place*

These investigations of the books used and the texts read in the elementary classroom give a good sense of *how* elementary Latin was taught in fourteenth-century Florence, but they do not fully answer the question of *why* the boys who studied Latin did so. It is true, and truistic, that the prestige of Latin and its use by professionals, churchmen, and intellectuals guaranteed a demand for Latin skills. Again, as I have several times remarked, Latin study had an initiatory quality for many Florentines. Some future merchants, bankers, and industrial entrepreneurs who had no expectations of Latin careers seem to have chosen to suffer the rigors of the grammar school course for the sake of acquiring a badge of honor of sorts, similar to the ritual cultural status that accrued to private school "old boys" down to our own century.

But surely this was not all. Grammar school students might also acquire genuine literary polish and even some substantial insight into the meaning of Latin high culture. This last achievement could be practical in addition to satisfying mere curiosity. Every trecento merchant dealt with rulers and other aristocrats, especially churchmen, who were well-versed in Latin culture or employed professional Latinists. These powerful people used Latin as an international medium of communication; their cultural outlook was highly latinized. So a wool merchant or banker could well use a smattering of Latin (and even more French) in social discourse, in legal matters, and in understanding the prejudices of his most highly educated clients.

Still, we have not yet fully evaluated the social meaning of Latin study. Granted that some sort of transformation of attitude was wrought in the student by the memorization, grammatical analysis, vocabulary study, and composition exercises of the Latin course, what was the new man thus made prepared to do? What could the Latin-literate person understand that others could not? What was the meaning of this new skill in social terms? Did Latin of itself offer status, or was it merely an ornament to one whose social position was defined in some other way? We may answer these questions by weighing the status of the grammar master and his skill in two ways, first by looking at how social and linguistic hierarchies functioned in a city where merchants and lawyers determined cultural status, and then by evaluating the economic and social realities of the grammar master's lifestyle. The grammar master lived by Latin alone; his living standard is the real measure of the prestige of the discipline he taught.

The most important skill of the Latin student, probably the only one that would stick with him from the rather short course that seems to have been normal, was the ability to decipher Latin texts, with more or less difficulty to be sure, but for himself and without need of a translator or other intermediary. This could be a practical skill, as in the case of reading certain legal documents, or it could open up a world of moral, devotional, technical, even merely entertaining texts. Some of the most accomplished of the Florentine merchant diarists make clear that reading had become their principal avocation and gave them a private intellectual world they valued as a source of solace and reflection. At issue was the ability to manipulate the ancient and medieval textual heritage of the West for personal ends.

In Florentine merchant society these personal goals only rarely concerned the universals of political power and even more rarely did they aim at esoteric wisdom. Those had been reasons for study (or implicit in the possession of literacy) at other times and places. The trecento merchant reader was more likely to look to classical and medieval Latin literature for help in improving his ability to make personal decisions morally. His goal was the wisdom of the paterfamilias whose duty was to create family harmony and prosperity and to advance the family's prospects in city politics. At their most ambitious, Florentines of the political class wanted to use rhetoric to promote the power of their city and political harmony within it.

But Latin literacy was also the model for much less ambitious projects. Above all, the Latin reader could make himself over into a translator, that is, he could read Latin texts for others and interpret for them the wisdom of the ancients, the lessons of Scripture, or the tales of pagan and Christian heroes.[1] This sense of personal interpretive mission underlay the flood of thirteenth- and fourteenth-century translations by both expert and only middling Latinists into Tuscan and other *volgare* dialects.[2] Over a hundred such translations that were made between 1250 and 1375 survive, 60 percent of them in Tuscan dialects. The subjects were classical, religious, and courtly.[3]

Translation, however, need not be understood merely in the formal sense of interpreting a literary text in a second language. Its truer and more general sense in our period was learning Latin to use it for personal interpretaion of the medieval and classical heritage, and, more socially, for spreading and popularizing ideas of the old elite cultures among a broader literate public. In this sense, preachers, politicians, Latin teachers, and some legal experts were all translators. Memorial techniques, scribal practices, and individual aptitudes determined how successful any given student of Latin was in this role, but the very fact of undertaking Latin study required the would-be Latinist to assume a threshold or liminal stance at least temporarily. Any student who took his Latin schooling seriously would retain his interpretive, translator's role life long.

In a hierarchically arranged society, especially one with somewhat fluid class boundaries, interpreters or translators of this sort were crucial figures even if they were not professionals in language use. There were also several levels of professionalization in Latin. The most professional and sophisticated users of the elite language were university scholars, churchmen involved in canon law courts and administration, and anyone engaged in international diplomacy. Below these we may rank notaries, lawyers, magistrates, and doctors for whom Latin was a necessary but not constant professional usage. In most Italian cities this professional elite

---

1. This is the real meaning of the contemporary terms *volgarizzatore* / *volgarizzamento* / *volgarizzare*, which I hereafter denote with the modern terms "translator" / "translation" / "translate." It is important to conceive of this activity, however, in a broad, trecento manner and not in the technical way we have understood it since the philological revolution of the fifteenth century. The essential studies of this important literary fact of the earliest Italian prose literature are Maggini, *I primi volgarizzamenti*; Folena, *"Volgarizzare"*; Copeland, *Rhetoric, Hermeneutics*; and Segre, *Volgarizzamenti*; the critical introduction to this latter volume is also available in Segre's *Lingua*, 49–78. An excellent, recent survey with invaluable bibliography is Guthmüller, "Die *volgarizzamenti*." Also useful is Bruni, "Traduzione, tradizione."

2. Folena, *"Volgarizzare,"* 78–79; cf. Copeland, "Rhetoric," 63–66.

3. These figures result from analyzing the translations listed by Guthmüller, "Die *volgarizzamenti*," 333–48, the best single list available.

had dominated local cultural activity for centuries, since the middle of the twelfth century at least. More or less on this same level were the pastoral clergy, most influential among them the members of mendicant orders. Clerics had liturgical functions that required some Latin and pastoral ones that might require both mastery of vernacular rhetoric and Latin training in theology. Latin teachers, insofar as they did not also belong to one of the above groups, earned their living from Latin but were in many ways less professionalized than those who used the language as the tool of a specific occupation. And at the bottom of the hierarchy of Latin professionalism were educated readers who knew Latin, sometimes quite well, more often only poorly, but who had no professional involvement with the language. A merchant diarist like Giovanni Morelli, whom we have cited repeatedly for his articulate sense of language, would fall into this last category.[4]

In fact, of course, Florence had not one linguistic hierarchy but many. It is important to understand this plurality of hierarchies, for in the complex urban society of late medieval Italy there were many parallel realms of social and intellectual discourse which only partially interpenetrated. The hierarchy of language that obtained in a law school might not apply in a law court, for example, and would have been even less applicable in a contract between merchants, even though these are all legal forums. Similarly, the role of the language specialists in each case would have varied. A given notary might be sole official actor in one case, expert witness or guarantor in another, and completely irrelevant to the activity of the third. A preacher, meanwhile, had to structure every sermon to offer food for thought to the most sophisticated members of his audience without losing the attention of less educated listeners or giving scandal to them.[5]

Then too, in any hierarchical scheme the individual's place in a rank order determines how much of the order she or he sees, understands, and embraces. To the average Florentine textile worker, say a spinner of wool, the Latin of Salutati and that of a neighborhood priest would have seemed much the same. She would have considered pretty much all Latin speakers

4. For a different range of language professionals, see Antonelli and Bianchini, "Dal *clericus*," 186–200.

5. These multiple levels of audience participation and authorial labor are often described in religious literature, e.g., the prologues to Domenico Cavalca's translation of the *Dialogues* of Gregory the Great and his *Pungilingua*. For more on the learned and popularizing traditions in trecento literature, see Delcorno, *Exemplum*, esp. 79–95, 229–38; Copeland, *Rhetoric, Hermeneutics*, 222–28.

in an undifferentiated linguistic caste well above her own. Insofar as she had dealings with such people at all it would have been their social standing that was important to her livelihood and salvation, not their linguistic achievements. A notary or an aristocratic nun, if they had cultural pretensions, might have been able to distinguish not only between Salutati and the local priest but also between the Latin of Salutati's circle and that of the Dominicans at Santa Maria Novella, between these latter and the notaries of the archbishop, and between all of these Latins and the usage of a visiting professor of medicine from Montpellier. For such an observer, the linguistically undifferentiated masses were those who had no Latin, and even there a distinction could be made between the relatively few cultivated speakers of the oligarchy and the large, illiterate or semiliterate populace.

A Florentine grammar master, assuming he was not university trained and had few ambitions, might have constructed a different sort of linguistic hierarchy. He would have become expert at distinguishing the linguistic abilities of his incoming students—his *non latinantes*—and at pushing them through his course to latinize as far as their abilities allowed. But his own latinity might have been relatively unsophisticated and his ability to deal with legal or theological Latin slim. He might well have recognized the existence of many higher Latins than his own but have remained either linguistically unable to rank them or socially unwilling to admit his own deficiencies with respect to other Latin professionals.

Social rank, needless to say, was not even roughly equivalent to rank in the linguistic hierarchy in trecento Florence or elsewhere. Language accomplishments were valued, often rewarded economically, but they did not lead to any certain improvement of social condition. Even in the church, with its hierarchy of skill, there were limits to the social mobility of many clerics.

The grammarian's position in these various hierarchies was no more fixed than anyone else's. If anything, it was more fluid and insecure, for the grammarian depended even more than most on the opinions of others, both the merchants whose children he taught and the Latin professionals who controlled the future careers of his students. For both the groups that determined his social status, the Latin teacher was merely a supervisor of beginners, a popularizer of a sort analogous to preachers and translators in that his job was to diffuse wisdom embodied in Latin literature.[6]

6. This analogy is developed at length in my essay "Preachers, Teachers, and Translators: Grammar and Society in Trecento Florence," forthcoming in *Viator* 25 (1994).

Werner Raith, in his 1979 study *Florenz vor der Renaissance*, attempted to sketch a picture of merchant attitudes toward education which were strongly secularizing and would have allied the early humanists with the commercial class against the conservative, religious outlook of mendicants and other churchmen.[7] The evidence presented in this and earlier chapters should make it clear that Raith's is an inadequate view. The practical bent of the merchant oligarchs of Florence did not for a minute mean that they were less pious. On the contrary, they favored stern Christian moralizing and firm orthodoxy without the frills and pomp of scholastic theology. The natural allies of the pragmatic merchants were the popularizing mendicants, precisely the self-confident group who would lead the attack on the Florentine civic humanists. In this they were joined by traditionalizing grammarians, dependent as they were on the patronage of merchants and the favor of mendicants.

What was the import of the view of grammar as popularization in trecento Florence? Especially in a city where Latin was sometimes treated as a finishing course inessential to commercial and political success, or a preparatory course for *ars dictaminis* (a "useful" form of Latin study), the grammar master suffered a prejudice against his popularizing role. Merchants and politicians sometimes saw Latin as a mere ornament; worse, they might view the grammar master as just another craftsman with a simple skill to teach. A similar attitude characterized early humanist critiques of medieval Latin teaching. Petrarch and Giovanni Conversini attacked the practice of forcing students to memorize trivial works, thereby overloading them with inanities and giving them no opportunity to appreciate important and beautiful works of the Latin heritage.[8] In arguing thus, the humanists were recalling grammar to its older, more moral mission, one they felt had been compromised away by attempts to make it a practical, pre-professional discipline.

Meanwhile, fully professional Latinists such as lawyers and medical doctors could also look down on the popularizing grammar master. Even though they acknowledged the importance of his work in educating new Latinists, they might think of him as one who could not make better use of his Latin. The city's numerous and powerful notaries were particularly susceptible to this sort of thinking. Men of law, organized in the prestigious Guild of Judges and Notaries, represented the most visible and

7. Raith, *Florenz,* 126–42.
8. Sabbadini, *Giovanni da Ravenna,* 130–32; Garin, *Pensiero,* xxii.

socially influential form of Latin culture active on the local level. Their professional latinity, closely circumscribed by traditional use and legal precedent, was a model of formal, technical use of language. Moreover, lawyers and notaries often trained in letter theory, *ars dictaminis*, which provided further models for the application of linguistic formulas to practical political and social needs. These men dominated the tradition of vernacular poetic writing in thirteenth-century Florence and made up a major part of the writers active in the city in the fourteenth.[9]

The roots of the cultural influence of the notaries and lawyers at Florence lay deep in the medieval history of the Italian communes. While in the twelfth and thirteenth centuries French schools were developing newly professional disciplines of grammar and logic, the schools of Italy were rediscovering the ancient legal corpus of Roman law and, almost contemporaneously, codifying the canon law. This development provided impetus in turn for studies of forensic rhetoric and Latin composition related to legal matters. As the numbers of lawyers and notaries multiplied, so did the general literacy rate in Italian towns. Sooner or later in every Italian city the notaries, lawyers, and judges formed sworn associations. By the beginning of the fourteenth century, the Guild of Judges and Notaries was among the most influential in Florence, even though the merchant guilds were far richer.

Much of the complexion of intellectual life in late medieval Italy, then, depended on the existence of what Ronald Witt has dubbed a legal culture of the book, which in the course of the eleventh and twelfth centuries challenged and eventually displaced the clerically dominated and grammatically based book culture of an earlier period.[10] This development pushed traditional grammar off to the side intellectually and resulted in decreased social prestige for the grammarians. Once the proud nucleus of the studies at flourishing cathedral schools, where it partook of the esteem granted to learned clerics with lucrative church appointments, grammar

9. Antonelli and Bianchini, "Dal *clericus*," 181–89, and Bec, "Lo statuto," 230–33, demonstrate a strong presence of legal professionals in the literary culture of Florence, though Bec's figures imply that this was relatively less the case in Tuscany than in the north and that the influence of notaries as writers declined across the fourteenth century. For Bec, the most characteristic aspect of the Tuscan literary scene was the strong presence of merchant writers in the thirteenth and early fourteenth centuries and of clerics, especially mendicants, in the later fourteenth century; see 240–42.

10. The details of this process are one major theme of Witt's forthcoming *Italian Medieval Culture and the Origins of Humanism*, which he has kindly shared with me while in progress.

was increasingly relegated to a preparatory school course taught by independent lay teachers or by parish clergy.

In Tuscany there is good evidence that, by contrast to the growing presence of men of law among the influential writers of the city, the teaching corps provided fewer and fewer writers across the fourteenth century, and those teachers who did contribute to the new vernacular literature were increasingly concentrated in advanced schools. Whereas lawyers increasingly dabbled in literature, elementary and intermediate teachers retreated into their classrooms.[11] This phenomenon argues for the continued, profound influence of legal Latin in the formation of the audience for nascent humanism. At the same time, it reinforces our sense of the marginalization of the traditional Latin teachers who aimed their program of study at broad, moral education and not at professional specialization. The elementary course, as we have seen in earlier chapters, remained strongly religious and ethical in content and took much of its internal logic from monastic studies of grammar in the early Middle Ages. But it was becoming harder for grammarians to claim to be teaching a useful skill of any merit in and for itself.

Notaries were themselves fully literate in one sort of Latin, and they seem also to have provided much of the basic Latin education that went on outside the independent grammar schools. This matter of notaries as teachers has been little studied, though the practice was widespread. There is good, early evidence that it was normal for notaries from places as far apart as Pavia and Palermo to have students, although before the thirteenth century we can rarely be sure about the level of instruction.[12] In thirteenth-century Padua, notaries taught grammar, probably privately and not at that city's distinguished university. Another thirteenth-century document, from Perugia, shows a payment for reading and writing instruction by a notary.[13] We know more about Venice than any other fourteenth-century city in this regard; there are at least nine clear cases of notaries teaching at the elementary level among the documents assembled by Bertanza. Similar evidence is to be found for Genoa and other Italian cities without universities.[14]

11. This, at least, is one way to read the figures supplied and interpreted by Bec, "Lo statuto," 233, 238–39.

12. Sóriga, *Statuta, decreta*, 147; Bresc, "Ecole et services," 12.

13. Marangon, "Scuole e università"; *Il Notariato*, 152.

14. Bertanza and Della Santa, *Documenti*, 4, 36, 43, 54, 87, 89, 103, 134, 216; Petti Balbi, *L'insegnamento*, 48–53, presents clear thirteenth-century evidence of elementary

For Florence, alas, we are less informed about teaching notaries. We can glimpse the practice in surviving records, but without details that would make it clear how the Florentine use might have differed from that in other towns. The Guild of Judges and Notaries expected candidates for membership to demonstrate two years' study in a professional office or in a school before being permitted to take a matriculation examination, according to a statute of 1344.[15] Conceivably, then, students could acquire all the necessary Latin in an office setting. We can document the presence of students as apprentices in notarial offices, but we cannot say for sure what they studied there or whether they were expected to have some Latin before entering an office as an apprentice.

Santorre Debenedetti cites at least one case of a Florentine notary who was also a *magister puerorum* in 1325, but he also points out that the statutes of the guild exclude from possible membership anyone who "taught boys the alphabet or psalter or such things."[16] Presumably this prohibition would not have extended to teaching grammar at more advanced levels, and the distinction is revealing. It suggests that the notaries did not consider extremely elementary tuition a worthy occupation but tolerated intermediate teaching of Latin among their members; it was in fact common for them to take on apprentices at an early age who were still in need of a Latin course. It is possible, too, that students apprenticed in notarial offices were rushed through the elements of Latin grammar and set early to studying formulaic Latin composition, *ars dictaminis*, and *ars notariae*. This might explain the existence in our census of copies of works by Geoffrey of Vinsauf in the form of elementary Latin readers.

In the view of notaries who taught in this way, the more traditional grammar masters who were not notaries would be respectable but inessential actors, especially for teaching professional Latin. Grammarians who prepared students for university careers might even seem frivolous to the most hidebound and practical of the notaries, the ones who had themselves trained as apprentices and not at the university. At the same time, the immense prestige of law as an academic discipline enlarged the pretensions and power even of notaries not university trained. At Flor-

---

instruction by notaries but is less informative on the practice of the fourteenth century, when increasing numbers of Genoese students went to Bologna to study the *ars notariae*, a professional course for which it was necessary to have a grammar school education.

15. *Il Notaio*, 29. This may be compared to similar statutes, but with more specific mention of grammar study, at Lucca and San Gimignano (Barsanti, *Il pubblico insegnamento*, 106) and at Pisa (Fabroni, *Memorie istoriche*, 161).

16. Debenedetti, "Sui più antichi," 335, 339; cf. Klapisch-Zuber, "Le chiavi," 774.

ence, moreover, legal professionals had thoroughly absorbed the commercial prejudices of other guildsmen. Legal Latin was practical and useful Latin; more advanced or literary levels of Latin study were not.

One way the legalistic and mercantile prejudices of Florentines circumscribed the pretensions of grammar masters to be real Latin professionals was in terms of the private contracts between parents and teachers. These differed significantly in tenor from the letters of appointment given to public teachers of grammar in smaller Tuscan cities or the documents of public appointments in the Florentine *studio*. Public appointments were framed in an elaborate rhetoric of civic pride. They almost always stressed the dignity of the discipline, the need of the city for educators, and the worthiness of the master in question before spelling out the specific terms of the appointment in days of residence, numbers of students, teacher performance, curriculum, and fees. As Robert Black has rightly pointed out, this rhetoric reflected both the high esteem provincial governors accorded to grammatical learning and the competitive labor market in smaller towns.[17] In the case of appointments to the Florentine *studio*, the strong language reflects the status of professional studies in law and medicine and, again, a competitive, international job market in these fields.[18]

The economic realities and legal rhetoric of the usual Florentine private contract between parents and teacher allowed for no such fancy language. The cost and the material to be covered or term of study were stated baldly and without deference to the master's educational pretensions or accomplishments. In form these contracts are indistinguishable from other contracts for artisan services, and the schoolhouse was even called a *bottegha*, just as if it were a shop of any other sort.[19] Payments could be for tuition for a given period of time, or the contract could name a fee for specific skills attained. In the latter case, the child was to be brought up to a specified and commonly understood level of language proficiency. In either case, the exchange was purely commercial. And the market was a buyers' one; parents had the advantage.[20]

The reasons for this difference in rhetoric are not far to seek. Florence's

17. Black, "Humanism and Education," 206–15.
18. On the ultimate failure of the Florentines to compete in this job market, clearly ascribable to the ambiguous attitude of the city fathers toward intellectual pursuits, see Brucker, "Florence and Its University."
19. Klapisch-Zuber, "Le chiavi," 774.
20. Cf. Davidsohn, *Firenze*, 200–201; Klapisch-Zuber, "Le chiavi," 774.

system of private schools differed substantially from the provincial ones in structure as early as the thirteenth century, and it engendered a different social view of the schoolmaster.[21] Provincial masters were on the public payroll and held a public trust; no such official status obtained in the private schools of Florence. Moreover, whereas grammar masters in small towns regularly undertook instruction at all levels from the most basic to the most advanced, Florentine masters specialized. The latter typically taught either reading and writing or grammar but not both. Debenedetti described this stratification and specialization as long ago as 1902. He claimed that the Florentine notaries, who redacted almost all the documents that survive to attest to the existence of schoolmasters, made a regular distinction between the two types of teacher. They differentiated *doctores puerorum*, who taught the alphabet and reading and writing and sometimes also taught Donatus, from grammar teachers, usually called *magistri grammatice*, who taught Latin as such. Debenedetti may have proposed too rigid a set of terms; he himself offers at least one case of a mixed-term *magister puerorum*, and others of his *doctores puerorum* seem more likely to have been grammarians than reading masters.[22] Still, it is clear that at Florence the two kinds of teacher and two kinds of school were distinct. Villani fully distinguishes between the masses of students learning reading and writing and the relatively few who studied in grammar schools, and so do the statutes of the notaries' guild.[23]

Still, the commercial nature of the exchange in the private school system of Florence meant that even grammar masters were not accorded the rhetorical status they would have had in provincial towns. For example, the termination document (*solutio*) of a 1302 contract between a certain Florentine *magister grammatice*, Bartolus, and his fifteen students is just barely complimentary. The document attests that *omnia et singularia fecerat et observaverit que dictis scolaribus promiserat circa studium predictum et . . . ipsum magistrum bene eos docuisse et instruxisse . . . et bene eis satisfactum esse de predicto studio* [he did and observed each and every thing that he had promised to do for the students in respect of their

---

21. On the institutionalization of public instruction, see Petti Balbi, "Istituzioni," 32–34.

22. Debenedetti, "Sui più antichi," 335, 348. The Florentine practice is unlikely to have been much more regular than that at Venice, where there was considerable flexibility; one schoolmaster who appears in eight documents recorded by Bertanza and Della Santa, *Documenti*, 65–129, has four different forms of title. In five of the eight cases there is no mention of grammar and in the remaining three Rainaldus de Filippo de Treviso is called either *doctor grammatice* or *rector grammatice*.

23. Villani, *Cronica*, 3:324 (xi.94); Debenedetti, "Sui più antichi," 339–40; Black, "Florence," 35, and "Curriculum," 139–40.

studies and . . . taught them and instructed them well . . . and he satisfied them well in their study].[24] The terms of the agreement are extremely vague in this termination document, and we may suspect that they were so in the original contract too. Perhaps because the master in this case had gone to teach children in Laterina, a village many miles outside Florence, his obligation was stated in terms of time and presence in the village and not in terms of the skills he was to teach. The lapidary prose here is not even subscribed by adults! The parties to the contract were the master and the fifteen students, and their names, not those of their parents, appear in the parchment, carefully put down by the notary.

Even this sort of a contract was tighter and more affirmative of the master's status than was usually the case in Florence, since Master Bartolus was contracting to be present in a suburban locality for the instruction of a set group of students. The more usual situation at Florence was a contract for an individual student's tuition and, to judge from the rarity of these, the most usual contract of all was not even a written one. By far the majority of the students must have been sent to the schools of masters in the immediate neighborhood of their homes on verbal agreements between their parents and the masters. Agreements of this sort occasionally survive in the form of a memorandum in the father's account book or family ledger, but often the arrangement was not even formalized to that degree. The student's progress was monitored according to the parents' level of interest; and the boy could be moved from one master to another as seemed appropriate to the parents. We know from the ex libris in schoolbooks that some students went from teacher to teacher at the same, latinizing stage of the curriculum while using a single textbook. The same practice was true for even more elementary students.[25]

The matter of localism, even *campanilismo* (strong neighborhood loyalty), was significant in the careers of grammar masters and students alike. I remarked in Chapter 2 that ownership marks in grammar school books indicate that new Latin readers were educated into identifying and being loyal to their families and their quarters of the city. This practice is consistent with the rare surviving contracts or memoranda from which it is possible to individuate the residences of both the student and the teacher: there are no surviving cases of students being sent across town to

24. Archivio di Stato di Firenze, SS. Annunziata, 1302.VII.26. This document was pointed out to me by Professor Franek Sznura of Florence, whom I thank cordially. Davidsohn, *Firenze*, 207, says this same master had taught in a similar school at Montevarchi in 1297.
25. Sapori, "Un bilancio," 355; Klapisch-Zuber, "Le chiavi," 766–69.

study grammar, although this must have happened sometimes when they were sent to the school of a particular religious order. Unfortunately, we have no sources for the local mentalities of the Florentine grammar masters themselves. We may speculate that one factor in the apparently poor job market for Latin masters in Florence was the unwillingness of Florentines to leave the city.

We can document local loyalties among masters outside Florence, as well as the restlessness of teachers who did leave their hometowns for the footloose life of a provincial grammar master. These men often changed jobs after a single annual contract or a few years' stay in one place. In town after town we also find the situation of a valued outside or foreign grammar master given a substantial municipal stipend to remain in service far from home while a local product who wants to teach in his hometown is given a humbler remuneration or none at all. At Prato in the 1330s, for example, an outsider and a local grammarian were paid 45 and 20 lire per year, respectively.[26] Among local masters, careers of twenty, thirty, even forty years were not uncommon. Sometimes we hear about these stay-at-homes primarily because they went to their city council and asked for a subsidy in consideration of their long service and present poverty.[27] Needless to say, the teachers at the bottom of the educational hierarchy, the reading and writing masters, especially the occasional women who taught, had no mobility at all. In general, the more local the teacher's aspirations, the more likely he or she was to end up in a state of poverty.

And yet these people very much wanted to stay at home. When the city of Pistoia went looking for a grammar master in the early 1380s, their hiring agent, Giovanni Ser Franceschi, surveyed the active grammarians in Tuscany. His notes are sketchy, but he usually says something about the age of the master and the size of his school or his reputation. Moreover, because he asked specifically whether each candidate would be willing to come to Pistoia and at what price, he has left us a precious snapshot of the mobility of the teaching corps.[28] The grammarians who were already

26. Piattoli, "Due osservazioni," 146.

27. The case of Maestro Anichino of Lucca, who found himself unable to pay the rent on his schoolhouse in the 1370s after twenty years of teaching, could be typical of this sort of gradual, genteel impoverishment of teachers with only local aspirations. The Lucca council, which a few years later would pay a salary of 100 lire (ca. 27 florins) to bring an *abbaco* teacher from Siena, could find only 36 lire (9 florins) toward the hapless Anichino's rent. See Fumi, *Regesti*, 2.2.671, 749, 814. Cf. Bertanza and Della Santa, *Documenti*, 12–35, 38, 63; Petti Balbi, "Istituzioni," 34.

28. Bacci, "Maestri," 88–90, edited this document. He dated it to ca. 1360, but Robert Black has found conclusive evidence that it must date from the early 1380s. My thanks to him for sharing this information with me.

teaching in their hometowns were much less willing to move than those who had appointments in "foreign" locations. Almost all the latter were clearly driven by monetary considerations and would consider an appointment with better pay in Pistoia; typically they asked 10 florins per year increase over their present salaries. But teachers with social standing and prominence in their home communities were adamant about not moving, or else they set prices so high that we may doubt the sincerity of their negotiations with the recruiter.[29] All three Pisan grammarians, who were from that city or nearby villages and had Pisan citizenship, refused to consider coming to Pistoia. We can almost hear the voice of the most senior of them, who had risen to serve his native city as chancellor, in the report that "he would not come even if the city [of Pistoia] offered him a thousand florins." A younger compatriot contented himself with saying "he would not now leave Pisa," presumably because of the large and successful school he had.[30]

These seem honest and straightforward answers from native sons well content with their situations at home. The Pistoiese envoy does not seem to have gotten nearly as frank a reply from another senior and native candidate:

> Master Piero da Ovile of Siena, poet and doctor in three sciences, grammar, philosophy, and rhetoric, with whom I spoke, is sixty years of age, and very active and flourishing. He has a two-year contract at Siena. He would come willingly to Pistoia because, although he is very rich, he is ill content at Siena. It would be necessary to gain the dissolution of his contract with the lord defenders [of the city of Siena] which he says the lord elders [of Pistoia] could do by sending ambassadors to the said lords. He asked a salary of one hundred florins yearly. This, he says, he could get from Florence. I think he would come for ninety or even eighty florins annually, which would seem as fair a price as one hundred for his services. He is the greatest teacher in Tuscany and would teach any text. He would also teach rhetoric.[31]

---

29. Of the eleven teachers described by the envoy, five were native to the place where they were teaching and six were not. Only one of the natives said he was willing to move, and only one of the "outsiders" was expressly unwilling to move.

30. Bacci, "Maestri," 89, for the text. Novati identified these two grammarians, both named Francesco, as Francesco Merolla da Vico and Francesco di Bartolo da Buti ("Due grammatici," 251–52), but this is clearly incorrect in light of Black's redating of the document. By the 1380s, Francesco da Buti, most famous as an early commentator on Dante, had also served as chancellor at Pisa, and so it may well be his remark about the thousand florins that we can hear in the record ascribed to "Maestro Francesco vecchio, poeta e doctore."

31. Bacci, "Maestri," 89, my translation.

There are several reasons for doubting the willingness of this candidate to move. He is probably to be identified with the Pietro di Chello who held a chair in grammar at the *studio* of Siena from 1349 onward, apparently without going to teach anywhere else.[32] Why would he want to do so at the age of sixty? Even the optimistic Pistoiese envoy, moreover, admits that Master Piero was overstating his own price for moving. It is hard to take his salary bid seriously, even as an opening position in a round of bargaining. The 100 florins he claimed he could have gotten from Florence (presumably for a university appointment) is fully 30 florins over the top price asked by any other candidate in the pool and double any recorded university salary for a grammarian at Florence.[33] The only explanation for such a difference, beyond the possibility of simple exaggeration, is that Piero felt his appointment at Siena was less well paid than it should be and that any new appointment should be at a university-level stipend worthy of his high self-opinion. If the envoy from Pistoia thought he could be hired for 80 florins, he could not have been making more than 70 at Siena.[34] This was generous for a grammar master of the period but not particularly so for a university professor; it may explain why Piero was rich but ill content. Master Piero, in short, seems a thorough Sienese, not really willing to move, and the sort of vain academic who needed constantly to be wooed from abroad to feel welcome at home.

The corollary to strong local loyalty among native teachers is the constant wandering of the masters who did not have jobs near home.[35] Only one of the six non-native grammarians interviewed by Giovanni Ser Franceschi was unwilling to come to Pistoia, and he was a Venetian who had just moved from a job in Pisa to one in Lucca. The other candidates either said they would come or seemed willing but had existing contracts that limited their ability to change jobs immediately. In these latter cases, however, all seem to have made a career move within the previous few years. Two, like the Venetian at Lucca, were reported to have accepted contracts in new towns between the time they were interviewed by the agent from Pistoia and the time his report was made.

These footloose grammarians, then, confirm the pattern of highly local, nativist loyalties. They moved about because they had not attained the real goal of most teachers, to set up school in one's hometown. The final

32. *Chartularium Studii Senensis*, 553–73.

33. Garfagnini, "Città e Studio," 116.

34. The records of the university at Siena are published only through 1357, at which time Pietro di Chello, whom I take to be the same as this Piero da Ovile, was being paid 50 lire.

35. Cf. Patrone Nada, "Super providendo," 72.

portion of the Pseudo-Boethian *De disciplina scolarium* is eloquent in this regard. It is a compilation of careerist advice about getting ahead as a grammarian and making money at it. The book culminates in a chapter that formulates exactly the distinction I have been making between stay-at-home and wandering grammarians. There are those who wander to Rome and "Athens" (the French writer probably meant Paris) and beyond in search of wide-ranging fame; but others seek livings in their own fatherlands out of a sense of duty to their compatriots or for sheer love of their native place.[36] The author's own preference for the stay-at-home course is clear. He warns wandering scholars to be careful of their dignity, always imperiled in a foreign land; but he assumes that the native teachers will be ever welcome and honored by their grateful compatriots. This last is a nostalgic wish, rather as if everyone should strive for an esteemed and prosperous old age as the grammar master back home. But there are some realistic considerations in this scene too. Even at home it is important, the medieval giver of advice tells us, to cut a good figure: to dress well, to eat nobly, and in general to comport oneself with dignity, like a local boy made good in the great world, now come home to educate the youth of his beloved patria.[37]

Although there is no specifically Florentine evidence for this psychology, I think we can assume that it was at work there too. Given the high degree of Florentine local pride and patriotic rhetoric, it would be strange indeed if Florence's native schoolmasters were not strongly attached to the city and to their own neighborhoods within it.[38] It may be that they were even more so than other Tuscans. Some few Florentines can be glimpsed as wandering teachers elsewhere, but their numbers are small compared with teachers from other, much smaller towns who elected this career path. Pisa had a relatively high number of native grammarians at two attested moments in her trecento history and a closer relation with Florence in this regard than other Tuscan towns. In 1328, four of the nine grammarians listed in the matriculation lists of the Pisan college of notaries were native, two were from Florence, two from Pistoia, and one from Volterra.[39] Later in the century, however, there were no Florentines and no other non-Pisans either.[40] By contrast, not one of the fourteen grammarians attested

36. Pseudo-Boethius, *De disciplina scolarium*, ed. Weijers, 123.
37. Text and commentary in Pseudo-Boethius, *Un saggio*, ed. Ducci, 143–47; text in Pseudo-Boethius, *De disciplina scolarium*, ed. Weijers, 130–34.
38. On neighborhood loyalty, see Cohn, *Laboring Classes*, 57–62.
39. Fabroni, *Memorie istoriche*, 178n16.
40. Bacci, "Maestri," 89.

at Pistoia from 1304 to 1399 and not one of the thirty-two grammar masters at Siena from 1241 to 1357 was Florentine, although these cities drew their teaching corps from throughout Tuscany and well beyond.[41] Nor did Giovanni Ser Franceschi find any Florentine grammarians in his survey of provincial Tuscany. He did not even visit Florence, the regional metropolis, while searching for a master. It seems clear that he had no hope of luring a Florentine even to nearby Pistoia. The large local market for elementary teaching must have encouraged most Florentines grammarians to stay at home, even on relatively unfavorable economic terms.

What were the economic realities of the Florentine grammar master? Again, we are at a considerable disadvantage in studying Florentines by comparison with those who worked in the provinces because of the lack of public appointments in Florence and the consequent shortage of documentation for individual cases. The provincial towns did offer lucrative contracts, although with considerable variation in levels of pay. The non-native grammarian at San Gimignano in 1360 was making fully 60 florins. The grammarian at Volterra a decade later, a man from Prato who had at least five annual contracts, was paid 50 florins each year. A similar teacher at Pistoia in 1375 had a salary equivalent to 77 florins. Giovanni Ser Franceschi's report to the elders of Pistoia concerning "experienced or adequately trained grammarians in Tuscany" lists actual salaries of 60 florins annually and realistic bids up to 70 about 1380.[42] Many teachers, however, could not do as well. In the 1370s a non-native grammarian at Colle di Valdelsa was paid 40 florins, and the great Convenevole da Prato, teacher of Petrarch, was paid less than 30 florins annually by his native town in 1336–37, the last years of his distinguished career.[43] In addition to these fixed sums, masters were allowed to charge fees, and they were

41. Zanelli, *Del pubblico insegnamento*, 10–28; *Chartularium Studii Senensis*. Almost the only Florentine masters we know had careers outside the city were professors at Bologna, or *abbaco* teachers, on whom see Debenedetti, "Sui più antichi," 344n2–3, and Raith, *Florenz*, 151. Debenedetti cites Bertanza and Della Santa, who give a thorough list of trecento teachers at Venice and record only six individuals from Florence. A much later source, the Venetian surveys for 1587–88 used by Grendler and Baldo, shows that even at the end of the Renaissance Florence supplied the Adriatic city with only about the same number of teachers as did tiny Arezzo. See Baldo, *Alunni*, 18, 43–81.

42. Vichi-Imbeciadori, "L'istruzione," 62; Battistini, *Il pubblico insegnamento*, 87–88; Zanelli, *Del pubblico insegnamento*, 120; Bacci, "Maestri," 88–89.

43. Archivio di Stato di Siena, Comune di Colle di Valdelsa, vol. 121, March 1368; this reference was supplied to me by Robert Black. Ser Convenevole's case is discussed at some length by Piattoli, "Due osservazioni," 146–49. It seems likely that this sum was intended as a sort of pension to honor the grand old man and not as a salary proper.

usually provided with a schoolhouse or meeting room and sometimes a residence at city expense. In Florentine terms, a salary of 50–60 florins was a steady, respectable income, adequate to maintain a normal household, though not to live extravagantly.[44] An individual with capital to invest could do better in almost any risk venture, even a small shop, but 50 florins was well in excess of the income of most wage earners.[45]

Small-town municipal salaries also compare reasonably well with Florentine civil servants' salaries of the day, probably a more logical comparison in terms of career expectations, educational level, and cultural pretensions than a measure against profit-making ventures or day labor. The highest ranking civil servant of the Florentine republic was the chancellor, and his salary was officially posted at 100 gold florins for most of the trecento. The chancellor himself, of course, was also at the center of an elaborate patronage network and could accumulate four to six times this amount. Minor public appointments at Florence rotated on a two- or four-month basis and carried highly varied salaries. Monthly rates at mid-century could range from 3 to 10 lire, the equivalent of 12 to 40 florins annually if it had been possible to serve for a whole year's time. Most such appointments, however, went to notaries who could also charge fees for some of the work involved and who would consider the salary a mere income supplement over and above their normal business. Another sort of public post was that of scribe. The scribe of the salt tax commission in 1370, for example, was appointed through the patronage of the city's chancellor, Nicolo di Ventura Monachi. The employees of such tax commissions were paid on the basis of the yield of the tax in any given period of work. We do not know the scribe's total income from the office, but it must have been considerable, because he paid the chancellor 42 florins as the portion of his earnings due to his patron for the six-month duration of the appointment. In other such dealings Nicolo di Ventura received as much as half the total earnings of his clients, so we might reckon that this scribe earned at least another 40 florins as secretary to the tax collectors. We might also compare the salaries of provincial grammar masters with

44. Park, *Doctors and Medicine*, 158. Patrone Nada, "Super providendo," 57–59, provides evidence on salaries in contemporary northern Italy which she characterizes as consistently *medio-bassi o bassi*.

45. Cipolla, *Monetary Policy*, 76, indicates that the value of the florin in the 1370s hovered around 75 soldi. At this rate, a salary of 60 florins would be equivalent to 215 lire. See also De la Roncière, "Pauvres et pauvreté," 673, 680, where the annual wage of a gardener in the 1370s was in the neighborhood of 150 lire and that of a skilled and prosperous master mason about 315 lire.

those earned by the few grammarians who had contracts at the University of Florence in the fourteenth century. Chronically underfunded, this institution was founded three times during the century and thrice allowed to die. The salaries actually paid to grammarians never exceeded 50 florins per year, respectable but not generous sums.[46]

Public salaries for elementary teaching were not generally available to grammar masters in Florence. To find a secure, steadily paying teaching job of this sort, it would have been necessary to relocate to one of the provincial towns. In Florence, both reading and grammar masters lived entirely on income from student fees unless they could also secure an ecclesiastical benefice or a second income as a notary, scribe, or other job. Putting together a living from student fees could make for a difficult and strenuous career. We have very few records of fees charged in Florence, but we do know about the fees allowed under municipal contracts elsewhere, and they do not make it seem likely that the Florentine masters earned much.

In one famous and fascinating Florentine case, in 1304, Mistress Clementia contracted to teach the basic course—reading, psalter, and Donatus—to the son of a prominent family for a fee of 40 soldi. The contract specifies that this is the only fee to be charged, meaning probably that it was for the tasks described, not for an annual period.[47] If the course took two years, this fee would amount to 20 soldi annually. Assuming Clementia could manage forty students or so a year, a heavy load, her total income from fees would amount to 800 soldi, little more than 12 gold florins at the date, not even a subsistence wage. Clementia's case, however, is not typical. She may have earned less as a woman, and she is described in the contract as married, so hers was probably not the only income of the household. Certainly she could not have supported a family on her own at this rate of pay. Even if the contract were for a single year's tuition, her total income could hardly have exceeded 24 florins, enough to support a widow perhaps, but not if she had many children.[48]

Clementia's contract may be compared with the school fees paid by the guardians of Perotto di Paghino Ammannati in 1290 and 1291. They are

46. Marzi, *La cancelleria*, 96–100; Marzi notes that officeholders complained that these salaries were hardly worth the work, but he also shows that such functionaries brought in considerable money over and above their salaries; Martines, *Social World*, 105–7. On the university, see Garfagnini, "Città e Studio," 113–16.

47. Debenedetti, "Sui più antichi," 333.

48. For the value of the florin at this date, see Cipolla, *Monetary Policy*, 31. A female teacher of small children is also recorded by Patrone Nada, "Super providendo," 72.

of roughly the same order of magnitude and confirm the small earning potential of reading masters. Little Perotto was destined to become a blacksmith's apprentice, and so he was given minimal training in reading and writing and did not go on to Latin. He had three masters in all, one for reading who was paid 1.5 soldi a month for most of a year, a second for writing at the rate of 2 soldi per month for one month only, and a third, for writing again, at 3 soldi monthly. Even this last fee would amount to just 36 soldi a year, and Perotto did not stay that long. Apparently the new teacher thought Perotto could be taught to write in three months' time and demanded full payment in advance. The boy's more elementary masters had been paid monthly. The account book specifies that the guardian gave these small monthly sums to Perotto himself, who carried them to the teacher.[49] At these fees, reading and writing masters would have needed large numbers of students to assemble a decent living.

Provincial contracts make it clear that higher fees were charged for more advanced levels of study. A grammar master who, on the Florentine pattern, taught only students at the latinizing level would have earned somewhat more than Clementia or Perotto's reading masters. It would also seem that fees rose considerably in the course of the century. Those recorded by Robert Black for Colle di Valdelsa run as high as 30 soldi per student per year at mid-century (for advanced latinizers) and up to 48 soldi in 1367; at San Gimignano and Arezzo at the end of the century, the most advanced students paid as much as one florin per year.[50] At Lucca in 1389 we find a contract with remarkably high fees of one florin per year for a student *non latinante* and two florins for each of the *latinantes*.[51] But these figures do not directly translate into fees at Florence in the same period, for small-town grammarians had small classes and charged these fees in addition to their comfortable municipal salaries. To make as much in Florence, a master with private students and no other income would have to have charged much more, or to have taught many more students each year, or both.

We might posit, for example, a completely hypothetical Florentine grammar master in 1350 with thirty to forty students a year each paying on average 40 soldi (both numbers are at the high end of what seems possible in a one-room, one-teacher school). This master would earn 20–27 florins, not even as much as the usual wage of a gardener in that

49. Sapori, "Un bilancio," 355, 361–62, 364.
50. Personal communication of Professor Black.
51. Barsanti, *Il pubblico insegnamento*, 115.

year. Only if such a teacher were able to manage fifty students, or if he could charge the smaller number 50 soldi, could his income approach 35 florins, the potential income of a construction laborer. As Charles-M. De la Roncière has shown, this income would support a family of four somewhat precariously.[52] If, again hypothetically (and based necessarily on provincial sources), tuition payments had risen above one florin per year at the end of the century at Florence, the grammar master might assemble a slightly more respectable income of 40–50 florins per year from student fees. This was comfortable, but just barely, and compares badly both with the possible salaries in smaller Tuscan towns and with the expectations of Florentine civil servants or notaries.

The numbers alone argue for a situation in which masters had to take on many more students than the twenty to thirty scholars usually suppose teachers had.[53] There is, moreover, a well-documented way teachers could deal with the limited resources offered by student fees, namely, by taking on larger numbers of students in schools with several staff members. Such partnerships are recorded at Florence as early as 1301 and seem to have been common there.[54] The four large grammar schools and the schools of *abbaco* described by Villani in 1338 must have been cooperative schools of this sort. Even if we do not take his enrollment figures literally, Villani's use of the adjective "large" implies two or more masters working together with several apprentice teachers and goodly numbers of students. Florence was, in these years just before the plague, at her highest premodern population. The pressure of the large school-age population might well have made unusually large schools possible.

52. De la Roncière, "Pauvres et pauvreté," 672–81. His raw sums in soldi per diem can be annualized assuming a 250-day year and thus compared directly with the fees received by teachers. But teachers, we must remember, also had fixed business expenses, principally the cost of rent. Rents did not increase significantly across the century, so the observable increases in fees were probably realized by the teachers; see Sapori, "Case e botteghe," 328; cf. Pinto, "I livelli di vita."

53. E.g., Grendler, *Schooling*, 73, who assumes a model with only one teacher or one teacher and one assistant per school and an average of only twenty-three students. This was not necessarily the most common case. A 1342 statute at Lucca considers twenty students the effective *minimum* for a full-time teacher, that is, one who would merit exemption from military service; Barsanti, *Il pubblico insegnamento*, 108. A Parma statute of 1347 sets a *maximum* of fifty students per *repetitore* in a school run by a qualified master of grammar; Frova, *Istruzione*, 111. Patrone Nada, "Super providendo," 66, offers evidence of a single master at Vercelli in 1348 with two hundred students; presumably he was assisted by *repetitores*. She also cites the case of an Ivrean master whose contract of 1428 stipulated that he would receive assistance once his enrollment exceeded eighty students.

54. Debenedetti, "Sui più antichi," 332; cf. ibid., 340–41; Davidsohn, *Firenze*, 206–7; Raith, *Florenz*, 153n218.

Even small schools sometimes included a senior grammarian and one or more *repetitores*, generally younger and unmarried teachers who could live with the master's family and make do with a small wage. Sometimes they were very young indeed. Cristofano di Gano di Guidino, who eventually became a notary in Siena, worked as a private *repetitor* or Latin tutor for six years, starting when he was twelve. He tells us that at his first such job he was paid his expenses, by which he meant clothing, room, and board; in a second instance he was also paid 6 florins a year. Both these positions were set up for him by his own grammar master. Working thus allowed him to secure further training in notarial Latin, so that he was able to matriculate as a notary in 1362, when he was eighteen.[55] Apprenticed *repetitores*, employed by either parents or teachers, carried the weight of the drills and memory work so central to medieval pedagogy. Intensively employed, they might allow for enrollments of fifty, sixty, or even more students per grammar master. In a partnership for a really large school with, say, two grammarians and five or six *repetitores*, it is possible to imagine total enrollments well over 150 students. Thus, if we assume a total staff of seven people, the schoolboys could be divided into seven sections of twenty-five to thirty students each, or 175–210 students. If, again, these students paid an average of 35 soldi per year, the total revenue of the school would be between 102 and 122 florins per year (at the value of the florin in 1350). These figures are entirely hypothetical but well within the limits attested by the sketchy documents available to us for Florence and other cities. Such a seven-member staff would allow each of the senior teachers a comfortable and relatively steady annual income in the 40–50 florin range even after the considerable expenses of operating so large an establishment were paid. Whatever the actual numbers, enlarging the staff and enrollment would increase the earning power of the grammar masters, a formula of which teachers in the period must have been aware.[56]

Another possible source of income was in selling or renting school supplies and books to students. I know of no documentary evidence for

55. Cherubini, *Signori, contadini*, 398.

56. Grendler, *Schooling*, 71–73, rejects such large enrollments as impossible because he is using comparative data from sixteenth-century Venice, where grammar masters seem to have had unusually small schools with one teacher and at most one *repetitor*. Cf. Davidsohn, *Firenze*, 206–7, who cites several examples of partnerships between senior masters and *repetitores* in the context of discussing Villani's "large schools." Even larger schools are anticipated in Parma (1347) by Frova, *Istruzione*, 111, and Genoa (1253) by Petti Balbi, *L'insegnamento*, 84. Denley, "Governments," 103, rightly stresses the crucial place of the *repetitor* in the economics of teaching.

this practice at Florence, but we do know of the case of Bonvesin de la Riva at Milan whose 1315 will makes provision for schoolbooks which he possesses in pawn, presumably because he was repurchasing them from students with an eye to resale.[57] Moreover, the books we examined in Chapter 2 have physical characteristics that suggest that this might have been the practice in Tuscany as well. Certainly more than one unrelated student sometimes used the same book successively, suggesting that it might have been resold by the master. We also have probate inventories for grammar masters that show they possessed multiple copies of commonly used textbooks.[58] These might have been distributed for use in the classroom, or they might have been intended for sale or resale. The strongly uniform design of the textbooks that survive from Florence also suggests that teachers had a hand in the making of the books, either directly or through collaboration with booksellers.[59] Even if grammarians did not sell books directly, they had the skills to work as scribes for pay, another income supplement.[60]

In the end, however, there are no solid figures for teachers' total incomes at Florence. We can only guess about the earning potential of teachers who were not on a municipal payroll, and our best guess must be that it was not great. We have slightly more information about teachers' net worth, though even here the data allow us only impressionistic conclusions. Perhaps the best relative measure of the wealth of the teaching corps as a whole comes from the tax on corporations levied in 1321. In that year, the Guild of Grammar and Abbaco Masters paid a total tax of 36 lire, compared to 32 lire levied against the Glaziers Guild or the Furriers Guild and 40 lire charged to the Shield Makers.[61] This would mean that the

57. The sum was considerable enough to warrant separate mention; Pecchiai, "Documenti," 121: *iudico quod omnes libri scolarium quos habeo in pignore assignentur fratribus de la Colombeta et omnes illi denarij quos debeo habere a scolaribus perveniant ipsis fratribus.*

58. This would seem to be the situation behind a lot of inherited books sold by the company of Orsanmichele in 1357 which contained three Donadellos and several other small grammar books; Carabellese, "La compagnia," 268. See Bertanza and Della Santa, *Documenti*, 25, for a Venetian grammarian who owned three Donatus manuscripts valued at about 10 grossi each in 1336. On the use of probate inventories and guardianship papers as sources for book ownership, see Bec, *Les livres*, and the cautions of Ciapelli, "Libri e letture."

59. There is parallel evidence from Bologna (Gargan, "Libri," 234–36) and from Venice (Bertanza and Della Santa, *Documenti*, 194).

60. See the remarkable brokering of manuscripts for copying by the Vallombrosan monk and schoolmaster Giovanni di Baldassare reported by Brentano-Keller, "Il libretto," esp. 149, where a Prosper is loaned.

61. Raith, *Florenz*, 86–87, 152.

intermediate, pre-university teachers as a group (reading masters were exempt from the tax) were in the same general economic category as skilled craftsmen in the other minor guilds.

Florentine teachers sometimes had enough resources to own real property, although of course we cannot say that because one teacher had available capital the teaching corps as a whole was equally well off. In this too, the teachers resemble small shopkeepers and craftsmen, for they could occasionally but not certainly acquire some property with luck and hard work. One of the earliest recorded *doctores puerorum* (probably a reading and writing master) is Ser Donato di Guido of the Santa Trinità quarter. He purchased a field with trees and a vineyard on the edge of the city in 1292 for the substantial sum of 12 florins. We do not know where Ser Donato acquired the capital for this purchase, but we do know that he still owned the property in 1302, so it seems not to have been an ill-considered or risky venture. Another piece of agricultural land was sold to a Florentine teacher in 1317 for 16 florins. In the next year, yet another elementary teacher entered into a curious three-way partnership with a mother and daughter (his kinswomen?) to cultivate a field rented from the monks of San Miniato. It is unlikely that any of these men worked their fields or gardens themselves; most likely they were looking to earn rents or agricultural produce to supplement their teaching income. In at least one case at Lucca in the 1290s, a grammar master sold feed grain to a wholesaler, implying either that he had agricultural property of his own or was paid a substantial amount in kind.[62]

I do not know of any cases in which an elementary school teacher was able to own his own schoolhouse or even his own residence in Florence, nor was this the usual case in provincial towns where contracts often include the cost of renting a house. Developed urban property was substantially more expensive than garden or agricultural land in and around the city. It was simply beyond the means of most teachers we know about to own houses, especially ones large enough to hold classes as well as to live in. This fact is a measure of the economic limits on those teachers who attempted to live on their earnings without independent means or patronage, for one way small-scale artisans and shopkeepers could get ahead was to own their own places of business. This was also true of intellectual

---

62. Debenedetti, "Sui più antichi," 330–34; Paradisi, *Libro memoriale*, 133. At Venice we know of schoolmasters who owned milk cows and vineyards; see Bertanza and Della Santa, *Documenti*, 38, 117. It was also common for masters to be paid in kind by parents without cash means; Patrone Nada, "Super providendo," 61.

laborers such as notaries and teachers, whose principal capital invest-
ments were in their educations and in places to work at their professions.[63] Teachers, especially, needed space in which to assemble their
students, and, predictably, we can find Florentine contracts for the rental
of shops or houses to teachers. This was a necessary cost of doing business, but it was not possible to convert the cost of housing into an
investment if the teachers could not hope to buy their schoolrooms or
homes. Sometimes these rentals imply fairly large amounts of space, and
they could get complicated, another evidence that some teachers had large
and flourishing schools.

In September 1300, for example, Ser Bino di Ser Accarigi rented a shop
and the adjoining garden in the parish of Santa Felicità from a certain
Casella di Bonaguida de Scorionibus, who owned a partial interest in the
house that contained the shop. The previous tenant was a barber. Master
Bino's rent was 15 soldi per year higher than the barber's, probably
because he intended to use the shop as a schoolroom, which might have
required remodeling and surely would have brought larger numbers of
people into the space. The schoolyear began in Florence at the end of
September, and it may be that the space turned out to be too small, for on
October 25 Ser Bino and his wife rented another property in the immediate neighborhood, a house that had at least two floors plus an upper loft
with a loggia or stair. On this very day Bino stood surety for someone who
was renting a shop and garden at the same address as the September lease,
from the same landlord. It is not absolutely certain that this is exactly the
same property, but it looks like it. If so, it would mean that Ser Bino had
found a substitute tenant for the first shop when he located the second,
larger property to use for his school. This second house had even more
room than Bino could use, for two days later he sublet the upper room to a
barber for about a third of the total rent he was paying for the property.
His annual expenses for the part of the house he and his wife used,
presumably both for living and teaching quarters, was 12 lire and 2 soldi,
roughly 3.5 florins.[64]

Some elementary teachers were substantial enough citizens to make

---

63. Sznura, *L'espansione*, 134–35.

64. Debenedetti, "Sui più antichi," 331–32, and Sznura, *L'espansione*, 137–38, have
each published extracts from some of the documents on this series of transactions. Raith,
*Florenz*, 147, speculates on the possible curricular uses of the garden in the first lease. The
case of Bino's second property is directly parallel to one described in 1394 in Venice in which
a house is described as having a *pars de supra pro una domus et pars de subtus pro una alia*;
Bertanza and Della Santa, *Documenti*, 209.

loans to others or to stand surety for them in small business matters. Usually these transactions involved members of the artisan class, and in one case we are explicitly told that the teacher's own brother was a *fabbro*, a blacksmith. This pair stood surety for a shoemaker in 1297–98 to the tune of 5 florins. In the course of that year-long business affair the teacher, Ser Albertino di Giunto, found it necessary to borrow a small sum from a local notary. Apparently he had some disposable cash but not much. Another teacher of the 1290s made a loan in the range of 3 florins to the wife of a tailor.[65]

In general, then, the rare documents that mention reading and writing masters and grammarians situate them socially in the same class as members of the minor guilds. These guildsmen were artisans and small merchants with a strong corporate structure and sense of entrepreneurial identity. They were capable of making a comfortable living most of the time and a few even became wealthy; but they did not form part of the political elite in trecento Florence. If grammarians did not have some other source of income, they were on the same economic level as small shopkeepers and skilled workers. Unless they were willing to move to other towns or capable of securing a prestigious university position, however, they were unlikely to become rich men. They could claim a higher educational status than artisans and shopkeepers, and they did, but the social realities were that they were not able to rise much above the modest economic status of minor guildsmen.

Teachers' limited economic horizons were only one source of tension within the profession. Several other aspects of Florentine society contributed as well to the uneasy status of the grammarian, among them the high level of violence, the social pretensions and aspirations of students, and even the rhetoric of ceremonial address in a society that took titles and honorifics with great seriousness. In particular, the remarkable level of violence in the schools may have contributed to the way schoolmasters were grouped socially with artisans. Our information on this is rather sketchy, but it is clear that Florentines tolerated violence among schoolboys and even encouraged it. Physical punishment of students was considered a normal and necessary part of teaching and learning throughout the period. Over and above this, however, the schoolboys of Florence in the late thirteenth and early fourteenth centuries were given to vandalism, quarreling, and street fighting. These activities were even institutionalized

65. Debenedetti, "Sui più antichi," 330–31.

in several ways. It was usual for the schoolboys of the town to participate in public executions by stoning condemned political criminals. On occasion, groups of students and other boys even subtracted condemned individuals from their official escorts and carried out the executions themselves.[66] The communal statutes of 1325, moreover, forbid the so-called boys' war or fighting game, apparently a practice that pitted school-age boys against each other in organized fistfights.[67]

Although encouraged and institutionalized in some ways, the violence among schoolboys put them in a group with the untrustworthy lower classes, at least as long as they remained out of control. Certainly a master who consistently failed to control his students' behavior would suffer in reputation for allowing them to associate with ruffians and low-life types. It may even be that the whole profession suffered from the habit of violence among students, although we must be careful not to overdraw this picture given the high level of violence in late medieval society generally. Still, the habit of violence in the schools is in sharp contrast to the moralizing themes of the Latin curriculum.

Yet another tension or ambiguity within the public reputation of the grammar masters was created because grammar students in many cases came from more prosperous and socially more ambitious families than the grammarians could expect to establish for themselves. Parents could look down on teachers in social terms, and their ability to do so must also have colored the grammar master's view of his own professional status. One index of the parents' attitude is the frequency with which they moved their children from school to school; parents wanted to see prompt results and were likely to assume that a lack of progress was the fault of the teacher rather than of the student.[68]

No wonder then that masters insisted on whatever marks of status they could claim. In early fourteenth-century documents, they are almost always granted the honorific *Ser*, otherwise reserved for clerics and notaries. It is unclear whether these teachers were also notaries or whether, as Davidsohn believed, the honorific was a real symbol of status for them. Later in the century, this honorific came more and more to refer to

---

66. Davidsohn, *Firenze*, 198–99; Raith, *Florenz*, 168–70.

67. Caggese, *Statuti*, 2:200. This provision immediately follows others concerned with public order, such as one providing fines for those who throw stones or cause disturbances at night. Patrone Nada, "Super providendo," 68–70, cites comparable evidence for northern Italy.

68. The case of Guerrieri di Tribaldo dei Rossi, detailed by Klapisch-Zuber, "Le chiavi," 766–69, is particularly poignant but entirely typical of this parental attitude.

notaries and priests only; and since it was the notaries who drew up all the documents that tell us about teachers, teachers who were not also notaries had to content themselves with *maestro* or *magister*.[69]

Elementary teaching was so tenuous and marginal a status that, whenever he could, a grammar or reading master would surely claim another, higher occupational title. As a result, relatively few members of the teaching corps appear as teachers in documentary sources. In particular, the large number of notaries and clerics who taught would almost always have appeared only with their higher-status clerical and professional titles. They would have no incentive to characterize themselves as *magistros* unless their teaching was an essential part of the logic of the document to hand. This situation also means that what documents we have on teachers are probably skewed somewhat toward the poorer and less employed teachers who could not claim any other title. The rich Florentine documentation of trecento everyday life is prejudiced against the researcher on this particular matter of economic status because of the relatively low esteem in which grammarians were held at Florence by comparison with their high status in smaller cities.[70]

A differential of status among elementary teachers definitely did exist. The statutes of the Guild of Judges and Notaries distinguish between the low-status reading and writing masters and others. In 1316, several grades of teachers banded together to pay city taxes, but within a few years the reading masters had been exempted from this obligation, probably in recognition that they simply did not earn enough to put them in a taxable category.[71] Grammar teaching, by contrast, was definitely more respectable. Grammar was a university discipline as well as an elementary one, and even elementary grammar teaching was sufficiently respectable that some members of good families could in good conscience engage in teaching at this level. Davidsohn remarks the late thirteenth-century case of Egidio de' Cantori, whose father had held the city's highest political office.[72] There are no comparable examples of grammar masters from prominent families in the fourteenth century, suggesting perhaps that the grammarian was already relegated to a somewhat lesser status by the time of Villani. But the distinction between grammarians and reading masters

69. Davidsohn, *Storia di Firenze*, 7:214; cf. Klapisch-Zuber, "Le chiavi," 774.

70. On the problems of inconsistent use of occupational titles in Florentine notarial documents, see Cohn, *Laboring Classes*, 48.

71. Debenedetti, "Sui più antichi," 339–40; Davidsohn, *Firenze*, 198; Raith, *Florenz*, 152.

72. Davidsohn, *Firenze*, 206n3.

remained.[73] The burden of moral education assumed by grammarians was part of their ability to claim a greater prestige than the lowly reading teachers.

The several tensions that existed between high educational and low economic status could also be resolved in some few cases when a teacher became a private tutor in a wealthy family. Such a teacher would own a dependent but relatively secure position within a well-understood framework of patronage. Moreover, a family that was willing to make an investment in a full-time teacher for its children was likely to have strong cultural interests that would provide the grammarian with a sense of esteem adequate to his own pretensions. Unfortunately for the grammarians, very few Florentines felt the need to educate their children privately, and even those that did would only employ a master for the six to twelve years it would take to educate all their children. A post in a family was likely to be considered ideal for a very young teacher, but not for one who had or wanted to start a family of his own.[74]

Every time we seek Florentine documents that would substantiate the grammarians' claims to high status, then, we are disappointed. This cannot be a coincidence. The economic and social reality was that grammarians could claim only a modest status. They were not as badly regarded as reading and writing masters, but neither could they achieve social prestige or economic independence. Education was valued in Florence, but apparently less so than in the nearby provincial towns of Tuscany. In particular, Latin education of the traditional, moralizing sort was marginalized or treated with some ambivalence at Florence, at least among the merchant oligarchy.

For merchant fathers, grammar was a course of study appropriate for those rare sons who showed promise in the linguistic skills needed for ecclesiastical, medical, notarial, or legal careers. One of the tensions imbedded in the grammar course, consequently, was that it was often preprofessional training for those boys who were in some sense about to reject (or get beyond) the merchant worldview of their own fathers. Although these fathers were the city's rulers, or at any rate made up most of its enfranchised, political class, both fathers and sons recognized the existence of a larger, mostly Latin culture that claimed a more universal

73. It persisted into the fifteenth century; Black, "Florence," 34–35.
74. Bec, *Les marchands*, 387. Black, "Florence," 34–37, portrays the widespread employment of private tutors in fifteenth-century Florence, a practice he traces to the turn of the century and the influence of the humanists in the generation after Salutati; he does not document any cases for the early or mid-fourteenth century.

rule than even the most pompous Florentine civic propaganda could claim. A son who chose a professional career with universalizing pretensions, even if he did so with the approval of his father, was setting out into a world beyond his parents' own comfortable horizons.

Perhaps even more compromising to the grammarian's prestige was the fact that grammar was not a subject valued in and for itself; at Florence it was too often merely pre-professional. Most trecento Latin professionals had a clearer place in society and a stronger sense of worth than grammar masters did. We know, for example, that many if not most notaries and lawyers were the sons of other notaries and lawyers. Strong family traditions enhanced these men's claim to an elevated place in Florentine society, even in the face of political failure and personal adversity.[75] But an elementary grammarian who had ambitions for his sons would almost surely have hoped that they would achieve a university degree and appointment, or perhaps that they would be able to move into the better-paying and more prestigious legal or other professions. We may imagine, then, that the grammarians owned a modest sense of personal achievement and a certain optimism for the future of their offspring, but by no means a secure sense of fixed place in society.

The Florentine grammarian surely thought of himself as part of the academic world, in contact with a pan-European intellectual elite. All his claims to be a useful part of society resided in his power to introduce his students to academic and professional language and to a worldview that extended beyond Florence. But, in the end, the grammar master's own mentality and social status were more typical of artisans or minor guildsmen than of the city's ruling elites. And even the Florentine ruling class did not value a broader view, unless it was that of international banking.

The economic constraints on the grammarians' claims to social status almost surely contributed to the extreme conservatism of their curricular program as well. As I have remarked earlier, the lack of a university at Florence made it difficult for the grammar masters there to insert themselves into an extended academic hierarchy and insulated them from the innovations undertaken in the university disciplines in the thirteenth and fourteenth centuries. Although this meant that they were immune from

---

75. The degree to which this could be a self-conscious and highly intellectualized sense of family and personal worth is proved by the remarkable pair of father and son treatises on nobility penned in the late 1370s by Lapo da Castiglionchio and his son Bernardo, *Epistola o sia ragionamento*. On this text, see the important essay of Guglielminetti, *Memoria*, 232–38.

much of the scholastic specialization of Latin study and less influenced by scholastic curricular reform, it also meant that they missed out on the new humanist ideals that were first nurtured in the university towns of the north.[76] Moreover, it isolated them from other intellectuals who would have been natural allies in the battle to preserve the status of Latin as a privileged language. Relegated as they were to middling social status and without the support of more prestigious university scholars, Florentine grammarians were unable to press any claims for a new curriculum with the parents of their students. Quite the opposite happened. They insisted on the age-old curriculum and modified it by making it less inclusive. In particular, they stripped the grammar course of any utility in teaching classical style and classical mythology and so made it less irrelevant, they thought, to the simple moralizing needs of the commercial ruling classes.

In terms of social and intellectual currents, this marginalization of Latin grammatical study meant that the sophisticated but anticlassicizing mendicant program was the strongest force in Florentine Latin culture. Grammar masters, if they did not wish to lose their students, had to ally themselves with this mendicant program of broad education in moral decision making and rigid Christian orthodoxy. This stance tended to align them against the supposedly secularizing tendencies of the humanists. Grammar, at Florence, became the mouthpiece of the mendicants; its status depended closely on the mission assigned to it by them.

76. On this theme, see Raith, *Florenz*, 155–57.

# CONCLUSIONS

The grammar masters of trecento Florence had only middling social status. In large part this was because they had inherited a discipline that had not yet transformed itself to serve urban culture in a way that made sense to middle- and upper-class parents. Florentine Latin teachers were employed directly by parents and were dependent on them, but the conservative discipline of grammar had evolved to serve a different cultural context altogether, that of the monasteries and secular clergy of the early and central Middle Ages. The bilingual culture of the trecento required skilled cultural translators *from* Latin, but most of the grammar teaching corps recognized only the older mission of Latin study, that of translating students *into* a Latin realm and out of the vernacular one. In the preceding chapters I have outlined a new picture of elementary education at Florence, one that takes account of the highly conservative nature of the basic grammar course and its practitioners in the Arno city.

The traditional Latin course and the needs of the city were at odds, and nothing short of an intellectual revolution could bridge the resulting gap. Several generations of humanists sought to effect such a revolution, but the outcome of the humanist reform was not the inevitable success subsequent historiography has presented. The humanists of the fifteenth century did succeed in one area where their trecento counterparts had not, in convincing the ruling classes of the need for a Latin-educated intelligentsia. But they did so most thoroughly in the north of Italy and by creating a new Latin elitism, not by broadening the application of Latin in Italian society.

At Florence the humanists' influence was always only partial; until the very end of the fourteenth century it hardly made a dent in the attitudes of most influential Florentines. This may seem curious, for in the thirteenth and early fourteenth centuries Florence was in the vanguard of vernacular literacy and record keeping and at the center of the vast movement of translation of classical and medieval literature. The city had one of the most advanced and differentiated urban economies in Europe. Its merchant oligarchy possessed both enormous self-confidence and a sense of cultural superiority that did not bow before the haughty claims of older, more universalizing cultural institutions, not even the Roman church or empire.

The advanced state of Florence's political and business culture, however, did not bring with it a vernacular high culture of distinction. The greatest "Florentine" intellectuals of the century all studied outside Florence and lived much of their productive lives away from the Tuscan metropolis. They deeply resented the lack of acclaim offered them by their native city. Dante, Petrarch, and Boccaccio all experienced political exile, either personally or in the circumstances of their birth. These, the city's greatest poets, developed an émigré culture, one that represented and embraced intellectual horizons much broader than those of the Florentines themselves. Of the prominent early humanists only Coluccio Salutati made a career at the center of the city's public life, and his achievement came only in the last years of the century. Salutati, moreover, was not a Florentine by birth, family, or education. Like humanism itself, the great chancellor was an import to Florence.

Inside the city, there evolved a strongly nativist, secularizing, and popularizing vernacular culture, one with distinct prejudices against Latin study and even a certain antiintellectualism. The most obvious single symptom of this complex of prejudices was the city's inability to found a lasting university. This was a direct result of a lack of political will or intellectual breadth on the part of the ruling oligarchy.[1] Latin grammarians at Florence, meanwhile, remained highly conservative. They stubbornly held onto a philosophy and certain methods of teaching that had developed in the monastic Middle Ages. Others of their ideals and methods had emerged in the early stages of urbanization in Italy, when Latin was still the only means of formal communication. These medieval modifications had adapted the ancient language to new ends: on the one hand, the spiritual and administrative needs of churchmen and, on the other, the record keeping and diplomatic requirements of increasingly

1. Cf. Garfagnini, "Città e Studio," 117–20.

complex urban governments. Although we might think of these as popularizing reforms in that they enlarged the role of Latin as the number of literate Italians grew, they were not really adequate to the new non-Latin literacy. They did not create a clear, unambiguous place for Latin study in the bilingual society of urban Italy.

Of course, all this was also true in many places outside Florence, but nowhere was the contrast of the old literacy with the new sharper or more crippling to the pretensions of grammarians. The principal symptom of this disjunction of needs is to be found in the remarkable expansion of the reading and writing schools described by Villani. Thousands of students were learning to read, most of them entirely without intending ever to study Latin, a language they did not need and could not use. Even the narrow, pre-professional courses in notarial arts and *ars dictaminis* were no longer enough to justify Latin training in the minds of many Florentine parents. The professional student still needed to study Latin, but his chances to use it outside school were fewer than ever. Merchants and artisans wanted most to be able to read the *volgare* ledgers, business letters, and legal instruments that concerned them directly. In such a world, Latin study was increasingly marginalized. It was forced to be elitist even if it claimed a universalizing mission.

Moreover, the grammarians of Florence responded to the tensions of the new urban environment by becoming more conservative and restrictive than ever in what they taught. The curriculum shrank in size and variety because teachers feared that the more purely literary texts would seem frivolous or immoral to the earnest, profit-oriented parents of their students. In particular, the lively neo-Ovidian and neo-Terentian texts of the central Middle Ages were dropped, because it was not easy to explain away their frank obscenity and their authors' obvious delight in moral ambiguities. Although these reductionist changes were probably aimed at buttressing the claims of grammarians to be offering a course in moral decision making, they impoverished the linguistic and literary content of the course and diminished even more its claims to have anything to do with everyday life.

This Florentine trend in grammar teaching was not by any means inevitable. Other, more creative paths were taken outside the Arno city. Most striking of these alternatives, because it happened so near Florence, was the case of the smaller Tuscan towns that established well-paying municipal chairs of grammar for the elementary instruction of their children and competed for the available pool of good teachers. Schools elsewhere in Italy embraced still other forms of the grammar curriculum.

At Genoa, a distinctive business Latin course had begun to develop in the thirteenth century. In the Po valley cities, university grammarians, influenced by the nascent humanism of Padua, began teaching classical poetry and rhetoric and slowly encouraged elementary grammarians to teach a more classicizing Latin too. Meanwhile, in Germany and England, where the demand for clerical education remained strong, the traditional grammar course had a continuing life well into the fifteenth century with a curriculum very like that of the High Middle Ages, dominated by Ovidianism hedged round by traditional practices of Christian devotion. In Catalonia in the early years of our period, moreover, Ramon Llull founded a radically new school of literary training based on a reform of scholastic grammatical and rhetorical teaching under the influence of monastic and mendicant spirituality. Idiosyncratic as it was, Llullism was immensely influential in creating a popular, latinate culture that was distinctly not classicizing and not humanistic and yet lasted well into the sixteenth century as a system of education.[2]

Even the rich mendicant intellectual tradition at Florence could not salvage a place for the impoverished Latin course offered by the city's lay grammar masters. The mendicants embraced a highly pragmatic form of Latin education, aimed at moving their students quickly along into Scripture study and theology. The object from the beginning of the course was to allow each friar to preach as effectively and learnedly as he could, given his particular stage in spiritual and intellectual life, but never to become sidetracked into literary study for its own sake. Nor, for that matter, were mendicants allowed to found elementary schools for lay folk: the education of children on a large scale would have been equally distracting to their fundamental preaching mission. When we look at the many translations undertaken by mendicants, we can see that their priority was not Latin study but rather the effective transfer of Latin moral categories into vernacular thought. Conversely, they carefully preserved a distinct Latin realm for speculative theology and scriptural commentary, fields their particular brand of education allowed them to dominate from the thirteenth century onward. Thus the mendicants had a clear, single-minded reason for studying Latin, and they set rigid limits to its study. It is no wonder that Dante, when his life took a philosophical turn, went to "the schools of the religious" at Florence for instruction.[3]

2. Johnston, *Spiritual Logic*, is the fundamental study of Llull's new system. The other phenomena here sketched are described in works already cited, especially those by Grendler, Petti Balbi, Witt, and Lucchi.

3. *Convivio* II.xii.2.

The single-mindedness of the mendicants effectively set them apart from both the traditionalist, lay grammar masters and the new humanists. We often forget that Giovanni Dominici's attacks on the humanist circle of Salutati were accompanied by a much more generalized concern that Latin schools had gone to the dogs. His advice to Bartolomea degli Olbizzi was to avoid lay schools for her children, and those run by clerics as well, on the grounds that the setting of such urban schools was not conducive to disciplined learning.[4] By this he implied that Latin study itself was dangerous in any but the closely supervised mendicant framework.

As an alternative for laymen, mendicants like Dominici proposed an entirely different sort of study quite outside the Latin schools. Moral precepts and the basics of dogmatics could be studied through private reading of vernacular translations of selected spiritual texts, frequent attendance at sermons, and frequent confession. Or, if laymen must study Latin, Dominici proposed, let it be on the basis of a strictly traditional and fully Christianized curriculum. Given the stature and eloquence of this sort of criticism, it is no wonder that the lay grammarians weighed their choice of texts carefully.

We can clearly see that Latin study was in a state of crisis brought on by its inability to adapt to century-long changes in Florentine society. We should not, however, imagine that the grammarians themselves were much aware of this crisis until the very end of the trecento. On the contrary, their defensive behavior in modifying the curriculum bears all the marks of a complacent and self-interested teaching corps, responding to some parental and ecclesiastical pressure to be sure, but nonetheless certain of the value and importance of doing things in the traditional way. It is always hard to write the history of conservatism, even more that of complacency, but it seems to me that here we have a classic case. Indeed, the grammarians' defensiveness seems to have been both a response to their relatively low social status and a reaction to mendicant-inspired zeal for the moral improvement of their charges. Certainly the mendicants transformed the culture of lay spirituality profoundly. This could not have failed to affect the expectations of parents. But mendicant pressure did not convert the grammarians into zealots for the cause of the new vernacular literacy. Quite the opposite happened. Those who chose to remain lay teachers were making a personal choice against joining one of the prestigious mendicant orders and in favor of an older sort of Latin literacy. They could not do so without accommodating the changed expectations

4. Dominici, *Regola*, ed. Salvi, 134–35.

of their public, but they also had to work against the more radical implications of the mendicant program.

Myopically, the conservative grammarians of Florence did not notice that they too were transforming tradition, leaving behind much of the breadth and depth of the universalizing Latin culture they claimed to represent. Trecento grammarians inherited a Latin program that had developed (at least potentially) into a carefully calibrated and broadly representative study of Latin literature from the ancient moral poets to modern spiritual and satirical authors. By subtraction and restriction, the Florentine masters transformed this program into the pallid and repetitive study of a few moral precepts embodied in the words of mediocre authors. This process began in eleventh-century Italy, when the emphasis on legal and notarial usage relegated Latin stylistics to a few forms such as letter writing. The process was Italy-wide. But the Florentine masters seem to have been particularly reductionist and unimaginative in choosing texts from the large number of possible readings.

Perhaps we should say merely that the masters and students of Florence were unambitious, for all the texts eliminated from the core course were still to be found in libraries and at stationers, and some advanced students continued to read them. A contributing factor to the small ambitions of the course was the high drop-out rate. Many students started the latinizing program and got one massive dose of memorization, rule making, and earnest moralizing in the form of Donatus and Cato. Rather fewer got the second due measure of Latin moralizing from Prosper and Aesop. Fewer still went on to anything requiring more careful and sophisticated study. Few indeed really learned Latin.

The narrowness of the curriculum at Florence may prompt us to wonder if the masters there did not also jettison the moral program of the medieval Latin course. Certainly, such mendicant critics as Giovanni Dominici accused elementary teachers of corrupting the young. Dominici's criticism, however, implies that moral education was still part of the expectations for Latin study in the last years of the trecento; he compares its current decadence to an ideal situated in his own youth only a generation earlier.

Although we will never find a source that says clearly and unambiguously that the medieval moral program for grammar was firmly and fully in place in trecento Florence, I think there are several good reasons for seeing its strong influence in elementary classrooms there. First of all, the particular choices made in narrowing down the reading course betray a sense of moral purpose that seems to have been a response to mendicant ideals rather than an original creation. The course represents, indeed, a rather earnest and unimaginative sort of moralizing that would seem to rule out any radical changes in the underlying philosophy of education. The Florentine masters were simply not that original or learned. It was easier to tinker with the reading list than challenge the status quo, easier to respond to specific criticisms than to rethink the entire curriculum.

Second, the neoplatonic spirit of literary training had changed relatively little during the Middle Ages, even though the curriculum itself had altered considerably. Latin reading was for Augustine and remained for Dante a multilevel, richly spiritual literary exercise. In the intervening millennium, this sense of mission had deepened and acquired a mystical and meditative dimension still clearly visible in the trecento use of Pruden-tius and the *Physiologus* in the basic course. Elementary Latin study had to provide entrée to this world; the many additions to the curriculum in the twelfth and thirteenth centuries were attempts to reflect this deepening Christian mission. The changes we can observe in that period, however, were additive, not radical, reforms. New texts were included in the tradi-tional curriculum, but there is little evidence that teaching techniques or goals changed. The reductive modifications of the Florentine masters were almost surely qualitatively the same.

Last, we can see the influence of the medieval moral program in all the early humanist works on grammar, and so we know that this theoretical program survived into the fifteenth century. There is no good reason to think that Christianized, neoplatonic educational theory had been lost in the meantime, although the restriction of the curriculum may well have diluted its impact. On the contrary, most of the restrictive modifications made at Florence in the fourteenth century can be explained as real if misguided reactions to the demands of a moral agenda for Latin. In particular, the Florentine masters displayed great concern for orthodoxy and control, both of the in-class behavior of their students and of their reading in general, because this last would affect their whole conduct of life (and what their parents saw of their education). This same sort of concern, though with different ends and means, would characterize the reforms of the humanist educators as well.

The most important single lesson of this book is that trecento Florence had a teaching corps, a teaching tradition, and a restricted Latin curricu-lum that were unique to itself. This and other localisms like it have been obscured in the traditional historiography of education because we have tended to see and stress the similarities between the practices of different times and places, not the differences, and perhaps because we have taken a bit too seriously the universalizing claims of Latin educators (beginning with our own high school Latin teachers in the twentieth century). Latin teachers *have* always claimed a universalizing ideal, but the content of the Latin universe has changed radically across the centuries. Florentine grammar masters backed themselves into a dead end in the history of Latin literature and Latin pedagogy, under the dual influence of their city's profoundly antiintellectual commercial culture and the vital but single-minded program of the mendicants. Outside Florence various medieval latinisms had continuing life. In the Arno city, and in much of Italy eventually, the Christianized moralizing of the medieval Latin curriculum was slowly supplanted by the civic and political moralizing of the humanists. Eventually, the Jesuit reformers of the sixteenth century swept away all moralizing in language education and gave us modern Latin, a philological rather than a philosophical construct, a skill and not a norm.

# A   P   P   E   N   D   I   X

# CENSUS OF
# READING BOOKS

The following descriptive census of elementary and intermediate Latin reading books written in Tuscany in the late thirteenth and fourteenth centuries is intended to offer summary descriptions of all the manuscripts of this type known to me. It grows out of a preliminary census published in *Scrittura e civiltà* 13 (1989), 411-40, and has been enlarged significantly with the help of scholars who responded to that essay. Still, no such list can be definitive, because manuscripts of this type survive in large numbers and do not always bear evidence of provenance.

I have chosen to be conservative in my principles of inclusion and so have described only manuscript readers of indisputable Tuscan origin or provenance, and only those that can be assigned to the late thirteenth or fourteenth centuries with a high degree of certainty. This core list forms Part I of this appendix and is referred to throughout this book as the census. Part II of the Appendix is a list of trecento Tuscan books designed similarly to those in Part I but significantly oversized. Part III lists manuscripts examined but excluded.

The division of the three lists follows codicological principles and not textual ones. I hope the fruits of this exercise in classification will demonstrate its value. Isolating the second group clearly shows how format reflects the way texts were used. Although the assignments were made purely on the basis of format, primarily size, this group consists almost entirely of advanced grammatical and rhetorical manuals, not of reading books as such.  It shows how the reader format could be adapted for other uses.

The parameters for the first group, however, need some further explanation, since I use this census in Chapter 2 as the basis for my generalizations on the nature of classroom practice. Conservative geographical principles of inclusion for this group, the census proper, ensure that we achieve a sense of what was peculiar to the Tuscan tradition in the period covered here.  In two cases (I.29 and I.38), I have included books of which I have seen photographs that make it clear that they are Tuscan.  In other cases, my examination of microfilms has been inconclusive, and these manuscripts I have relegated to Part III.  Other books in the third list are clearly of the period and format that interests us, but they come from other parts of Italy.   Doubtful cases bear the indication "Tuscan?"  I excluded texts that occur in any of these manuscripts in the totals for frequency given in Chapter 2, because including them would dilute the regional sample I have aimed for throughout this study.

I have also excluded from the census many copies of the school authors that do not conform to the format described in Chapter 2, because for the most part books of other sorts cannot be said with any degree of certainty to have been used for reading instruction.   The list of books examined but excluded includes manuscripts in other formats, which I have labeled auct or ref or inst, a practice I hope will clarify my principles of description and selection on design grounds.   The books marked auct (*auctores*-level), for example, are genuine schoolbooks but do not follow the format pattern of the books in the census.  They may or may not have been designed for use in the classroom, but they show clear traces of student use at a relatively advanced level.  Excluding these books helps the census reflect the earlier part of the Latin curriculum, the latinizing stage.  At more advanced levels, students used many books not designed specifically for school reading. Moreover, we know that at all periods, especially in the early Middle Ages before the development of schoolbooks designed as such, some students were given adult books to use in learning to read even at the most elementary levels.  This practice surely continued to be the case in Trecento Florence, perhaps especially in clerical schools. Inevitably, then, my conservative principles of inclusion prejudice the sample somewhat against the most sophisticated and precocious students, against the least orthodox teachers, and against students studying in monastery schools. The census also tends to focus on schools that used texts and books available from stationers.

The sample is better and more useful for this inherent prejudice; a more inclusive census would quickly become vague and amorphous. It would not let us see what the real prejudices of the lay teaching corps were, because we could not be sure that all the books included were really used in the classroom or used regularly there. Such a large sample would also reflect many opportunistic and merely occasional uses of available books and would not give due consideration to those books deliberately designed for school use. By focusing only on what I can be sure was used in the classroom in a deliberate way, I describe a real phenomenon in the history of pedagogy and book production both. Consequently, we achieve a more limited but more solid understanding of choices actually made by teachers. I hope that in this way we also avoid modern prejudices in favor of pedagogical originality and broadly inclusive curricula, prejudices that simply did not exist in the late Middle Ages.

The entries in the census are not full-dress codicological descriptions, but they do attempt to offer enough detail to fill out the summary of the Latin reader format provided in Chapter 2. Within descriptions, Roman numerals distinguish the parts of composite manuscripts so as to describe clearly the units that survive from the fourteenth century. Descriptions do not include data on the subsequent history of the manuscripts (present bindings, later reader's marks, etc.) except as these evidence the Tuscan provenance or early history of the book in question. Bibliographical references are selective and usually include only significant descriptions of the manuscripts or those cases in which critical editors of the texts have made use of these manuscripts.

Each entry begins with the location and press mark of the manuscript, followed on the next line by the usual indications of membrane, century (in Roman numerals), and overall size. The contents of the manuscript are then listed by folio numbers using the commonplace name of the texts. Standard editions of the texts are given in the Bibliography. No collations of texts against printed editions have been attempted, but obviously fragmentary copies are indicated. Texts not originally part of the manuscript and added in a later hand are marked with an asterisk (*). Unidentified texts are described generically and an incipit is given. Foliation follows that actually in the manuscript, with inaccuracies noted at the beginning of the physical description of each book.

In the next paragraph, a collation of the gatherings is provided in the usual form; where there is more than one medieval manuscript in a composite book, the break between the separate parts is indicated in the collation with a semicolon. The remainder of this paragraph describes the book as designed and written, including information on the ruling, script, and decoration. In some cases, aspects of the decoration are not described here but left to the following paragraph. My aim in this is to distinguish clearly between the design of such readers and the subsequent history of these heavily used little books.

A separate paragraph follows, where appropriate, to indicate evidence that bears on the subsequent use of the book in the fourteenth or early fifteenth centuries. This paragraph includes information on readers' notes, annotation not part of the design of the book, decoration obviously added later than the writing of the book, and ownership marks.

PART I. LATIN READING BOOKS WRITTEN IN TRECENTO TUSCANY

The following are Latin readers properly speaking, that is, single texts or anthologies of texts designed for teaching reading at the Latinizing level.

I.1  **Cortona, Biblioteca Comunale e dell'Accademia Etrusca.  MS 82** Parchment, dated 1335, 22 x 15.9 cm

Poetic and epistolary miscellany compiled by a student, including:

| | |
|---|---|
| 17-38r | *Ilias latina.* |
| 47r-v | *Anon., *Epistola leonis ad asinum.* |
| 52-54v | Anon., *De casu mundi.* |
| 55-56v | *Pseudo-Ovid, *De lombardo et lumaco.* |

(Access restrictions precluded my preparing a more detailed listing of contents; cf. that in Mazzatinti, *Inventarii* vol. 18, 42-43).

56 numbered leaves: 1-7⁸. 25 lines per page. Single column ruled in lead from prickings, except 17-24v ruled from ink dots, 14 x 9.2 cm, double line at left margin. The young scribe, Galeazzo di Floriomonte de Brognolis, identifies himself in three colophons on 38, 46v, and 54v. He writes an accomplished round gothic book hand and has supplied rubrics, red flourishes for line initials, minor initials, and three rather clumsy major initials decorated with birds or monsters on 1, 17, 49. The *Ilias latina* was begun (17r-v) in a separate round gothic book hand and continued by Galeazzo.

The *Ilias latina* has interlinear and marginal glosses of an historical and mythological sort, written in a neat, small, contemporary gothic hand, possibly that of Galleaccio. Additions on 47 and 55-56 in a *mercantesca* (XIVᵉˣ). Sparse index marks and lexical notes (XV) elsewhere.

*See:* Gehl, "Latin Readers ," 413-14; Mancini, *I manoscritti*, 46; Bonacina, "De lombardo et lumaco," 111-12.

**I.2. Cambridge.** University Library. MS Ee.VI.34
Paper fragment, XIV (Tuscan?), 19.5 x 13 cm

The flyleaves of this manuscript contain two leaves of a Tuscan Prosper. 27 or 28 lines per page. Single column ruled in ink, 14 x 9 cm. Expert round gothic book hand. Single flourished initial in red.

Minor interlinear and marginal annotation.

*See:* University of Cambridge, *Catalogue* 2:272-73.

**I.3.  Eton.  Eton College Library.  MS 202**
Parchment fragments, XIV[1],  11.7 x 9.2 cm

1-4 (flyleaves)   Prosper of Aquitaine, *Epigrammata* (fragment).

4 unnumbered leaves inserted sideways as front flyleaves to a
small personal copy (XIV/XV) of the *Doctrinale* of Alexander of
Villa Dei.   They constitute two leaves, probably originally a
bifolium.   31 or 32 lines per page originally; we may estimate the
original size of the leaves at ca. 25 x 20 cm.   Single column ruled
drypoint, 16.1 x 11.2 cm.   Expert round gothic book hand, rather
narrow and upright in look.   Alternating red and blue initials with
very simple flourishing.   Frequent corrections over erasures in hand
of scribe.

Ownership mark (XV) in margin of 2r:   *Franceschiolo.*
*See*:  Ker, *Medieval Manuscripts* 2:777-78.

**I.4.  Florence, Archivio di Stato.  Carte Strozziane III[a] ser., 72**
Parchment, XIV[2], 20.8 x 14.6 cm

1-20          Henry of Settimello, *Elegia.*
20v           blank

20 numbered leaves: 1-2[8], 3[4].   26 lines per page.   Single
column ruled drypoint, 14.5 x 9.5 cm, double line at left margin.
Expert,  handsome  round  gothic  book  hand;  rubrics  in  hand
contemporary to that of text.   Multicolored initial Q on 1.
Alternating red and blue minor initials.

Two erased ownership marks of schoolboy sort, 20v, where
also many other scribbles.   Annotation (XIV) consists of elementary
grammatical notes throughout, extensively only on 1-2v, and
rhetorical *divisiones* in margins on 1, 1v, 2, 5v.   Scratch graffiti of
male genitalia, 6v.   Pressmark on front fly: Carte Strozzi-Uggucioni,
72.

*See*:  Gehl, "Latin Readers," 414; Cremaschi, *Elegia*, 19;
Guasti, *Carte Strozziane*, 3:206.

**I.5. Florence, Biblioteca Medicea-Laurenziana. Plut. 33,32**
Parchment, XIVex, 24.2 x 17 cm

1-25v          Henry of Settimello, *Elegia*. Provided with a careful, thorough marginal commentary in hand of text, inc. (opposite line 7), *In parte precedenti signa posuit henricus*. . .
    25 numbered leaves: 1-2⁸, 3³ (binion less one; stub before 17), 4⁶. 20 lines per page. Single column ruled in ink, 14 x 8.5 cm., triple rule at right margin, double at left. Expert, upright round gothic, slightly nervous in feel. No initials, but spaces provided.
    *See*: Gehl, "Latin Readers," 415; Cremaschi, *Elegia*, 21; Bandini, *Catalogus* 2:128-29.

**I.6. Florence, Biblioteca Medicea-Laurenziana. Plut. 37, 24**
Parchment, XIV, 19.6 x 13.2 cm

1-22          Prosper of Aquitaine, *Epigrammata*.
22v           blank
    22 numbered leaves plus one unnumbered pastedown at front: 1² (pastedown plus fol. 1), 2⁷ (quaternion less one; stub after 2), 3⁸, 4⁶. 27 lines per page. Single column ruled drypoint, 12.4 x 8.8 cm. Uneven and inexpert round gothic book hand. Alternating red and pale blue initials painted over sketches in brown ink. Catchwords added in later (XV?) hand 8v, 16v.
    Bound with Horace, *Ars poetica* written in German gothic book hand (XIII).
    *See*: Gehl, "Latin Readers," 415; Bandini, *Catalogus* 2:258.

**I.7. Florence, Biblioteca Medicea-Laurenziana. Plut. 77, 16**
Parchment, XIV¹, 21.8 x 16 cm

I.
1-24v         Henry of Settimello, *Elegia*.
25r-v         blank

II.

26-33v          John the Abbot, *Liber de septem virtutibus*.

33 numbered leaves: 1[8], 2[9] (includes 3 leaves of paper supplied in XV as present fols. 9, 10, and 16), 3[8]; 4[8]. 22 lines per page (exceptionally 23 in I only). I: Single column ruled in lead, 16 x 10 cm, double line right and left. II: Single column ruled in lead, 15 x 9.5 cm. Both I and II in expert round gothic book hands, that of II slightly more angular. Folios supplied to second gathering written in hand imitating that of I. Decoration for the two sections is the same, possibly supplied at the time of their assembly in present form (XV?). Major initials in red and blue; yellow wash over line initials. II had earlier decoration of some minor initials in red and black.

Minor etymological annotation on first folios of each text.

*See*: Gehl, "Latin Readers," 416; Cremaschi, *Elegia*, 21; Bandini, *Catalogus* 3:138; Klein, "Johannis abbatis *Liber*," 182.

### I.8.  Florence, Biblioteca Medicea-Laurenziana.  Plut. 91, sup. 4
Paper, composite variously XIV and XV, 21.2 x 14.3 cm

Ia.

| | |
|---|---|
| 1-22 | *Ilias latina*. |
| 22v | [Coluccio Salutati], *Elegia*. |

II.

| | |
|---|---|
| 23-27v | *Physiologus*. |
| 28-33 | Theodulus, *Ecloga*. |
| 33v-34v | Coluccio Salutati, *Fabula de uulpo et cancro*. |

Ib.

| | |
|---|---|
| 35-36v | *Chartula*. |
| 37-40v | Prudentius, *Dittochaeon*. |
| 41-49 | *Facetus*, inc. *Moribus et vita*. |
| 49-65 | Prudentius, *Psychomachia*. |
| 65-66 | Anon. argumenta for Statius, *Achilleid*. |
| 66-77 | Giovanni Bonandrea, *Ars dictaminis*. |
| 77-89 | Avianus, *Fabulae*. |
| 89v | *Fragment of *Chartula*. |

| | |
|---|---|
| 90-92v | blank |
| III. | |
| 93-117v | Claudian, *De raptu Proserpinae.* |
| 118-120r | blank |
| 120v | *annotations (see below). |

120 numbered leaves: $1^{12}$, $2^{10}$ (pages disordered); $3^{12}$; $4^{10}$, $5$-$8^{12}$; $9$-$10^{12}$, $11^{4}$. 25 to 28 lines per page. Single column throughout, ruled in lead, 14.5 x 7.1 cm. Expert round gothic book hands, except for inserted fragment on 89v in an inexpert book hand imitating the hand of the rest of I. Hands of I and II are XIV/XV, that of III is XV$^{in}$. Watermarks: Scissors in all paper of III. Bow and arrow throughout II and in second gathering of I. A variety of other marks also in I. Hand of part I has supplied catchwords throughout I and II. Most major initials have ink sketches for geometrical or figured decoration; only that on 23 and author portrait on 1 are colored, both clumsily in red and dark green. Catchword on 12v decorated with a sketch of a fantastical bird; other catchwords framed in brown ink.

Ownership mark (XV) on 120v: *Iste liber est Pauli Morelli de Morellis. Isti sunt libri qui continentur in isto volumine nomina eorum infra descripta* . . . There follows a list of the contents of the entire volume, excepting the fragment on 89v. Items in the table are numbered with Arabic numerals and the corresponding numbers appear in the rest of the manuscript in one of two ways, either on the upper left corner of the folios on which the text begins (23, 35), or in the lower left corner of the first folio of the gathering inside which the text begins (e.g. number 2 on fol. 1, no. 6 on 35, no. 7 on 45).

*See*: Gehl, "Latin Readers," 416-17; Thiel, "Neue Handschriften," 258-63; Banker, "Giovanni di Bonandrea," 3-20; idem, "The Ars dictaminis," 153-68; Jenson and Bahr-Volk, "Fox and Crab," 162-75; Scaffai, "Tradizione," 262 (where part I is dated XV); Bandini, *Catalogus* 3:745-47.

I.9.  Florence, Biblioteca Medicea-Laurenziana.  Plut. 91, sup. 38
Parchment, XIV/XV, 23.7 x 16.8 cm

| | |
|---|---|
| 1-23 | Prosper of Aquitaine, *Epigrammata.* |
| 23v | Prayer to Virgin Mary. |
| 24-24v | blank |

24 numbered leaves:  1-2$^8$, 3$^6$, 4$^2$ (this gathering once a wrapper for the whole book).  30 lines per page.  Single column ruled drypoint, 15.8 x 11.7 cm.  Compact, expert round gothic book hand with hairline flourishes.  The book is provided with an elaborate decorative program including two major initials (on 1 and 12) in gold, orange, green, and purple; a full-page border on 1 with coat of arms (black and white lion rampant on red shield) at base; red and blue flourished minor initials; yellow wash line initials; two catchwords and two major headings in large gold and blue letters; and on 23v, originally the back cover of the wrapper, a vernacular prayer to the Virgin arranged in serpentine fashion.

Very minor annotation in *volgare* on 9 and 17v only; one marginal note on 14v.  The whole book was badly water damaged at some early date and parts of the text rewritten in a hand nearly contemporary to that of the original scribe on 1v, 3v, 6, 14.

I.10.  Florence, Biblioteca Medicea-Laurenziana.  Conv. Soppr. 416
Parchment, XIV$^2$, 22 x 16 cm

| | |
|---|---|
| 1-33 | Pseudo-Boethius, *De vita scholastica* with extensive gloss to Book I only. |
| 33v | blank |

33 numbered leaves:  1-4$^8$, 5$^1$ (present 33 pasted to modern paper fly).  16 lines per page to 14v, thereafter 17 or 18 lines per page ruled in lead, 13.9 x 9.8 cm with additional ruling in all margins to define space for gloss.  Highly calligraphic round gothic book hand for text, small gothic for commentary.  Simple, elongated red initials with white highlights throughout.

*See*: Gehl, "Latin Readers," 417-18.

**I.11. Florence, Biblioteca Medicea-Laurenziana. Conv. soppr. 521**
Parchment, XIV, 21 x 14.4 cm

| | |
|---|---|
| 1-46 | Boethius, *Consolation of Philosophy*. |
| 46v | blank |

46 numbered leaves: 1-5[8], 6[6]. 30 lines per page. Single column ruled drypoint, 15.3 x 9 cm. Regular catchwords except on 32v, where apparently trimmed off. Expert, smallish round gothic book hand. Alternating red and blue flourished initials.

Annotation limited to a few interlinear grammatical glosses, frequent *nota* hands and other signs for notabilia. Ownership marks on 46v: *Iste liber est. . . magistri petri. deo gratias* (XIV[2]), and (erased but partially legible) *Iste liber est F[rancesci] petri. Deo [gratias]*. Below text on 4: *Iste liber est loci nemoris* [i.e., priory of Bosco dei Frati].

*See*: Gehl, "Latin Readers," 418; Black, "Curriculum," 148.

**I.12. Florence, Biblioteca Medicea-Laurenziana. Acquisti e Doni 467**
Parchment, XIV, 18.8 x 12.5 cm

I.

| | |
|---|---|
| 1-23v | Aesop, *Fables*. |

II.

| | |
|---|---|
| 24-29v | Prudentius, *Dittochaeon*. |
| 29v-31 | Unidentified *Regulae fugitivae Magistri Siffani*. |
| 31v | blank |

III.

| | |
|---|---|
| 32-62 | Prosper of Aquitaine, *Epigrammata*. |
| 62v-83 | Tebaldo, *Regulae grammaticales*. |
| 83v-85 | Bartolomeo de Lodi, *Regulae grammaticales*. |
| 85v-87 | Anon. *Regulae grammaticales*. |
| 87v | blank |

87 numbered leaves: 1-2[8], 3[7] (a quaternion less one; stub after 23); 4[8]; 5[6] (a binion with two added leaves, viz., 36 and 37, which connect to stubs before present 32), 6-11[8], 12[2]. I: 16 lines

per page on first folio only, thereafter a change of pen allows of compressing 23-26 lines per page. Single column ruled in ink, 13 x 8.5 cm. Expert, upright round gothic book hand; rubrics in same hand, centered. Inexpert red initials, paragraph marks, and line-initial flourishes. II:  21 lines per page. Single column ruled drypoint, 14.2 x 9.5 cm. Scribe identifies himself 31v as Mathiolus. He writes an accomplished but not highly expert, upright round gothic book hand, somewhat angular in overall appearance; rubrics in same hand, centered. Single major red initial on 24. Flourishes to this initial and to line initials throughout in same brown ink as that used for corrections to rubrics. III:  23 or 24 lines per page. Single column ruled drypoint, 12.8 x 8.5 cm. Expert, upright round gothic book hand with very short ascenders and descenders.  Two highly expert major initials on 32 and 62 in red, green, and lavender. Minor initials also in red, green, and lavender. Paragraph marks in red.

Minor annotation to texts.  Much schoolboy scribbling on 23v, including the name *Francesco* and an explanation in *volgare* of a Latin declensional paradigm.  Additional schoolboy notes on 31v (including illegible ownership mark) and 87v; reader notes scattered throughout in hands as late as eighteenth century. Catchwords regular in single hand (XIV?) framed in decorative shields. Foredge title *ESOPO* (XV?).

*See*: Gehl, " Latin Readers," 418-19; Black, "Curriculum," 162.

I.13.  Florence, Biblioteca Medicea-Laurenziana.  Strozzi 80
Parchment, XIII/XIV, 21.8 x 15.3 cm

| | |
|---|---|
| 1-29v | *Ianua.* |
| 29v-35v | *Disticha Catonis.* |
| 35v-60 | Prosper of Aquitaine, *Epigrammata.* |
| 60v-72 | Tebaldo *Regulae grammaticales.* |
| 72v | blank |
| 73-91 | Aesop, *Fables.* |
| 91v | blank |

91 numbered leaves: 1-9⁸, 10⁴, 11⁸, 12⁸ (a quaternion less one; stub after 91). 27 to 29 lines per page. Single column ruled in ink, 15 x 9 cm for prose works, 15 x 9.5 cm for poetic ones. Compact, square, expert round gothic book hand. Alternating red and blue initials throughout.

Minor annotation on Prosper and Aesop only, some in *volgare*; extensive syntax markers in letter form on six of the Aesopian fables. 91v much scribbled up, including a scribbled picture of an hermaphrodite and various paraphrase exercises.

*See*: Gehl, "Latin Readers," 419-20; Black, "Unknown"; Bursill-Hall, *Census*, 79; *Disticha*, ed. Boas, lxii, lxx.


**I.14. Florence, Biblioteca Nazionale Centrale. Conv. soppr. C.4.2870**
Paper, XIV, 22.5 x 14.5 cm

| | |
|---|---|
| 1 | flyleaf |
| 2-12 | *Physiologus*, with extensive commentary. |
| 12v | blank |
| 13-46 | Prudentius, *Dittochaeon*, with commentary. |
| 46v-47v | blank |

47 numbered leaves: 1¹, 2-3¹⁰, 4¹², 5¹⁴ (a gathering of twelve with two added folios, 36 and 37, connecting to stubs between 46 and 47). Single column ruled margins only in ink, 14.8 x 9.2 cm. Formatting of page very informal: 23-28 lines of text before fol. 35, with various portions of the text spaced by eye. Thereafter, 30-32 lines of script in a tight text block. Hand is probably the same throughout but clearly engaged in making a personal copy. Most of the text copied in a large, rather loose *mercantesca*, but stretches are attempted in a stiff and inexpert round gothic. Important words and lemmata within commentary washed with yellow or underlined. Watermarks unclear: horse's head(?), chalice(?).

Front flyleaf: *Iste liber est Simoneti Andree de...*
*See*: Gehl, "Latin Readers," 423-24.

I.15.  Florence, Biblioteca Nazionale Centrale.  Magliabecchi I, 45
Parchment composite, XIII and XIII/XIV, 22 x 15.1 cm

I.

| | |
|---|---|
| 1-15v | *Ianua* |
| 15v-21 | *Disticha Catonis.* |

II.

| | |
|---|---|
| 22-29r | Theodulus, *Ecloga.* |
| 29v-34v | Prudentius, *Dittochaeon.* |
| 34v-42 | *Chartula.* |
| 42-48v | *Physiologus.* |
| 48v-69 | Bonvesin de la Riva, *Vita scholastica.* |
| 69-91v | Aesop, *Fables.* |
| 91v-93v | blank |
| 94-96 | *Pseudo-Jerome, *Liber de contemptu mulierum.* |

100 leaves, i + 96 + iii: $1^1$ (unnumbered flyleaf), $2-3^8$, $4^4$, $5^1$ (originally connected to front fly? presently folded around following gathering so stub appears after 29v); $6-14^8$, $15^6$ (including three unnumbered flyleaves).  Single column throughout ruled in ink.  I: 31 lines per page, 11 x 15.3 cm.  Expert round gothic book hand (XIII/XIV).  Decoration of simple, lumpy red and blue alternating initials.  Large initial P on fol. 1 very clumsily decorated.  Catchwords at bottom center.  II: 24 lines per page, 9.5 x 13.8 cm.  Two expert round gothic book hands (XIII).  Catchwords centered and enclosed in elaborate lozenge-shaped frames and decorated with red dots and yellow ochre wash.  Rubricator has added titles and pious invocations, including a Marian formula at the beginning of each work and invocations to Christ at the end of each.  Pseudo-Jerome added in a nervous, inexpert round gothic book hand.  Elegant, simple red and blue alternating initials, some flourished, including one at the beginning of the added text, Pseudo-Jerome; thick yellow ochre wash over initial letters of every line.

*See*:  Black, "Unknown," 109-10; Gehl, "Latin Readers," 420-21; Bursill-Hall, *Census*, 82; Garin, *Pensiero*, 92; Galante, "Index, " 328-29; Vidmanovà-Schmidtovà, *Quinque claves*, xxxix; Schmitt, *Ianua*, 50

I.16.  Florence, Biblioteca Nazionale Centrale.  Magliabecchi VII, 931
Parchment, XIII, 19.5 x 12.4 cm

1-5          *Physiologus.*
5v-16v       Aesop, *Fables* (fragmentary).
        16 numbered leaves: 1-2⁸.  32 lines per page; considerable variation and compression toward end, where eventually fully 43 lines are regular.  Single column ruled variously in lead and ink from ink dots still visible in margins of first gathering, and drypoint from prickings visible in second gathering.  Written space varies considerably, but averages about 15.5 x 7 cm.  Expert, somewhat angular round gothic book hand throughout.  A second, looser gothic book hand has added rubrics and red initials.  Additional initials in brown ink added clumsily.
        Numerous, careful interlinear notes in small gothic hand to both texts.  Aesop also has numerous marginal notes in several hands (XIII to XV[in]).
        *See*:  Gehl, "Latin Readers," 421; Mazzatinti, *Inventarii* 13:198.


I.17.  Florence, Biblioteca Nazionale Centrale.  Magliabecchi VII, 1064
Parchment, XIV/XV, 24.5 x 17.3 cm

1-6v         *Disticha Catonis.*
7-32v        Prosper of Aquitaine, *Epigrammata.*
33-39v       *Ilias latina.*
40-44        Prudentius, *Dittochaeon.*
44v-61       Bonvesin de la Riva, *Vita scholastica.*
61-68v       Pseudo-Jerome, *Liber de contemptu mulierum.*
68v-71v      Pseudo-Boethius, *De disciplina scholastica.*
        71 numbered leaves: 1⁹ (5 connects to stub visible before 6), 2⁶, 3-9⁸.  28-30 lines per page.  Single column ruled drypoint, 17 x 10 cm.  Two highly expert round gothic bookhands, change of hand on 40.  Rubrication in third hand is unitary for both sections of the

codex.   Careful, elegant decoration of red and blue alternating initials throughout.

See: Gehl, "Latin Readers," 421-22; Black, "Curriculum," 150, 162 (where XV); Galante, "Index," 354; Vidmanovà-Schmidtovà, *Quinque claves,* xxxviii; Scaffai, "Tradizione," 262 (where XV).

**I.18.   Florence, Biblioteca Nazionale Centrale.   Magliabecchi VII, 1070**
Paper, XIV$^2$, 21.8 x 14.2 cm

1-18v   Bonvesin de la Riva, *Vita scholastica*
18 numbered leaves:   1$^{10}$, 2$^8$ (quinternion lacking last two leaves). Watermark unclear.   27 lines per page.   Single column, ruled drypoint from prickings, 14.9 x 14 cm.   Expert but unlovely round gothic book hand, upright in feel.

Minor interlinear annotation in hand of text scribe, who has also supplied a few marginal *divisiones* on 1, 9, 9v and 10.

**I.19.   Florence, Biblioteca Nazionale Centrale.   Nuovi acquisti 293**
Parchment, XIV, 24.5 x 17.5 cm

1-41v   Boethius, *Consolation of Philosophy.*
42-42v blank
41 numbered leaves plus one rear flyleaf:   1-41$^{10}$, 5$^2$.   30 lines per page.   Single column ruled in ink, 17.3 x 11.5 cm.   Expert round gothic book hand.   Alternating red and blue initials throughout; major initials decorated with bands of crosshatching decorated with yellow, blue, and grey dots.

Minor interlinear and marginal notation.   Rear flyleaf much scribbled up by schoolboys:   various short poems and acrostics; a list of sums; a roughly drawn armored knight.   Coat of arms (unidentified) on bottom of fol. 1.

See: Gehl, "Latin Readers," 414.

I.20. Florence, Biblioteca Nazionale Centrale. Panciatichi 68
Parchment, XIV², 21 x 15.1 cm

I.

| 1-13v | Goro d'Arezzo, *Vocabula* (some text missing). |
| 13v-20 | Goro d'Arezzo, *Regulae* (some text missing). |
| 20v-22v | blank |

II.

| 23-48v | Prosper of Aquitaine, *Epigrammata.* |
| 49-62v | Aesop, *Fables* (fragmentary at end). |

III.

| 63-64v | blank |
| 65-66 | *Chartula* (fragmentary). |
| 67-71v | Prudentius, *Dittochaeon.* |
| 72 | blank |
| 73-79 | *Physiologus.* |
| 79v | blank |
| 80-82v | Vitalis of Blois, *Geta* (fragmentary). |

82 numbered leaves plus one unnumbered flyleaf at front
and at back, the whole comprising a composite manuscript, parts of
which are missing substantial numbers of leaves. 1⁸, 2⁴ (once a
quaternion?), 3-4² (once parts of a single quaternion?), 5⁶; 7-11⁸; 12-
13² (two bifolia, first blank, second with *Chartula* fragment), 14-15⁸.
26-31 lines per page. I: The works of Goro d'Arezzo are written in
two columns ruled in lead (margins only), 11.5 x 16 cm with
considerable variation. The expert round gothic book hand of the
Goro d'Arezzo section is compact and closely fitted into the text
block space. II: Single column, ruled as in I, written in a slightly
angular hand, widely spaced and regularly utilizing only 28 or 29
lines per page. III: Single column, 11.5 x 16.2 cm, written in a
broadly spaced round gothic. Decoration is regular and careful but
extremely simple throughout the manuscript; alternating red and
blue initials and simple rubrics for each work, and for the
subsections of the Aesop and *Physiologus*; rubrics frequently
supplied above the ruled space.

Considerable wear to all parts of the manuscript; many
leaves reinforced at the gutters. Front flyleaf contains proverbs and

*probationes pennae* reported by Morpurgo et al. Also there, the ownership note of Filippo di Bartolomeo di Filippo Valori (XV²) and that of Bernardo di Filippo Valori (XVI).

　　*See*: Gehl, "Latin Readers," 422-23; Morpurgo, *Codici Panciatichiani*, 123-24.

**I.21. Florence, Biblioteca Riccardiana. MS 350**
Parchment, XIV, 15 x 13.8 cm

| | |
|---|---|
| 1-30v | Prosper of Aquitaine, *Epigrammata*. |
| 30v-52v | Aesop, *Fables*. |
| 53r-v | blank |

　　53 numbered leaves: 1-6⁸, 2⁵ (53, a flyleaf, connects to stub before 49). 24 lines per page. Single column ruled in lead, 13.7 x 8.8 cm, double line at left margin. Expert, rather square and upright round gothic book hand. Line initials decorated with hairline flourishes. Catchwords on 24v, 32v, 40v, and 48v. Rubrication begun to both texts but left incomplete in both cases.

　　Numerous, inexpertly written interlinear glosses in a hand that has also made corrections to text. Syntax markers over some lines on 12v. Several ownership marks only partly visible on 53 r-v, e.g., *Iste liber est Simone mio fratello el quale a me* . . .[illegible]. Repeated name of Piero and/or Piero di Zacharia Gionesce(?).

**I.22. Florence, Biblioteca Riccardiana. MS 381**
Parchment, XIV² (part I) and XIVⁱⁿ (part II), 19.3 x 14 cm

I.

| | |
|---|---|
| 1-6v | Prudentius, *Dittochaeon*. |
| 7-17v | Vitalis of Blois, *Geta*. |
| 17v-24 | *Physiologus*. |
| 24v | blank |
| 25-32v | *Doctrina rudium*. |

II.

| | |
|---|---|
| 33-51r | Prosper of Aquitaine, *Epigrammata* (fragmentary at end). |
| 51v-52v | various fragmentary notes (see below). |

52 numbered leaves: 1-4 [8]; 5 [8] (36 and 37 pieced together), 6 [8], 7 [4] (once a binion; 51 and 52 cut away to mere strips but numbered). I: Coarse and scrappy parchment, some reused. 24 lines per page. Single column ruled drypoint from several rows of prickings in outer margins, 14.2 x 10.2 cm. Loose and nervous round gothic book hand on 1-6v. Thereafter, an unlovely but expert round gothic book hand. Initials supplied irregularly and inexpertly. II: Badly rubbed, darkened, and water damaged parchment. 34 lines per page. Single column ruled drypoint, 15.6 x 9.9 cm. Small, expert round gothic book hand. Initials added clumsily in pinkish red ink.

Numerous notes and scribbles in II, some of apparent classroom origin, e.g., 49v in right margin: *Queritur utrum sit bonum latinum Ego petrus lego* . . . Elsewhere on same folio parallel texts in Latin and *volgare*. Schoolboyish drawings of monsters 42v and 46.

*See*: Gehl, "Latin Readers," 425; Vidmanovà-Schmidtovà, *Quinque claves*, xiii-xiv.

## I.23. Florence, Biblioteca Riccardiana. MS 427
Paper, XV (part I) and XIV [ex] (part II), 19 x 14 cm

I.

| | |
|---|---|
| 1-24 | Bonvesin de la Riva, *Vita scholastica*, here attributed to Theobaldus. |
| 24v | blank |

II.

| | |
|---|---|
| 25-32 | *Chartula.* |
| 32v | blank |

32 numbered leaves: 1-3 [8], 4 [8]. I: 20 lines per page. Single column ruled in lead, 12.5 x 9 cm, double line at left margin only.

Inexpert humanist book hand. II: 25 lines per page. Single column ruled in ink, 13.8 x 8 cm, double line both left and right. Loose but expert round gothic book hand. Watermarks: scissors in I; none apparent in II.

Considerable minor annotation on 24v and 32v. Ownership mark (XV) on 32v: *Iste liber est Marci iohannis[?] neri de Chambis cives Florentinus.*

*See*: Gehl, "Latin Readers," 425-26; Black, "Curriculum," 150; Vidmanovà-Schmidtovà , *Quinque claves*, xxxviii.

### I.24.  Florence, Biblioteca Riccardiana.  MS 552
Parchment, XIV², 25.8 x 18.5 cm

| 1-46v | Boethius, *Consolation of Philosophy.* |
| 46v | *Prudentius, *Dittochaeon* (fragment). |
| 47r-v | flyleaf |

One unnumbered flyleaf plus 47 numbered leaves: $1^1$ (flyleaf), $2-6^8$, $7^7$ (quaternion less one ancient flyleaf missing after present 47). 30 lines per page. Single column ruled in lead, 18 x 13 cm, double line at left margin only. Spacious round gothic book hand, practiced but not expert, and betraying considerable inattention after first few folios.

Prudentius fragment added in clumsy gothic book hand by an early owner. Frequent interlinear annotation of elementary grammatical sort on the poems and to the Greek passages in Boethius. Rare elsewhere. A few marginal notes with elementary mythological and historical content. Much annotation and scribbling. Several ownership marks: front flyleaf, v: *Iste liber et mei Dominici andree [this name over erasure] morantis in iscolis magistri Nicholai d'aretio in camera[?] ser Benincase de Sancta maria in balneum . . .* 47r: *Ego bartolomeus quondam filippi de sancto miniato notarius Florentie . . .* 47r: *Iste liber est petri tommasi de minnettis[?].* 47v: *Questo libro e di Zuchettio[?] borsi . . .[?].*

*See*: Gehl, "Latin Readers," 426-27; Black, "Curriculum," 148.

**I.25. Florence, Biblioteca Riccardiana. MS 607**
Parchment, XIV², 23.8 x 16.5 cm

1-16v   Aesop, *Fables*.
   Early, unnumbered flyleaves front and back, 16 numbered leaves: 1-2⁸. The flyleaves constitute a bifolium, once the wrapper for these two gatherings, but not, it seems, original, since there is considerable wear to 1, 8v, 9, and 16v. 34 lines per page. Single column ruled in ink, 18.2 x 9 cm. Large, expert round gothic book hand. Simple, expertly drawn red and blue flourished initials. Three inexpert but charmingly drawn illustrations on fol. 1: Aesop[?] kneels to pluck a flower; hen and thistle; wolf and sheep.
   In addition to wear, some of the folios of the first gathering show evidence of creasing. Various ownership marks. Front flyleaf, r: *Francesco*. Front fly, v (largely illegible, XVI?): *questo libro e di Guiglielmo di Chardina Rucella* . . . Rear fly, v: *Antonio Piero di Giovanni Antonii*.
   *See*: Gehl, "Latin Readers," 427.

**I.26. Florence, Biblioteca Riccardiana. MS 630**
Parchment, XIV², 20.9 x 14.6 cm

| | |
|---|---|
| 1-6v | *Disticha Catonis*. |
| 7-12v | *Chartula*. |
| 13-16v | Prudentius, *Dittochaeon*. |
| 17-22v | *Physiologus*. |
| 23-28v | Theodulus, *Ecloga*. |
| 29-44v | Bonvesin de la Riva, *Vita scholastica*. |
| 45-64v | Prosper of Aquitaine, *Epigrammata*. |
| 65-80v | Aesop, *Fables*. |
| 81-112 | Filippo di Naddo, *Regule grammaticales*. |

110 leaves incorrectly numbered 1-112: 1-2⁶, 3⁴, 4-5⁶, 6-8⁸, 9¹⁰, 10-15⁸. 34 lines per page for poetic works, 35 lines per page for Filippo di Naddo. Single column ruled in lead, 14.8 x 8.8 cm, with additional ruling added as needed for diagrams within the last text. Expert round gothic book hand. A single design

throughout, decorated uniformly with simple red initials and line-initial flourishes, large red or blue flourished initial at start of each text. Catchwords in the hand of the scribe are provided only where a single text runs from one gathering to the next. Remaining catchwords added by a second hand (XIV or XV).

Annotation rare, but there are a few schoolboyish interlinear glosses in *volgare*.

*See*: Gehl, "Latin Readers," 427-28; Bursill-Hall, *Census*, 83; Vidmanovà-Schmidtovà, *Quinque claves*, xxxi (where s. XV ).

### I.27.  Florence, Biblioteca Riccardiana.  MS 640
Parchment, XIV², 20 x 13.8 cm

I.

| | |
|---|---|
| 1-6 | *Disticha Catonis*, here called  Liber Senece. |
| 6v | blank |
| II. | |
| 7-29 | Aesop, *Fables*. |
| 29v | blank |

29 numbered leaves:  1⁶; 2-3⁸, 4⁷ (quaternion less one; rear flyleaf missing?). I:  30 lines per page. Single column ruled in lead, 15.8 x 9 cm, double line at left margin. Expert round gothic book hand; heavy, coarse parchment. II:  24 lines per page.  Single column ruled in lead, 15.5 x 9 cm, triple line at left margin (for line initials set out into margin).  Highly expert, upright round gothic book hand; fine, medium-weight parchment.  Rubrics in hand of text.

Syntax markers in letter form on 7; at least three distinct hands (XV and XVI?) have annotated the whole.  Minor scribbles and scratch gloss (male genitalia?) on 6v.

*See*: Gehl,  "Latin Readers," 428.

**I.28. Florence, Biblioteca Riccardiana. MS 643**
Parchment, XIV², 18 x 13.2 cm

| | |
|---|---|
| 1-58 | Boethius, *Consolation of Philosophy.* |
| 58v | blank |

58 numbered leaves: 1-6⁸, 7¹⁰. 20-21 lines per page. Single column except for some of the poems in double column ruled drypoint, 11.5 x 8.5 cm. Expert round gothic book hand. Red and blue flourished initials. A few small decorations in margins.

Catchwords added by later hand, possibly the same one that has added a few minor annotations in a small, nervous gothic. Each catchword decorated with animal, monstrous, or human figures usually holding scrolls to contain the words.

*See:* Gehl, "Latin Readers," 428-29.

**I.29. Florence, Biblioteca Riccardiana. MS 644** (not seen)
Parchment, XIV, dimensions unknown

1-48 Boethius, *Consolation of Philosophy.*

24 lines per page, single column. Both proses and verses have heavy interlinear annotation (XIV and XV); there are also some notes of a historical and mythological sort in the margins.

**I.30. Florence, Biblioteca Riccardiana. MS 725**
Parchment, XIV¹, 19.8 x 14.5 cm

| | |
|---|---|
| I. | |
| 1-25 | Aesop, *Fables.* |
| 25v-30v | *Physiologus.* |
| 31-32v | blank |
| II. | |
| 33-40v | Theodulus, *Ecloga.* |
| III. | |
| 41-64v | Henry of Settimello, *Elegia.* |

64 numbered leaves: 1-4⁸; 5⁸; 6-8⁸. I: 21 lines per page through 16v, thereafter 26 lines per page. Single column ruled in lead; reruled to accommodate larger number of lines after 16v, 12.8 x 7 cm. Smallish, expert round gothic book hand. Catchwords in hand of scribe on 8v, 16v, 24v. II: 22 lines per page. Single column ruled in ink, 14 x 9 cm. Expert round gothic book hand not equal to that of I. III: 21 lines per page. Single column ruled in ink, 13 x 8 cm. Expert round gothic book hand. Catchwords in hand of this scribe on 48v and 56v. Decoration throughout is unitary, of well-drawn and highly decorated major and minor initials imitative of early medieval styles. Line initials in each section are distinctive (and predate the present assembly?): yellow wash in I and III, red flourishing in II (possibly the same hand as that of the overall program of initials).

Elementary, interlinear annotation (XIV), some in *volgare*, in Aesop and Theodulus, where also scattered notes (XV). III systematically annotated between lines and with occasionally extensive glosses arranged in blocks in margin. Gathering 4 (fols. 25-32) has a horizontal crease through all folia. Catchwords on 32v and 40v added by later gothic *notula* hand. Erased, illegible ownership mark, 40v. Signature marks (XVI?) on first folio of each gathering in Arabic numerals, beginning with 13 on 1r and continuing to 20 on 57r.

*See*: Gehl, "Latin Readers," 429-30; Cremaschi, *Enrico*, 22 (where sec. XV in. ).


I.31. Florence, Biblioteca Riccardiana. MS 732
Parchment, XIVᵉˣ, 20.5 x 14.5 cm

1-19v   Henry of Settimello, *Elegia.*
Unnumbered flyleaf plus 20 numbered leaves: 1¹, 2⁸, 3¹². 26 lines per page. Single column ruled in lead, 16 x 9.5 cm. Expert, upright and rather large round gothic book hand. Very simple decoration in red of a few initials, paragraph marks, and regular strokes on line initials.

Extensive annotation on 1-2v of historical and mythological

names; thereafter very little annotation though there are some *volgare* notes passim on 1-5v. Marginal note erased and illegible on 11. Various ownerships marks: Front flyleaf, r: *Iste liber est mei Georgius ser Amerigi de Vespucci.* Same leaf, v: *Iste liber est mei ser Amerigo Stasii de Vespucci.* 19v: *Anibaldus.* 20r: *Iste liber est Anibaldi de Johanis* and again *Iste liber est miei ser Amerig. Stasii de Vespuccis de Florentie.*

See: Gehl, "Latin Readers," 430; Cremaschi, *Elegia*, 21.

### I.32.  Florence, Biblioteca Riccardiana.  MS 2795
Parchment fragment, XIV², 21.4 x 14 cm

This is a modern composite manuscript containing fragments of many periods. Of interest here:

68-69v          Aesop, *Fables* (fragment).

One bifolium. 34 lines per page. Single column ruled in lead, 15 x 10 cm. Large, expert round gothic book hand. Simple red initials and rubrics for each fable; initials decorated with human faces in brown ink. A roughly sketched duck in brown and red inks at bottom of 69v.

See: Gehl, "Latin Readers," 430-31.

### I.33.  London, British Library.  MS Royal 15.A.28
Parchment, XIV/XV, 22 x 15.5 cm

1-16r          Aesop, *Fables.*
16v          blank

16 numbered leaves: 1-2⁸. 35 lines per page. Single column, margins ruled in ink, individual lines in crayon, 16.4 x 10.2 cm. Expert, upright gothic book hand. Initials and paragraph marks in red and blue.

Numerous rough drawings (XV?) of animals from the tales added to margins 1-5v in brown ink. Later (XV²?) decoration of initial C on 1r, a clumsily drawn picture of a student and teacher with foliate decoration in red, green, silver, and gold by the same

amateur artist who decorated British Library MS Royal 15.E.15. Ownership mark (XV?) twice on 16v, *Cheryte pertinet*.
See: British Museum, *Royal and King's* 2:150.


**I.34. London, British Library. MS Royal 15.E.15**
Parchment, XIV, 22.9 x 15.6 cm.

| | |
|---|---|
| 1r-v | blank (a wrapper or flyleaf conjugate with 20) |
| 2-20 | Prosper of Aquitaine, *Epigrammata* (fragmentary at end; last 7 lines of text supplied in later hand on 20). |
| 20v | blank |

20 numbered leaves: $1^2$ (wrapper, i.e. fols 1 and 20), $2^{10}$, $3^8$. 37 lines per page. Single column ruled in ink, 15.6 x 8.2 cm. Several expert round gothic book hands; a few corrections in the hand of scribe on 3 and 5. Red and blue alternating initials throughout.

Very little annotation. Later ($XV^2$?) decoration of first page with foliate forms in red, green, silver and gold by same inexpert hand as found in British Library MS Royal 15.A.28.
See: British Museum, *Royal and Kings* 1:117.


**I.35. London, British Library. MS Additional 10093, part II**
Parchment, XIV, 16.8 x 11.6 cm

| | |
|---|---|
| I. (n. Italian?) | |
| 1-6v | *Disticha Catonis.* |
| 7-17v | Tebaldo, *Grammatica.* |
| 18-40v | Prosper of Aquitaine, *Epigrammata.* |
| 41-56v | Boethius, *Consolation of Philosophy.* |
| II. (Tuscan) | |
| 57-65v | Aesop, *Fables* (fragment). |
| 66r-v | blank |

66 numbered leaves: $1^6$, $2^8$, $3^6$, $4^{10}$, $5\text{-}6^8$, $7^{10}$; $8^8$, $9^1$, $10^1$. I: 29 lines per page. Single column ruled in ink, 11.6 x 8.1 cm. Expert, fine, small round gothic book hand. Minor initials and

paragraph marks in dark blue; major initials in red and blue. II: 30 lines per page. Single column ruled in ink, 13.1 x 7.5 cm. Rubrics in hand of text. Catchword at bottom of 64v does not match text on 65r, the single leaf that follows.

Annotation, in I only, is mostly XV and XVI. On 6v the figure of a bearded man in a tunic holding a hoe or scythe, now erased. Ownership marks and titles (XVIII) on 1r.

*See*: Bursill-Hall, *Census*, 108.

## I.36. London, Lambeth Palace Library. MS 431
Parchment, XIV, 21.4 x 15.5 cm

An eighteenth-century composite of various small books. Of interest, three units toward the center, all probably Tuscan:

I.

| | |
|---|---|
| 89 | Prosper of Aquitaine, *Epigrammata* (first few lines only). |
| 89v | blank except for *ownership mark of *Johis. Stywarde.* |

II.

| | |
|---|---|
| 90-115 | Prosper of Aquitaine, *Epigrammata*. |
| 115v | *Prayer. |
| 116-136v | Aesop, *Fables*. |

III.

| | |
|---|---|
| 137-141v | Prudentius, *Dittochaeon*. |
| 141v | *arms of John Styworde (cf. 89v). |
| 142-143 | *Bernard of Clairvaux, *Super re familiari gubernanda*. |
| 143v | blank |

I: Single leaf ruled drypoint for a single column of 29 lines, 15.5 x 10.2 cm. Written one side only in small, expert round gothic book hand. Space left for major initial I of Prosper. Apparently a spoiled sheet from the same workshop that produced II. II: 47 leaves: 1-2$^{10}$, 3$^7$ (quaternion lacking one, stub after 115), 4-5$^{10}$. 27 lines per page. Single column ruled in violet ink, margins only, double lines right and left, 15 x 11.3 cm. Small, expert round gothic book hand. Minor initials in red and blue. Paragraph marks in ink and hand of text re-drawn in red in same hand as rubrics (Prosper only). Catchwords supplied by scribe. III: 1$^8$. 25 lines per page. Single column ruled in violet ink, 15.2 x 10.2 cm. Expert round gothic book hand, slightly larger and looser than that of II.

Present fols. 89-136 foliated in red (XV?), xxxi to lxxviii. English ownership mark (XVI) on 89v. Rubrics to III supplied later following marginal instructions in a spidery hand (XV?).

See: James, *Lambeth Palace*, 594-99.

### I.37.  Lucca, Biblioteca Statale.  MS 1400
Parchment, XIV, 24.8 x 18.1 cm

| I. | |
|---|---|
| 1-3 | numbered flyleaves, all cut back to narrow strips |
| 4-7 | Petrus de Riga, *Historia de S. Susanna.* |
| 7v | Index of chapters to Boethius. |
| II. | |
| 7-50 | Boethius, *Consolation of Philosophy* |
| 50v-51 | Anon. verses on the *Consolation*, inc. Conqueritur fortuna. |
| 51v-55v | *Theodulus, *Ecloga*, with gloss. |
| 56r-v | blank |

56 numbered leaves:  1$^1$ (stub follows immediately after 1, a half-width page), 2$^6$ (2 a mere stub connected to 7; 3 a half-width page); 3-8$^8$, 9$^1$. Fols. 1 and 56 of a different, heavier parchment than the rest of the book, probably an early wrapper provided to the whole after the Theodulus and Petrus de Riga had been added to the Boethius to form this school miscellany. I: 31 lines per page. Single column ruled drypoint from prickings in outer margins. Expert round gothic book hand same as that of the Theodulus. II: 29 lines per page for Boethius and verses on it.  42 lines per page for Theodulus.  Single column throughout, ruled drypoint from prickings in outer margins. Spacious, expert round gothic book hand for Boethius, writing alternately in red and black in the added verses. Rubrics in hand of text. Smaller round gothic book hand

identical to that of I but more crowded for Theodulus. Decoration of Boethius in red and black, that of other texts in red.

Marginal and interlinear glosses in several hands throughout. Various notes in Latin and *volgare* on 1, 3, and 56. Ownership marks of ser Bartolomeo (XIV), 55v; of Johannes Petri (XV), 1 and 56v. Rough drawing of male and female genitalia, 56v.

*See*: Gehl, "Latin Readers," 431-32; Sturlese et al, *Catalogo*, 5:117-18.

**I.38. Madrid, Biblioteca Nacional. MS 141** (not seen)
Parchment, XIV, 22 x 15.5 cm

| | |
|---|---|
| 1-2 | grammatical notes. |
| 2v-25 | Prosper of Aquitaine, *Epigrammata*. |
| 25v-41v | Aesop, *Fables*. |

41 numbered leaves; collation and most other physical details unknown. Written space measures 15 x 9.5 cm.

Numerous marginal notes, some in Italian.

*See*: Gehl, "Latin Readers," 432; Biblioteca Nacional, *Inventario General*, 1:119-20.

**I.39. Oxford, Bodleian Library. MS Additional A.171**
Parchment, composite, XIII and XIV, dates and sizes noted below.

I. (XIV, 21 x 15.5 cm)

| | |
|---|---|
| 1-20v | Aesop, *Fables*. |
| 20v-24v | Prudentius, *Dittochaeon*. |
| 24v-30v | *Chartula*. |

II. (XIII¹, 20.7 x 15.3 cm)

| | |
|---|---|
| 31-36 | Theodulus, *Ecloga*. |
| 36v-38v | blank |

III. (XIII/XIV, 20.9 x 15.3 cm)

| | |
|---|---|
| 39-46v | *Facetus*, inc. *Moribus et vita*. |

IV. (XIV, 20.9 x 15.4 cm)

| | |
|---|---|
| 47-53v | John the Abbot , *Liber de septem virtutibus*. |

53 numbered leaves:   1⁸ (2 and 7 supplied on diff.
parchment in XV), 2-3⁸, 4⁶; 5⁸; 6⁸; 7⁷ (quaternion less one; no stub
visible). I: 25-27 lines per page on gatherings 1-3; 30 lines per page
on gathering 4. Single column ruled drypoint, 13.7 x 10 cm in first
three gatherings, 15.8 x 10 cm in fourth. Expert but unlovely round
gothic book hands. Awkward, bright red initials, paragraph marks
and rubrics squeezed into margins on 1-8; thereafter these appear in
spaces left for them by the scribe. A later hand has added
flourishing to major initials. II: 34 lines per page. Single column
ruled drypoint, 14.2 x 8.5 cm. Last two leaves unruled. Small,
loose early gothic book hand. III: 35 lines per page. Single column
ruled drypoint, 15.4 x 9 cm. Small, graceful round gothic book
hand. Alternating orange-red and dark blue-green initials; red
flourishes to line initials. Single major initial on 38r is amateurish.
IV: 25 or 26 lines per page of very poor quality parchment. Single
column ruled drypoint, 15.5 x 8 cm. Expert, compact round gothic
book hand.

Extensive marginal and interlinear notes in several hands.
One, a fine, small gothic (XIV²) has added marginal notes in Latin to
the Prudentius. All of section I has also been extensively corrected
by a reader (XV) who erased and added to some of the earlier
corrections in the Prudentius. A hairline *mercantesca* (XIV²) has
added extensive interlinear glosses to Prudentius and Chartula in I
and to the last folios of John the Abbot in IV. A gothic hand
(XIII/XIV) added many notes to the Theodulus in II. Added
decoration (XV?) to I in the form of an illustration to the first
Aesopian tale, fol. 1. Several ownership marks. 38v (XIV): *Iste
liber est mei simonis petri* . . . 46v (XIV), partly legible: *Iste liber est
mei Christophori . . . de luca.* . . Also 46v (XV): *Antonio Piero in*
in imitation of Greek script. 1r bott.: *G. Nott MDCCCXVII.*

I.40.  Rome, Biblioteca Angelica. MS  1461
Parchment, XIV and XIV/XV, 24.1 x 17.1 cm

An eighteenth- or nineteenth-century composite of which the first
two parts are of interest to us. The remainder of the codex formed

an earlier composite from the collection of Domenico Passinea, but these two pieces do not seem to come from that library, nor do they seem to have been together before the formation of the present miscellany.

I. (XIV, Tuscan)
3-4v          Prosper of Aquitaine, *Epigrammata* (fragment).
II. (XIV/XV, Tuscan?)
5-32          Claudian, *De raptu Proserpinae.*
32v-34v       blank

    I: two leaves of coarse, flawed parchment, apparently the outer leaves of a quaternion. 44 lines per page. Single column ruled drypoint from prickings, 17.9 x 11.2 cm. Written in black ink in a small, upright, expert round gothic book hand. Major initial decorated in red, violet, green, light blue, and dark blue; simple red and blue initials; border of four lines of red and blue on 3r. II: 30 leaves of reused parchment, apparently from a large folio, theological or canon law manuscript (XIII/XIV) in two columns: 1-$3^8$, $4^6$. 20 lines per page. Single column ruled in lead from prickings, 19 x 10.8 cm. Written in a very large, regular but inelegant and unprofessional hand, probably that of a good student scribe, with much self-correction, several blottings, etc. Ownership mark 3r, *de Griolami de Siena,* seems to be in the same hand as the annotations to the Prosper.

    Both sections annotated by different hands in XIV/XV. The notes on Prosper are almost exclusively syntax markers in the form of suprascript letters, but there are also a few lexical notes and paraphrases, some in *volgare.* Claudian annotation extends through the first fifteen folios only and consists of two parts: the usual elementary lexical and syntactical notes (at least one in the vernacular) inserted interlinearly, and an uneven set of rhetorical *divisiones* in the margins of 8-21.

## I.41.   Vatican City, Biblioteca Apostolica Vaticana. Arch. S. Pietro G.46

Parchment, XIII, 14.8 x 10.3 cm

A fourteenth-century composite consisting of a thirteenth-century copy of John the Abbot (part I), to which is added a separate, contemporary miscellany of grammatical and meditative texts (part II; for contents see Pellegrin) and a somewhat later copy (XIII/XIV) of Henry of Settimello (part III). Part II appears northern Italian; the others appear to be Tuscan:

I.

| | |
|---|---|
| 1-7v | John the Abbot, *Liber de septem virtutibus.* |
| 7v-8v | *various additions (see Pellegrin) |

III.

| | |
|---|---|
| 79-96v | Henry of Settimello, *Elegia.* |

I: 8 numbered leaves: 1⁸. Expert round gothic book hand. Simple red and blue initials. III: 18 numbered leaves: 1⁸, 2¹⁰. 29 lines per page. Single column ruled in lead from prickings, 11.3 x 6.4 cm. Compact, expert round gothic book hand. Decoration amateurish and limited to a few red capitals and flourishing to line initials. Blank spaces passim left by scribe of rubrics never supplied.

Rare annotation in several hands (XIV).

*See*: Gehl, "Latin Readers," 432-33; Pellegrin, *Manuscrits,* 1:38-39.

## I.42.   Vatican City, Biblioteca Apostolica Vaticana. Barb. lat. 48

Parchment, XIV², 19.2 x 13.3 cm

| | |
|---|---|
| 1-8 | *Disticha Catonis.* |
| 8v | blank |

8 numbered leaves: 1⁸. 24 lines per page. Single column ruled drypoint, 13.8 x 8.9 cm. Inelegant but professional round gothic book hand; some folios rewritten. One initial only on 1, blue with expertly done flourishing. Line initials flourished throughout.

Frequent annotation in several hands (XIV and XV). Last

folio much worn and torn, with numerous scribblings and *probationes pennae*, including at least one badly rubbed ownership mark, *Alberti filii panne* [?].

See: Gehl, "Latin Readers," 435; Pellegrin, *Manuscrits,* 1:103; *Disticha,* ed. Boas, lxii, lxx.

I.43. Vatican City, Biblioteca Apostolica Vaticana. Barb. lat. 426
Parchment, XIV[1], 18.5 x 12.6 cm

1-24          Prosper of Aquitaine, *Epigrammata.*
24v-28v      *Prudentius, *Dittochaeon* (fragment).
          28 numbered leaves: 1-2[10], 3[8]. 29 lines per page, 1-24, thereafter 19 lines on page ruled for 20. Single column throughout, ruled in ink 1-24 and drypoint 25-28 from prickings throughout, 12.3 x 9.2 cm. Three hands. That of the Prosper is an expert, small round gothic book hand; the Prudentius fragment was begun in a spacious and stiff round gothic book hand (24v only) and continued in a loose, nervous round gothic book hand. Decoration by later hands: Elaborate but inexpert major initial on 1 with leafy borders and monsters in margins; small red initials 3v-24; thereafter large, clumsy initials. Sparse, mostly etymological annotation in *volgare* to Prudentius only. Nota hands and other readers' marks in margins.
          See: Gehl, "Latin Readers," 433.

I.44. Vatican City, Biblioteca Apostolica Vaticana. Ottob. lat. 1534
Parchment, XIV, 22 x 16.6 cm

1-26v          Prosper of Aquitaine, *Epigrammata.*
          26 numbered leaves: 1-2[8], 3[10]. 27 lines per page. Single column ruled in ink, 16.6 x 11 cm. Expert, round gothic book hand with hairline finishing strokes. Decoration of simple red initials fols 1-6 only; single, ambitious initial (XV?) on fol. 1 embellished with face and foliage in margins.
          See: Gehl, "Latin Readers," 434.

I.45.  Vatican City, Biblioteca Apostolica Vaticana.  Ottob. Lat. 2879
Parchment, XIVᵉˣ, 19.6 x 15.5 cm

I.

| | |
|---|---|
| 1-8v | *Disticha Catonis.* |
| 9-39v | Prosper of Aquitaine, *Epigrammata.* |
| 40r-v | blank |

II.

| | |
|---|---|
| 41-63r | Aesop, *Fables.* |
| 63v-64v | blank |
| 65-86v | Bonvesin del la Riva, *Vita scholastica.* |

88 leaves incorrectly numbered 1-86: 1-5⁸, 6-7¹⁰, 8⁶, 9-
10¹⁰, 11². 22 lines per page throughout. I: Single column ruled
drypoint, 14.2 x 9 cm. Expert, compact round gothic book hand.
Major and minor initials in red and blue with flourishing to 9;
thereafter red initials only. No rubrics. II: Single column ruled
drypoint, 13.4 x 9.5 cm. Expert, spacious round gothic book hand,
which has also supplied rubrics. Simple red initials and paragraph
marks; line initials flourished in red.

Minor interlinear annotation (XV) at beginnings of texts.
Pellegrin notes owner's mark incompletely visible under ultraviolet
radiation on 86v.

*See*: Gehl, "Latin Readers," 434; Pellegrin, *Manuscrits*,
2.1:813; Vidmanovà-Schmidtovà, *Quinque claves*, xxxviii; *Disticha*,
ed. Boas, lxii, lxx.


I.46.  Vatican City, Biblioteca Apostolica Vaticana.  Reg. lat. 282
Parchment, XIV², 15.3 x 7.7 cm

1-20v  Prosper of Aquitaine, *Epigrammata* (fragmentary both
within and at end).

20 leaves, incorrectly numbered 1-15: 1-2⁸, 3⁴ (several
folios lacking, probably two at the beginning and two at the end of
this gathering). 30 lines per page. Single column ruled in ink, 16.3
x 10.7 cm. Expert round gothic book hand with hairline finishing
strokes. Red initials and flourishes to line initials.

No annotation. Damp and mud stains along top edge.
*See*: Gehl, "Latin Readers," 435; Wilmart, *Codices Reginenses*, 2:90-91.


**I.47. Vatican City, Biblioteca Apostolica Vaticana. Rossi 165**
Parchment, XIVex, 25.5 x 19 cm

| | |
|---|---|
| 1-20r | Prosper of Aquitaine, *Epigrammata*. |
| 20v | blank |

20 numbered leaves: 1-2¹⁰. 35 lines per page. Single column ruled in ink, 18.3 x 11.5 cm. Expert, spacious round gothic book hand. Single catchword in hand of scribe, 10v. Red and blue alternating initials with flourishes in blue and red.

Lexical and grammatical glosses interlinear on 1-6 only. A few marginal notes (XV) on 1 and 2. Ownership mark (XV): *Iste liber est mei Matteii filii magistri Donati de cesa*, written first in a neat firm hand and then repeated in a trembling and inexpert one.

*See*: Gehl, "Latin Readers," 435.


**I.48. Vatican City, Biblioteca Apostolica Vaticana. Urb. lat. 677**
Parchment, XIV, 20.7 x 14.3 cm

I.
| | |
|---|---|
| 1-74v | Boethius, *Consolation of Philosophy* (original text damaged; several folios supplied in later hand). |

II.
| | |
|---|---|
| 75-103r | Prosper of Aquitaine, *Epigrammata*. |
| 103v | blank |

III.
| | |
|---|---|
| 104r-v | blank |
| 105-125 | Aesop, *Fables* (fragmentary at end; last two folios supplied in later hand). |
| 125v | blank |

125 numbered leaves: $1^{10}$, $2\text{-}4^8$, $5\text{-}6^{10}$, $7\text{-}8^8$, $9^4$; $10^{10}$, $11^8$, $12^{10}$; $13^1$ (104, supplied by binder), $14^7$ (105 loose, once glued to 106), $15^{12}$, $16^1$ (supplied with missing text), $17^1$ (supplied with missing text). I: 20 lines per page. Single column ruled in ink, 13.9 x 9.1 cm. In one gathering only, the seventh, space has been ruled for marginal glosses in outside and bottom margins. Two tight, expert round gothic book hands. Simple, rather clumsy red initials outlined in brown ink. II: 25 lines per page except 98, where 26 lines. Single column ruled in ink, 15.1 x 5.8 cm. Some parchment reused. Expert round gothic book hand. Red initials outlined in brown as in I. III: 24 or 25 lines per page (25 regularly on 104, 124, and 125). Single column ruled in ink, 16.4 x 8.3 cm (16.4 x 10.5 cm on 104, 124 and 125). Spacious, expert round gothic book hand. Decoration of heavy, dark red initials and roughly drawn paragraph marks also in red.

Catchwords to I and II supplied in one hand (XV), some decorated with drawings of monsters. This same hand may be responsible for rewriting some faded or rubbed text in II. Boethius Book V is supplied with an extensive marginal gloss (XIV). Remainder of I has only sparse interlinear annotations (XIV and XV). Many interlinear and short marginal notes and conventional symbols of uncertain meaning (XV and XVI) in II, some in hand of catchword artist. Ownership mark (XVI?), 125v: *Peregrinus*.

*See*: Gehl, "Latin Readers," 435-36.

## I.49. Volterra, Biblioteca Guarnacci. MS XLIX.33
Parchment, $XIV^1$, 21.5 x 15 cm

1-15v        Prosper of Aquitaine, *Epigrammata*.
16           blank

16 numbered leaves: $1\text{-}2^8$. 28 or 29 lines per page. Single column ruled in ink from prickings, 14.3 x 10 cm. Expert, graceful round gothic book hand. Careful, relatively elaborate program of decoration including red initials and flourished line initials. Initials are flourished in red and blue on alternating page openings, except 8v-9 where the pattern is broken; the result is a pattern regular

within each of the two gatherings and such that the outside of one gathering has red flourishes front and back and the second gathering has blue flourishes on the single outer page with text.

Annotation of text limited to marginal notes on a few folia (XIV). Index letters (XIV) of unidentified significance above top text line on 3, 4, 5, 7, 8, 9, 10, 11, 13 and 14. Numerous scribbles in margins including drawings of coats of arms. Ownership mark (XIV), 15v: *Iste liber . . . chellocci magistri petri deo gratias*, repeated 16v: *Iste liber est chollocci magistri petri de gap . . .* Various other scribblings on 15v and 16r-v in hands of XIV to XVI.

*See*: Gehl, "Latin Readers," 436-37; Mazzatinti, *Inventarii*, 2:234 (no. 255).


PART II. OVERSIZE MANUALS IN READER FORM

The following books, largely grammar and rhetoric manuals, are redacted in copies very similar in design to Tuscan elementary readers of the fourteenth century but are for the most part larger in overall format. Only summary entries are provided here.

**II.1. Cambridge, Gonville and Caius College. MS 720/747**
Parchment, XIV
>Boethius, *Consolation of Philosophy*.
>*See*: James, *Gonville and Caius*, 691.

**II.2. Florence, Bibiloteca Medicea-Laurenziana. Acquisti e Doni 362**
Parchment fragment of 18 leaves only, XIV[2]
>Alexander of Villa Dei, *Doctrinale*.
>*See*: Gehl, "Latin Readers," 437; Bursill-Hall, *Census*, 79.

**II.3. Florence, Biblioteca Nazionale Centrale. Magliabecchi I, 47**
Parchment, XIV[in]
>Alexander of Villa Dei, *Doctrinale*. In overall appearance and decoration very similar to Census I.11.
>*See*: Gehl, "Latin Readers," 438; Garin, *Pensiero*, plate I.

### II.4. Florence, Biblioteca Nazionale Centrale. Panciatichi 69
Parchment, XIVex
> Geoffrey of Vinsauf, *Poetria nova.*
> *See*: Gehl, "Latin Readers," 438; Morpurgo, *Codici Panciatichiani*, 125-26.

### II.5. Florence, Biblioteca Riccardiana. MS 315
Parchment, XIV
> Prosper of Aquitaine, *Epigrammata.* Very similar in format to a regular reading copy, with extensive notation in Latin and volgare of the sort that goes with teaching reading, but significantly oversize. Ownership marks 22v indicate early monastic provenance.
> *See*: Black, "Curriculum," 153.

### II.6. Florence, Biblioteca Riccardiana. MS 682
Parchment, XIVex
> Geoffrey of Vinsauf, *Poetria nova.*
> *See*: Gehl, "Latin Readers," 438.

### II.7. Florence, Biblioteca Riccardiana. MS 789
Parchment, XIV
> Alexander of Villa Dei, *Doctrinale.* Ruled to receive elaborate marginal gloss.
> *See*: Gehl, "Latin Readers," 438; Bursill-Hall, *Census*, 84.

### II.8. Florence, Biblioteca Riccardiana. MS 809
Parchment, XIV
> Eberhard of Bethune, *Graecismus.*
> See: Gehl, "Latin Readers," 439; Bursill-Hall, *Census*, 84.

### II.9. Florence, Biblioteca Riccardiana. MS 874
Parchment, XIV
> Geoffrey of Vinsauf, *Poetria nova.* Ownership mark on 39v: *Iste liber est Antonii Arnalti morantis in scholis magistri Spaliatri*[?].
> *See*: Gehl, "Latin Readers," 439.

**II.10. Florence, Biblioteca Riccardiana. MS 1189**
Parchment, XIII²

Geoffrey of Vinsauf, *Poetria nova.*
*See*: Gehl, "Latin Readers," 439.

**II.11. London, British Library. MS Burney 129**
Parchment, XIV

Boethius, *Consolation of Philosophy.* Ownership mark at bottom of last folio, verso: *Explicit liber boecii franceschini de Anicinis.*

**II.12. Vatican City, Biblioteca Apostolica Vaticana. Chigi I.IV.145**
Parchment, XIV/XV

Geoffrey of Vinsauf, *Poetria nova.* Extensive annotation (XV) makes this seem a grammar-course book taken on to a University-level course.
*See*: Gehl, "Latin Readers," 439.

**II.13. Zurich, Private Collection**
Parchment, XIV

Geoffrey of Vinsauf, *Poetria nova.* Several ownership marks, now illegible except for that (XV) of Antonio di Francisco di Zanobi on back flyleaf (unnumbered).
*See*: Gehl, "Latin Readers," 440.

PART III. MANUSCRIPTS EXAMINED AND EXCLUDED

The following list includes manuscripts consulted in the course of this study but excluded from the lists above. There is room here for only the most summary listing; location and shelf mark are given in abbreviated form, followed by the contents of potential interest for our study. After a double colon (::) are brief notes indicating the reason for exclusion. Needless to say, these notes are not merely descriptive; they represent my conclusions after examining the evidence available to me. I hope the list will be of some interest to scholars wishing to pursue the subject of medieval and Renaissance schoolbooks.

These abbreviations are used:

| | | |
|---|---|---|
| XV | = | Fifteenth century. |
| Ital | = | Written in Italy but almost surely not in Tuscany. |
| Tuscan? | = | Possibly but not certainly written in Tuscany. |
| auct | = | *auctores* level book, that is, one that I judge was used for classroom instruction in grammar but which does not follow the standard reader form. |
| inst | = | Institutional copy, not intended primarily for private study or teaching. |
| ref | = | Reference copy, probably intended for personal ownership and use but not for reading instruction. |
| # | = | Not seen. These manuscripts are reported on the basis of published descriptions or microfilm. |

**Arezzo, Comunale. Confraternità dei Laici 181.** Commonplace book with fables :: XV.

**Arezzo, Comunale. Confraternità dei Laici 424.** Seneca :: XV.

**Arezzo, Comunale. Confraternità dei Laici 429.** Ovid :: XV, ref.

**Bergamo, Civica. MA 97.** Theodulus, Prudentius, *Physiologus* :: Ital.

**Bergamo, Civica. MA 187.** Theodulus :: Ital.

**Bergamo, Civica. MA 321.** Prosper :: Ital.

**Bergamo, Civica. MA 355.** Prosper :: XV, Ital.

**#Bologna, Archiginnasio. A.918.** Prosper, Isidore :: inst.

**Bologna, Universitaria. 1206.** Henry of Settimello :: XV, Ital.

Bologna, Universitaria. 2749. Aesop :: Ital.

Bologna, Universitaria. 2795. Aesop :: Ital.

Cortona, Accademia Etrusca. 33. Boethius, Hugh of St. Victor, etc. :: ref.

Cortona, Accademia Etrusca. 262. Grammatical miscellany :: ref.

Cortona, Accademia Etrusca. 263. *Doctrinale* :: inst.

Cortona, Accademia Etrusca. 264. Grammatical miscellany :: XV.

#El Escorial. S.III.9. *Ianua*, Cato :: Tuscan?

Eton College. 136. Seneca :: ref.

Ferrara, Ariostea. II,175. Henry of Settimello, etc. :: XV.

Ferrara, Ariostea. II,216. Aesop, Cato :: XV.

Florence, Medicea-Laurenziana. Plut. 22, 12. Priscian :: ref.

Florence, Medicea-Laurenziana. Plut. 23, 22. Petrus de Isolella :: inst.

Florence, Medicea-Laurenziana. Plut. 29, 39. Isidore :: inst.

Florence, Medicea-Laurenziana. Plut. 38, 35. Theodulus, Statius :: Ital, XV.

Florence, Medicea-Laurenziana. Plut. 52, 26. Miscellany :: ref.

Florence, Medicea-Laurenziana. Plut. 89, sup. 61 (Gaddi). Seneca, Cato, vernacular poetry :: XV.

Florence, Medicea-Laurenziana. Plut. 91, sup. 49 (Gaddi). *Doctrinale*, Vergil, Pseudo-Cicero :: XV.

Florence, Medicea-Laurenziana. Acquisti e Doni 28. Avienus, Pseudo-Ovid :: XV.

Florence, Medicea-Laurenziana. Acquisti e Doni 208. Virgil :: auct.

Florence, Medicea-Laurenziana. Acquisti e Doni 343. *Sententiae* :: ref.

Florence, Medicea-Laurenziana. Ashburnham 243. Filippo di Naddo, anon. *dictamen* treatise :: ref.

Florence, Medicea-Laurenziana. Ashburnham 247. Isidore, moral commonplaces :: ref.

Florence, Medicea-Laurenziana. Ashburnham 258. Guido da Bologna :: ref.

Florence, Medicea-Laurenziana. Conv. soppr. 65. *Graecismus* :: inst.

Florence, Medicea-Laurenziana. Conv. soppr. 444. Macrobius :: ref.

Florence, Medicea-Laurenziana. Conv. soppr. 546. Virgil :: auct.

Florence, Medicea-Laurenziana. Conv. soppr. 609. Aesop :: XV.

Florence, Medicea-Laurenziana. Strozzi 140. *Doctrinale* :: Ital.

Florence, Naz. Centr. I.I.2. Huguccio :: inst.

Florence, Naz. Centr. II.I.73. Seneca :: inst.

Florence, Naz. Centr. II.II.67. Proverbs :: ref.

Florence, Naz. Centr. II.IV.158. Prosper :: Ital.

Florence, Naz. Centr. Conv. soppr. B.3.500. Proverbs, Seneca, biblical *flores* :: ref.

Florence, Naz. Centr. Conv. soppr. C.9.2916. Proverbs, grammatical miscellaney :: ref.

Florence, Naz. Centr. Conv. soppr. E.4.784. Bernard of Naples :: inst or ref.

Florence, Naz. Centr. Conv. soppr. G.8.1557. Metrical treatises :: inst.

Florence, Naz. Centr. Conv. soppr. I.1.34. *Graecismus* :: inst.

Florence, Naz. Centr. Conv. soppr. I.4.2. Seneca :: ref.

Florence, Naz. Centr. Conv. soppr. I.6.17. Horace, Geoffrey of Vinsauf :: inst.

Florence, Naz. Centr. Conv. soppr. da ordinare, Vallombrosa 22 (311). Quintilian :: XV.

Florence, Naz. Centr. Conv. soppr. da ordinare, Vallombrosa 40 (329). Moral/rhetorical miscellaney :: inst.

Florence, Naz. Centr. Magliabecchi I, 2. Anon. grammar :: ref.

Florence, Naz. Centr. Magliabecchi I, 10. Grammatical miscellaney :: ref.

Florence, Naz. Centr. Magliabecchi I, 50bis. Priscian :: ref.

Florence, Naz. Centr. Magliabecchi I, 52. Priscian :: ref.

Florence, Naz. Centr. Magliabecchi I, 53. *Doctrinale* :: XV.

Florence, Naz. Centr. Magliabecchi VI, 152. *dictamen* treatises. :: ref.

Florence, Naz. Centr. Magliabecchi VII, 1. Prosper, Cato, *Ilias latina*, Prudentius, Bonvesin, Pseudo-Boethius :: XV.

Florence, Naz. Centr. Magliabecchi VII, 177. Cicero, Martianus Capella :: XV.

Florence, Naz. Centr. Magliabecchi VII, 932. Miscellaney of fragments including Terence, Seneca :: auct?

Florence, Naz. Centr. Magliabecchi VII, 1018. Virgil :: French?

Florence, Naz. Centr. Magliabecchi VII, 1035. Boethius :: inst.

Florence. Naz. Centr. Magliabecchi VII, 1063. Statius, *Illias latina*, Vergil :: auct.

Florence, Naz. Centr. Magliabecchi VII, 1088. Statius, *Ilias latina*, Henry of Settimello, other poetry :: XV.

Florence, Naz. Centr. Magliabecchi XXIII, 136. Valerius Maximus :: ref.

Florence, Naz. Centr. Nuovi acquisti 96. Grammatical miscellany :: ref.

Florence, Naz. Centr. Nuovi acquisti 812. Seneca :: auct?

Florence, Naz. Centr. Nuovi acquisti 1091. moral miscellaney :: ref.

Florence, Riccardiana. 150. *Ilias latina*, anon. grammar :: XV.

Florence, Riccardiana. 268. Boethius :: inst.

Florence, Riccardiana. 364. Prosper, Cato, Prudentius :: XV.

Florence, Riccardiana. 418. *Physiologus*, Virgil, Prudentius' *Psychomachia* :: XV?, auct.

Florence, Riccardiana. 581. Macrobius :: XV.

Florence, Riccardiana. 588. Horace :: auct?

Florence, Riccardiana. 641. Boethius :: ref.

Florence, Riccardiana. 642. Boethius :: inst or ref.

Florence, Riccardiana. 649. Petrus de Isolella :: ref.

Florence, Riccardiana. 808. Lorenzo d'Aquila :: ref.

Florence, Riccardiana. 987. Sallust :: ref.

Florence, Riccardiana. 1221. *Ilias latina* :: Ital.

#Ivrea, Capitolare. 7. Prudentius, *Doctrina rudium*, *Geta* :: Ital.

London, British Library. Additional 11979. Valerius Maximus :: inst.

London, British Library. Additional 27625. Aesop :: XV.

London, British Library. Arundel 266. Boethius :: XV, inst.

London, British Library. Arundel 394. *Doctrinale*, *Graecismus*, Pseudo-Boethius :: inst.

London, British Library. Burney 129. Boethius :: Ital, inst.

London, British Library. Burney 130. Boethius :: Ital, inst.

London, British Library. Burney 131. Boethius :: Ital, inst.

London, British Library. Burney 247. Prudentius :: XV.

London, British Library. Burney 316. Anon. Lat. grammar :: XV.

Lucca, Statale. 370. Henry of Settimello, Boethius, Prosper :: inst.

Lucca, Statale. 1407. Boethius :: ref.

#Milan, Braidense. A.D.X.43. *Geta*, Aesop, Prosper, Henry of Settimello, etc. :: XV.

Milan, Trivulziana. 498. Prosper :: Ital.

Milan, Trivulziana. 629. Theodulus :: XV.

Milan, Trivulziana. 662. *Chartula* :: Ital.

Milan, Trivulziana. 676. *Ianua* :: Ital.

Milan, Trivulziana. 702. Boethius :: Ital.

Milan, Trivulziana. 762. Geoffrey of Vinsauf :: Ital.

Modena, Estense. Alpha K.5.25. Boethius :: XV, Ital.

Modena, Estense. Alpha O.6.2. *Ianua*, Cato :: XV, Ital.

Modena, Estense. Alpha P.8.1. *Ianua*, Cato :: XV, Ital.

Modena, Estense. Alpha Q.7.27. Bonvesin :: Ital.

Modena, Estense. Alpha Q.9.5. Aesop :: XV.

Modena, Estense. Alpha T.6.4. Boethius, *Doctrinale* :: XV?, Ital.

Modena, Estense. Alpha U.5.13. *Ianua*, Cato, Conrad of Pontremoli :: XV, Ital.

Modena, Estense. Alpha W.2.20. *Graecismus* :: ref or auct.

Montecassino. Cod. lat. 227P. Aesop :: Ital.

Oxford, Bodleian. Canon. lat. 72. Theodulus :: Ital.

Oxford, Bodleian. Lat. misc.d.70. Huguccio of Pisa :: ref.

Oxford, Bodleian. Lat. misc.e.52. Francesco da Buti :: XV.

Oxford, Bodleian. Add. A.171. Theodulus :: Ital, inst.

Oxford, Christ Church College. 507. Ovid :: Ital.

Oxford, Christ Church College. 508. Ovid :: XV.

Pisa, S. Caterina. 79. Seneca :: inst.

Pisa, S. Caterina. 124. Boethius, etc. :: inst.

Pisa, S. Caterina. 140. Isidore :: inst.

Pisa, S. Caterina. 182. Francesco da Buti :: ref.

Pistoia, Forteguerriana. A.27. Priscian :: ref.

Pistoia, Forteguerriana. A.28. Boethius :: auct.

Pistoia, Forteguerriana. A.31. Horace :: ref or auct.

Pistoia, Forteguerriana. A.36. Juvenal :: ref or auct.

Ravenna, Classense. 358. Cato, Prudentius, Aesop, John of Soncino :: Ital, ref.

Rovigo, Accademia dei Concordi. Silv. 310. *Physiologus, Chartula* :: XV?, Ital.

Siena, Comunale degli Intronati. H.VII.4. Boethius :: inst.

Siena, Comunale degli Intronati. H.VII.5. Boethius :: inst.

Siena, Comunale degli Intronati. H.VI.23. Miscellany :: XV, ref.

Siena, Comunale degli Intronati. J.VI.26. Miscellany including Boethius :: ref.

Siena, Comunale degli Intronati. K.V.22. Prosper, *Ianua*, Cato, Aesop :: inst.

Siena, Comunale degli Intronati. K.V.24. Geoffrey of Vinsauf :: inst.

Toledo, Cathedral. MS 102-11. Ovid, *Pamphilus* :: Ital.

Vatican. Chigi L.IV.98. *Ianua* :: XV.

Vatican. Ottob. lat. 1297. Prudentius, Avianus :: inst.

Vatican. Ottob. lat. 1967. *Ianua* :: XV.

Vatican, Ottob. lat. 3325. Bonvesin, *Chartula*, Ovid, *Geta*, Aesop :: XV.

Vatican. Ottob. lat. 3327. Prosper :: Tuscan?, inst.

Vatican. Pal. lat. 1611. *Ilias latina* :: Ital., XV.

Vatican. Reg. lat. 270. Prosper :: XV.

Vatican. Reg. lat. 2080, fragment 1. Terence :: XV?

Vatican. Reg. lat. 2080, fragment 5. Lucan :: inst.

Vatican. Rossi 410. Priscian :: Ital, inst.

Vatican. Vat. lat. 2868. Henry of Settimello, Aesop, Prudentius, Theodulus, *Chartula*, Vitalis of Blois :: inst.

Vatican. Vat. lat. 5158. *Chartula, Doctrina rudium*, Henry of Settimello :: XV, Tuscan?

Vatican. Vat. lat. 9295. *Ianua* :: XV.

Vatican. Vat. lat. 9657. Boethius, Ovid, Pseudo-Ovid, Henry of Settimello :: Ital.

Vatican. Vat. lat. 10504. Boethius, Prosper :: Ital.

Verona, Civica. MS 1209-10. Prosper :: Ital.

Verona, Civica. MS 1880. John of Soncino :: XV.

Verona, Civica. MS 2197. Prosper :: XV, ref.

#Vienna, Nationalbibliothek. 154. *Ianua*, Cato :: Tuscan?

Volterra, Comunale Guarnacci. LVI.4.3. Persius, Horace :: XV, auct.

# BIBLIOGRAPHY

Printed sources are given in abbreviated form in the notes and fully here. Manuscript and archival sources are cited in full in the notes or referred to fuller descriptions offered in the Appendix.

## Printed Primary Sources

Aesop. *See* Hervieux.

Arrigo da Settimello. *See* Henry of Settimello; Cremaschi.

Augustine of Hippo. "Christian Instruction." Trans. John J. Gavigan, O.S.A. In *Writings of Saint Augustine.* Vol. 4. New York: Fathers of the Church, 1947.

———. *Sancti Aurelii Augustini De doctrina Christiana.* Ed. Joseph Martin. Corpus Christianorum Series Latina 32. Turnhout: Brepols, 1972.

Avianus. *See* Hervieux.

Bartolomeo da S. Concordio. *Ammaestramenti degli antichi raccolti e volgarizzati.* Milan: Società tipografica de' Classici italiani, 1808.

Bertanza, Enrico, and Giuseppe Della Santa, eds. *Documenti per la storia della cultura in Venezia.* Vol. 1: *Maestri, scuole e scolari in Venezia fino al 1500.* Monumenti storici publicati dalla R. Deputazione Veneta di storia patria, ser. 1, vol. 12. Venice: R. Deputazione Veneta di storia patria, 1907.

Boas, Marcus. *See Disticha Catonis.*

Boccaccio, Giovanni. *Le lettere edite e inedite di Messer Giovanni Boccaccio.* Ed. Francesco Corazzini. Florence: Sansoni, 1877.

Boethius. *The Consolation of Philosophy.* Trans. S. J. Tester. Loeb Classical Library 74. Cambridge, Mass.: Harvard University Press, 1978.

Pseudo-Boethius. *De disciplina scolarium: Edition critique, introduction et notes.* Ed. Olga Weijers. Studien und texte zur Geistesgeschichte des Mittelalters 12. Leiden: E. J. Brill, 1976.

——. *Un saggio di pedagogia medievale: Il 'De disciplina scolarium' dello Pseudo-Boezio.* Ed. Edvige Ducci. Turin: Società editrice internazionale, 1967.

Bonacina, M., ed. "De lombardo et lumaco." In *Commedie latine del XII e XIII secolo.* Ed. Ferruccio Bertini. Vol. 4. Pubblicazioni dell'Istituto di filologia classica e medievale dell'Università di Genova 79. Genoa: Università di Genova, 1983. Pp. 111–12.

Bonvesin de la Riva. *Le meraviglie di Milano.* Trans. and ed. Ettore Verga. Milan: F. Cogliati, 1921.

——. *Volgari scelti: Select Poems.* Trans. Patrick S. Diehl and Ruggero Stefanini. American University Studies, ser. 2, vol. 58. New York: Peter Lang, 1987.

——. *See also* Vidmanovà-Schmidtovà.

Branca, Vittore, ed. *Esopo toscano dei frati e dei mercanti trecenteschi.* Venice: Marsilio, 1989.

——, ed. *Mercanti scrittori: Ricordi nella Firenze tra medioevo e rinascimento.* Milan: Rusconi, 1986.

Caggese, Romolo, ed. *Statuti della Repubblica Fiorentina.* 2 vols. Florence: E. Ariani, 1910, and Tipografia Galileiana, 1921.

*Catonis Disticha. See Disticha Catonis.*

Ceffi, Filippo. *Le Dicerie di ser Filippo Ceffi notaio fiorentino.* Ed. Luigi Biondi. Turin: Chirio e Mina, 1825.

*Chartula.* Ed. Jean Mabillion as "Carmen paraeneticum ad Rainaldum" in *S. Bernardi Clarae-vallensis Abbatis . . . opera omnia.* Patrologiae cursus completus series latina 184. Paris: J.-P. Migne, 1854. Cols. 1307–14.

*Chartularium studii senensis.* Ed. Giovanni Cecchini and Giulio Prunai. Vol. 1: (1240–1357). Siena: R. Università degli Studi, 1942.

Claudian. *Claudian: De raptu Proserpinae.* Ed. John Barrie Hall. Cambridge: Cambridge University Press, 1969.

Cremaschi, Giovanni, ed. *Enrico da Settimello Elegia.* Orbis Christianus 1. Bergamo: Istituto italiano Edizioni Atlas, 1949.

Dante Alighieri. *Il Convivio.* Ed. and commented by Giovanni Busnelli and Giuseppe Vandelli. Opere di Dante, nuova edizione sotto gli auspici della Fondazione Giorgio Cini. 2d ed. Florence: Le Monnier, 1964.

*De disciplina scolarium. See* Pseudo-Boethius.

*De lombardo et lumaco. See* Bonacina.

*Disticha Catonis.* Ed. Marcus Boas and Heinrich Johann Botschuyver. Amsterdam: North-Holland, 1952.

*Disticha Catonis.* Trans. Wayland Johnson Chase as *The Distichs of Cato. A Famous Medieval Textbook.* University of Wisconsin Studies in the Social Sciences and History 7. Madison: University of Wisconsin, 1922.

*Doctrina rudium. See* Vidmanovà-Schmidtovà.

Dominici, Giovanni. *Iohannis Dominici Lucula noctis.* Ed. Edmund Hunt. Publications in Mediaeval Studies 4. Notre Dame, Ind.: University of Notre Dame, 1940.

——. *Regola del governo di cura familiare.* Ed. Donato Salvi. Florence: Angiolo Garinei, 1860.

Eden, P. T., ed. *Theobaldi Physiologus Edited with Introduction, Critical Apparatus, Translation and Commentary.* Leiden: Brill, 1972.

*Facetus. See* Garin, *Pensiero,* 94–95.

Fasoli, Gina. *Statuti del comune di Bassano dell'anno 1259 e del anno 1295.* Monumenti storici pubblicati dalla R. Deputazione di storia patria per le Venezie, n.s. 2. Venice: R. Deputazione di storia patria, 1940.

Fierville, Charles. *Un grammaire inédite du XIIIe siècle* [that of Petrus de Isolella]. Paris: Imprimerie nationale, 1886.

Fumi, Luigi, ed. *R. Archivio di Stato in Lucca: Regesti.* Vol. 2: *Carteggio degli Anziani.* Lucca: Alberto Marchi, 1903.

*Geta. See* Vitalis of Blois.

Henry of Settimello. *Henrici Septimellensis Elegia sive de Miseria.* Ed. Aristides Marigo. Scriptores Latini Medii Aevi Italici 1. Pavia: A. Draghi, 1926.

——. *See also* Cremaschi.

Hervieux, Lèopold. *Les fabulistes latins depuis le siècle d'Auguste jusqu'à la fin du moyen âge.* 4 vols. Paris: Firmin-Didot, 1890–1898.

Huygens, R. B. C., ed. *Bernard d'Utrecht Commentum in Theodolum (1076–1099).* Spoleto: Centro italiano di studi sull'alto medioevo, 1977.

*Ilias latina. See* Scaffai.

Pseudo-Jerome. *De contemptu mulierum.* Patrologiae cursus completus series latina 30. Paris: J.-P. Migne, 1846. Col. 288.

John the Abbot. *See* Klein.

Klein, Heinz-Willi. "Johannis abbatis *Liber de VII viciis et VII virtutibus.*" *Mittellateinisches Jahrbuch* 9 (1974), 173–247.

Lapo da Castiglionchio. *Epistola o sia ragionamento di Messer Lapo da Castiglionchio celebre giuresconsulto del secolo XIV colla vita del medesimo composto dall'abate Lorenzo Mehus.* Bologna: Girolamo Corciolani ed Eredi Colli a S. Tomaso d'Aquino, 1753.

Latini, Brunetto. *La rettorica.* Ed. Francesco Maggini. Florence: Galetti e Cocci, 1915.

Pseudo-Ovid. *See* Bonacina.

*Pamphilus.* Ed. Franz G. Becker. Beihefte zum Mittellateinischen Jahrbuch 9. Ratingen: A. Henn, 1972.

*Pamphilus.* Ed. Stefano Pittaluga. In *Commedie latine del XII e XIII secolo.* Vol. 3. Pubblicazioni dell'Istituto di filologia classica e medievale dell'Università di Genova 68. Genoa: Università di Genova, 1980. Pp. 13–137.

Paolino Minorita. *Trattato de regimine rectoris.* Ed. Adolfo Mussafia. Vienna: Tendler, 1867.

Passavanti, Jacopo. *Lo Specchio della vera penitenzia.* Ed. F.-L. Polidori. 2d ed. Florence: Le Monnier, 1863.

Petrus de Isolella. *See* Fierville.

*Physiologus. See* Eden.

Prosper of Aquitaine. *Epigrammatum ex sententiis S. Augustini Liber Unus.* Patrologiae cursus completus series latina 51. Paris: J.-P. Migne, 1846. Cols. 498–532; 611–16.

———. *Sancti Prosperi Aquitani Liber Sententiarum*. Ed. M. Galasso. Corpus Christianorum Series Latina 68A. Turnhout: Brepols, 1972.

Prudentius. *Dittochaeon*. In *Prudence*. Ed. M. Lavarenne. Vol. 4. Paris: Budè, 1951.

———. *Dittochaeon*, or *Tituli historiarum*. Ed. H. J. Thomson. In *Prudentius*. 2 vols. Cambridge, Mass.: Harvard University Press, 1953. Vol. 2, pp. 346–71.

Salutati, Coluccio. *See* Jenson.

*Theoduli Ecloga*. Ed. J. Osternacher. Urfahr bei Linz: Collegium Petrinum, 1902.

*Theoduli Ecloga*. *See also* Huygens.

Velluti, Donato. *La cronica domestica*. Ed. Isidoro del Lungo and Guglielmo Volpi. Florence: G. Sansoni, 1914.

Vidmanovà-Schmidtovà, Anežka, ed. *Quinque claves sapientiae*. Leipzig: Teubner, 1969.

Villani, Giovanni. *Cronica*. Ed. F. Gherardi Dragomanni. 4 vols. Florence: Sansone Coen, 1844–1845.

Vitalis of Blois. *Geta*. Ed. Ferruccio Bertini. In *Commedie latine del XII e XIII secolo*. Vol. 3. Pubblicazioni dell'Istituto di filologia classica e medievale dell'Università di Genova 68. Genoa: Università di Genova, 1980. Pp. 141–241.

———. *Der "Geta" des Vitalis von Blois: Kritische Ausgabe*. Ed. A. Paeske. Cologne: n.p., 1976.

## Secondary Works

Ageno, Franca. "Tradizione favolistica e novellistica nella fraseologia proverbiale." *Lettere italiane* 8 (1956), 351–84.

Alessio, Gian Carlo. "Brunetto Latini e Cicerone (e i dettatori)." *Italia medioevale e umanistica* 22 (1979), 123–69.

———. "La grammatica speculativa e Dante." In *Letture classensi*. Vol. 13. Ed. Maria Corti. Ravenna: Longo, 1984. Pp. 69–88.

———. "Le istituzioni scolastiche e l'insegnamento." In *Aspetti della letteratura latina nel secolo XIII: Atti del primo convengo internazionale di studi dell'Associazione per il Medioevo e l'Umanesimo latini, Perugia, 3–5 Ottobre 1983*. Ed. Claudio Leonardi and Giovanni Orlandi. Perugia: Regione Umbria and La Nuova Italia, 1986. Pp. 3–28.

Alexandre-Bidon, Danièle. "La lettre volée: Apprendre a lire a l'enfant au Moyen Age." *Annales: Economies, Sociétés, Civilisations* 44 (1989), 953–92.

Amsler, Mark. *Etymology and Grammatical Discourse in Late Antiquity and the Early Middle Ages*. Amsterdam Studies in the Theory and History of Linguistic Science, ser. 3, vol. 44. Philadelphia: John Benjamins, 1989.

Antolín, Guillermo, O.S.A. *Catalogo de los códices latinos de la Real Biblioteca del Escorial*. 4 vols. Madrid: Imprenta Helénica, 1910–1916.

Antonelli, Roberto, and Simonetta Bianchini. "Dal *clericus* al *poeta*." In *Letteratura italiana*. Ed. Alberto Asor Rosa. Vol. 2: *Produzione e consumo*. Turin: Einaudi, 1983. Pp. 171–227.

Aurigemma, Marco. *Saggio sul Passavanti*. Saggi di letteratura italiana 9. Florence: Le Monnier, 1957.

Avesani, Rino. "Leggesi che cinque sono le chiave della sapienza." *Rivista di cultura classica e medioevale* 7 (1965): 62–73.

———. "Il primo ritmo per la morte del grammatico Ambrogio e il cosidetto *Liber Catonianus*." *Studi medievali*, 3d ser., 6 (1965), 455–88.

———. *Quattro miscellanee medioevali e umanistiche*. Note e discussioni erudite 11. Rome: Edizioni di storia e letteratura, 1967.

Bacci, Orazio. "Maestri di grammatica in Valdelsa nel secolo XIV." *Miscellanea storica della Valdelsa* 3 (1895), 88–95.

Bäuml, Franz H. "Varieties and Consequences of Medieval Literacy and Illiteracy." *Speculum* 55 (1980), 237–65.

Bagni, Paolo. "Artes dictandi e techniche letterarie." In *Retorica e poetica tra i secoli XII e XIV: Atti del secondo convegno internazionale di studi dell'Associazione per il Medioevo e l'Umanesimo . . . Trento e Rovereto, 3–5 ottobre 1985*. Quaderni del Centro per il Collegamento degli studi medievali e umanistici nell'Università di Perugia 18. Perugia: La Nuova Italia, 1988. Pp. 201–20.

———. "L'inventio nell'ars poetica latino-medievale." In *Rhetoric Revalued: Papers from the International Society for the History of Rhetoric*. Ed. Brian Vickers. Medieval and Renaissance Texts and Studies 19. Binghamton, N.Y.: Center for Medieval and Early Renaissance Studies, 1982. Pp. 99–114.

Baldelli, Ignazio. "Le lingue del rinascimento da Dante alla prima metà del Quattrocento." *Rassegna della letteratura italiana* 87 (1983), 5–28.

Baldo, Vittorio. *Alunni, maestri e scuole in Venezia alla fine del XVI secolo*. Como: New Press, 1977.

Bandini, Angelo Maria. *Catalogus Codicum Manuscriptorum Bibliothecae Mediceae Laurentianae*. 5 vols. Florence: 1764–1777.

Banker, James R. "The *Ars dictaminis* and Rhetorical Textbooks of the Bolognese University in the Fourteenth Century." *Medievalia et Humanistica*, n.s. 5 (1974), 153–68.

———. "Giovanni di Bonandrea and Civic Values in the Context of the Italian Rhetorical Tradition." *Manuscripta* 18 (1974), 3–20.

Barsanti, Paolo. *Il pubblico insegnamento in Lucca dal secolo XIV alla fine del secolo XVIII*. Lucca: Alberto Marchi, 1905.

Battistini, Mario. *Il pubblico insegnamento in Volterra dal secolo XIV al secolo XVII*. Volterra: n.p., 1919.

Bec, Christian. *Les livres des Florentins (1413–1608)*. Biblioteca di Lettere italiane, Studi e testi 29. Florence: Olschki, 1984.

———. *Les marchands écrivains, affaires et humanisme à Florence 1375–1434*. Civilisation et sociétés 9. Paris: Mouton, 1967.

———. "Lo statuto socio-professionale degli scrittori (Trecento e Cinquecento)." In *Letteratura italiana*. Ed. Alberto Asor Rosa. Vol. 2: *Produzione e consumo*. Turin: Einaudi, 1983. Pp. 229–67.

Bernardo, Aldo S. "Petrarch, Dante, and the Medieval Tradition." In *Renaissance*

*Humanism: Foundations, Forms, and Legacy.* Vol. 1: *Humanism in Italy.* Ed. Albert Rabil, Jr. Philadelphia: University of Pennsylvania Press, 1988. Pp. 115–37.

Bianchini, Simonetta. "Arrigo da Settimello e una sua fonte oitanica." *Studi medievali,* 3d ser., 30 (1989), 855–63.

Biblioteca Nacional, Madrid. *Inventario General de Manuscritos de la Biblioteca Nacional de Madrid.* 4 vols. Madrid: Biblioteca Nacional, 1953–1958.

Billanovich, Giuseppe. "Auctorista, humanista, orator." *Rivista di cultura classica e medioevale* 7 (1965), 143–63.

———. "Petrarca, Pietro da Moglio e Pietro da Parma." *Italia medioevale e umanistica* 22 (1979), 367–95.

———. *I primi umanisti e le tradizioni dei classici latini.* Discorsi universitari, n.s. 14. Freiburg: Edizioni Universitarie, 1953.

Black, Robert. "The Curriculum of Italian Elementary and Grammar Schools, 1350–1500." In *The Shapes of Knowledge from the Renaissance to the Enlightenment.* Ed. Donald R. Kelley and Richard H. Popkin. International Archives of the History of Ideas 124. Dordrecht: Kluwer Academic Publishers, 1991. Pp. 137–63. The author has supplied important typescript *corrigenda* to many copies.

———. "Florence." In *The Renaissance in National Context.* Ed. Roy Porter and Mikulas Teich. Cambridge: Cambridge University Press, 1992. Pp. 21–41.

———. "Humanism and Education in Renaissance Arezzo." *I Tatti Studies* 2 (1987), 173–237.

———. "Italian Renaissance Education: Changing Perspectives and Continuing Controversies." *Journal of the History of Ideas* 52 (1991), 315–34.

———. "An Unknown Thirteenth-Century Manuscript of Ianua." In *Church and Chronicle in the Middle Ages: Essays Presented to John Taylor.* Ed. Ian Wood and Graham A. Loud. London: Hambledon Press, 1991. Pp. 101–15.

Boas, Marcus. "De librorum Catonianorum historia atque compositione." *Mnemosyne* 42 (1914), 17–46.

Bonaventure, F. "The Teaching of Latin in Later Medieval England." *Medieval Studies* 23 (1961), 1–20.

Bonilla y San Martín, Antonio. "Una comedia latina de la edad media (El liber Panphili): Reproducción de un manuscrito inédito en versión Castellana." *Boletín de la Real Academia de la historia* 70 (1917), 395–467.

Brentano-Keller, Nelly. "Il libretto di spese e di ricordi di un monaco vallombrosano per libri dati o avuti in prestito." *La Bibliofilía* 41 (1939), 129–58.

Bresc, Henri. "Ecole et services sociaux dans les cités et les 'terres' siciliennes (XIIIe–XVe siècles)." In *Città e servizi sociali nell'Italia dei secoli XII–XV.* Dodicesimo convegno di studi del Centro Italiano di Studi di Storia e d'Arte, Pistoia, 9–12 ottobre 1987. Pistoia: Centro Italiano di Studi di Storia e d'Arte, 1990. Pp. 1–20.

British Museum. *Catalogue of Western Manuscripts in the Old Royal and King's Collections.* Comp. George F. Warner and Julius P. Gilson. 4 vols. London: The British Museum, 1921.

Brucker, Gene. "Florence and Its University." In *Action and Conviction in Early Modern Europe: Essays in Memory of E. H. Harbison*. Ed. Theodore K. Rabb and Jerrold E. Siegel. Princeton: Princeton University Press, 1969. Pp. 220–36.

Bruni, Francesco. "Boncompagno da Signa, Guido delle Colonne, Jean de Meung: Metamorfosi dei classici nel Duecento." In *Retorica e poetica tra i secoli XII e XIV: Atti del secondo convegno internazionale di studi dell Associazione per il Medioevo e l'Umanesimo . . . Trento e Rovereto, 3–5 ottobre 1985*. Quaderni del Centro per il Collegamento degli studi medievali e umanistici nell'Università di Perugia 18. Perugia: La Nuova Italia, 1988. Pp. 79–108.

———. *L'italiano: Elementi di storia della lingua e della cultura. Testi e documenti.* Turin: UTET, 1984.

———. "Traduzione, tradizione e diffusione della cultura: Un contributo alla lingua dei semicolti." In *Alfabetismo e cultura scritta nella storia della società italiana.* Perugia: Università degli Studi, 1978. Pp. 195–234.

Buck, August. *Die Rezeption der Antike: Zum Problem der Kontinuität zwischen Mittelalter und Renaissance.* Wolfenbütteler Abhandlungen zur Renaissanceforschung 1. Hamburg: Hauswedell, 1981.

Bultot, Robert. "La *Chartula* et l'enseignement du mépris du monde dans les écoles et les universités médiévales." *Studi medievali*, 3d ser., 8 (1967), 787–834.

———. *La doctrine du méprise du mond en Occident de s. Ambroise á Innocent III.* Vols. 4.1 and 4.2 of *Christianisme et valeurs humains.* Louvain: Nauwelaerts, 1963–1965.

Burdach, Konrad. *Rienzo und die geistige Wandlung seiner Zeit.* Vol. 2.1 of *Vom Mittelalter zur Reformation: Forschungen zur Geschicthe der Deutschen Bildung.* 2 vols. Berlin: Weidmann, 1913–1928.

Bursill-Hall, Geoffrey. *A Census of Medieval Latin Grammatical Manuscripts.* Grammatica speculativa 4. Stuttgart: Frommann-Holzboog, 1981.

Capello, Giuseppe. "Maestro Manfredo e Maestro Sion grammatici vercellesi del Duecento." *Aevum* 17 (1943), 45–70.

Carabellese, Francesco. "La compagnia di Orsanmichele e il mercato dei libri in Firenze nel secolo XIV." *Archivio storico italiano*, 5th ser., 16 (1895), 267–73.

Cardini, Franco. "Alfabetismo e livelli di cultura nell'età comunale." In *Alfabetismo e cultura scritta.* Ed. A. Bartoli-Langelli and A. Petrucci. Quaderni storici, n.s. 38. Ancona: Il Mulino, 1978. Pp. 488–522

———. "Intellectuals and Culture in Twelfth- and Thirteenth-Century Italy." In *City and Countryside in Late Medieval and Renaissance Italy: Essays Presented to Philip Jones.* Ed. Trevor Dean and Chris Wickham. London: Hambledon Press, 1990. Pp. 13–30.

Carruthers, Mary. *The Book of Memory: A Study of Memory in Medieval Culture.* Cambridge: Cambridge University Press, 1990.

Ceva, Bianca. *Brunetto Latini: L'uomo e l'opera.* Milan: Ricciardi, 1965.

Chadwick, Henry. *Boethius: The Consolations of Music, Logic, Theology, and Philosophy.* Oxford: Clarendon Press, 1981.

Cherchi, Paolo A. *Andrea Cappellano, i trovatori e altri temi romanzi.* Biblioteca di cultura 128. Rome: Bulzoni, 1979.

——. "Jacopo Facciolati and the Canon of Latin Authors." *Storia della Storiografia* 9 (1986), 46–61.

Cherubini, Giovanni. *Signori, contadini, borghesi: Ricerche sulla società italiana del basso medioevo.* Florence: La Nuova Italia, 1974.

Ciapelli, Giovanni. "Libri e letture a Firenze nel XV. secolo, le 'ricordanze' e la ricostruzione delle biblioteche private." *Rinascimento* 29 (1989), 267–91.

Cicchetti, Angelo, and Raul Mordenti. "La scrittura dei libri di famiglia." In *Letteratura italiana.* Ed. Alberto Asor Rosa. Vol. 3: *Le forme del testo.* Turin: Einaudi, 1984. Pp. 1117–1159.

Cipolla, Carlo M. *The Monetary Policy of Fourteenth-Century Florence.* Berkeley: University of California Press, 1982.

Clogan, Paul M. "Literary Genres in a Medieval Textbook." *Medievalia et Humanistica,* n.s. 11 (1982), 199–209.

Cohn, Samuel Kline, Jr. *The Laboring Classes in Renaissance Florence.* New York: Academic Press, 1980.

Colini Baldeschi, Luigi. "L'insegnamento pubblico a Macerata nel trecento e quattrocento." *Rivista delle biblioteche e degli archivi* 11 (1900), 19–26.

Constable, Giles. "The Popularity of Twelfth-Century Spiritual Writers in the Late Middle Ages." *Renaissance Studies in Honor of Hans Baron.* Ed. Anthony Molho and John A. Tedeschi. DeKalb: Northern Illinois University Press, 1971. Pp. 3–28.

Copeland, Rita. "Rhetoric and Vernacular Translation in the Middle Ages." *Studies in the Age of Chaucer* 9 (1987), 41–75.

——. *Rhetoric, Hermeneutics, and Translation in the Middle Ages: Academic Traditions and Vernacular Texts.* Cambridge: Cambridge University Press, 1991.

Courcelle, Pierre. "Etude critique sur les commentaires de Boèce (IXe–XVe siècles)." *Archives d'histoire doctrinale et littèraire du Moyen Age,* 1939, 5–141.

Cremaschi, Giovanni. "Enrico da Settimello e la sua Elegia." *Atti dell'Istituto veneto di scienze, lettere ed arti, Classe di scienze morali e lettere* 108 (1949–50), 177–206.

Curtius, Ernst Robert. *European Literature and the Latin Middle Ages.* Trans. W. R. Trusk. Evanston, Ill.: Northwestern University Press, 1953.

D'Alatri, Mariano. "Panorama geografico, cronologico e statistico sulla distribuzione degli *Studia* degli ordini mendicanti. Italia." In *Le Scuole degli ordini mendicanti (secoli XIII–XIV).* Convegni del Centro di studi sulla spiritualità medievale 17. Todi: Accademia Tudertina, 1978. Pp. 49–72.

Davidsohn, Robert. *Firenze ai tempi di Dante.* Trans. Eugenio Duprè-Theseider. Florence: R. Bempoard e Figlio, 1929.

——. *Geschichte von Florenz.* 8 vols. Berlin: 1896–1927. Trans. Eugenio Duprè-Theseider as *Storia di Firenze.* 8 vols. Florence: Sansoni, 1972–1973.

Davis, Charles T. "The Early Collection of Books of S. Croce in Florence." *Proceedings of the American Philosophical Society* 107 (1963), 399–414.

——. "Education in Dante's Florence." *Speculum* 40 (1965), 415–35. Rev. and repr. in *Dante's Italy.* Philadelphia: University of Pennsylvania Press, 1984. Pp. 137–65.

——. "The Florentine *Studia* and Dante's 'Library'." In *The Divine Comedy and the Encyclopedia of Arts and Sciences*. Acta of the International Dante Symposium, 13–16 Nov. 1983, Hunter College, New York. Ed. Giuseppe C. Di Scipio and Aldo Scaglione. Philadelphia: John Benjamins, 1988. Pp. 339–66.

——. "Remigio de' Girolami O.P. (d. 1319), Lector of S. Maria Novella in Florence." In *Le scuole degli ordini mendicanti (secoli XIII–XIV)*. Convegni del Centro di studi sulla spiritualità medievale 17. Todi: Accademia Tudertina, 1978. Pp. 281–304.

Davis-Weyer, Caecilia. "Komposition und Szenenwahl im Dittochaeum des Prudentius." In *Studien zur spätantiken und byzantinischen Kunst Friedrich Wilhelm Deichmann gewidmet*. Ed. Otto Feld and Urs Peschlow. Teil 3. Bonn: Dr. Rudolf Habelt, 1986. Pp. 19–29.

Debenedetti, Santorre. "Sui più antichi 'doctores puerorum' a Firenze." *Studi medievali* 2 (1902), 327–51.

De La Mare, Albinia C. *The Handwriting of Italian Humanists*. Oxford: Association internationale de bibliophile, 1973.

——. "The Shop of a Florentine Cartolaio in 1426." In *Studi offerti a Roberto Ridolfi*. Ed. Berta Maracchi-Biagiarelli and Dennis E. Rhodes. Florence: Olschki, 1973. Pp. 237–48.

De la Roncière, Charles-M. "Pauvres et pauvreté à Florence au XIVe siècle." In *Etudes sur l'histoire de la pauvreté*. 2 vols. Ed. Michel Mollat. Publications de la Sorbonne, Etudes 8. Paris: Université de Paris IV–Paris Sorbonne, 1974. Pp. 661–745.

Delcorno, Carlo. *Exemplum e letteratura tra medioevo e rinascimento*. Bologna: Il Mulino, 1989.

——. "Predicazione volgare e volgarizzamenti." *Mélanges de l'Ecole française de Rome, Moyen age temps modernes* 89 (1977), 679–89.

Denley, Peter. "Governments and Schools in Late Medieval Italy." In *City and Countryside in Late Medieval and Renaissance Italy: Essays Presented to Philip Jones*. Ed. Trevor Dean and Chris Wickham. London: Hambledon Press, 1990. Pp. 93–107.

Dolezalek, Gero. "La pecia e la preparazione dei libri giuridici nei secoli XII–XIII." In *Luoghi e metodi di insegnamento nell'Italia medioevale (sec. XII–XIV)*. Ed. Luciano Gargan and Oronzo Limone. Galatina: Congedo, 1989. Pp. 201–17.

Dufner, Georg. *Die Dialoge Gregors der Grossen im Wandel der Zeiten und Sprachen*. Miscellanea erudite 19. Padua: Antenore, 1978.

Endlicher, Stephanus. *Catalogus codicum philologicorum latinorum Bibliothecae Palatinae Vindobonensis*. 2 vols. Vienna: F. Beck, 1836.

Fabroni, A. et al. *Memorie istoriche di più uomini illustri pisani*. Pisa: Ranieri Prosperi, 1790–1792.

Federici Vescovini, Graziella. "Due commenti inediti del XIV secolo al *De consolatione philosophiae* di Boezio." *Rivista critica di storia della filosofia* 13 (1958), 384–414.

Filosa, Carlo. *La favola e la letteratura esopiana in Italia dal medio evo ai nostri giorni*. Milan: Vallardi, 1952.

Fiumi, Enrico. "Economia e vita privata dei fiorentini nelle rilevazioni statistiche di Giovanni Villani," *Archivio storico italiano* 111 (1953), 207–41.

Folena, Gianfranco. "*Volgarizzare e tradurre*, idea e terminologia della traduzione." In *La traduzione, saggi e studi*. Trieste: Lint, 1973. Pp. 59–120.

Frova, Carla. *Istruzione e educazione nel medioevo*. Turin: Loescher, 1973.

———. "La scuola nella città tardomedievale: Un impegno pedagogico e organizzativo." In *La città in Italia e in Germania nel medioevo: Cultura, istituzioni, vita religiosa*. Ed. Reinhard Elze and Gina Fasoli. Annali del Istituto storico italogermanico, Quaderno 8. Bologna: Il Mulino, 1981. Pp. 119–43.

Frugoni, Arsenio. "Giovanni Villani *Cronica* XI,94." *Bullettino dell'Istituto storico italiano per il medioevo* 77 (1965), 229–55. Repr. in *Incontri nel Medioevo*. Bologna: Il Mulino, 1979. Pp. 263–87.

Galante, Aloysius. "Index codicum classicorum Latinorum qui Florentiae in Bybliotheca Magliabechiana adservantur." *Studi italiani di filologia classica* 10 (1902), 323–58, and 15 (1907), 129–60.

Garfagnini, Gian Carlo. "Città e studio a Firenze nel XIV secolo: Una difficile convivenza." In *Luoghi e metodi di insegnamento nell'Italia medioevale (sec. XII–XIV)*. Ed. Luciano Gargan and Oronzo Limone. Galatina: Congedo, 1989. Pp. 101–20.

———. "Da Seneca a Giovanni di Salisbury: *Auctoritates morali* e *vitae philosophorum* in un MS Trecentesco." *Rinascimento* 20 (1980), 201–47.

Gargan, Luciano. "Libri, librerie e biblioteche nelle università italiane del Due e Trecento." In *Luoghi e metodi di insegnamento nell'Italia medioevale (sec. XII–XIV)*. Ed. Luciano Gargan and Oronzo Limone. Galatina: Congedo, 1989. Pp. 219–46.

Garin, Eugenio. *L'educazione in Europa (1400–1600)*. Bari-Laterza, 1957.

———. *Il pensiero pedagogico dello umanesimo*. I classici della pedagogia italiana, n.n. Florence: Giuntine and Sansoni, 1958.

Gehl, Paul F. "An Augustinian Catechism from Fourteenth-Century Florence." *Augustinian Studies* 19 (1988), 93–110.

———. "Latin Readers in Fourteenth-Century Florence: Schoolkids and Their Books." *Scrittura e civiltà* 13 (1989), 387–440.

*Gesamtkatalog der Wiegendrucke*. Leipzig (later Stuttgart): Hiersemann, 1925–.

Glei, Reinhold. "Dichtung und Philosophie in der Consolatio Philosophiae des Boethius." *Würzburger Jahrbücher für die Altertumswissenschaft*, N.F. 11 (1985), 225–38.

Graff, Harvey J. *The Legacies of Literacy*. Bloomington: Indiana University Press, 1987.

Grafton, Anthony, and Lisa Jardine. *From Humanism to the Humanities: Education and the Liberal Arts in Fifteenth- and Sixteenth-Century Europe*. Cambridge, Mass.: Harvard University Press, 1986.

———. " 'Studied for Action': How Gabriel Harvey Read His Livy." *Past and Present* 129 (November 1990), 30–78.

Grassi, Ernesto. *Renaissance Humanism: Studies in Philosophy and Poetics*. Medieval and Renaissance Texts and Studies 51. Binghamton, N.Y.: Medieval and Renaissance Texts and Studies, 1988.

Grayson, Cecil. *Cinque saggi su Dante.* Bologna: Pàtron, 1972.

Green, R. P. H. "The Genesis of a Medieval Textbook: The Models and Sources of the Ecloga Theoduli." *Viator* 13 (1982), 49–106.

Grendler, Paul F. "Reply to Robert Black." *Journal of the History of Ideas* 52 (1991), 335–37.

——. *Schooling in Renaissance Italy: Literacy and Learning, 1300–1600.* Baltimore: Johns Hopkins University Press, 1989.

Gruber, Johann. *Kommentar zu Boethius De Consolatione Philosophiae.* Texte und Kommentare 9. Berlin: De Gruyter, 1978.

Guasti, Cesare, ed. *Le Carte Strozziane del R. Archivio di Stato di Firenze.* 3 vols. Florence: Tip. Gallileane, 1884.

Guglielminetti, Marziano. *Memoria e scrittura: L'autobiografia da Dante a Cellini.* Turin: Einaudi, 1977.

Guthmüller, Bodo. "Die *volgarizzamenti.*" In *Die italienische Literatur im Zeitalter Dantes und am Uebergang vom Mittelalter zur Renaissance.* Vol. 2: *Die Literatur bis zur Renaissance.* Ed. August Buck. Grundriss der Romanischen Literaturen des Mittelalters 10. Heidelberg: Carl Winter, 1989. Pp. 201–54, 333–48.

Hamilton, George L. "Theodulus, a Mediaeval Textbook." *Modern Philology* 7 (1909), 169–85.

Hazelton, Richard. "The Christianization of 'Cato': The *Disticha Catonis* in the Light of Late Mediaeval Commentaries." *Mediaeval Studies* 19 (1957), 157–73.

Henkel, Nikolaus. *Studien zum Physiologus im Mittelalter.* Tübingen: Niemeyer, 1976.

Ising, Erika. *Die Herausbildung der Grammatik der Volkssprachen in Mittel- und Osteuropa.* Veröffentlichungen des Instituts für deutsche Sprache und Literatur der Deutsche Akademie der Wissenschaften zu Berlin 47. Berlin: Akademie-Verlag, 1970.

James, M. R. *A Descriptive Catalogue of the Manuscripts in the Gonville and Caius College.* 2 vols. Cambridge: Cambridge University Press, 1907–8.

——, and C. Jenkins. *A Descriptive Catalogue of the Manuscripts in the Library of Lambeth Palace.* 5 vols. Cambridge: Cambridge University Press, 1930–1932.

Jed, Stephanie H. *Chaste Thinking: The Rape of Lucretia and the Birth of Humanism.* Bloomington: Indiana University Press, 1989.

Jenson, Richard C., and Marie Bahr-Volk. "The Fox and the Crab: Coluccio Salutati's Unpublished Fable." *Studies in Philology* 73 (1976), 162–75.

Johnston, Mark D. *The Spiritual Logic of Ramon Llull.* Oxford: Clarendon Press, 1987.

Jones, W. R. "Franciscan Education and Monastic Libraries: Some Documents." *Traditio* 30 (1974), 435–45.

Kaeppeli, Tommaso. "Opere latine attribuite a Jacopo Passavanti, con un appendice sulle opere di Nicoluccio di Ascoli, O.P." *Archivum fratrum praedicatorum* 32 (1962), 145–79.

Kelly, Louis G. "Medieval Philosophers and Translation." In *History and Histo-*

riography of Linguistics: Papers from the Fourth International Conference on the History of the Language Sciences, Trier, 24–28 August 1987. Ed. Hans-Josef Niederehe and Konrad Koerner. Amsterdam Studies in the Theory and History of Linguistic Science, ser. 3, vol. 51. Philadelphia: John Benjamins, 1990. Pp. 205–18.

Ker, Neil R. *Medieval Manuscripts in British Libraries.* 3 vols. Oxford: Oxford University Press, 1969–1983.

Klapisch-Zuber, Christine. "Le chiavi fiorentine di barbablù: L'apprendimento della lettura a Firenze nel XV secolo." Trans. Maddalena Santini. In *Bambini.* Ed. E. Becchi. Quaderni storici, n.s. 57. Ancona: Il Mulino, 1984. Pp. 765–92

Knoespel, Kenneth J. *Narcissus and the Invention of Personal History.* New York: Garland, 1985.

Kohl, Benjamin G. "Humanism and Education." In *Renaissance Humanism: Foundations, Forms, and Legacy.* Vol. 3: *Humanism and the Disciplines.* Ed. Albert Rabil, Jr. Philadelphia: University of Pennsylvania Press, 1988. Pp. 5–22.

Kristeller, Paul Oskar. *Renaissance Thought and Its Sources.* New York: Columbia University Press, 1979.

Lanza, Antonio. *Polemiche e berte letterarie nella Firenze del primo Rinascimento (1375–1449).* 2d ed. Biblioteca di cultura 383. Rome: Bulzoni, 1989.

Lassandro, D. "Note sugli epigrammi di Prospero di Aquitania." *Vetera Christianorum* 18 (1971), 211–22.

Law, Vivien. "Originality in the Medieval Normative Tradition." In *Studies in the History of Western Linguistics in Honour of R. H. Robins.* Ed. Theodora Bynon and F. R. Palmer. Cambridge: Cambridge University Press, 1986. Pp. 43–55.

——. "Panorama della grammatica normativa nel tredicesimo secolo." In *Aspetti della letteratura latina nel secolo XIII: Atti del primo convengo internazionale di studi dell'Associazione per il Medioevo e l'Umanesimo latini, Perugia, 3–5 Ottobre 1983.* Ed. Claudio Leonardi and Giovanni Orlandi. Perugia: Regione Umbria and La Nuova Italia, 1986. Pp. 125–45.

Lerer, Seth. *Boethius and Dialogue: Literary Method in the Consolation of Philosophy.* Princeton: Princeton University Press, 1985.

Lesnick, Daniel R. *Preaching in Medieval Florence: The Social World of Franciscan and Dominican Spirituality.* Athens: University of Georgia Press, 1989.

Lorch, Maristella. "Petrarch, Cicero, and the Classical Pagan Tradition." In *Renaissance Humanism: Foundations, Forms, and Legacy.* Vol. 1: *Humanism in Italy.* Ed. Albert Rabil, Jr. Philadelphia: University of Pennsylvania Press, 1988. Pp. 71–94.

Lucchi, Piero. "La Santacroce, il salterio e il Babuino: Libri per imparare a leggere nel primo secolo della stampa." In *Alfabetismo e cultura scritta.* Ed. A. Bartoli-Langelli and A. Petrucci. Quaderni storici, n.s. 38. Ancona: Il Mulino, 1978. Pp. 593–630.

Luzzati Laganà, Francesca. "Un maestro di scuola toscano del Duecento: Mino da Colle di Valdelsa." In *Città e servizi sociali nell'Italia dei secoli XII–XV.* Dodicesimo convegno di studi del Centro Italiano di Studi di Storia e d'Arte, Pistoia, 9–12 ottobre 1987. Pistoia: Centro Italiano di Studi di Storia e d'Arte, 1990. Pp. 83–113.

McGregor, James H. "Ovid at School: From the Ninth to the Fifteenth Century." *Classical Folia* 37 (1978), 28–51.

Maggini, Francesco. *I primi volgarizzamenti dai classici latini*. Florence: Le Monnier, 1952.

Maierù, Alfonso. "Tecniche di insegnamento." In *Le scuole degli ordini mendicanti (secoli XIII–XIV)*. Convegni del Centro di studi sulla spiritualità medievale 17. Todi: Accademia Tudertina, 1978. Pp. 305–52.

Manacorda, Giuseppe. *Storia della scuola in Italia: Il Medioevo*. 2 vols. Milan: R. Sandron, 1914.

Mancini, G. *I manoscritti della libreria del comune e dell'Academia Etrusca di Cortona*. Cortona: Academia etrusca, 1884. Repr. in Mazzatinti, Sorbelli et al., vols. 18 and 20.

Mandruzzato, Enzo. "L'apologo 'della rana e del topo' e Dante (*Inf.* XXIII,4–9)." *Studi danteschi* 33 (1955–56), 147–65.

Mannelli, Girolama. "La personalità Prudenziana nel *Dittochaeon*." *Miscellanea di studi di letteratura cristiana antica* 1 (1947), 79–126.

Manzi, Adele. "L'exemplum nella *Vita scholastica* di Bonvesin de la Riva." *Aevum* 23 (1949), 1–27.

Marangon, Paolo. "Scuole e università a Padova dal 1221 al 1256: Nuovi documenti." *Quaderni per la storia dell'Università di Padova* 12 (1979), 131–36.

Marshall, J. H. *The Donatz Proensals of Uc Faidit*. London: Oxford University Press, 1969.

Martines, Lauro. *The Social World of the Florentine Humanists, 1390–1460*. Princeton: Princeton University Press, 1963.

Marzi, Demetrio. *La cancelleria della repubblica fiorentina*. Rocca S. Casciano: Licinio Cappelli, 1910.

Mauro, Alfredo. *Francesco del Tuppo e il suo "Esopo"*. Città di Castello: "Il Solco," 1926.

Mazzatinti, Giuseppe, Antonio Sorbelli et al. *Inventarii dei manoscritti delle biblioteche d'Italia*. Forli: Bordonini (later Florence: Olschki), 1890–.

Melis, Federigo. *L'economia fiorentina del Rinascimento*. Ed. Bruno Dini. Florence: Le Monnier, 1984.

Migliorini, Bruno. *Storia della lingua italiana*. Florence: Sansoni, 1960.

Morpurgo, Salomone, et al. *I Codici Panciatichiani della R. Biblioteca Nazionale Centrale di Firenze*. Indici e cataloghi 7. Rome: 1887–1953.

Mueller-Goldingen, Christian. "Die Stellung der Dichtung in Boethius' Consolatio Philosophiae." *Rheinishes Museum für Philologie*, n.s. 132 (1989), 369–95.

Murphy, James J. "The Teaching of Latin as a Second Language in the Twelfth Century." *Historiographia Linguistica* 7 (1980), 159–75.

Najemy, John M. *Corporatism and Consensus in Florentine Electoral Politics, 1280–1400*. Chapel Hill: University of North Carolina Press, 1982.

Nardelli, Enrico. *Catalogus codicum manuscriptorum praeter grecos et orientales in Bibliotheca Angelica*. Rome: L. Cecchini, 1893.

Norton, Glyn P. *The Ideology and Language of Translation in Renaissance France and Their Humanist Antecedents*. Travaux d'Humanisme et Renaissance 201. Geneva: Droz, 1984.

*Il Notaio nella civiltà fiorentina, secoli XIII–XVI: Mostra nella Bibliotecca Medicea Laurenziana.* Florence: Vallecchi, 1986.

*Il Notariato a Perugia: Mostra documentaria e iconografica per il XVI Congresso del Notariato.* Ed. Roberto Abbondanza. Fonti e strumenti per la storia del notariato italiano 1. Rome: Consiglio Nazionale del Notariato, 1973.

Novati, Francesco. "Due grammatici pisani del sec. XIV: Ser Francesco Merolla da Vico e Ser Francesco di Bartolo da Buti (Lettera al prof. dott. Orazio Bacci)." *Miscellanea storica della Valdelsa* 5 (1897), 251–54.

———. "Le serie alfabetiche proverbiali e gli alfabeti disposti nella letteratura italiana de' primi tre secoli." *Giornale storico della letteratura italiana* 15 (1890), 337–401.

Ong, Walter J., S.J. "Latin Language Study as a Renaissance Puberty Rite." In *Rhetoric, Romance, and Technology.* Ithaca: Cornell University Press, 1971. Pp. 113–41.

Orlandelli, Gianfranco. *Il libro a Bologna dal 1300 al 1330.* Studi e ricerche di storia e scienze ausiliare 1. Bologna: Zanichelli, 1951.

Osternacher, Johannes. "Die Ueberlieferung der Ecloga Theoduli." *Neues Archiv der Gessellschaft für altere deutsche Geschichtskunde* 40 (1915–16), 331–76.

Paccagnella, Ivano. "Plurilinguismo letterario: Lingue, dialetti, linguaggi." In *Letteratura italiana.* Ed. Alberto Asor Rosa. Vol. 2: *Produzione e consumo.* Turin: Einaudi, 1983. Pp. 103–67.

Padoan, Giorgio. "Il *Liber Esopi* e due episodi dell'*Inferno.*" *Studi danteschi* 41 (1964), 75–102.

Pandimiglio, Leonida. "Giovanni di Pagolo Morelli e la continuità familiare." *Studi medievali,* 3d ser., 22 (1981), 129–81.

Paradisi, Paola. *Il libro memoriale di Donato: Testo in volgare lucchese della fine del Duecento.* Lucca: Maria Pacini Fazzi, 1989.

Park, Katharine. *Doctors and Medicine in Early Renaissance Florence.* Princeton: Princeton University Press, 1985.

Patrone Nada, Anna Maria. " 'Super providendo bonum et sufficientem magistrum scolarum': L'organizzazione scolastica delle città nel tardo Medio Evo." In *Città e servizi sociali nell'Italia dei secoli XII–XV.* Dodicesimo convegno di studi del Centro italiano di studi di storia e d'arte, Pistoia, 9–12 ottobre 1987. Pistoia: Centro italiano di studi di storia e d'arte, 1990. Pp. 49–81.

Pecchiai, Pio. "I Documenti sulla biografia di Buonvicino della Riva." *Giornale Storico della letteratura italiana* 78 (1921), 96–127.

Pelaez, M. "Un compendio in prosa latina con commento morale verseggiato in volgare veneto delle Favole attribuite a Walterius." *Atti dell'Academia nazionale dei Lincei: Memorie delle classe di scienze morali, storia e filologie.* ser. 8, vol. 4. Rome: Accademia nazionale dei Lincei, 1951.

Pellegrin, Elisabeth. *Les manuscrits classiques latins de la Bibliothèque Vaticane.* 2 vols. Paris: CNRS, 1975–1982.

Percival, W. Keith. "The Grammatical Tradition and the Rise of the Vernaculars." In *Current Trends in Linguistics.* Vol. 13: *Historiography of Linguistics.* Ed. Thomas A. Sebeok. The Hague: Mouton, 1975. Pp. 231–75.

———. "The Historical Sources of Guarino's *Regulae grammaticales.*" In *Civiltà dell'Umanesimo.* Ed. Giovannangiola Tarugi. Florence: Olschki, 1972. Pp. 263–84.

——. "A Hitherto Unpublished Medieval Grammatical Fragment on Latin Syntax and Syntactic Figures." In *De Ortu Grammaticae: Studies in Medieval Grammar and Linguistic Theory in Memory of Jan Pinborg.* Ed. G. L. Bursill-Hall, Sten Ebbesen, and Konrad Koerner. Amsterdam Studies in the Theory and History of Linguistic Science, ser. 3, vol. 43. Philadelphia: John Benjamins, 1990. Pp. 271–84.

——. "On Priscian's Syntactic Theory: The Medieval Perspective." In *Papers in the History of Linguistics: Proceedings of the Third International Conference on the History of the Language Sciences, Princeton, 19–23 August 1984.* Ed. Hans Aarsleff, Louis G. Kelly, and Hans-Josef Niederehe. Amsterdam Studies in the Theory and History of Linguistic Science, ser. 3, vol. 38. Philadelphia: John Benjamins, 1987. Pp. 65–74.

——. "Renaissance Grammar." In *Renaissance Humanism: Foundations, Forms, and Legacy.* Vol. 3: *Humanism and the Disciplines.* Ed. Albert Rabil, Jr. Philadelphia: University of Pennsylvania Press, 1988. Pp. 67–83.

——. "Renaissance Grammar: Rebellion or Evolution?" In *Interrogativi dell'Umanesimo.* Ed. Giovannangiola Tarugi. 3 vols. Florence: Olschki, 1976. Vol. 2, pp. 73–90.

——. "Textual Problems in the Latin Grammar of Guarino Veronese." *Res publica litterarum* 1 (1978), 241–54.

Petrucci, Armando. "Il libro manoscritto." In *Letteratura italiana.* Vol. 2: *Produzione e consumo.* Ed. Alberto Asor Rosa. Turin: Einaudi, 1983. Pp. 499–524.

Petti Balbi, Giovanna. *L'insegnamento nella Liguria medievale: Scuole, maestri, libri.* Genoa: Tilgher, 1979.

——. "Istituzioni cittadine e servizi scolastici nell'Italia centro-settentrionale tra XIII e XV secolo." In *Città e servizi sociali nell'Italia dei secoli XII–XV.* Dodicesimo convegno di studi del Centro Italiano di Studi di Storia e d'Arte, Pistoia, 9–12 ottobre 1987. Pistoia: Centro Italiano di Studi di Storia e d'Arte, 1990. Pp. 21–48.

Piattoli, Renato. "Due osservazioni ai recenti studi su Convenevole da Prato, maestro del Petrarca." *Bullettino dell'Istituto storico italiano per il medio evo* 85 (1974–75), 145–50.

Pillinger, Renate. *Die Tituli historiarum oder das sogennante Dittochaeon des Prudentius: Versuch eines philologisch-archäologischen Kommentars.* Denkschriften der Oesterreichischen Akademie der Wissenschaften, philosophisch-historische Klasse 142. Vienna: Oesterrichische Akademie, 1980.

Pinto, Giuliano. "I livelli di vita dei salariati cittadini nel periodo successivo al tumulto dei Ciompi (1380–1430)." In *Il tumulto dei Ciompi, un momento di storia fiorentina ed europea.* Florence: Olschki, 1981. Pp. 161–98.

Quinn, Betty Nye. "Ps. Theodolus." In *Catalogus translationum et commentariorum.* Vol. 2. Washington, D.C.: Catholic University of America Press, 1971. Pp. 383–408.

Quondam, Amadeo. "Nascita della grammatica: Appunti e materiali per una descrizione analitica." In *Alfabetismo e cultura scritta*. Ed. A. Bartoli-Langelli and A. Petrucci. Quaderni storici n.s. 38. Ancona: Il Mulino, 1978. Pp. 555–92.

Raith, Werner. *Florenz vor der Renaissance: Der Weg einer Stadt aus dem Mittelalter*. Frankfurt: Campus-Verlag, 1979.

Reeve, Michael D. "The Circulation of Classical Works on Rhetoric from the 12th to the 14th Century." In *Retorica e poetica tra i secoli XII e XIV, Atti del secondo convegno internazionale di studi dell Associazione per il Medioevo e l'Umanesimo . . . Trento e Rovereto, 3–5 ottobre 1985*. Quaderni del Centro per il Collegamento degli studi medievali e umanistici nell'Università di Perugia, 18. Florence: La Nuova Italia, 1988. Pp. 109–24.

Richter, Michael. "Kommunikationsprobleme im lateinischen Mittelalter." *Historische Zeitschrift* 222 (1976), 43–80.

Rizzo, Silvia. "Il latino nell'Umanesimo." In *Letteratura italiana*. Ed. Alberto Asor Rosa. Vol. 5: *Le questioni*. Turin: Einaudi, 1986. Pp. 379–408.

Roos, Paolo. *Sentenza e proverbio nell'antichità e i Distici di Catone*. Brescia: Morcelliana, 1984.

Rossi, Paolo. *Clavis universalis: Arti mnemoniche e logica combinatoria da Lullo a Leibnitz*. Milan: Riccardi, 1960.

Rossi, Vittorio "Un grammatico cremonese a Pavia nella prima età del Rinascimento." *Bollettino della Società pavese di storia patria* 1 (1901), 16–46.

Sabbadini, Remigio. *Giovanni da Ravenna, insigne figura d'umanista (1343–1408)*. Como: Ostinelli, 1924.

Saenger, Paul. *A Catalogue of the pre-1500 Western Manuscript Books at the Newberry Library*. Chicago: University of Chicago Press, 1989.

Salsano, Roberto. *Il volgarizzamento Cavalchiano della "Vita Beati Antonii Abbatis."* Florence: Le Monnier, 1972.

Sanford, Eva Matthews. "The Use of Classical Latin Authors in the *Libri Manuales*." *Transactions and Proceedings of the American Philological Association* 55 (1924), 190–248.

Sapori, Armando. "Un bilancio domestico a Firenze alla fine del Dugento." In *Studi di storia economica (secoli XIII–XIV–XV)*. 3d ed. Florence: Sansoni, 1955. Pp. 353–71.

———. "Case e botteghe a Firenze nel Trecento: La rendita della proprietà fondiaria." In *Studi di storia economica (secoli XIII–XIV–XV)*. 3d ed. Florence: Sansoni, 1955. Pp. 305–52.

———. "La cultura del mercante medievale italiano." In *Studi di storia economica (secoli XIII–XIV–XV)*. 3d ed. Florence: Sansoni, 1955. Pp. 53–93.

Scaffai, Marco. "Tradizione manoscritta del *Ilias latina*." In *In uerbis uerum amare: Miscellanea dell'Istituto di filologia latina e medioevale dell'Università di Bologna*. Ed. Paolo Serra Zanetti. Pubblicazioni della Facoltà di Magistero dell'Università di Bologna, n.s. 5. Florence: La Nuova Italia, 1980. Pp. 205–77.

Scaglione, Aldo. "Dante and the *Ars Grammatica*." In *De Ortu Grammaticae: Studies in Medieval Grammar and Linguistic Theory in Memory of Jan Pinborg*. Ed. G. L. Bursill-Hall, Sten Ebbesen, and Konrad Koerner. Amsterdam Studies in the Theory and History of Linguistic Science, ser. 3, vol. 43. Philadelphia: John Benjamins, 1990. Pp. 305–19.

Scalon, Cesare. *Libri, scuole e cultura nel Friuli medioevale.* Medioevo e umanesimo 65. Padua: Antenore, 1987.

Schiaffini, Alfredo. "Esercizi di versione dal volgare friulano in latino nel secolo XIV in una scuola notarile cividalese." *Rivista della Società filologica friulana* 3 (1922), 87–117. Also issued as a separate paginated 1–31 (Udine: Società filologica friulana, 1922).

———. "Frammenti grammaticali latino-friulani del secolo XIV." *Rivista della Società filologica friulana* 2 (1921), 3–16, 93–95. Also issued as a separate paginated 1–29 (Udine: Del Bianco, 1921).

Schmidt, Wieland. *Untersuchungen zum "Geta" des Vitalis Blesensis.* Beihefte zum Mittellateinischen Jahrbuch 14. Ratingen: A. Henn, 1975.

Schmitt, Wolfgang O. "Die Ianua (Donatus), ein Beitrag zur lateinischen Schulgrammatik des Mittelalters und der Renaissance." *Beiträge zur Inkunabelkunde,* 3d ser., 4 (1969), 43–80.

Scolari, Antonio. "Un volgarizzamento trecentesco della *Rhetorica ad Herennium*: Il *Trattatello di colori rettorici.*" *Medioevo romanzo* 9 (1984), 215–66.

Segre, Cesare. *Lingua, stile e società: Studi sulla storia della prosa italiana.* Milan: Feltrinelli, 1963.

———. *Volgarizzamenti del due e trecento.* Turin: UTET, 1953.

Smith, M. *Prudentius' Psychomachia: A Reexamination.* Princeton: Princeton University Press, 1976.

Sóriga, Renato. *Statuta, decreta et ordinamenta Societatis et Colegii notariorum Papie reformata (1255–1274).* Biblioteca della Società storica subalpina 129/2. Turin: Società storica subalpina, 1932.

Spagnesi, Enrico. *Utiliter edoceri: Atti inediti degli ufficiali dello studio fiorentino (1391–96).* Pubblicazioni della Facoltà di Giurisprudenza dell'Università di Firenze 34. Milan: Giuffrè, 1979.

Stock, Brian. *The Implications of Literacy: Written Language and Models of Interpretation in the Eleventh and Twelfth Centuries.* Princeton: Princeton University Press, 1983.

Stolt, Birgit. "Das Werk eines pädagogischen Genies: Die Ars Minor des Donat im Codex Ups. C 678." *Daphnis* 8 (1979), 309–20.

Stotz, Peter. "Dichten als Schulfach: Aspekte mittelalterlicher Schuldichtung." *Mittellateinisches Jahrbuch* 16 (1981), 1–16.

Sturlese, A., et al. *Catalogo di manoscritti filosofici nelle biblioteche italiane.* Florence: Olschki, 1980–.

Sznura, Franek. *L'espansione urbana di Firenze nel Dugento.* Florence: La Nuova Italia, 1975.

Tavoni, Mirko. "The Fifteenth-Century Controversy on the Language Spoken by the Ancient Romans." In *The History of Linguistics in Italy.* Ed. Paolo Ramat, Hans-J. Niederehe, and Konrand Koerner. Amsterdam Studies in the Theory and History of Linguistic Science, ser. 3, vol. 33. Philadelphia: John Benjamins, 1986. Pp. 23–50.

Thiel, E. J. "Neue Handschriften der mittellateinischen Nachtdichter von Ovids *Ars amatoria* und *Remedia amoris* und Nachträge." *Mittellateinisches Jahrbuch* 9 (1973), 248–68.

Trexler, Richard C. *Public Life in Renaissance Florence.* New York: Academic Press, 1980.

Ullman, Berthold Louis. "Some Aspects of the Origin of Italian Humanism." In *Studies in the Italian Renaissance.* Rome: Edizioni di storia e letteratura, 1955. Pp. 27–40.

University of Cambridge. *A Catalogue of the Manuscripts Preserved in the Library of the University of Cambridge.* 5 vols. Cambridge: University Press, 1866–1867.

Vance, Eugene. "The Differing Seed: Dante's Brunetto Latini." In *Mervelous Signals: Poetics and Sign Theory in the Middle Ages.* Lincoln: University of Nebraska Press, 1986. Pp. 230–55. The same essay may be consulted in *Vernacular Poetics in the Middle Ages.* Ed. Lois Ebin. Studies in Medieval Culture 16. Kalamazoo: Medieval Institute Publications, 1984, and in *Mimesis: From Mirror to Method, Augustine to Descartes.* Ed. S. G. Nichols and J. Lyons. Hanover, N.H.: University Press of New England, 1982.

Velli, Giuseppe. "Petrarca, Boccaccio e la grande poesia latina del XII secolo." In *Retorica e poetica tra i secoli XII e XIV: Atti del secondo convegno internazionale di studi dell Associazione per il Medioevo e l'Umanesimo . . . Trento e Rovereto, 3–5 ottobre 1985.* Quaderni del Centro per il Collegamento degli studi medievali e umanistici nell'Università di Perugia 18. Florence: La Nuova Italia, 1988. Pp. 239–56. A briefer version of the same study appeared as "Petrarca e la grande poesia latina del XII secolo." *Italia medioevale e umanistica* 28 (1985), 295–310.

Verde, Armando. *Lo studio fiorentino, 1473–1503.* 4 vols. Florence: Istituto nazionale di studi sul Rinascimento, 1973–1985.

Vichi-Imbeciadori, J. "L'istruzione in San Gimignano dal secolo XIII al secolo XX." *Miscellanea storica della Valdelsa* 86 (1980), 59–122.

Viscardi, Antonio. "Lettura degli *auctores* moderni nelle scuole medievali di grammatica." In *Studi in onore di Angelo Monteverdi.* Modena: Società tipografica editrice modenese, 1959. Pp. 867–73.

Vitale-Brovarone, A. "Testo e attitudini del pubblico nel *Roman de Renart.*" In *Epopée animale, fable, fabliau: Acts du IVe Colloque de la Société international Renardienne, Evreaux, 7–11 Septembre 1981.* Ed. Gabriel Bianciotto and Michel Salvati. Publications de l'Université de Rouen 83. Paris: Presses Universitaires de France, 1984. Pp. 669–85.

Voight, E. "Das erste Lesebuch des Triviums in den Kloster- und Stiftschulen des Mittelalters (11.–15. Jahrhundert)." *Mitteilungen der Gesellschaft für deutsche Erziehungs- und Schulgeschichte* 1 (1891), 42–53.

Vredeveld, Harry. "Pagan and Christian Echoes in the *Ecloga Theoduli*, a Supplement. *Mittellateinisches Jahrbuch* 22 (1987), 101–13.

Wieland, Gernot R. "The Glossed Manuscript: Classbook or Library Book?" *Anglo-Saxon England* 14 (1985), 153–73.

——. *The Latin Glosses on Arator and Prudentius in Cambridge University Library MS Gg.5.35.* Studies and Texts 61. Toronto: Pontifical Institute of Mediaeval Studies, 1983.

Wieruszowski, Helene. *Politics and Culture in Medieval Spain and Italy.* Rome: Edizioni di storia e letteratura, 1971.

Wilmart, A. *Bibliothecae Apostolicae Vaticanae Codices Manuscripti recensuit . . . Codices Reginenses Latini.* 2 vols. Vatican City: Biblioteca Apostolica Vaticana, 1945.

Witt, Ronald G. *Hercules at the Crossroads: The Life, Works, and Thought of Coluccio Salutati.* Duke Monographs in Medieval and Renaissance Studies 6. Durham, N.C.: Duke University Press, 1983.

——. "Medieval Ars Dictaminis and the Beginnings of Humanism: A New Construction of the Problem." *Renaissance Quarterly* 35 (1985), 1–35.

——. "Medieval Italian Culture and the Origins of Humanism as a Stylistic Ideal." In *Renaissance Humanism: Foundations, Forms, and Legacy.* Vol. 1: *Humanism in Italy.* Ed. Albert Rabil, Jr. Philadelphia: University of Pennsylvania Press, 1988. Pp. 29–70.

——. "The Origins of Italian Humanism: Padua and Florence." *Centennial Review* 34 (1990), 92–108.

Zanelli, Agostino. *Del pubblico insegnamento in Pistoia dal XIV al XVI secolo.* Rome: Loescher, 1900.

# INDEX

305

universities (*cont.*)
  Pisa, 15
  Siena, 15
*urbanitas* (rhetorical notion), 127

Valerius Maximus, 283
Vallombrosans, 41, 224
Valori, Bartolomeo di Niccolo dei, 43, 85, 86
Velluti, Donato, 23
Venice, 21, 22, 40, 42, 173, 209, 212, 225–26
vernacular languages, 10, 16, 27–29, 32, 34–
    37, 76–79, 83–84, 102, 234
versification, 80, 100, 107, 109, 122, 137–39,
    141, 188
Villani, Filippo, 181
Villani, Giovanni, 20, 21, 23–26, 33, 41, 222,
    223
violence, 196, 227–28

Virgil, 29, 38, 54, 57, 74, 104, 108, 128, 134,
    141, 166, 169–70, 180, 200, 281–
    83
Viscardi, Antonio, 180
Vitale-Brovarone, A., 135
Vitalis of Blois, 43, 53, 178–79, 190–93,
    257–58, 283–85
Vittorino da Feltre, 47, 173
Volterra, 102–3, 217–18

Walter the Englishman, 43, 110–12, 122, 131.
    *See also* Aesop
Witt, Ronald, 4, 10, 43, 77, 208
women, 6, 24, 32–33, 57, 80, 117, 128–30,
    132, 142, 161, 205, 206, 214, 225
  as readers, 117
  as teachers, 220
wordplay, 52, 124–27, 187